Christophe Pichaud

Professional C++

Philosophy and Principles

Guidelines From C++ Renaissance To Modern C++ For Every Developers

1st Edition – 402 Pages – November 2022 –
With Love For Mini-Mini, Maggie & Didou.

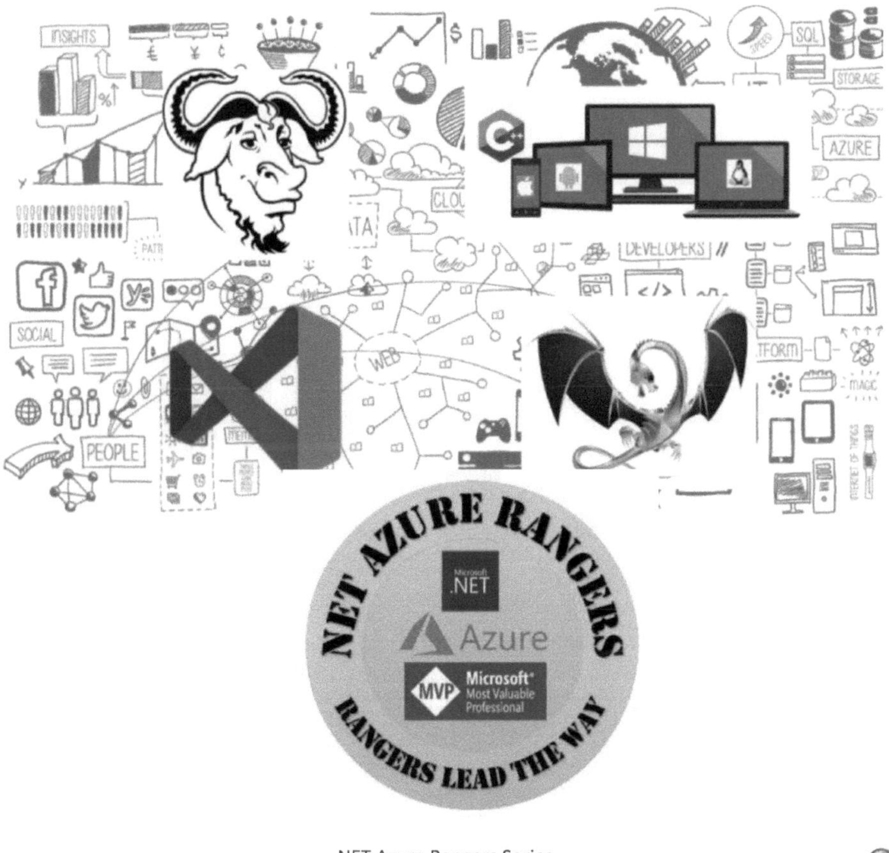

.NET Azure Rangers Series

Professional C++ - Philosophy and Principles

Professional C++

Philosophy and Principles

Guidelines From C++ Renaissance To Modern C++ For Every Developers

402 Pages – 1st Edition

This project of a book is the synthesis of software development activities since 1994.
Without MSDN July 1994, I would not have the chance to embrace such a career.
I am a Microsoft Windows Win32 developer since a long time now.

Like an old red wine, my objectives are to belong to an ISO C++ perfect professional.

For me, it's a long run because my world has been driven by DOS, Win16, CL.EXE, C, C++, COM, MFC, DCOM, ATL/COM, MAPI, MFC, OLE2, Visual Basic, VBA, VBS, WinRT, NET , C#, CoreCLR and now Azure…

Without Microsoft, I would not be able to have written such materials because I had so many chance.
With all the competitor MS had during the last 3 decades, it makes me learn other things, others realities, others way "to cook" software meals and solutions big restaurants stuff.

This books is my way "to transfer" learning things for the field from a lot of people on various projects. Real stuff. From debugging with or without debuggers, live or post-mortem, with daemon without any human of it during 768 days, making a series of software that are reliable and stable for decades. From communication layers to embedded devices carrying your software and nobody can't give you any news because you don't have the required security level approved to know anything about what you have developed…

Technologies are weapons.
Do you think Satellites, Airplanes, F35 or Rafale multirole fighters are done with Java or .NET? I doubt about that.
Just for kidding: Try just to make a real-world application like a browser with all those productive languages and I pay you beers for the entire of your life.

Rust is coming. We are declared as dinosaurs by all those funny Iznogoud[1] people. I am waiting. It's not because something new is considered superior than anything else that it will become the best product(s). I know that because I work for Microsoft directly or not or other ways (you won't know) since 3 decades. 😊

Herb Sutter says: **"The World is Built On C++"**.
Bjarne Stroustrup says: **"C++ is The invisible Foundation Of Everything"**.
These 2 guys are living legends. Everybody should consider that. I have the chance they looked at my book.

---

[1] Iznogoud want to be Kalif to replace the existing Kalif. It's a famous comic strip in France.

Introduction

This book is dedicated to my parents Jean-Marc and Mireille, who have always believed in me. The support of my daughters Edith (Didou), Lisa (the mini-mini) and Lilly (Maggie) was also important.

Jerome (little Lulu), this is the 6th opus and I think that I will able to offer you the Porshe and the Toni's Michella job of your dream in Redmond, San Francisco or in Texas... or Canada !

Vive le Québec libre !

Vive le Général !

Professional C++ - Philosophy and Principles

My little sweetheart female cat named Bébé is the first to have told me
"Yep, I don't understand a word about C++ but without me, you would never have finished. I am the Boss."

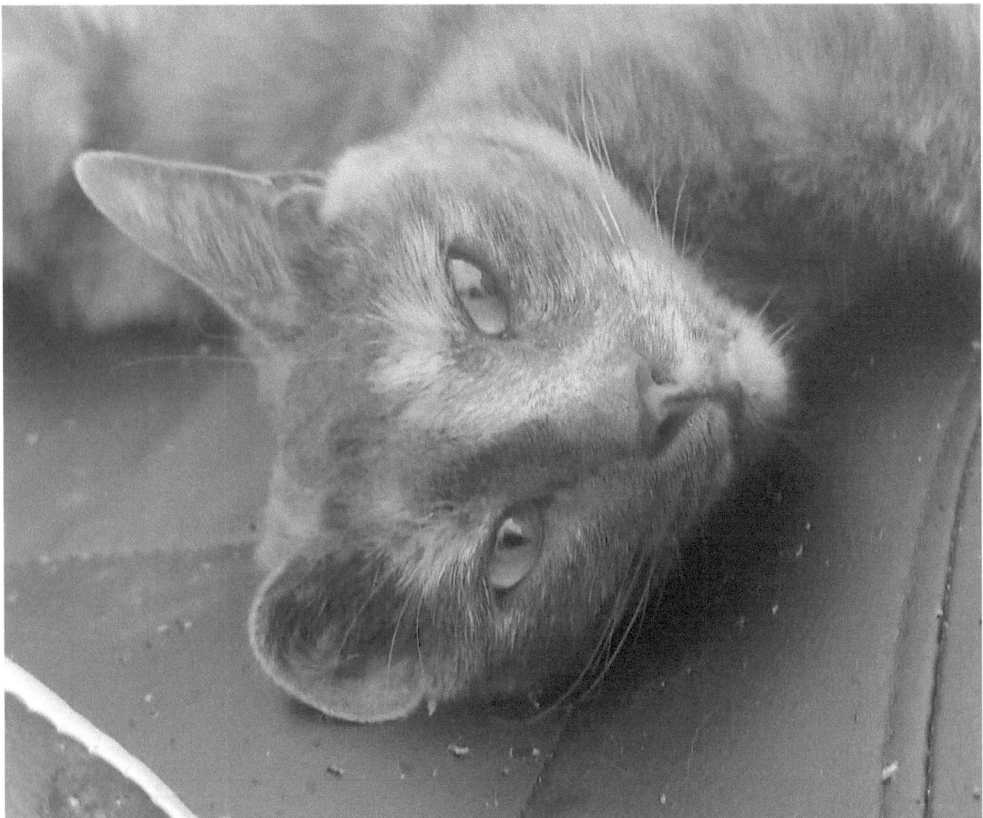

Figure 1- Bébé - Queen of Egypt like Cleopatra

This book is sponsored by Microsoft, United States Agencies (CIA, FBI, DEA, NSA), China, Russia, India, Pakistan and North Korea. Warning[2].

But some friends told me a lot of State hackers and Gov agencies like Microsoft but not the same way[3]. Some like it because it communicates a lot, and some like to communicate in not the same way it communicates. The fact is that it communicates. I hope it makes you smile.
But now you have this book, it would be not cool to not try to see if there any jokes in?

---

[2] Please stay calm. Don't call the police. It's a joke.

[3] Excuse me again. It's also a joke. Keep calm, there is no more f*** jokes. I promise.

Professional C++

I do not promise anything except if you are young, you could have a life or joy and creativity, adrenaline and a lot of special emotions just by learning the infinite piece of software that exists today in the industry, in the open-source, and that now, everything is possible to learn for free, or at minimal cost.
ENJOY READING. ENJOY LEARNING. ENJOY SHARING.
LET'S MAKE A SAFER WORLD. LET'S FACE NEW CHALLENGE THAT ARE COMING.
TO BE MORE AND MORE _____[4] WHEN TIME IS RUNNNING THAN YESTERDAY.

Table of Contents

Introduction 3

In France, we cut the head of the king (1789) 17

Preface 19
    About the Author 19
    Why Read this Book? 22
    Examples of Code and Prerequisites 22
    About the Compilers 22
    Structure of the Book 23
    Foreword 24
    Author's Note 25
    Acknowledgements 26
    Acknowledgements bis (The Kiss of Death) 26

1.   Introduction to Modern C++ 30
    Why C++ and What is Modern C++ ? 30
    C++ Myths and Reality 32
    C++ is Multi-Platform and Multi-Devices 36
    The TIOBE Index 38
    Performance and Optimization Orientations 39
    Microsoft Inspiration and its Cooking Guide 39
    Microsoft is committed to C++ 41
    The Key is performance 42
    Anatomy of applications 43
    Myths and realities 44

---

[4] It's up to you to choose the word(s). For me, it's "confident in the way we will be better"

C/C++ is portable and native 44
The documentation 45
Some Resources For Students or Cookbook Books to carry in your bag or SD card 47
The STL (Standard Template Library) 48

2. Essential C++ Cookbook – Quick Learning 62

Classes and OOP 71
KEY Concepts of Object-Oriented Programming 79
Templates with C++ 82
The Standard Template Library 93
C++ Language Features and Standard Library Components 104
  C++11 Language Features *104*
  C++14 Language Features *105*
  C++17 Language Features *105*
  C++20 Language Features *105*
  C++11 Standard Library Components *106*
  C++14 Standard Library Components *107*
  C++17 Standard Library Components *107*
  C++20 Standard Library Components *107*

3. Modern C++ : C++ 11, 14, 17, C++20 and upcoming C++23 109

Modern C++ 109
Dynamic memory, vector<T> and smart pointers via shared_ptr<T>... 118
Latest Features from C++ 14, C++ 17 and C++ 20 126
  Using auto instead of explicit types *126*
  Creating objects: () and {} *127*
  Use nullptr instead of 0 and NULL *127*
  Use deleted functions instead of private ones *127*
  Use override instead of virtual for functions *128*
  Use const_iterator instead of iterator *130*
  Use noexcept for functions *130*
  Use the Pimpl Idiom *130*
Advanced Topics for Modern C++ (C++17 and C++20) 134
  Move Semantic, Perfect Forwarding et Rvalue References *134*
  std::move and std::forward *134*
  std::move *134*
std::forward 135
Forwarding references and rvalue references 136

    Best Practices for std::move and std::forward *138*
    Avoid copies when returning objects *139*

4.   The future standard C++20 and upcoming C++23 140

   Modules 140
   Coroutines 141
   Concepts 142
     The header<concepts> *142*
   Span 144
     The <span header> *144*
   C++20 AND STL20 Features in The Area of Performance 145

5.   PERFORMANCE MEASURE AND TOOLS 146

   Drawbacks of the C++ language 146
   Portability 146
   Development time 146
   Time to Market 147
   Security and safe-code 147
   Security Features in Microsoft C Runtime 148
   Microsoft SAL Annotations 148
   General Tips & Tricks 149
   When it is not necessary to optimize 149
   Use a profiler 150
   Shared Modules 150
   Processing Files 150
   EFFICIENT LIBRARIES FOR PERFORMANCE 151
     Private and System Database *152*
     Databases *153*
     Graphics *155*
     Network, Middlewares and Brokers *155*
   Others Performance Considerations 157
   The 90/10 Rule in Optimization 159
     The Visual Rule *159*
     The Logger is Your Best Friend *160*
     Measuring time *160*
     Tracing operations *162*
     List of Logging Libraries *162*
     Overview of Log4cpp *162*
     Logging Usage *164*

Build Your Own Tracing GUI Tool 164
Excellence in Tracing 167
The Compiler Code Profiler 167
Unit Tests and DevOps 169
List of Unit Tests Library 170
Overview of CPPUnit.. 170
Anatomy of a test application 173
Conclusion 173

6. Containers... 175
   Hardware and Memory 175
   The header <iterator>... 175
   Iterators 175
   Access features 177
   The header <vector>.. 177
   std::vector.. 177
   The header <array>.. 178
   std::array 178
   The headers <list> et <forward_list>.. 178
   std::list and std::forward_list.. 178
   Container operations 179
   Iterators 179
   Size and capacity 181
   access 182
   Changes 183
   Non-member functions 184
   The header<bitset> 185
   std::bitset... 185
   access 185
   Operations 185
   The header<queue> 186
   std::tail 186
   std::p riority-tail 186
   std::stack 186
   references.. 186
   The header<map> 187
   std::map 187
   std::multimap 187
   The header<set>.. 187
   std::map and std::multiset 187
   Search operations 187

Moving knots 187
Container merger 188
reference 188
Iterators 188
waist 188
Access and Search 189
Changes 190
Non-member functions 190
The headers <unordered_map> and <unordered_set> 190
Hash Map 190
references 191
Observers 191
Interface Bucket 191
Hash Policy 191
Non-member functions 192

7. Algorithms 193

The header <algorithm> 193
for_each 193
Transform 193
Check for items 193
Find items 194
Find Min/Max items 195
Binary search 195
Search other 195
Comparison sequences 196
Generation sequences 196
Copy, Move, Exchange 197
Delete and Replace 198
Reversal and Rotations 198
Partying 199
sort 199
Sampling and Shuffling 200
Operations on sorted rows 200
permutation 201
Heaps 201
The header <numeric> 202
Reductions 202
scalar product 202
Amounts and differences 202
The header <memory> 202

Memory algorithms 202
The head <execution> 203
Parallel algorithms 203
The header <iterator> 203
Iterator adapters 203

8. Memory Managment 205

Basic usage... 205
Prefer passing pointers or reference 205
Pass Objects by Reference 205
Smart Pointers 205
A closer look at shared_ptr 206
Using smart pointers 206
Prefer make_unique and make_shared instead of new................ 208
The C routines alternative.. 208
Game Development and Embedded Devices Specific Cases 209
Game Development... 209
Portable Development and Memory Allocation 210
Windows Specific Development... 210
 The Microsoft Press Windows API Reference Book 210
 Win32 Virtual Memory Functions – [EXTRACT FROM MICROSOFT.COM]
 210
 Win32 VirtualAlloc Reference API Documentation 211
 Comparing Memory Allocation Methods by Microsoft.................. 212
Linux Development 213

9. EASTL study 215

Credits And Maintainers 215
License 216
EASTL Modules 217
 Module List... 217
 Module Behaviour 219
Glossary for the STL.. 221
A High Performance STL 232
Design of the EASTL... 232
 Motivations 232
 Prime Directives... 233
 Thread Safety... 234
EASTL Design 234
 Motivations 234

Prime Directives...235
Thread Safety...236
Containers Efficiencies..237
Algorithms Better Implementation..238

10. Applied Optimizations in EASTL using ISO C++ 241

EASTL Best Practices 241
List all the others items 241
Consider intrusive containers..242
Consider fixed-size containers. 242
Consider custom allocators..243
Consider hash tables instead of maps. 243
Consider a vector_map (a.k.a. sorted vector) for unchanging data. 243
Consider slist instead of list. 244
Avoid redundant end() and size() in loops. 244
Iterate containers instead of using operator[]. 244
Learn to use the string class appropriately. 245
Cache list size if you want list::size() to be O(1). 246
Use empty() instead of size() when possible...246

Use vector::reserve. 247
Use vector::set_capacity to trim memory usage. 247
Use swap() instead of a manually implemented version. 248
Consider storing pointers instead of objects. 248
Consider smart pointers instead of raw pointers.....................................248
Use iterator pre-increment instead of post-increment. 249
Make temporary references so the code can be traced/debugged. 249
Consider bitvector or bitset instead of vector<bool>. 250
Vectors can be treated as contiguous memory..250
Search hash_map<string> via find_as() instead of find().................250
Take advantage of type_traits (e.g.
EASTL_DECLARE_TRIVIAL_RELOCATE). 250
Name containers to track memory usage. 252
Pass and return containers by reference instead of value. 255
Consider using reset_lose_memory() for fast container teardown. 255
Consider using fixed_substring instead of copying strings. 256
Consider using vector::push_back(void). 256

11. Multithreading using ISO C++ 257
   Basics of threads 257
      Passing arguments to a thread 258
      Returning result from a thread 258
      Sharing Data 259
      Mutexes 260
      Tasks 262
      future and promise 262
      async 262
      Optimization of Locks 263
      Read/Write Lock 264
      Condition Variable 265
      Parallel Algorithms 265
      Windows API and specific issues 266
   Optimizing Concurrency – Tips and Tricks 267
      Avoid ctor and dtor 267
      Always use a multithreaded logger 268
      Create async tasks instead of threads 268
      Implement a thread pool mechanism 268
      Create as many threads as Cores 268
      Make a wall between compute and I/O 268
      Use or implement a middleware or a messaging pipeline 268
      Enhance your locks 268
      The thread pool can server the whole earth 269
      Resources need to be managed carefully 269
      Avoid infinite wait 269
      Don't create your own lock types 269
      Concurrency Libraries 269
      Write lock-free applications 269
   Boost and Lock-free Mecanism 270
      Properties of Non-Blocking Data Structures 271
      Performance of Non-Blocking Data Structures 271
   Introduction to Intel TBB 271
   Introduction to Microsoft Concurrency Runtime 278
      Introduction to Parallel Patterns Library 278
      Example of PPL code 279
      Others PPL Topics 281
      General considerations on PPL 281

Advice 282

12. Multithreading on Windows 283

    Introduction 283
    A variant in Runtime C 284
    The termination of a thread... 286
    Suspending or summarizing a thread................................ 286
    The interlocked routines 287
    Threads synchronization in User mode............................. 287
    Threads synchronization in Kernel mode 288
    The Concurrency Runtime alias ConcRT 289

13. Multithreading with Linux 294

14. Web Services and Web API using Modern C++............................ 302

    The Microsoft REST SDK CPP 302
    Casablanca alias C++ REST SDK....................................... 302
    A simple REST http server.. 302
    The body of the GET handler 305
    Generation of the JSON 307
    The client part 309
    Web API in C++ with the CPP Rest SDK............................... 311
    A simple REST http server.. 311
    The body of the GET handler 313
    Generation of the JSON 315
    The client party 317
    What is the Performance & Optimization point to remember? 318

15. Introduction to The Boost C++ Libraries 319

    How do I get Boost?.. 319
    Build Boost 319
    Introduction to Boost.Serialization 319
    The result of XML serialization 320
    Writing the data... 324
    Conclusion 326

16. I/O Async with Boost 327

    Introduction 327

Multi-threading + synchronous I/O 327
  Single-threading + asynchronous I/O 328
  Combining both synchronous and asynchronous models 329
  Choose an I/O model 329
  Choose an implementation 330

17. Boost ::Asio 331

  Presentation 331
    Benefit from modern concepts about I/O and its management 331
    Ignore the particularities of the OS or hardware platform 331
    Minimize implementation differences between different types of I/O ... 332
    Use a unified interface for error handling 332
    Benefit from utility classes for common operations 333
    Use a robust and high-performance implementation 333
  ASIO Main Concepts 333
    io_context 333
    Endpoint 334
    socket 334
    Resolver 335
  ASIO Examples 336
    Hello asynchronous TCP server 336
    Hello Asynchronous TCP Client 336

18. C++ and Docker Containers on Azure 337

  Introduction 337
  Software Architecture 337
  Run in local 338
  Implementation of Docker 338
  Local run under Docker 339
  Run in Azure 339
  Network issue 346
  Comments on Docker 348
  What we have learned 348

19. Migrate your C++ code to 64 bits 349

  The necessary tools 349
  The std::string & std::wstring conversions 353
  Alternate Windows solution via MFC and ATL/MFC 354
  The C++ x64 project type 354

Naming of modules 355
Additionals Reminder 356
Command line compilation 356
Conclusion 357

20. Tests in C++ 358
CPPUnit 358
Google Test Adapter 362
Boost.Test 366
Continuous integration 367

21. C++ Core Guidelines 368

Abstract 370

22. Herb Sutter's CPPCon 2022 Talk "Can C++ be x10 Simpler and Safer" 372

23. Herb Sutter's Work on CPP2 376
Goals and History 377

ANNEXES 378

Bibliography 379

ANNEXE A - Interview with Bjarne Stroustrup (24th Feb 2020 – 19:00 GMT+) 382

Beginning – General questions 384

Core C++ Questions 386

Various questions 389

ANNEXE B – BJARNE STROUSTRUP'S ARTICLE in ACCU Overload No 161 . 392
Acknowledgements 392

C++ – AN INVISIBLE FOUNDATION OF EVERYTHING 392

Overview 392
Aims and means 393
Use 394
Evolution 395
Guarantees, language, and guidelines 396
People 397
References and resources 398
Appendix: The C++ language 399
Acknowledgements 400

ANNEXE C – LINUS TORVALD .... : C++ is CRAP LANGUAGE   401

Linus Torvalds Says Rust Closer for Linux Kernel Development, Calls C++ 'A Crap Language' (itwire.com) 401

ANNEXE D – RUST WILL REPLACE C AND C++ as System Programming Language ? 402

IN FRANCE, WE CUT THE HEAD OF THE KING (1789)

My little sweet heart female cat named Bébé is the first to have told me
"yep, I don't understand a word about C++ but without me, you would never have finished. I am the Boss."

This book is sponsored by Microsoft, United States Agencies (CIA, FBI, DEA, NSA), China, Russia, India, Pakistan and North Korea. Warning[5] .
But some friends told me a lot of State hackers and Gov agencies like Microsoft but not the same way[6]. Some like it because it communicates a lot, and some like to communicate in not the same way it communicates. The fact is that it communicates. I hope it makes you smile.

But now you have this books, it would be not cool to not try to see if there any jokes in?
I do not promise anything except if you are young, you could have a life or joy and creativity, adrenaline and a lot of special emotions just by learning the infinite piece of software that exists today in the industry, in the open-source, and that now, everything is possible to learn for free, or at minimal cost.

ENJOY READING. ENJOY LEARNING. ENJOY SHARING.
LET'S MAKE A SAFER WORLD. LET'S FACE NEW CHALLENGE THA ARE COMING.
TO BE MORE AND MORE _____[7] WHEN TIME IS RUNNNING THAN YESTERDAY.

Christophe (@windowscpp) | christophep@cpixxi.com

---

[5] Please stay calm. Don't call the police. It's a joke.

[6] Excuse me again. It's also a joke. Keep calm, there is no more f*** jokes. I promise.

[7] It's up to you to choose the word(s). For me, it's "confident in the way we will be better"

PREFACE

About the Author

Christophe Pichaud is a French C/C++ developer based in Paris. In his career, he built large banking infrastructures and opened the first online bank (Banque Populaire) and participated in the construction of banking services for 2500 Société Générale branches (MAIA, URTA). It also performs C++ migrations and implements hybrid applications with the Microsoft .NET. Past clients include Accenture, Avanade, Sogeti, Cap Gemini, Palais de l'Elysée (Presidency of the French Republic), SNCF, Total, Danone, CACIB, Bnp Paribas. It has MCSD and MCSD.NET. In addition, he participates in Microsoft events as a speaker (TechDays, DevDays) and MVP on the Ask The Expert stands. He has been a regular contributor to Programmez *magazine* since 2011. He is also the Community Manager of ".NET Azure Rangers[8]", which has 28 members, including 8 MVPs, whose activities include facilitating technical sessions, writing technical articles and books and promoting Microsoft or Cloud technologies. NET Azure Rangers is officially a Microsoft Partner in France, UK and US with its local subdivisions SAS NET Azure Rangers in France, NET Azure Rangers LLC in DE, US and NET AZURE RANGERS Limited in London, UK.

About the NET Azure Rangers Community
The .NET Azure Rangers was created by François MERAND, a Microsoft France veteran who managed the Enterprise Architects in the 2000 to 2010, focusing on .NET Technologies promotion and evangelism about the .NET Platform ad Tools like Visual Studio, Windows Server and SQL Server or any server products to interact with.
When François left Microsoft, he asked Microsoft if the Rangers word could be used for custom software development, ALM (Application Lifecycle Management) and Azure. He was told OK, Rangers was reserved for Exchange Server specialists but Corp was Ok because the term was still in the Microsoft family. From 2011 to 2017, we have made a lot of strategic Microsoft Consulting missions and projects following the MCS guidelines:
- High rate per hour
- High skills and Solid Delivery

Our group was composed of the best .NET guys in France, HQ located in Paris Great Area, in Issy-Les-Moulineaux, where Microsoft HQ in France are located. We had Lyon, Strasbsourg, Bordeaux and some others place of battle fields for our Rangers. Lyon was the primary work force with an external service, not a Rangers camp, but a Business Unit lead by a Rangers, Keelan CLECH.
When François was fired from Sogeti (Capgemini group) for a fuzzy reason, he asked me to continue the Soaoul & Quest of the .NET Rangers as a public community. François get back in Nantes, in Loire Atlantique

When I took the Rangers on my own, I created the web site, the WordPress blog and because I was a technical writer since more than a decade, I filled the blog with ton of articles and stuff from my personal blog and real missions with information about anonymization data and sample softwares architecture case studies. Now, in May 2021, we are a group of former Sogeti/Capgemini Rangers veterans and some of the best IT guys I worked with since I joined Microsoft in 2017.

We are a group of 28 members and 8 MVPs. I upgraded our status from an association to a real company in September 2019. We are a Microsoft Partner and also a Linux/Cloud native member. We Company and we have opened virtual offices in France, UK and USA.

---

[8] www.netazurerangers.com

Professional C++ - Philosophy and Principles

SAS NET Azure Rangers
2 rue Henri Wallon
94120 Fontenay sous Bois
APE: 6202A
Conseil en systèmes et logiciels informatique

NET Azure Rangers LLC
16192 Coastal Highway
Lewes, Delaware 19958 USA

CPIXXI LIMITED
Company number 12299260
130 Old Street
London England
EC1V 9BD

The logo of the company is composed with the following pillars:

- The Microsoft .NET logo
- The Azure logo
- The MVP award logo

When he doesn't read books or develop software, Christophe spends his time with his three daughters, Edith, Lisa and Audrey and also his parents, Jean-Marc and Mireille who are in Burgundy. Every day, Christophe try to be a good guy with Patsy, it's young 10 months lovely tittle female cat.

You can join me on my email: christophep@cpixxi.com

My blog posts are dispatched randomly and spited and/or duplicated on the following URLs with some contents either in French or English :

- (En-us) http://www.christophep.com

Professional C++ - Philosophy and Principles

- (Fr) http://www.netazurerangers.com/blog/
- (Fr) https://christophepichaud.home.blog/

Why Read this Book?

The Modern C++ is expanding. We find it on:

- Connected Objects (IoT)
- The smartphones
- The desktops
- The servers
- The Cloud and AI

C++ is the most powerful and fastest language. It takes maximum advantage of hardware architecture and processors with a limited memory footprint.

Its modernity is characterized by a semi-automatic memory management with intelligent pointers (smart pointers), algorithms and lambdas, auto, the standard library STL (Standard Template Library), its data structures (containers), etc.

Compilers such as GCC, Clang, Intel Compilers or Visual C++ ones are using the latest processors and all hardware architectures (ARM, x86, amd64, PPC, MIPS, Alpha, IA64).

Examples of Code and Prerequisites

Code examples are freely available for download at http//www.windowscpp.com.

To compile the examples, you must have Visual Studio or GCC under MinGW64 or WSL (Windows Subsystem for Linux). On Linux, a compiler like GCC or Clang is sufficient. This is C++ ISO so portable and multiplatform.

About the Compilers

At the time of writing this book (December 2020), the compiler versions are:

- Visual C++ 2019 v16.9.6
- GCC 9.0
- Clang & LLVM 11

C++17 support is complete for all compilers. C++20 is complete for Visual Studio 2019 since this last days (21 May 2021)

Structure of the Book

There are specialized chapters.

- The C++ langage topics
    - Focus on C++11 révolution
    - Focus on Modern C++
- The Standard Library (STL)
- Some C++ magic stuff like
    - Lambdas
    - Templates
    - Smart Pointers
    - Memory Management
- Multithreading
    - On Widows
    - On Linux
- The ERA of Web Services and Web API on ALL Platforms
- The Unit Tests
- Classes and OOP
- The management of memory
- The lambdas
- The 64 bits
- The World of Web Services
- The Windows Services
- The Containers and Azure

Professional C++ - Philosophy and Principles

Foreword

Why learn C++ in 2021?

The world belongs to Microsoft Experts.

With their blog (http://www.netazurerangers.com/blog/), the .NET Azure Rangers address all important themes of our Microsoft ecosystem such as:

OSS, Linux, Kubernetes, NET Legacy, NET Core, NET 5, Azure, Windows Server, AD, O 365, Identity, WIF, oAuth, etc.

C+++? Why C/C++? Yes ... Because everything is done in C/C++.

Java and . NET (Microsoft .NET Developer) runtime are made in C/C++. Windows, Linux, Office, Chrome, SQL Server, Oracle, Exchange, Azure Service Fabric, etc.

Microsoft makes 95% of its products in C/C++. So, we discuss it and it's cool !

C/C++ runs the Cloud, the Servers, the Desktop. What else? (As George Clooney says.) 😊

Olivier Favre-Simon

Architect and C++ Developer since 1989

Author's Note

> The World is built on C++.
>
> Herb Sutter

C++ is deeply rich and intense as a language. Over time, it became elegant and modern. Despite spending billions on marketing, it has not been replaced by so-called "productive" languages. Operating systems like Microsoft Windows, Mac OS or Linux are always made with it. Office suites like Office also… Video games…

In 2018, I contacted DUNOD to propose them this book project because there is only a few books on the Modern C++, that is to say the C++ post C++11, date on which appeared a whole set of features like smart pointers, the automatic type deduction (auto) and the supremacy of the standard STL library with its strings, containers and algorithms among others.

Many C++ books speak of C++03/C++11/C++20 but do not detail the features of the latest standards for Performance and Optimization in mind. Buidling High-Scalable Application is dedicated vision of C++ for the Servers and the Cloud. It's the future. We already live in.

This book allows you, through an approach by example, to know all its features.

As a C++ development professional, I am MVP C++ since 2017 – Nov 2020 and have access to the source code of the latest Windows O.S. . To give you a quick idea, Microsoft has always made its O.S. and its software in C++. For Microsoft, C++ is natural, it's like electricity. There is no debate. We want to develop a product, we do it in C++.

Christophe Pichaud

Paris, France.

Sunday 31 January 2021 - 07:00 PM

Professional C++ - Philosophy and Principles

Acknowledgements

This book is the synthesis of my entire professional carrer begun in 1995 and its chapters were reviewed and corrected between September 2020 and February 2021 by many friends and work relations.

Among them, special thanks to Eric Mittelette (Microsoft Corp.), Alain Zanchetta (Microsoft Corp.) and Jean-Christophe Godefroy (ALTRAN) for their moments of truth and accuracy.

Thanks also to Eric Vernié (Microsoft France), Raphael Mansuy (CALYATIS), Daniel Begue (Orano), Fréderic Steczycki, Jean-Pierre Gervasoni (SYDEV), Michel Foucault (freelance) and Sylvain Pontoreau.

I would also like to thank my former colleagues from Sogeti and Capgemini, François Merand, Keelan Clech, Jean-Baptiste Bron and Cédric Georgeot.

My best friends are also to thank because I did not spare them during these years of writing: Philippe Rogie (Johnbry), Philippe Brand (freelance), Emeric Blumberger (SocGen).

I would also like to thank the best of us on C++, namely my friend Olivier Favre-Simon who made me discover Gentoo, Ubuntu, GCC, Boost and with whom I am looking forward to doing Cigare & Whisky parties again.

Acknowledgements bis (The Kiss of Death)

~~This book is the synthesis of my entire professional carrer begun in 1995 and its chapters were~~ Finally, Thanks to People at APress like 'Mark Powers' <MarkPowers@apress.com>; Matthew Moodie matthewmoodie@apress.com and Steve Anglin steveanglin@apress.com who allowed me to do my first book on C++ in English about a fabulous topic which is Performance and Optimization for High Available Software. There are not so many titles like this one. When I signed my APress contract, I was so happy. Thank you APress.

Things and the Weather has changed for a lot of reasons and the project was cancelled. It was very cool to know that Herb Sutter has accepted to write the foreword and then, for some reasons, Microsoft told us there was some "conflict of interests" so everything was cancelled on the Microsoft way. The final story is that Apress decided to stop the entire project of publishing the book. I was late but like any book author on a real and entire life project like this book represents for me. They tried to tell me some insane sentences about the quality of the books bla bla bla... I was shocked and completely disappointed and I was in a mindset to kill the entire humanity like a Dark Vador adept for the injustice that was given to me.

Professional C++

../..
 it does not meet the quality standards the manuscript needs to adhere to in order for it to be published by Apress.
../..
Per the email you sent us dated September 28, you still have not addressed our concerns and you have no intention to do so.
So, we have decided to terminate your publishing agreement.
../..
Sincerely,
Steve Anglin, Sc.M.
Assoc. Editorial Director, Acquisiti ons
Programming Languages/Topics

I wrote in this book by trying to explain the knowledge of 25 years of intense C++ battlefield missions that were sold between 420€ and 2350 € per day, including a lot of Microsoft missions as a contractor, a partner, a fireman, a life insurance guy, a co-architect or an employee. So my reaction at first glance was a feeling of injustice or surprise… like "You are kidding me or not ? I am not sure to really understand that what it is…"

So the Review was a little not funny when a little press man tell me : I don't know that, you may remove it from the script please, I do not even thing to delete any piece of letters nor any line. This book is what the industry gave me to earn a life, the respect of a lot of people and the proud and the reward of so many customers in trouble with softwares, desktop, servers, trouble shooting and so many debugging processes. I can't even deal with a guy who ever never done a compilation of helloworld.c trying to give me not publishing or writing stye advices but a judgement of the quality of

Professional C++ - Philosophy and Principles

my work. It's not a romance novel, it's a series of facts, best practices, tips and tricks and very documented stories about how to handle complex missions. Those guys have no ethic no shame but, they control the publishing of their branded books so I had to accept the fact it was cancelled. It took time to accept that decision. All the materials we belonging to them. To make me the owner of my own material, I had to sign a paper where I recognized that my draft was a shit 300 pages job. It was very complicated for me.

I had already published 5 books since 2019. You can check on Amazon for example.

Cf.https://www.amazon.fr/s?i=stripbooks&rh=p_27%3AChristophe+Pichaud&s=relevancerank&text=Christophe+Pichaud&ref=dp_byline_sr_book_1

It took me 12 months to sign this f**** paper and get my materials back to me. I signed it closing my eyes and my noise because I wanted to publish it as is. My readers will tell me rapidly whether or not they like it or not.

All the thing I believe in are in this book. It's 25 years of my life in this book and because emotions are important in that project, I can't resign for 2 or 3 jokers trying to tell me I am a Professional C++ Clown.

As a simple but experienced man, I try to understand my own emotions and to not deny or avoid it. It's the way it goes. Life is cruel and you have to fight hard to move your items on the Chess Game play. My relation with Microsoft is a 1994 begun love story and sometimes, I pushed it the hard way to survive on the battlefield and I can be proud to say, that I was always trying to find a good candidate option to making a win-win between the customer and Microsoft. I must admit that I have made millions of dollars of loss in Business for a lot of Microsoft Consulting Services stuff but... Millions of dollars of loss in consulting is a win when you stop the shipping process of some bad stuff delivery (software or critical solutions) to keep your level of integrity and professionalism for your customer.

I can't really give details on stuff that are covered in any NDA or shut-your-mouth budy case study but the fact is that the today business is going over complex and that technologies are not used the way they should be when politics and big money is the ultimate goal. Every consultant has to face the reality of what the customer wants and the constraints of the budget, the planning, the team and the necessary objective to ship it all the way it's written in the Business Agreement, the contract.

The difference between Consulting and Software Products Makers is that on the second side, the quality and the key indicators to take decisions and a battle plan are always clear because it's an engineering job. In the world of Consulting, politics is winning at all the layers of the life of a project. It will the topic of another book because it's so out of topic of this current book but it is definitively changing the way to solve a problem in a R&D department and in a open-space for a big Tech consulting company.

> C++ has been enormously influential. ... Lots of people say C++ is too big and too complicated etc. etc. but in fact it is a very powerful language and pretty much everything that is in there is there for a really sound reason: it is not somebody doing random invention, it is actually people trying to solve real world problems. Now a lot of the programs that we take for granted today, that we just use, are C++ programs.
>
> Brian Kernighan - 2018

Professional C++ - Philosophy and Principles

1. Introduction to Modern C++

This book is focused on Modern C++ with performance and optimization in mind. The different chapters cover techniques and advices to make your code better and presents best practices to enhance the performance of your applications. First, let's go back in a recent past to understand the context and the revolution of Modern C++, also called C++ Renaissance. Before Modern C++, C++ was an object-oriented language shipped with its Standard Template Library (STL) and *voilà*. It was the era of C++98 and next C++03. It was the final evolution of C with Classes[9]. C++ is managed by an ISO committee[10] called WG21. The current ISO C++ standard is officially known as ISO International Standard ISO/IEC 14882:2017(E) – Programming Language C++. The latest C++ standard[11] is available on Github in the ISO C++ repository[12]. The standard is a book containing 1800 pages that contains the whole documentation of C++. Here is how the scope of the book is described:

This document specifies requirements for implementations of the C++ programming language. The first such requirement is that they implement the language, so this document also defines C++. Other requirements and relaxations of the first requirement appear at various places within this document.

C++ is a general purpose programming language based on the C programming language as described in ISO/IEC 9899:2018 Programming languages — C (hereinafter referred to as the C standard). C++ provides many facilities beyond those provided by C, including additional data types, classes, templates, exceptions, namespaces, operator overloading, function name overloading, references, free store management operators, and additional library facilities.

Why C++ and What is Modern C++ ?

Modern C++ is covered by C++11, C++14 , C++17 and C++20. But let's look back in the mirror to see what is the DNA of C++, and how the creator C++, Bjarne Stroustrup, created and made evolutions to C++:

---

[9] In 1982, Stroustrup started to develop a successor to C with Classes, which he named "C++"

[10] The ISO C++ committee is called WG21, officially ISO/IEC JTC1 (Joint Technical Committee 1) / SC22 (Subcommittee 22) / WG21 (Working Group 21). WG21 was formed in 1990-91, and consists of accredited experts from member nations of ISO/IEC JTC1/SC22 who are interested in C++ work.

[11] https://github.com/cplusplus/draft/releases/download/n4861/n4861.pdf

[12] https://github.com/cplusplus/draft

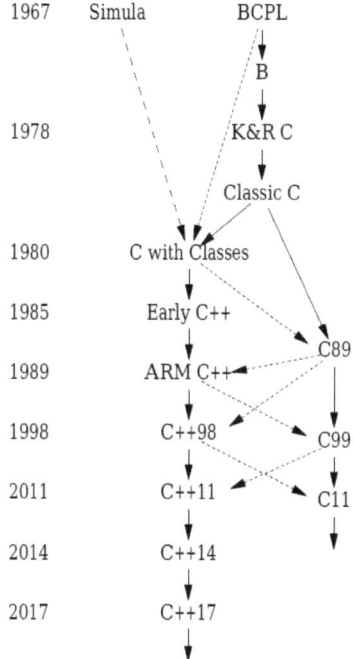

Figure 2 - C++ is inspirated by existing languages

As you can see on the diagram, there is gap of 13 years between C++98 and C++11. C++11 was previously named C++0x but it was shipped later than expected. A partial shipment was done in 2005 with somewhat was called TR1 (Technical Report 1) but the full features of C++ was included in C++11 and it became Modern C++. The new wave for C++: a renaissance.

Modern C++ means usage of STL containers, lambdas, algorithms, auto type deduction and smart pointers usage for example. This kind of coding is completely different of traditional C++ (old C++98 or C++03). C++ is the best language for abstraction, low-level and high-level code, object-oriented programming and template programming. In one of its presentation dated from 2011, Herb Sutter, Partner Architect working at Microsoft Corp. and Chairman of ISO C++, presented this picture of C++11 during a public conference:

Professional C++ - Philosophy and Principles

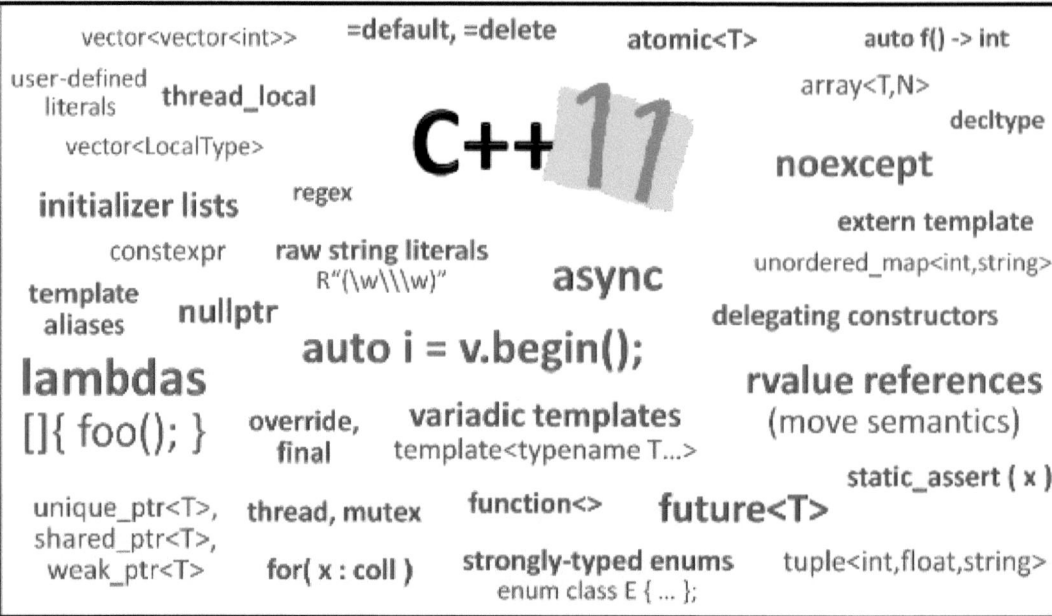

Figure 3 - Modern C++, myths and reality

One punchline of Herb was "Power and Performance" for describing C++ in 2011. C++ is the language of choice because of its power, its size and its experiences.

C++ Myths and Reality

Based on the previous image, I have created another picture in 2012 for illustrating the pitfalls of C++ and the urban legend propaganda on C++. I named this slide "Myths & Reality". It contains some sentences like:

- Pointers
- Macros and goto
- Difficult to learn
- Code is difficult to maintain
- Non secure, dangerous
- Ugly code
- C with structs
- Non productive

It was in 2012 for a Microsoft TechDays conference in Paris, France. A lot people are aware that C and C++ can drive you into high performance but few of the crowd know that C++11 was a revolution to the C++ world and most of them are staying with facts that were covering C++98 and C++03 and some reflections about C.

C++, myths & reality

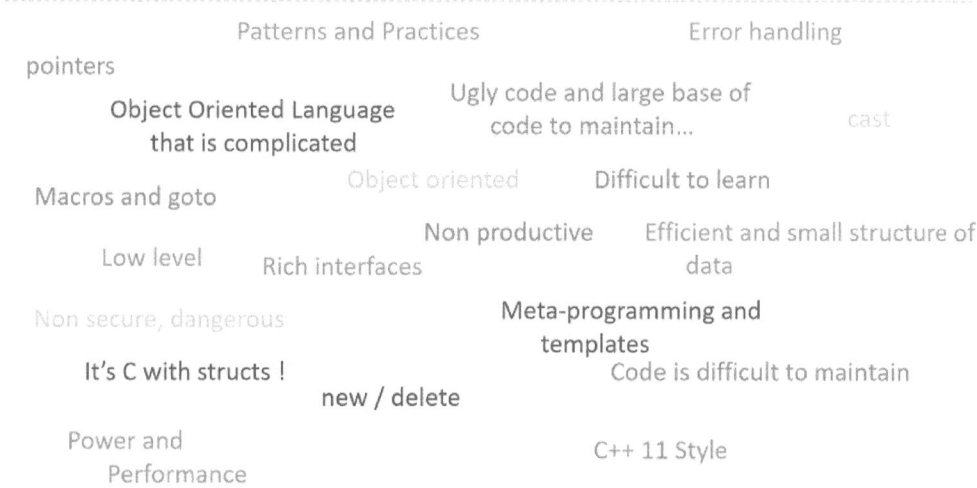

Figure 4 - C++, Myhs and Reality

Some are true, some are wrong but some people think this is real, it's a pity. But the evolution of C++ has changed everything. Since 2011, people are considering C++ has a top player in the software development world, moreover than before. The years of productivity languages has not accomplished all the miracles it was supposed to. The truth appeared in front of every developer that want an application on the server or one a mobile. If you want something that is reasonably fast, you need native stuff. Have you ever been patient for an application that makes 20 seconds to start on a mobile phone ? Do you think it is reasonable to upgrade your hardware because an application is slow ? More, your processor has multiples core and an application is not able to take advantage of it ? When you need concurrency, low resource usage (CPU, RAM), the choice is native[13]. On mobile, desktop and servers, most of the times, the choice is C/C++.

Some companies like Facebook, for example, has tried to make Java, PHP optimization and then, after several attempts, returned to C++ because it is the most genuine choice. One popular employee of Facebook, has written that:

*"The going word at Facebook is that '**reasonably written C++ code just runs fast**,' which underscores the enormous effort spent at optimizing PHP and Java code. Paradoxically, C++ code is more difficult to write than in other languages,*

---

[13] I admit there are also others languages that are native like Go, Rust or Objective C/C++. Some platform like Apple's iOS and Mac OS makes the promotion of Objective C/C++ and recently, Swift. You can also notice that LLVM has others front-end for producing native modules.

Professional C++ - Philosophy and Principles

but
efficient code is a lot easier." – Andrei Alexandrescu

In the previous slide from Herb Sutter, the goal was to cover all the aspects of Modern C++ with the upcoming of C++11. C++11 was a revolution with so many features, presented in this picture. In the same presentation, Herb presented also a slide called Why C++ ?

power: driver at all scales: on-die, mobile, desktop, datacenter

size: limits on processor resources: desktop, mobile

experiences: bigger experiences on smaller hardware; pushing envelope means every cycle matters

Figure 5 - Herb Sutter in 2011 about C++ Renaissance

In this presentation, Herb also made a review of previous years where productivity[14] was the only keyword "à la mode". But in 2011, date of the presentation, C++ is back on the sunlight of the actuality. On the popular Channel9 web site from Microsoft, the video "C++ Renaissance[15]" was the beginning of a wave. Here is an extract of the video description:

<< C++ is currently undergoing a renaissance. This means that, by definition, the language, compilers and compositional tooling are evolving and coalescing into a state that maximizes native developer efficiency, productivity, and creativity across hardware and software domains (PCs, mobile devices, embedded systems, operating systems, user applications, services, etc). C++ is a powerful "systems" programming language, but it's more than that. It's object oriented, but it's more than that. At Microsoft, most of our flagship products are written in C++ (and C, like the Windows kernel...). As somebody with a keen interest in programming languages and software engineering, generally, I wanted to get some answers to broad questions concerning the language that consistently ranks near the top of the most widely used general purpose programming languages in the world. Who better to talk to than some key technical leaders driving Microsoft's Visual C++ business? >>

This description let us remember that Microsoft is doing most of its applications with C and C++ (95%). Windows, Office (Word, Excel, PowerPoint, Outlook, Access), SQL Server, Exchange, Windows Server, Biztalk, .NET CLR, etc. Every Team at Microsoft is doing C/C++.

The C++ revolution was done without any Corporation (GAFAM) support nor extra Marketing events. Time has done its effect on productive languages. Herb said that Coffee based languages (Java and C#) been adopted so widely that developers realized that there were no options to optimize your code and have a gain of 20% or 50% using standard options like in C++. Why? The architecture of these languages is based on automatic memory management, virtual machine execution engine and low-level managed assembly code. One line of coffee-based language is executed when 1000 lines of "plumbing" is executed and fully managed. There is a sand box like architecture for running all the managed code. In Microsoft NET Technologies, the CoreCLR is hosting all the NET assemblies. More, the difference between Release and Debug Mode is very close so traditional developers are lost with existing old-school methods used in System Programming for decades to make enhancements either in performance or optimization.

In the others company, C/C++ is also the king. Oracle, Google, IBM, Adobe and others are developing software with millions of lines of C/C++. When C++11 was released[16], there are so many features that the C++ community was widely

---

[14] It was the years for Java and C# languages, the evidence of Framework and high-level features and virtual machine runtime controlling JIT compiling, Garbage Collector mechanism, application isolation, safety and security. Java was the first Application platform with byte-code and virtual machine execution and multiplatform features. In 2002, Microsoft shipped the .NET Framework, the C# language and the CLR, which is a copy of the Java platform but running only on Windows. Now, .Net Core enable to run on Windows, Mac and Linux.

[15] https://channel9.msdn.com/Shows/Going+Deep/Craig-Symonds-and-Mohsen-Agsen-C-Renaissance

[16] C++11 was approved by International Organization for Standardization (ISO) on 12 August 2011.

Professional C++ - Philosophy and Principles

enthusiasts are there was a massive adoption and growing evolution of the number of C++ developers even if C++ is not powered by a big marketing machine or owned by a company.

Some people say that C++ does not have Reflection features not Garbage Collector. Bjarne Stroustrup answered that *"C++ is the best language for garbage collection principally because it creates less garbage."*

C++ is Multi-Platform and Multi-Devices

C++ allows you to code on one platform and you can recompile your code on another platform. You share the source because between the different target architecture and compile with various compilers, each dedicated to target a specific architecture (Processor type / Mode 32 bit or 64bits), for example:

- Visual C++ on Windows (shipped with Visual Studio)
- CLang (LLVM) on Linux and Mac.
- GCC on Linux
- Intel compiler on Linux and Windows

Multiple compilers, multiple processors, multiples operating system and multiple devices:

The logo for C++ is looking like that:

Professional C++

I have added the Apple, Android and Linux logos. You can notice that the image shows different devices with different OS but also with different sizes.

With C/C++, you optimize the number of source code lines shared between the different architectures and platforms. The code is smaller, you reuse often and better and you have direct access to the underlying Operating Systems because they are made with C for the kernel, and C++ for others parts. Native APIs are directly exposed to C/C++ as APIs and you link with object files shipped by the Platform SDK.

Example of popular multi-platform, multi-device application : Chrome. The web browser from Google and also, Chromium[17] the open-source version of the project with few restrictions.

Another topic we will cover in this book is the processor. If you want to take advantage of extended instructions in new processor, you need C/C++ with some explications to proceed but it's not very complex and you can achieve a serious and significant step to the light.

---

[17] http://www.chromium.org/

Professional C++ - Philosophy and Principles

The TIOBE Index

Another source of inspiration about the wide adoption of C++ is the TIOBE Index[18]. The TIOBE index is a popular metric and is built with information from search engines[19]. At the time I am writing this chapter, the TIOBE Index is October 2020 and C++ is ranked 4th with 7% and C is ranked 1st with 17%. It means 24% for C/C++. Let's round to 25%. The world of software development is dominated by C/C++. It's a fact.

Oct 2020	Oct 2019	Change	Programming Language	Ratings	Change
1	2	^	C	16.95%	+0.77%
2	1	v	Java	12.56%	-4.32%
3	3		Python	11.28%	+2.19%
4	4		C++	6.94%	+0.71%
5	5		C#	4.16%	+0.30%
6	6		Visual Basic	3.97%	+0.23%
7	7		JavaScript	2.14%	+0.06%
8	9	^	PHP	2.09%	+0.18%
9	15	^	R	1.99%	+0.73%
10	8	v	SQL	1.57%	-0.37%

Figure 6 - The TIOBE Index

---

[18] https://www.tiobe.com/tiobe-index/

[19] The TIOBE Programming Community index is an indicator of the popularity of programming languages. The index is updated once a month. The ratings are based on the number of skilled engineers world-wide, courses and third party vendors. Popular search engines such as Google, Bing, Yahoo!, Wikipedia, Amazon, YouTube and Baidu are used to calculate the ratings. It is important to note that the TIOBE index is not about the best programming language or the language in which most lines of code have been written.

Performance and Optimization Orientations

This book is focused on enhancing **performance** of your applications and giving you the maximum of the best practices for making **optimizations** in your code whether you use traditional C++ or Modern C++. We will examine and make a deep dive into the following items:

- Algorithms
- Data Structures
- Language features
- Libraries
- Compiler Optimizations
- System Architecture
- Case studies

I hope that you will enjoy reading this book as much I had pleasure to write it. I made several researches to cover a wide aspect of Performance and Optimizations from various sources:

- The official documentation of compilers from Visual C++, to GCC and Clang (LLVM)
- Microsoft Docs and MSDN Library
- Linux Kernel Documentation from kernel.org
- cppreference.com
- some comments on Stack Overflow even if I don't recommend this site for unexperienced developers because there are too many bad advice or not appropriated solutions
- Best Sellers from Herb Sutter's Red Books from Addison Wesley
- Bjarne Stroustrup Books
- Some Github repositories

It was very excited to cover all those aspects because after 25 years of software development experiences, from consulting, training, audit and software development of products for customers, I have seen so many faces of the industry and so many different ways to design and build software. Making software auditing is one advantage in this business : you can see how a project, that was achieved during several months or years, was done and designing with all its source code in 1 week. The source code does not lie. From poor abstraction, C-like programs, to OOP systems, to middleware and plumbing layers, from UI to shared modules, I have a passion for reading source code.

Microsoft Inspiration and its Cooking Guide

Since 2002, I had the chance to read the Windows source code written with C and C++. At this time, it was possible because a leak of Windows NT4 source code appeared on P2P networks. The file was named *windows_nt_4_source_code zip* and if you use your favorite search engine, you will find it on Torrents network or even in some Github repositories ! The size of the zip archive is 235MB, and when the files are extracted, its size is 956MB. It's a huge base of code. You have the kernel, the NT RTL, the shell, the user, COM, OLE, a lot of things. In the ntos folder, you can browse the ke folder containing the kernel and you can look at diamonds like David N. Cutler source code, dated from 1989. Here is the banner comments from threaobj.c:

```
/*++

            Copyright (c) 1989  Microsoft Corporation

            Module Name:

                threadobj.c

            Abstract:

                This module implements the machine independent functions to manipulate
                the kernel thread object. Functions are provided to initialize, ready,
                alert, test alert, boost priority, enable APC queuing, disable APC
                queuing, confine, set affinity, set priority, suspend, resume, alert
                resume, terminate, read thread state, freeze, unfreeze, query data
                alignment handling mode, force resume, and enter and leave critical
                regions for thread objects.

            Author:

                David N. Cutler (davec) 4-Mar-1989

            Environment:

                Kernel mode only.

            Revision History:

--*/
```

In the beginning of year 2003, another leak appeared on P2P network, it was named *w2sc.zip* and it contains the Windows 2000 source code. Archive file is 208MB and extracted, its size is 658MB.

I have spent so many hours reading this huge source code and I continue event now. I was considering this source code as the state of the art of software development and I was reading and reading, learning and learning to be able to write code like Microsoft does. Even in 2020, at the times I write this book, I still have access to the latest Windows Source Code via my MVP[20] award membership[21] and the Microsoft Shared Source Initiative[22] that gives me access to Windows

---

[20] https://mvp.microsoft.com/

[21] https://mvp.microsoft.com/en-us/PublicProfile/5003105

[22] https://www.microsoft.com/en-us/sharedsource/default.aspx

10 latest source code. I have always considered Microsoft as best software development company and my love for products like Windows and Visual C++ always inspired me to take like a model the way they build their own products.

Microsoft is committed to C++

From Windows NT3.51 to Windows 10, the source code techniques have evolved a lot and there are different ways to express things with C++, whether you have support only to C++03 or C++17. With the latest source code of Windows 10, there is more C++ than ever and the direction is clearly about Modern C++.

Without breaking the NDA that I have signed with Microsoft, I can tell you that Windows 10 source contains:

- Templates programming
- Heavy STL usage
- Modern C++ with auto and lambdas
- Smart Pointers
- And a lot of C++ tips & tricks

The latest evolutions of Windows 10, the Windows Runtime, COM evolutions, latest accessories applications are made completely with Modern C++. Reading the Windows source code requires some information before the reading experience and a little time of adoption because you need to know how to parse the hierarchy of folders. But it is very comfortable to read. There are not so many comments but the code is very well written, in my opinion.

If you want to grab some Microsoft source code, you have the underground way of Torrents network or you can open a Github repository like the .NET Framework CLR[23], the Windows Terminal[24] project or Azure Service Fabric[25]. There is a lot of others repositories in the Microsoft root space on Github[26].

Herb Sutter, the Chairman of ISO C++ is working for Microsoft and he makes the promotion of ISO C++ instead of private extensions[27] or proprietary things.

---

[23] https://github.com/dotnet/runtime

[24] https://github.com/Microsoft/Terminal

[25] https://github.com/Microsoft/service-fabric

[26] https://github.com/Microsoft

[27] C++/CX is an example with its ^ (hat) usage. A nightmare.

Professional C++ - Philosophy and Principles

The Key is performance

7 years ago, I was doing an inventory of an old-school laptop and was asking myself why I don't throw it away to the garbage... There reason was that for a very limited Hardware set of components:
- Intel Celeron Quad Core Processor
- Intel HD Graphics
- 4 GB RAM
   500 GB Disk

As a reminder, all the software I used on my laptop were written in C/C++:
- Windows and its 3400 DLL and 650 EXE
- File Explorer
- The Task Manager
- MS Paint
- My media players VLC and WinAmp
- Web browsers (Chrome, Firefox, Internet Explorer, Edge)
- Office Suite (Word, Excel, PowerPoint, Outlook, etc) and Libre Office on Linux Ubuntu 20.10 LTSC
- Notepad++
- Acrobat Reader
- My old MSDN Library 2008 SP1
- My legendary MSDN July 1994 MSDN Library CD[28]

The only exception I have on my PC is Visual Studio which is a hybrid C/C++ application. NET COM. The laptop was used to write technical articles ; it was a low-cost laptop manufactured by Acer purchased in 2015. And yet with a low-cost PC, I can still use Windows at the same time, a browser, Word, MS Paint, Visual Studio and listen to music in the background. And I never had performance issues; Proof of this is the Task Manager:
Of course, this PC will not do video editing or diverse and varied compression... But on the other hand, for standard use, it allows me to work.
For serious research and compilation required and performance issues and measure, I soon jump on a €900 Laptop Dell Windows 10 Pro Core i7, 8 GB RAM and 1 TB Disk and 128 GB SSD Windows System Partition Disk. To be fully honest, extracting boost.zip archive, compiling it with bjam with dedicated flags liked Debug, Release, UNICODE and 64 bits with Visual C++ compiler (VS 2019 v16.8x) on the cmd.exe Window took around 8 minutes compared to 2 hours on the 300€ Celeron machine. But most people are standard users, so performance is key for users to continue to use an existing hardware.

Figure 7 - An Old PC configuration

---

[28] Thanks to Replay Software Corp and Olivier Dagguet and Jean-Claude Lavoignat in 1994 to have given me this and ... THE PASSSION of Microsoft stuff ☺. Olivier is now owning an company in Nice, France who sells Consulting, Softwares and Services like Document SharePoint style Company for Trial Court Office named « Greffes des Tribunaux » in French

Professional C++

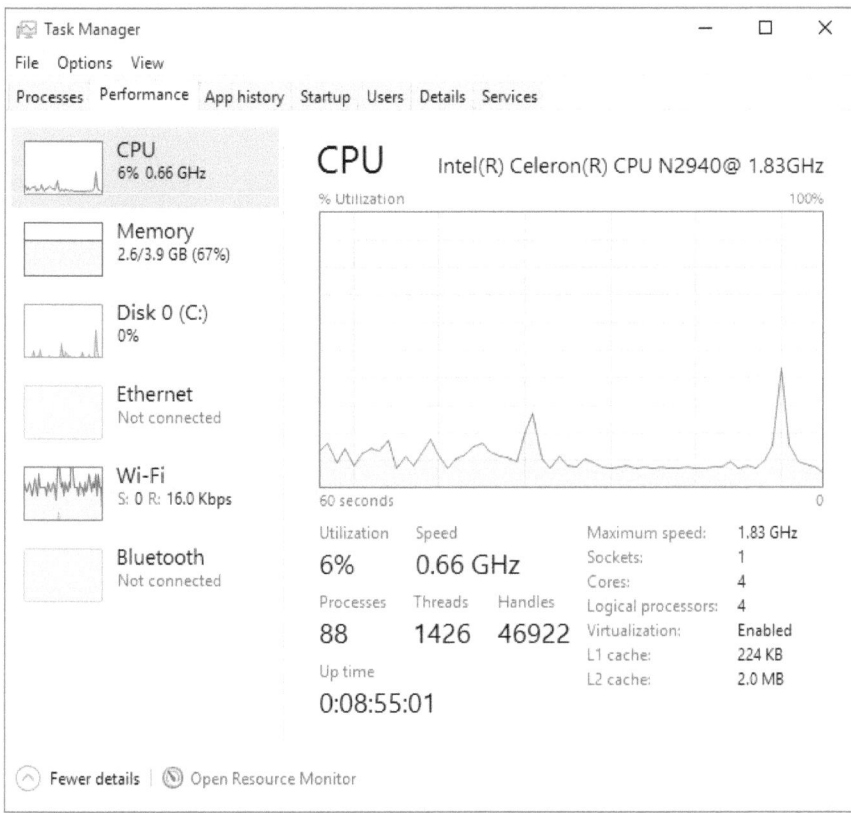

Modern computing usage is made with only one central application: a web browser. It's because Google Chrome is made with C/C++ that you can open 25 tabbed panes with one web site in each tab that Chrome memory consuming effort is less than that 1 or 2 GB. Modern web site relies a lot on JavaScript files and V8's Google JS Engine is making miracles for Chrome to work on either a Core i7 32GB RAM with Windows 10 or on Android devices with 1GB of RAM sold by Xiaomi for less than $150.

Anatomy of applications

The applications I run use little memory and are reactive. Why? Because they use directly the APIs of the operating system that is Windows. Windows APIs can be used from a simple C/C++ compiler. Just enter #include <windows.h> and you have access to thousands of functions. Each edition of Visual Studio distributes the Windows SDK. The applications consume little memory and this is the key to success.

Professional C++ - Philosophy and Principles

Myths and realities

You will tell me, yeah, but making an application in C++ *from scratch*, it's difficult and it's not productive. I reply to pay attention to the marketing discourse and prejudices...

Indeed, to develop an application, Microsoft recommends doing C#, VB.NET or JavaScript. Yes, but well... the question is: why doesn't Microsoft make its applications in . NET? We were told that Microsoft *practices dog-fooding*: that is, when MS releases a technology, MS reuses it in its products. Oh yes, but it's a little more complex than that. For Microsoft, C++ is electricity, it's natural. For marketing, .NET is the clear choice. So, who to believe? If you want to make an application that only works on Windows, yes. NET may be an alternative but be careful, you have to redistribute the .NET. You will say yes, but with . NET Standard 2.0, we can compile on Windows, Mac and Linux. I'm going to make it short... Ten years ago, there was a package called Mono that allowed to do C# under Linux. It was a flop. Now that Microsoft bought Xamarin and . NET Standard 2.0 is out, marketing sends its sirens to make mobile and desktop applications via . NET and C# across multiple platforms... Beware of ad effects because it's not as simple as it says. Do your own experiment. In C/C++ under Windows, simply redistribute MSVCRedist.exe which is 10 MB. This package contains the runtime of C, STL, DLLs of MFC. In addition, Windows already contains several versions of these modules.

To make an application of good standing, you have to be able to provide an elegant graphical interface, libraries that consume little memory and operations that do not push the processor into its last recesses. And here, it is the principle of onions. If you develop with a runtime and a framework, there will be several layers to go through before your code joins the operating system APIs or your processor's instructions. The fashion is to preserve the battery, relieve the discs, and consume little memory. Only the C/C++ allows you to do this. At the level of language C, we find the following fundamentals:
- Memory management with malloc/free functions
- I/O management: stdio. h and the functions open, close, read, write, fopen, fprintf, fread, fwrite
- Management of int * ptr pointers;
- Etc

The C++ provides a more abstract level via the STL (Standard Template Library) which manages:
- Automatic memory management: avoid new/delete via unique_ptr<T> and shared_ptr<T>
- Managing strings and buffers with string, wstring and streams
- Container management (array, vector, list, map, set, etc.)
- Of algorithms
- Etc

Instead of presenting my low-cost laptop PC, I could tell you about Linux distributions running on old machines. Why? Everything is done in C/C++ at 99%. In short, we position the cursor on the following elements:
- Manage the battery
- Manage memory
- Manage the processor

With so-called productive languages, you have no way of optimizing these 3 factors because you are in the high spheres of a runtime (CLR or JRE) that does a lot of things on its own... On a desktop, you can hide that, but on a mobile, the penalty is immediate. If the application taxes the battery or if an application spends its time heating the battery, it is not good and the application will not be very successful.

C/C++ is portable and native

On each system (Windows, Linux, Mac), there is a C/C++ compiler. It is thus possible to make portable code. Of course, the code that uses Windows APIs will not compile on Linux but the business code, POCO (Plain Old Class Object) classes

and third-party *libs* compile. The advantage of C/C++ is that the operating system is made with C. The other APIs of the third-party *libraries* are also made in C/C++. So what's the advantage? On Windows, for example, you want to send encrypted messages; Nothing prevents you from recovering an encryption library on Linux, recompiling it, and using it on Windows. The combinations are infinite.
In addition, the C/C++ compilers are free.

The documentation

If you want to start, there is a free and excellent resource, not so deprecated: MSDN Library 2008 SP1. This set of articles contains all the resources to develop under Windows. There are also articles on C/C++ and MFC.
Download this 2.8 GB ISO file from the *Microsoft Download Center* and install it.

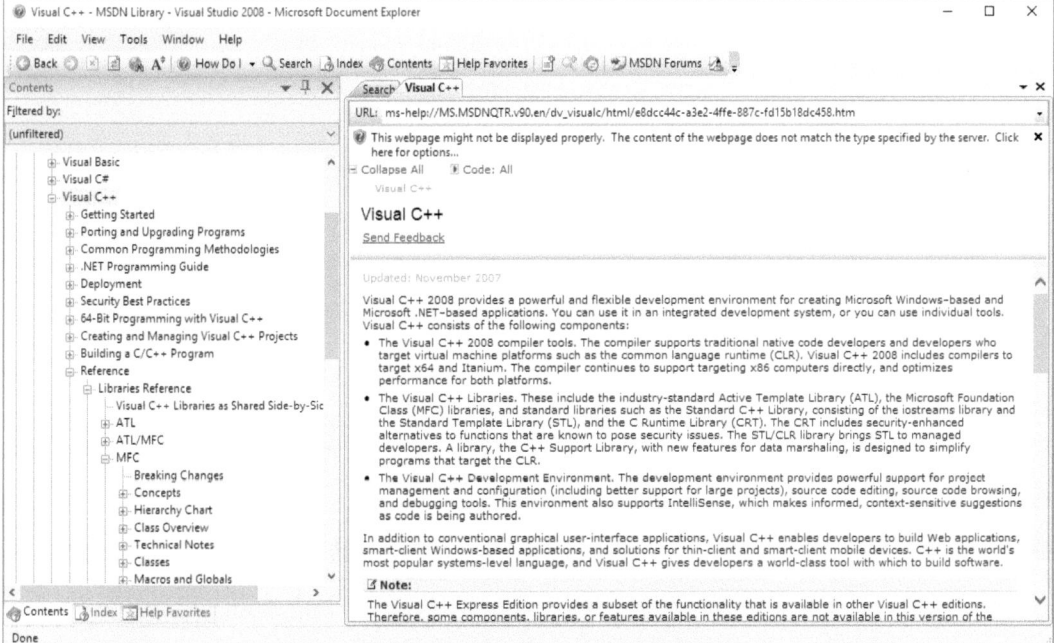

Figure 8 - MSDN Librray - Visual Studio 2008 SP1 Edition available on MSDN Download Center

There is also a more recent version of the Microsoft documentation. With Visual Studio, there is *an application called* Help Viewer in which you can download different sections of the help (.NET, Visual C++, SQL Server, etc).

Professional C++ - Philosophy and Principles

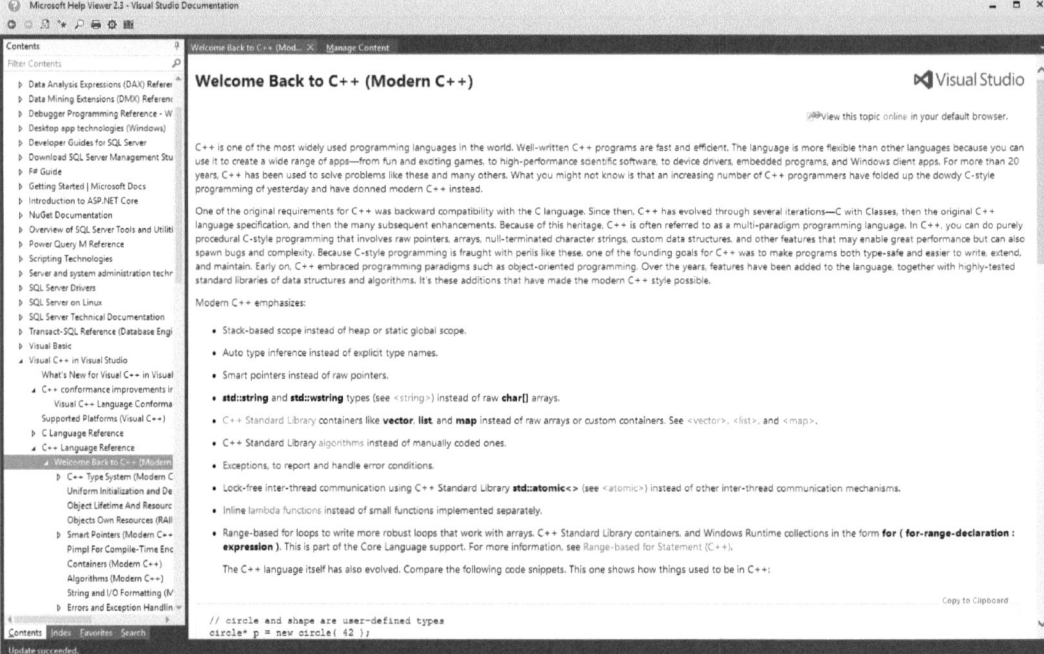

Figure 9 - MSDN Help Application shipped with Visual Studio 2017 and Visual Studio 2019

Here, the choice is Visual Studio. VS is available as a free Community Edition. This version is the calling product to the paid version of VS as VS Pro. The cost of the product is about $500 or €500.
The Visual Studio IDE is very comfortable but you must understand that this product contains many features. The problem with Visual Studio is that it's getting heavier and so you have to be patient if your development machine is not very fast... In short, you are warned!

Professional C++

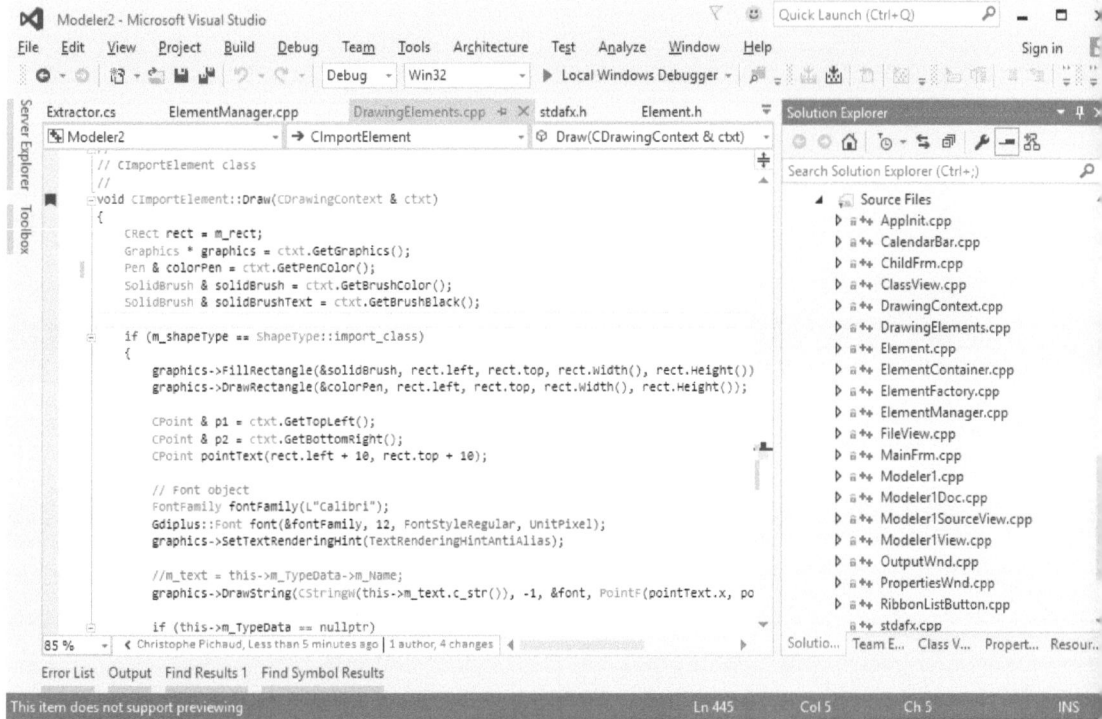

Figure 10 - Visual Studio 2019 with a C++ Project

It is also possible to use VS Code but it is not the same. VS Code allow you to call G++ or Clang but you run your commands manually on a Terminal Window with a Linux Shell and some basic IDE with features implemented by a TS/JS community more excited to promote the JS message rather than giving C+= developers a real text Experience. Running also possible either in VS Code Shell or in WSL2 via the wonderful Windows Terminal[29] Project provided Open-Source by Microsoft.

Some Resources For Students or Cookbook Books to carry in your bag or SD card

The first step is to learn the language in its version C++ 11 or C++ Modern. A good book, written by the language creator, is available since 2014: *A Tour of C++* by Bjarne Stroustrup.

---

[29] https://github.com/microsoft/terminal

47

Professional C++ - Philosophy and Principles

Figure 11 - A Tour of C++, by Bjarne Stroustrup, Inventor of C++

The STL (Standard Template Library)

The STL is the C++ library. It contains many header files. The evolution of the compiler is inseparable from the evolution of the STL. The STL provides template classes to satisfy all major needs: from algorithms to containers, from strings to threads, etc. Here are the header files:

<algorithm>	copy(), find(), sort()
<array>	array
<chrono>	duration, time_point
<cmath>	sqrt(), pow()
<complex>	complex, sqrt(), pow()
<forward_list>	forward_list
<fstream>	fstream, ifstream, ofstream
<future>	future, promise
<ios>	hex,dec,scientific,fixed,defaultfloat
<iostream>	istream, ostream, cin, cout
<map>	map, multimap
<memory>	unique_ptr, shared_ptr, allocator
<random>	default_random_engine, normal_distribution
<regex>	regex, smatch
<string>	string, basic_string
<set>	set, multiset
<sstream>	istrstream, ostrstream
<stdexcept>	length_error, out_of_range, runtime_error
<thread>	thread
<unordered_map>	unordered_map, unordered_multimap
<utility>	move(), swap(), pair
<vector>	vector

The classes
It is possible to create concrete or abstract types. To create an abstract class, simply declare a pure virtual method. Inheritance can be simple or multiple.

The templates

A template is a class that takes one or more types as a parameter. The template is evaluated at compilation. There are also template functions.

The Modern C++
The main elements of modern C++ are:
- Using the stack instead of the heap
- Using auto to hide the actual type
- Using smart pointers instead of normal pointers
- Using std::string or std::wstring instead of char[]
- Use of STL vector, list and map containers instead of customs structures
- Using SSD algorithms instead of customs routines
- Using Exceptions to escalate errors
- Using STL std::atomic<> instead of custom IPC mechanisms
- Use of inline *lambdas instead of small separately declared functions*
- Use of the range for the journey of the tables and other containers

The use of the auto keyword allows to hide complex types to be used. So to declare an iterator on a shared_ptr<T> vector, you no longer have to write:
vector<shared_ptr<MyClass>::const_iterator it = v.begin();
Instead we write this: auto it = v.begin();

With modern C++ there is no need to use the new/delete mechanisms to allocate or free memory. Instead, smart pointers such as unique_ptr<T> or shared_ptr<T> are used to free the memory automatically.

Cross-platform development
Let's go back to two definitions that are overused: the native and the multi-platform. When we talk about native development, we are talking about development that uses the same language as the one that made it possible to make the operating system. Concretely it's C/C++. Under Windows, Linux and Mac, it's like that.
This means that operating system APIs are used directly in the . h headers provided by the OS SDK. For a Windows program, this means that it loads kernel32.dll, user32.dll and gdi32.dll. From the moment you use a language like C# that contains a garbage collector and uses a runtime, you are not in the native. Unfortunately, marketing is full of crap...

C++ /CLR hybrid development
On Windows, it is possible to make C++ code that calls .NET classes via C++/CLI. To do this, the project must support the *Common Language Runtime Support*/clr option. It is thus possible to make reference additions to *assemblies* . NET in a C++ project. If you have code. NET, you can reuse it and it is done very easily. The advantage is that if you have XML or ADO.NET needs, you will immediately have the support of the . NET Framework at your fingertips.

Graphic framework
To develop a graphical application, you need APIs to display controls, windows, menus, dialog boxes, etc. Each system (Windows, Linux, Mac) provides APIs for this.

There are also different Frameworks to make windowed applications:
- GTK
- Qt
- MFC
- WTL
- AppKit, Cocoa
- WxWidgets

On Windows, there are 3 options:
- GDI32: Window Management History API C

Professional C++ - Philosophy and Principles

- MFC: Microsoft Foundation Classes
- WTL: Windows Template Library

Personally, I started with GDI32 to learn the basics. Nowadays, I am a fan of MFC because I am very productive with it. The framework provides the basics of modern applications at the output of the Wizard. With GDI32, you have to code everything and it takes time. In addition, MFC provides sophisticated controls such as docking pane, grid properties, ribbon, MDI with document-view model; It's a little different from MVC but the principles are the same.

Here are the types of applications that can be easily done with MFC:

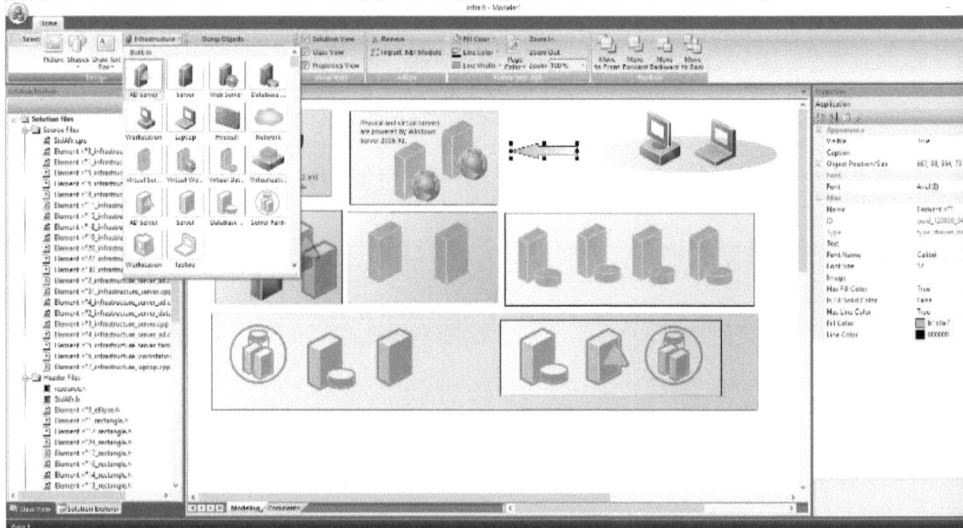

Figure 12 - A Very Complex Windows Application. Available on www.ultrafluid.net

This application has all the graphic controls that are sexy and functional.

Back-end in C++
It is possible to build the server part of an application via several technologies. It is possible to build:
- A Windows service with CPIs
- An XML-RPC custom server
- An API Web server that returns JSON via the REST SDK

The advantage of the REST SDK is that it can return data in JSON format for a front that is not necessarily in C++. The C++ server made with the REST SDK will be the subject of a separate article.

The Redmond Way on Modern C++ and the 25th Anniversary of cl.exe, the Microsoft Visual C++ Compiler
On Windows, the Visual C++ compiler is celebrating its 25th anniversary! He's never been more powerful. The Modern C++ opens up great possibilities because the code is easier to write, easier to read and more efficient. The STL has many features to use like containers, smart pointers. In short, the language is very affordable even if you have Java or C# bases because these are only descendants of C++...

A synthesis recap on C++ basic elements and Modern C++ (post ISO C++ 11 era)

Professional C++

I voluntary apologize to the reader who read the 5 or 6 following pages because it contains stuff every modern developer knows about: classes, OOP, and inheritance and polymorphism. But even in Bjarne Stroustrup's latest book[30], the students or the new coming developers to C/C++ is helped to reach our C++ community and mark some sites[31] and reference web site as favorites.

Here are several ways to use C++. You can be a class user or a class designer. In both cases,
There are several ways to use C++. You can be a class user or a class designer. In both cases, defining, designing and implementing classes are the primary activities of C++ developers. Where do we start? In general, we start with an abstraction or a concept. You look at something to be coded and then you try to see how you're going to manage your function or functions, what's internal and what's public and how you're going to use it— At the start of this reflection, we must put qon the hat of the one who will use the class. Our concept example will be a graphic element to draw like a line, a rectangle, an ellipse, etc. In English, it is a *shape*.

```
// This is a class statement
class CShape;

// This is the future way I want to draw Shapes
bool Draw(const CShape& item);

Then we look at the class as a whole:
class CShape
{
public:
    // public interface

private:
    // private implementation
};
```

What is put in private/public and how will it be structured. We start small arm and then the class takes volume.

Constructor and Destructor

The first question that comes to mind is how I will create my object and do I need to provide it with parameters. With my CShape class, you might say, I don't need it, but I need it. The two possibilities exist! Either it is a known figure -> hence an enumeration for known types and other possibility that is to draw an image and there I need a filename; everything is open!

```
enum ShapeType
{
    line,
    circle,
    rectangle,
    left_arrow,
```

---

30 A Tour of C++, 2nd Edition, Bjarne Stroustrup, 2014, Addison Wesley

31 https://isocpp.org | https://en.cppreference.com/w | https://www.boost.org | https://herbsutter.com

Professional C++ - Philosophy and Principles

```
        right_arrow,
        picture
};
```

The advantage of listing is that it is evaluated at compilation. There can be no error on the naming because it is an explicit type unlike a simple string. Let's take a look at how this famous CShape class could be built...

```cpp
class CShape
{
public:
    CShape();
    CShape(int x, int y, int xx, int yy, ShapeType type);
    CShape(int x, int y, int xx, int yy, std::string fileName);
    virtual ~CShape();

private:
    std::string m_fileName;
    ShapeType m_type;
};
```

I see two ways of creating a shape. Either from the list or from a file for the images. For the moment, I don't know how to organize the shape design. Should I put it inside the classroom or outside? I don't know.... It takes time to look at what's going to be the most natural way to do this. In the Windows GDI+ world, to draw an element you need a particular handle that has all the drawing primitives. Thinking about how to draw an element, we can consider including a Draw method in the CShape class. The first thought is to say, I will implement all possible cases in Draw with a construction that looks like this:

```cpp
void Draw(const CDrawingContext& ctxt) const
{
    if (m_type == ShapeType::line)
    {
        ctxt.Line(m_rect.left, m_rect.bottom,
                  m_rect.top, m_rect.right);
    }
    if (m_type == ShapeType::rectangle)
    {
        ctxt.Rectangle(m_rect);
    }
    // TODO
}
```

In the class, it is important to mark methods that do not modify private data. To do this, they are added the const keyword at the end as indicated on the Draw method.

Moreover, when an argument is passed that is not intended to be modified, it is passed as a const reference. As can be seen above, the definition of a class is an iterative work in which the best ideas drive away those of before or comfort them. If a class is well designed, the reading of its public members is clear because we go to the essentials. Attention, private members also explain a lot about implementation details. Now, let's put ourselves in a context where there are

several classes and the principles seen above are not enough to make an object model. We need more sophisticated mechanisms to connect classes with each other.
Classes have associations and behaviors and it is here that Jedi position themselves to design an elegant, easy-to-use, service-oriented model.
Our Draw method is not OOP because if I add a type in the enumeration, I have to add an if() in the Draw() method and code the implementation. We can do better, much better.

The concepts of OOP
The two pillars of OOP are inheritance and polymorphism. Inheritance allows classes to be grouped into families of types and allows operations and behaviors and data to be shared. Polymorphism triggers operations in these families at a unit level. So adding or deleting a class is not too much of a problem.
Inheritance defines a parent/child relationship. The parent defines the public interface and the private implementation is common to all its children. Each child chooses whether to inherit a unique behavior or to overload it. In C++, the parent is called "base class" and the child is called "derived class". The parent and children define a class hierarchy. The parent is often an abstract class and children implement pure virtual methods for the whole to work.
In an OOP program, classes are manipulated via a pointer on the base class rather than on derived objects.

An abstract class
Let's go back to the CShape class... The next step in design is to create an abstract class to identify the operations specific to each item – which involves operations with an implementation based on a derived class. These operations are pure virtual functions of the base class. A pure virtual method is an abstract method. There is no body. This implies that the class becomes abstract too. It is not possible to create an object from an abstract class. The Draw() method must be defined as pure virtual because there are several types of drawing to do and each drawing is specific to a given class. The body of Draw() does not exist, which is why it is said that the class is abstract; there is at least one pure virtual method.
So here's how it's done:

```cpp
class CShapeEx
{
public:
    CShapeEx() {}
    CShapeEx(ShapeType type, RECT rect, const std::string &fileName)
        : m_type(type), m_rect(rect), m_fileName(fileName) {}
    virtual ~CShapeEx() {}

public:
    virtual void Draw(const CDrawingContext& ctxt) const = 0;
    virtual void DrawTracker(const CDrawingContext& ctxt) const = 0;

private:
    std::string m_fileName;
    ShapeType m_type;
    RECT m_rect;
};
```

And we will now declare derived classes from CShapeEx:

```cpp
class CRectangle: public CShapeEx
{
```

```cpp
public:
    CRectangle() {}
    virtual ~CRectangle() {}

public:
    virtual void Draw(const CDrawingContext& ctxt) const
    {
        // TODO
        std::cout << "Rectangle::Draw" << std::endl;
    }

    virtual void DrawTracker(const CDrawingContext& ctxt) const
    {
        // TODO
    }
};

class CLine: public CShapeEx
{
public:
    CLine() {}
    virtual ~CLine() {}

public:
    virtual void Draw(const CDrawingContext& ctxt) const
    {
        // TODO
        std::cout << "Line    ::Draw" << std::endl;
    }

    virtual void DrawTracker(const CDrawingContext& ctxt) const
    {
        // TODO
    }
};
```

If you want to add an item to draw in the hierarchy, just add a derived class! Now let's see how this virtual mechanism works...

```cpp
    CDrawingContext ctxt;

    CRectangle * pRect = new CRectangle();
    CLine * pLine = new CLine();

    CShapeEx * ptr = nullptr;

    ptr = pRect;
```

```
        ptr->Draw(ctxt);

        ptr = pLine;
        ptr->Draw(ctxt);
```

We start by declaring 2 items to draw. Then the manager, a pointer to the CShapeEx base class is declared. Whenever it points to an object of a derived class, the virtual function Draw() called is that of the derived class because this function is defined as virtual.

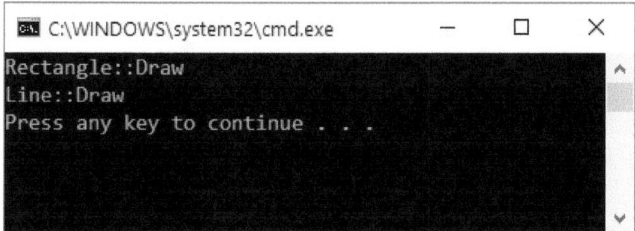

Figure 13 - CMD (Command Prompt) and cout display in console application

Now we are missing something that is very useful and that will avoid gas plants for building derivative objects. We need a factory! A mechanism for creating objects.

The factory

```
class CFactory
{
private:
      CFactory();

public:
      static CShapeEx * CreateObject(ShapeType type)
      {
              if (type == ShapeType::line)
              {
                      CLine * pObj = new CLine();
                      pObj->m_type = type;
                      return pObj;
              }

              if (type == ShapeType::rectangle)
              {
                      CRectangle * pObj = new CRectangle();
                      pObj->m_type = type;
                      return pObj;
              }

              // TODO
```

Professional C++ - Philosophy and Principles

```
            return nullptr;
        }
};
```

This class allows using a static method to create an object according to its type in the enumeration. The type is assigned as a member variable of the created object. Note that the constructor is private, which means that you cannot declare a CFactory object. You can only use the static CreateObject method. Except, the compilation falls in error:

```
146     static CShapeEx * CreateObject(ShapeType type)
147     {
148         if (type == ShapeType::line)
149         {
150             CLine * pObj = new CLine();
151             pObj->m_type = type;
152             return pObj;
153         }
154
155         if (type == ShapeType::rectange)
156         {
157             CRectangle * pObj = new CRectangle();
158             pObj->m_type = type;
159             return pObj;
160         }
161
162         // TODO
163
164         return nullptr;
165     }
166 };
```

Code	Description
E0265	member "CShapeEx::m_type" (declared at line 96 of "d:\Dev\CPP\Programmez\OOP\C
E0265	member "CShapeEx::m_type" (declared at line 96 of "d:\Dev\CPP\Programmez\OOP\C
C2248	'CShapeEx::m_type': cannot access protected member declared in class 'CShapeEx'
C2248	'CShapeEx::m_type': cannot access protected member declared in class 'CShapeEx'
C2248	'CShapeEx::m_type': cannot access protected member declared in class 'CShapeEx'
C2248	'CShapeEx::m_type': cannot access protected member declared in class 'CShapeEx'

Figure 14 - Compilation errors output in Visual Studio

The m_type member is inaccessible due to its level of protection... So we will add something to the CShapeEx class:

```
class CShapeEx
{
public:
      CShapeEx() {}
      CShapeEx(ShapeType type, RECT rect, const std::string &fileName)
              : m_type(type), m_rect(rect), m_fileName(fileName) {}
      virtual ~CShapeEx() {}

public:
      virtual void Draw(const CDrawingContext& ctxt) const = 0;
      virtual void DrawTracker(const CDrawingContext& ctxt) const = 0;

private:
      std::string m_fileName;
      ShapeType m_type;
      RECT m_rect;

      // The CFactory class can access members...
      friend class CFactory;
};
```

We add at the end of class that the CFactory class is friends of the CShapeEx class. And there, there is no more compilation error! Purists like AlainZ in Redmond will tell you that it violates object mechanics and that it's an exotic construction and it's better to go through the builder to pass the type— I don't think so. I think it's elegant to sprain for the factory. Here is the code that calls the factory:

```
      CDrawingContext ctxt;

      CShapeEx * pRect = CFactory::CreateObject(ShapeType::rectangle);
      CShapeEx * pLine = CFactory::CreateObject(ShapeType::line);

      CShapeEx * ptr = nullptr;

      ptr = pRect;
      ptr->Draw(ctxt);

      ptr = pLine;
      ptr->Draw(ctxt);
```

And the result is equivalent.

Compilation under Linux

Professional C++ - Philosophy and Principles

For those who don't know, the C++ language is ISO standardized. On the Linux platform, where everything is done in C/C++, the language has several compilers including the famous GCC. You can use Visual Studio Code that Microsoft provides as an IDE to compile under Linux via the terminal.
You have to install the C++ extension. I installed Cygwin and MSYS. So I have Linux commands.

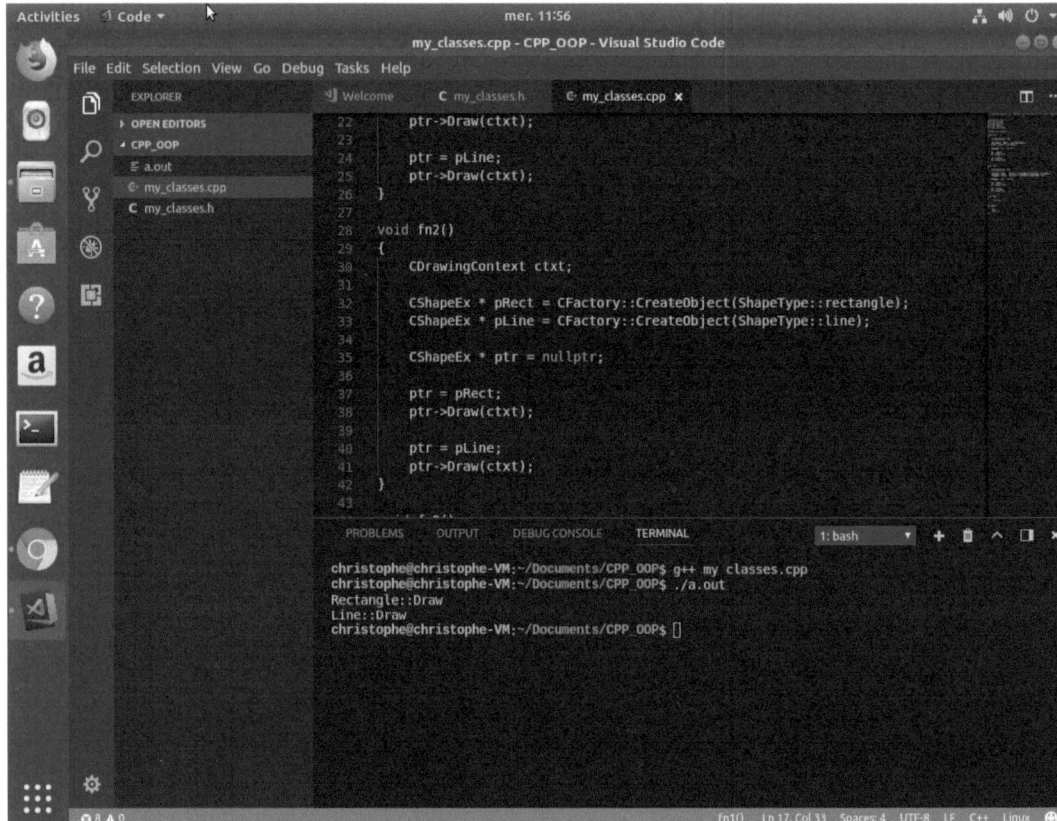

Figure 15 - Visual Studio Code and bash Terminal integration

One touch of C++ 11
We will try to continue our drawing application by materializing the drawing area. It looks like a set of shapes on a drawing support. First step when you think about the concept of the drawing board is what? Storing graphics in an STL container. Yes Sir, when you want to store something, you go through the STL containers. We will therefore use the std::vector<T> of the STL. We will store some rather special shapes that are shared shapes. Shared? By who, by whom? In a real drawing software, we display the properties in a grid and the drawing is on the central panel so we share our objects and it's not just the display. I'll show you the result.

58

Professional C++

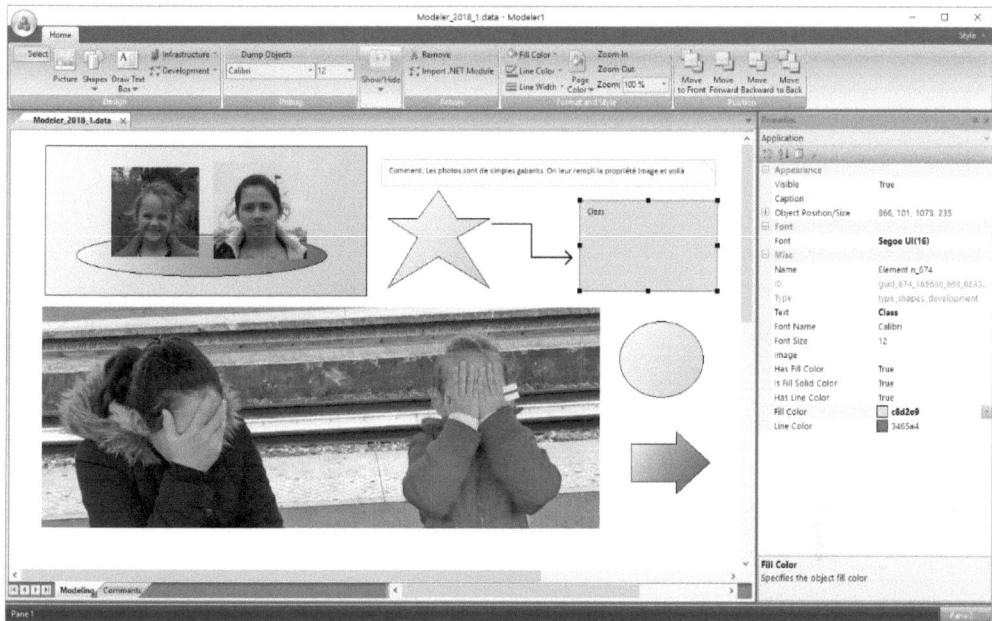

Figure 16 - Selecting UI Objects, Moving, Sizing

On this screen, we see that the selected blue rectangle has its attributes directly in the properties grid but also on the Ribbon. How do I share the data between the drawing panel, the ribbon and the properties grid? Do we make copies of the objects? Yes, but we make copies of pointers and not copies of objects. To do this, one uses the shared pointer mechanism of the STL. Let's see its use. First, we'll design the drawing area.

The drawing area
This area contains the shape objects to draw. We will therefore create a vector<shared_ptr<CShapeEx>>. The container vector is defined in <vector>. We're gonna have a collection of CShapeEx shared items. This way, we can store this particular pointer where we want without worrying about the release of memory. The drawing area is an MDI child view in Windows jargon. It has two scrollbars, one vertical and one horizontal. If you want to manage shared_ptr<T>, you have to change the factory:

```
static std::shared_ptr<CShapeEx> CreateObject(ShapeType type)
{
        std::shared_ptr<CShapeEx> pObj = nullptr;

        if (type == ShapeType::line)
        {
                pObj = std::make_shared<CLine>();
                pObj->m_type = type;
                return pObj;
        }

        if (type == ShapeType::rectangle)
        {
```

59

```
                pObj = std::make_shared<CRectangle>();
                pObj->m_type = type;
                return pObj;
            }

            return nullptr;
    }
```

We no longer make a new() but a call to std::make_shared<T>().
Moreover, in the use of objects, it gives this:

```
    CDrawingContext ctxt;

    std::shared_ptr<CShapeEx> pRect =
CFactory::CreateObject(ShapeType::rectangle);
    std::shared_ptr<CShapeEx> pLine = CFactory::CreateObject(ShapeType::line);

    std::shared_ptr<CShapeEx> ptr = nullptr;

    ptr = pRect;
    ptr->Draw(ctxt);

    ptr = pLine;
    ptr->Draw(ctxt);
```

There is even a way to let the compiler determine the type of variable used using auto:

```
    CDrawingContext ctxt;

    auto pRect = CFactory::CreateObject(ShapeType::rectangle);
    auto pLine = CFactory::CreateObject(ShapeType::line);

    auto ptr = pRect;
    ptr->Draw(ctxt);

    ptr = pLine;
    ptr->Draw(ctxt);
```

Let's go back to our class design. The shapes container is just a std::vector<T> collection of std::shared_ptr<CShapeEx>:

```
class CElementContainer: public CObject
{
private:

public:
```

```
        DECLARE_SERIAL(CElementContainer);
        CElementContainer();
        virtual ~CElementContainer(void);

// .. /.
// overridden for document i/o
virtual void Serialize(CElementManager * pElementManager, CArchive& ar);
// Debugging Operations
public:
        void DebugDumpObjects(CModeler1View * pView);

// MFC operations like
public:
        std::shared_ptr<CElement> GetHead();
        int GetCount();
        void RemoveAll();
        void Remove(std::shared_ptr<CElement> pElement);
        void AddTail(std::shared_ptr<CElement> pElement);

// Attributes
private:
        vector<std::shared_ptr<CElement>> m_objects;
};
```

There, I show you a real code and the elements are materialized by the CElement class but it's the same as CShapeEx. Note that the management functions associated with the vector are helpers methods in this class. This class must now be integrated into the Windows windowing mechanics.

Professional C++ - Philosophy and Principles

2. Essential C++ Cookbook – Quick Learning

We have a series of chapters on the practice of C++ for you to get started. No need to pay a round to practice as everything is free. Whether it's the old Visual Studio Express, Visual Studio Community Edition 2019 or GCC, or CLang via Linux or MinGW, it costs nothing. The main thing is to have a recent compiler to benefit from the C++ 11 alias C++ Modern. C++ 11 brings a lot of change to C++ 03 and C++05TR1 and this is why there is a huge craze around C++ 11. It's the rebirth of C++. C++ is the essential language to make apps on Android, iOS, Died Windows Phone but also to make apps on Windows, Linux and Mac. And yet we don't advertise it much. It's an open secret; Marketing tries to orient you to languages like C#, VB.NET or Java but do you know that the applications you use every day are made in C/C++. The operating system, the Internet browser, your video player, your music player, the Office Automation suite, your database server and of course, your favorite apps like facebook or twitter on mobile...

The C++ language
C++ is a standardized language by an ISO committee that constantly improves the STL (Standard Template Library) standard language and library. The ISO Committee is preparing the C++23 version (following the C++11, C++14, C++17 and C++20 versions).

The predefined types
There are many predefined types:

Type	Sense	Minimum size
bool	Boolean. True or false.	NA
char	Character	8 bits
wchar_t	Broad character	16 bits
char16_t	Character Unicode	16 bits
char32_t	Character Unicode	32 bits
short	Whole short	16 bits
int	Whole	16 bits
long	Longint	32 bits
long long	Longint	64 bits
float	Single precision floating	6 digits
double	Double precision floating	10 digits
long double	Double precision floating	10 digits

Types can be signed or not via the signed or unsigned specifier. The types-are all signed by default. The size of a variable can be obtained via sizeof(t).

The variables
A variable is declared as follows:
<type> variable name = initialization value;
Initialization is not mandatory but if it is missing, the content of the variable is undefined. In DEBUG mode, it will be 0 or null but in RELEASE it is undefined. Tip: you must initialize your variables.

The references
A reference points to an object. It's a reference to something. It's an alias, sir.

```
void Sample_References()
{
```

```
    int a = 10;
    int &b = a;
    a++;
    cout << "b=" << b << endl;
}
```

The display will be: b=11.
References are like pointers but with limited power. (Itchy?).

The pointers
A pointer is used to designate a memory space that points to something, an object or a variable. It is like a reference except that it does not have to be initialized at the declaration.

```
void Sample_Pointer()
{
    int a = 10;
    int * ptr = nullptr;
    ptr = &a;
    a++;
    cout << "ptr adress=" << ptr << " value=" << *ptr << endl;
}
```

The display will be:
ptr adress=0x0062FE20[32] value=11

In this example, set the pointer to nullptr. Then we indicate that ptr is the (via &) address of a. The value of a is its memory location and the contents of the pointer can be accessed via *.

const
Using const on a variable prevents this variable from being changed. However, it must be detailed in the declaration.

```
void Sample_Const()
{
    int a = 100;
    a++;            // error
    a = 200;        // error
}
```

By default, const objects are local to a .cpp file for compilation. To define and share a const object, you must declare this variable as extern otherwise the compiler will say not to find the variable with a message of the style «var is undefined.».

References const
There are also references const. These are refrences that cannot be changed.

---

[32] This memory address was the result of one application run. Of course, every run gives a different address.

Professional C++ - Philosophy and Principles

```
void Sample_ConstRef()
{
    int a = 10;
    const int & aref = a;
    int b = 20;
    aref = b; // error aref is const
}
```

Alias of types

It is possible to define an alias on a type. Why? It's to make the program more readable.

```
typedef std::string String;
typedef vector<string> MesFilles;
typedef vector<string>::iterator IT;

void Sample_Typedef()
{
    String maggie = "my name is Maggie and I am almost 5 years old and I love Dad";
    cout << maggie << endl;

    MesFilles girls;
    girls.push_back("Edith");
    girls.push_back("Lisa");
    girls.push_back("Audrey Maggie");
    for (IT = begin(girls); it!= end(girls); ++it)
    {
        cout << *it << endl;
    }
}
```

In this example, I created 3 aliases: on std::string, vector<string> and iterator.

The auto keyword

Available from C++ 11 «modern C++», the auto keyword allows the compiler to deduce the type of an object. This is the var of C# for those who know.

```
void Sample_auto()
{
    MesFilles girls = { "Edith", "Lisa", "Audrey" };
    for (auto it = begin(girls); it!= end(girls); ++it)
    {
        cout << *it << endl;
    }
}
```

You notice that I initialized the string vector (typedef MesFilles) with {}. It is C++ 11 that allows this.

The structures

To create a user type that contains variables, the simplest is to create a structure.

```
struct Book
{
    string name;
    int price;
    string comments;
};

void Sample_Book()
{
    Book CPPPrimer5ThEdition = { "C++ Primer", 50, "the bible"};
    cout << "book:" << CPPPrimer5ThEdition.name << endl;
    cout << "price: " << CPPPrimer5ThEdition.price << endl;
    cout << "comments : " << CPPPrimer5ThEdition.comments << endl;
}
```

In this example, the structure is declared outside the function and the definition of a variable of this type is done with {}. We could also have initialized the limbs one by one.

```
Book ref;
ref.name = "The C++ language";
ref.price = 50;
ref.comments = "by Bjarne Stroustrup, the creator of C++";
```

A structure is like a class where all members are public while they are private for a class. Another way to understand : in a structure, everything is public.

The . h (or .hpp) headers

A program can contain multiple .cpp. And it is necessary to share information knowing that when the compiler takes a file, all type declarations must be known. So we write header (.h) files that contain all the statements we're going to use. If I want the Book structure to be accessible by several . cpp files, I have to define it in a header. h and that I make a #include at the beginning of the . cpp file that wants to use it so that the compiler can do its job.
Here is the "clean" version of the sample that uses the book structure:

```
#include "Book.h"
void Sample_Book()
{
    Book CPPPrimer5ThEdition = { "C++ Primer", 50, "the bible"};
    ....
```

The precompiled headers

By convention, we put the #include at the beginning of the .cpp. To optimize compilation time, there is something called precompiled headers. Just put all its header files into a single header (stdafx.h for Visual C++) and set the project to say that this header must be precompiled as well, the stdafx.cpp file contains the #include stdafx. h and that's it. So, the file that contains all the parsed headers once and that's it.

The preprocessor

Inherited from the C language, the preprocessor allows you to change the content of the program. #include just injects the source into the program and to include the same file multiple times in a source, we use barriers. I explain myself... In reality, we don't put all the headers in the precompiled headers, we just put the headers for the files . h defined by the operating system and third-party libraries. The structures we define must have a structure that looks like this:

```
// Book. h - this header contains the definition of an entity Book
#ifndef BOOK_HEADER
#define BOOK_HEADER
#include <string>

struct Book
{
    string name;
    int price;
    string comments;
};
#endif
```

For a compiler that does not support precompiled headers, the file can be included several times, it will only be parsed once just with the tip of an ifndef.

The std namespace
It is possible to define types in namespaces. To do this, simply declare a namespace block <name> {...} and all types will be in it. It's useful for separating things. The C++ standard library (STL alias Standard Template Library) defines all its types in the std (standard) namespace. To include name resolution in a program, simply write using namespace <name> ;

The string type
The STL defines the string type. It is a template class that allows to manage strings. Before you can use string, you must add the statement #include <string>.

string is defined in the std namespace. The string type is a class so there are methods to manipulate strings. We can even use the + operator to concatenate strings. You can use the c_str() method to get the const pointer on the string as in C.

```
void Sample_String()
{
    string audrey = "I am a naughty girl";
    string maggie = audrey + string("a sa maman");
    if( !maggie.empty())
    {
        cout << "size: " << maggie.size() << endl;
    }
    for (auto c: maggie) // for each characteristic
    {
        cout << c;
    }
    cout << endl;

    const char * pChar = maggie.c_str();
```

```
        printf("%s \n", pChar);
}
```
The string class is simple to use.

The vector type
This is the best known type of STL with string. vector<T> stores contiguous elements. If you are looking to store items in memory, use the vector<T>

```
void Sample_Vector()
{
    vector<int> v = { 1, 2, 3, 4, 5, 6 };
    vector<string> girls;
    girls.push_back("Edith");
    girls.push_back("Lisa");
    girls.push_back("Audrey Maggie");

    Lacoquine string = girls[2]
    cout << "naughty is " << lacoquine << endl;

    for (auto & f: girls)
    {
            cout << f << endl;
    }
}
```

The Iterators
The STL introduces the concept of iterators which, like a pointer, allows indirect access to an object. In the case of an iterator, the object is an element in a container or string. An iterator allows you to retrieve an item and pass the next position. Like a pointer, an iterator may or may not be valid.
The begin() function is used to obtain the first position of the iterator and end() indicates the last invalid position. If the container is empty, begin() and end() will have the same value.

```
void Sample_Iterator()
{
    vector<string> girls = { "didou", "mini-mini", "mega teuteuteuteute" };
    vector<string>::const_iterator cit = begin(girls);
    cout << "my 12y baby is " << *cit << endl;
    ++cit;
    ++cit;<<<<<<<<<<<<<<<<<<<<<<<<<<<<<<<<<<<<<
    cout << "super maggie is " << *cit << endl;
    ++cit;
    if (cit == end(girls))
    {
            cout << "iterator is end..." << endl;
    }

    // it is a vector<string>::iterator
    for (auto it = girls.begin(); it!= girls.end(); ++it)
```

Professional C++ - Philosophy and Principles

```
    {
            cout << *it << endl;
    }
}
```

In this example, I use a const iterator and a normal iterator. Here are the possible operations on a container iterator:

Operation	Explanation
*iter	Returns a reference to the object pointed by iter
Iter->mem	Accesses the memory object
++iter	Advance a position to the next object
--iter	Moves back one position to have the previous object
Iter1==iter2	Compares two iterators
Iter1!=iter2	Compares two iterators

There are two types of iterators: const_iterator and iterator. Operations begin() and end() can be written in two ways:

```
auto it1 = begin(girls);
auto it2 = girls.begin();
if (it1 == it2)
{
        cost << "it1 == it2" << endl;
}
```

Operations (we pass quickly)
A C++ block starts with { and ends with }. There are the following operations: if, switch, while, do while and for. The C++ 11 introduces the simplified forum alias range-for:

```
void Sample_For()
{
        vector<string> girls = { "didou", "mini-mini", "maggie" };
        for (auto & girl: girls)
        {
                cout << girl << endl;
        }
}
```

Other operations exist as break, continue or goto.

Managing Exceptions
The exceptions are managed via a try.. block catch with the exception type to catch. It is possible to throw an exception via a throw. The STL defines the exception class for the main problems. Exceptions are defined in std::except.

The functions and the linker (link edition)
To define a function, you need a name, a return type and possibly arguments. Because programs can become complex, functions are created in . cpp files and used in other files. This is the principle of separate compilation. To be able to use

this mechanism, the function must be defined in a .h or .cpp file with just its declaration with one; (called the prototype). This allows the compiler to know that a call is made to a function and it is the link editor (the link) who will be responsible for solving the stuff to build an executable.

Passage of argument by references
With C, you can pass a parameter with a pointer parameter to modify it via the * symbol in the declaration and the & symbol in the calling syntax. With C++, you just pass a reference using the & symbol in the declaration and nothing in the calling context.

```
void Reset_Int_Ptr(int * i)
{
    *i = 0;
}

void Reset_Int_Ref(int & i)
{
    i = 0;
}

void Sample_Function()
{
    int a = 10;
    Reset_Int_Ptr(&a); // pass the address of a
    cout << a << endl;
    int b = 200;
    Reset_Int_Ref(b); // b is passed by reference
    cout << b << endl;
}
```

Manage the command line
The command line is simple to manage. The first argument gives the number of elements and the second is an array of strings containing the parameters.

```
int main(int argc, char **argv) { ... }
```

Functions with variable parameters
Introduced with C++ 11, variable parameter functions take advantage of initializer_lists. An initializer_list type is a type of a STL that represents an array. It is present in the initializer_list header.

```
void error_msg(initializer_list<string> ii)
{
    for (auto beg = il.begin(); beg!= il.end(); ++beg)
        cout << *beg << " ";
    cout << endl;
}

void Sample_Initializer_List()
{
```

Professional C++ - Philosophy and Principles

```
        initializer_list<string> params = { "I am happy", "with a beer", "at
6PM" };
        error_msg(params);
}
```

Default function arguments
It is possible to give a default value to the parameters of a function. This must be specified in the function declaration (header) in a specific header file.

Inline functions
Inherited from C, a function can be annotated inline. This means that with each call in the source code, the function will be broken up in bulk with its code. It is to gain success in performance but it is often used. Do not despise me.

The macros of the preprocessor
There are 4 macros that are super useful in debugging:
__FILE__ : name of the source file
__LINE__ line number
__DATE__ : date of compilation
__TIME__ Compilation time

The function pointers
A function pointer is a standard pointer except that instead of pointing to an object, it points to a function. More precisely, it points to a function that has a return type and arguments of a certain type. The function name is not relevant to the pointer.

```cpp
bool CompareInteger(const int & a, const int & b)
{
        if (a > b)
                return true;
        else
                return false;
}

void Sample_FunctionPointer()
{
        // function pointer declaration
        bool(*pFn)(const int&, const int&);

        // ptr association
        pFn = &CompareInteger;

        if( (*pFn)(100, 99) == true )
        {
                cout << "superior!" << endl;
        }
}
```

The rest is heavy...

Professional C++

In the next sub-chapter, we will discuss the classes that are the essence of C++. We will see simple types, builders, destructors, virtual methods, simple and multiple inheritance, friendly classes and also templates.

Classes and OOP

We have a series of chapters on the practice of C++ for you to get started. In C++, we use classes to define our own data types.

This sub-chapter will give you an idea of the support of abstraction and resource management in C++. How to define new types defined by the user and also basic properties, implementation techniques and language possibilities for concrete classes, abstract classes and class hierarchies. The language supports object-oriented and generic programming style (with templates).

The main feature of the C++ language is the class. A class is a user-defined type that represents a concept in the code of a program.

Any design of a program has concepts, ideas, entities, etc., that we try to translate into class in such a way that the readability, maintenance and evolution of the program is improved. A program is a set of user-defined classes to do a specific job. Libraries are sets of available classes.

There are two categories of developers: the one who makes the classes and the one who uses them. The approach is completely different. Most programming techniques talk about how to design and implement class types. There are 3 kinds of classes: concrete classes, abstract classes and classes in class hierarchies.

We will focus on the importance of data abstraction, which makes it possible to separate the implementation of an object from the operations that this object can perform. Objects can be copied, moved or destroyed. It is even possible to define its own operators. The fundamental ideas behind classes are data abstraction and encapsulation. Data abstraction is a programming technique based on the separation of interface and implementation. The class interface presents the operations that a class user can perform. The implementation contains the member data of the class, the body of functions present in the interface and all the functions internal to the class to do its job. Encapsulation allows the class interface to be separated from its implementation. A class hides its implementation and users of this class do not have access (sometimes) to its implementation. This is the mechanism of the libraries in which we only have the dot . h (header) of the class and the implementation is provided as a binary (.dll).

A class has a header; it's a header file. h and a body, it's a cpp file. By convention, headers may be deposited into an INCLUDE directory and CPP files into a SRC folder. You are going to tell me "yep, but in java or C#, we put everything in the class and that's it!" Yes it is true but in C++ we do not do it like that.

Let's look at a simple log class through its header. The class is prefixed with the name of the company for which it was made (Cerius) in 1995. This class uses a CString type. This is a type that comes from a well-known library made by Microsoft called MFC (Microsoft Foundation Classes).

```
class CerLog
{
public:
        CerLog(const CString& path);
        ~CerLog();
```

```
        BOOL Log(ORB_REQUETE * pReq);

private:
        CString m_path;                 // Log Directory
        static long m_stCompt;
};
```

This class is in a CerLog. h file which is in the INCLUDE directory. What do we notice? It has a manufacturer named after the class. This constructor will be called upon the creation of an object. The ctor takes a string as a parameter. It is mandatory; There is no empty ctor. The first part of the class is in a public block but at the end we see private which implies that it is member data that we will not be able to use. It's for the class. So, in this class, we have a ctor, a dtor (destructive) and a log method, that's all. Let's open the code of this CerLog class:

```
#include "cerlog.h"

long CerLog::m_stCompt = 0;

CerLog::CerLog(const CString& path) : m_path(path)
{
        SECURITY_ATTRIBUTES    sa;
...
        ::CreateDirectory(m_path,&sa);
}

CerLog::~CerLog()
{}

BOOL CerLog::Log(ORB_REQUETE * pReq)
{
        HANDLE hFic;
...
        bDone = ::WriteFile(hFic,(LPSTR) pReq,
                        (DWORD) pReq->usLgRequete,
                        &dwBytesWritten,
                        NULL);
        ::CloseHandle(hFic);
return TRUE;
}
```

We notice that the static member is initialized and we find the code of the ctor, the dtor and the Log method. Let's go into the details of how a class works.

Define a member function

You can set the signature in the header and put the implementation in the cpp file. But for some members, they can be defined in the header. Thus simple properties have their place in the header.

Here is how we would have designed the CerLog2 classes for simple use:

```cpp
void Discover_Class()
{
    CerLog2 log("c:\\temp");
    log. Log("hello the logger");
}


class CerLog2
{
public:
    CerLog2(const string &path): m_path(path) {}
    ~CerLog2() {}

    string GetPath() const
    {
        return m_path;
    }

    void Log(string message)
    {
        //...
    }

private:
    string m_path;
};
```

And now you're telling me, "but it looks like Java or C#!" Indeed, if we put all the code in the header... But generally we propose a solution with two different characters. There is the one who builds and designs the class and there is the one (or the one) who uses it.

Introduction to this and const

This represents a pointer to the object within a class.

Professional C++ - Philosophy and Principles

```
string GetInternalPath() const { return this->m_path;            }
```

Specifying that the member function is const indicates that the values of the member data cannot be changed. This becomes a this const. Objects that are const and references or pointers to const objects can only call const member functions.

It should be noted that when writing a member function outside the header, it is necessary to specify the name of the class with:: and respect the parameters of the function.

Define a function that returns the "this" object

Let's add a Merge method in the MyLogger class to merge a logger.

```cpp
class MyLogger
{
...
public:
    MyLogger& Merge(const MyLogger &logger);
...
};
Here is the implementation:
MyLogger& MyLogger::Merge(const MyLogger &logger)
{
    m_path = logger.m_path;
    return *this;
}
```

The logger sets the path and returns a this object in its entirety with the * on this. It is a reference that is returned.

Defining Non-Class Functions

Sometimes it is necessary to create auxiliary functions (read, write, print) that work with our class. In this case, you must define the function in the same header as the class.

In the header:

```cpp
void LogAMessage(string message);
```

In the cpp:

```cpp
void LogAMessage(string message)
{
    MyLogger logger("c:\\temp");
    logger.Log(message);
}
```

The builder

By default, the compiler defines a ctor that does nothing. Each class defines how objects are initialized. Classes control the initialization of objects by defining one or more member functions that bear the name of the class and these are constructors (ctor). The ctor initializes the member data of a class object. A constructor is executed when the object of a class is created. Manufacturers do not have a return type and can be an empty block. A class may have several constructors that differ in their parameters. A constructor cannot be marked const. The MyLogger class can have the following ctor:

```
MyLogger()
{
        m_path = "c: temp";
}

MyLogger(string path)
{
        m_path = path;
}
```

The ctor and list initialization

It is possible to provide a list to the ctor. It is the C++ 11 that allows this.

In the header:

```
MyLogger(string path, initializer_list<string> log_headers);
```

In the cpp:

```
MyLogger::MyLogger(string path, initializer_list<string> log_headers)
{
    m_path = path;
    for (auto it = log_headers.begin(); it!= log_headers.end(); ++it)
    {
            Log(*it);
    }
}
```

And here's how to use this ctor:

```
    MyLogger log4("c:\\temp", { "begin log", "1 June 2015", "Application Totor"});
```

Professional C++ - Philosophy and Principles

```
    log4.Log("the logger log4");
```

Access control and encapsulation

When we define an interface for our class, nothing forces the user to respect calls in the right order or the choice of methods. This is why we hide the implementation in private blocks. Access control ensures encapsulation. Members defined after public are accessible in all parts of the program. Public members define the class interface. Members defined after private are accessible to class member functions but are not accessible to the code that uses the class. The private encapsulent (cache) sections implement.

Class or struct, you have to choose

Class and struct have the same meaning if only in struct by default everything is public and in class everything is private by default. But it's the same thing.

Functions or classes friend

Let's take the MyLogger class and add a private member for security (an example):

```cpp
class MyLogger
{
...
private:
    string m_path;
    SECURITY_ATTRIBUTES sa;
};
And let's define the LogAsAdministrator function:
void LogAsAdministrator(string message)
{
    MyLogger logger("c:  temp");
    // fake function:)
    logger.m_sa = ::CreateRestrictedToken(Windows::Administrator);
    logger. Log(message);
}
```

This function must access the private m_sa member which is the security token. Problem, this function is not in the class. Therefore, she must be declared a friend (friend) and thus she will have the right to access all members of the class. Magic!

```cpp
class MyLogger
{
```

```
        friend void LogAsAdministrator(string message);
...
```

The mechanics are the same for friend classes.

I'm going to add a class that provides the fictitious administrator privilege.

In the MyLogger header:

```
        void LogAsAdministrator(const string & message);
private:
        CSecurityHelper m_sec;
};
```

In the MyLogger cpp:

```
void MyLogger::LogAsAdministrator(const string & message)
{
        m_sec.m_sa = m_sa;
        m_sec.EnableAdministratorMode();
        Log(message);
}
```

The MyLogger class through its LogAsAdministrator method will inform a private member of CSecurityHelper who is m_sa by providing their own to request a privilege elevation.

To be able to access the private member, the MyLogger class must be a friend of CSecurityHelper whose header is:

```
#pragma once

class CSecurityHelper
{
        friend class MyLogger;

public:
        CSecurityHelper() {}
        ~CSecurityHelper() {}

        void EnableAdministratorMode();

private:
        SECURITY_ATTRIBUTES m_sa;
};
```

Here is the cpp:

Professional C++ - Philosophy and Principles

```
#include "stdafx.h"
#include "MyLogger.h"
#include "SecurityHelper.h"


void CSecurityHelper::EnableAdministratorMode()
{
    // use m_sa
    // fake function:)
    m_sa.lpSecurityDescriptor = NULL;
//:::CreateRestrictedToken(Windows::Administrator);

}
```

For this to compile, you have to do a #include of MyLogger. h for the compiler to know the definition of the friend class.

Types in the classes

To define user types, we sometimes use the typedef inside a class. This makes the class more readable. Let's go back to the MyLogger class which has headers before logging and which we will store in a vector<string>. We can store the vector in private and declare the iterators as typedef with a simpler name... Here's what it looks like:

```
class MyLogger
{
...
public:
    typedef vector<string> HEADERS;
    typedef vector<string>::const_iterator CIT;

private:
    HEADERS m_headers;
```

Typedef is here to help you make types more readable.

The resolution of names

The compiler spends most of its time searching for matching function names. From time to time in the code there is a line of code like::WriteFile(); this means that the scope sought is global and that this is not in the class in which this function is used.

The static members

A class may have static members but they must be initialized explicitly in the cpp file.

Example: In the header file:

```
class NewLogger
{
public:
    static void Log(const string& message);
    static string m_path;
};
```

In the cpp:

```
string NewLogger::m_path = "c:\\temp";

void NewLogger::Log(const string& message)
{
    cout << message << endl;
}
```

In the program that uses it:

```
NewLogger::Log("here is a static logger");
```

There is nothing complicated.

Overload of operators

It is possible to override all ++ operators by going through -> through [] or ==.

```
bool operator==(const MyLogger &left, const MyLogger &right)
{
    return left.GetPath() == right.GetPath();
}
```

KEY Concepts of Object-Oriented Programming

The key ideas in object-oriented programming are data abstraction, inheritance, and legacy and dynamic binding. With data abstraction, we can define classes that have a separation between the interface and their implementation. Through inheritance, we can define classes that form a model of relationship with similar types. With dynamic binding, you can use objects with types whose differences from the base class are unknown. Let's take a simple example that explains inheritance, abstract classes and virtual functions. There is the abstract class Animal and two derived classes that are Cat and Dog:

Professional C++ - Philosophy and Principles

```cpp
class Animal
{
public:
        Animal() {}
        virtual ~Animal() {}
public:
        virtual void Eat() = 0;
        virtual string Type() { return "Animal"; }
};

class Cat: public Animal
{
        virtual void Eat()
        {
                cout << "whyskas croquettes for Cat" << endl;
        }
        virtual string Type() { return "Cat"; }
};

class Dog : public Animal
{
public:
        virtual void Eat()
        {
                cout << "whyskas croquettes for Dog" << endl;
        }
        virtual string Type() { return "Dog"; }
};
```

I voluntarily put everything in the header to make more concise. Here's what to remember: the Animal class is an abstract class because it contains the Eat() method which is pure virtual (=0); It means that any class that inherits Animal has an obligation to redefine the Eat method. The destructor is annotated virtual: it is mandatory for dtor in parent and derived classes.

```cpp
        Animal * ptrAnimal;
        Cat c1;
        Dog d1;
        // Point on the Cat
        ptrAnimal = &c1;
        cout << ptrAnimal->Type() << endl;
        ptrAnimal->Eat();
        // Point on the Dog
        ptrAnimal = &d1;
```

```
        cout << ptrAnimal->Type() << endl;
        ptrAnimal->Eat();
```

This little piece of code shows how to bind with a pointer to the abstract class. One does not have the right to declare a type Animal because it is an abstract class; On the other hand, we have the right to use it as a pointer and to point to children. We point to a Cat and then a Dog and the virtual methods are magically called.

The key concept: polymorphism in C++

The key idea behind OOP is polymorphism. This word is derived from a Greek word that means many forms. We talk about inheritance-related types as polymorphic types because we can use many forms of these types while ignoring the differences between them. When we call a function in a base class through a reference or pointer of the base class, we do not know the type of the object on which this member is called. The object may be an object of the base class or an object of the derived class. If the function is virtual, then the decision to know which function will run is postponed to run. The version of the running virtual function is defined by the object type with which the reference is linked or for a pointer to the object type being pointed. On the other hand, calls to non-virtual functions are determined at compilation.

Access control and inheritance

As in a class to hide its own members, each class controls whether its members are accessible to a derived class.

A class uses protected for members it wants accessible to its derived classes but wants to protect from general access. Protected access is positioned between the private and the public. As private, protected members are inaccessible to users of this class. As a public, protected members are accessible to members and friends of the derived classes of this class. A member of a derived class or friend can access protected members of the base class only through a derived object. The derived class has no special access to protected members of objects in the base class.

Conclusion

In C++, the class is the inseparable object-oriented programming ally. This article focuses on how to simply experiment with the features offered by a class. There is still a lot to be understood, such as the semantics of moving, the redefinition of operators, virtual functions. With this article, you have the basics to make your own construction. Create classes, assemble them and don't forget: C++ developers wear 2 hats on their head, the one that designs the class and the one that uses it. It is much simpler to be a user than a class designer. Mastering the principles of object programming requires training and experience. In C++, there are never (or almost never) deprecated classes. So once created, the class is there and for a long time. Take the MFC class framework; Developed around 1990, this framework continues to grow and evolve. When you do C++, you have in mind that the code will work for a long time. This is an exercise that we do not encounter with modern languages like Java nor C#.

In C++, we keep everything. The pyramid grows, but you don't throw anything away. Look to the Linux world: GTK, Kde, Xfce, all these libraries have been evolving for years and it is still used. Looking at QT, it's never been better. ISVs love QT because it makes it possible to make multi-platform GUI madness. Come on, let's go!

Professional C++ - Philosophy and Principles

Templates with C++

The templates represent the generic programming part of the C++ language.

Object-oriented programming (OOP) and generic programming work with types that are not known at the time the program is written. The distinction between the two is that OOP works with known types only at runtime while generic programming uses types that are known at compilation.
Containers, iterators and algorithms are examples of generic programming. When writing a generic program, the code is independent of the types it manipulates. When using a generic program, we provide the types or values on the instance of the program that will run.
For example, the standard library provides a simple generic definition of each container, such as vector. We can use the generic definition to define several types of vector, each being different from the others depending on the type it contains. Templates are the foundation of generic programming in C++. We can use them without understanding how they are defined. A template is a "formula" for creating classes or functions. When we use a generic type like vector, or a generic function like find, we provide the type information needed to execute this class or function to the declaration.
Example: vector<string> v.

Concepts and generic programming

Why are templates made? What programming techniques are implemented when using templates? The templates offer:
- The ability to pass types (values and templates) as arguments without loss of information.
- The type check done at the instanciation.
- The ability to pass constant values as arguments. This involves doing calculations at compilation.

Templates provide a powerful mechanism for compile-time computation and type manipulation that allow to have an efficient and very compact code. Remember that types (classes) may contain code and values. The first and most common template use scenario is generic programming support, which is, a programming model that emphasizes the design, implementation and use of general algorithms. Here, "general" means that an algorithm can be designed to accept a wide range of types as long as they are passed into arguments. Templates are (compile-time) a mechanism of parametric polymorphism.
Consider the function sum:

```
template<typename Container, typename Value>
Value sum(const Container& c, Value v)
{ for ( auto x: c ) v+=x;
return v;
}
```

It can be invoked for any data structure that supports begin() and end() so that the range-for can run. Such standard library structures (Standard Template Library) such as vector, list and map do the trick. To go further, the element type of this data structure is only limited by its use: it must be a type to which we can add a Value argument. The examples are ints, doubles and matrices. We can say that the sum() algorithm is generic in 2 dimensions: the type of data structure to store the elements (the container) and the type of its elements. So, sum() requires the first argument to be a sort of container and the second argument to template to be a kind of number. Such prerequisites are called concepts. Good and valuable concepts are fundamental for generic programming. The examples are integers and floating-point numbers (as defined even in classical C) and more generally mathematical concepts such as vector and containers. They represent the fundamental concepts for a field of application. Identification and formalization to a degree necessary for effective generic programming can be a challenge. For basic use, consider the Regular concept. A type is regular when it behaves like an int or a vector.
A regular type object:
- Can be built by default
- Can be copied using a builder or assignment

- Can be compared using == and !=
- Does not suffer from technical problems in use

A string is another example of a regular type. As int, string is also Ordered. This means that 2 strings can be compared with <, <=, >, >= with the appropriate semantics. Concepts are not just syntactic concepts, they are basically semantics.

The templates functions

Let's imagine a compare function that works with all types, how will we write this:

```
template <typename T>
int compare(const T &v1, const T &v2)
{
  if (v1 < v2) return -1;
  if (v2 < v1) return 1;
  return 0;
}
```

The return 0 is just there to look pretty because you have to finish the function and return something...
It is a simple function and takes two types T as a parameter. Notice the elegance of the style. In a template definition, the list of template parameters cannot be empty. A template definition starts with the template keyword followed by a list of template parameters that are separated by commas and are between token < and >.

Instantiation of a template function

When calling a template function, the compiler uses the call arguments to deduce the template arguments for us. When calling to compare, the compiler uses the argument type to determine which type to associate with the T template parameter.

```
cost << compare(1, 0) << endl;    // T is int
vector<int> vec1{1, 2, 3}, vec2{4, 5, 6};
cost << compare(vec1, vec2) << endl; // T is vector<int>
```

For the first call, the compiler will write and compile a version of compare with T replaced by int:

```
int compare(const int &v1, const int &v2)
{
    if (v1 < v2) return -1;
    if (v2 < v1) return 1;
    return 0;
}
```

For the second call the function will be generated with vector<int>.

The template type parameters
It is possible to use the template parameter as the function arguments. Example:
```
template <typename T> T foo(T* p)
{
  T tmp = *p;
```

Professional C++ - Philosophy and Principles

```
    // ..
    return tmp;
}
```

Each type parameter must be preceded by the keyword class or typename.

```
template <typename T, U> T calc(const T&, const U&);
template <typename T, class U> calc (const T&, const U&);
```

The compilation of templates

When the compiler sees the definition of a template, it does not generate any code. It only generates code when you instantiate a specific instance of a template. The fact that the code is generated only when the template is used (not when it is defined) affects how we organize the source code and how errors are detected. It also goes to the size of the exe or lib or dll library.

When calling a function, the compiler needs to see only the declaration of the function. When using a class type object, the class definition must be available but the definition of member functions need not be present. So, we put class definitions and function declarations in header files (.h) and class member functions definitions in source code (.cpp).

The templates are different. To generate an instantiation, the compiler needs the code that defines a template function or a template class member function. So, the header (.h) for templates contain their definitions and their statements and member functions.

Template compilation errors

The detection of errors on the templates can sometimes be a real obstacle because the compiler checks several things when the template is instantiated. One of the most common errors is that encountered on types. Example: A template requires a cost operation <<. Compilation does not detect an error until instantiation on a type is performed. If the type does not support the << operator for iostream cost on the object passed in the parameter, the error is immediately detected.

Example:

```
template <typename T> void Echo(const T & t)
{
    cost << t << endl;
}

void Template1()
{
    string t = "My Lisa";
    Echo(t);  // OK
    Echo(9);  // OK

    vector<string> girls = { "edith", "lisa", "audrey" };
    Echo(girls); // KO, binary << no operator found in vector<T>...
}
```

Build error: binary '<': no operator found which takes a right-hand operand of type 'const std::vector<std::string,std::allocator<_Ty>>' (or there is no acceptable conversion)

In our example, there is no << operator defined in vector<T> that can work with the cost function defined in iostream of the STL. The Echo function only costs << but this is not possible on vector<T>. It was possible on string and int but not on vector<T>.

A good practice is to try to minimize the number of prerequisites requested on the type of argument.

It is up to the template designer to check that the arguments passed to the template support all the operations that the template uses and that these operations behave correctly in the context that the template uses.

The class templates

A class template is used to generate classes. Class templates differ from function templates in that the compiler cannot deduce the template parameter types for a class template. To use a class template, we need to provide additional information in the token (< and >) right after the template name. The extra information is the list of template arguments to use for this template.

Define a class template

Like function templates, class templates start with the template keyword followed by a list of template parameters. Here is a template for handling pointers. No need to delete, the template supports it.

```cpp
template<typename T>
class MyPtr
{
public:
    MyPtr()
    {
        m_count = 0;
        m_ptr = nullptr;
        cost << "No Pointer catched" << endl;
    }

    MyPtr(T* ptr): m_ptr(ptr)
    {
        m_count = 0;
        m_count++;
        cost << "Pointer catched" << endl;
    }

    virtual ~MyPtr()
    {
        m_count--
        if (m_count == 0)
        {
            delete m_ptr;
            cost << "Pointer deleted!" << endl;
        }
```

```cpp
        }

        T& operator*(void)
        {
                return *m_ptr;
        }

        T* operator->(void)
        {
                return m_ptr;
        }

        MyPtr& operator=(MyPtr<T> &ptr)
        {
                if ( m_ptr!= nullptr)
                        delete m_ptr;
                m_ptr = ptr.m_ptr;
                m_count++;
                return *this;
        }

        MyPtr& operator=(T* ptr)
        {
                if (m_ptr!= nullptr)
                        delete m_ptr;
                m_ptr = ptr;
                m_count++;
                return *this;
        }

private:
        T * m_ptr;
        int m_count;
};
```

The MyPtr template has a template parameter type named T. We can use this parameter anywhere to represent the type MyPtr holds. For example, we define the return type of an operation that provides access to the MyPtr element as T&. When a developer instantiates this template, the uses of T will be replaced by a specific template argument.

Instantiation of the class template
To instantiate the class template, you must explicitly provide a parameter type to the template such as, for example, an CElement class which is a dummy class to designate elements to be drawn:

```cpp
MyPtr<CElement> pElement(new CElement(10));
pElement->Draw();
```

It is possible to have as member data a storage of elements in vector for example by using the type parameter of the template:

```
std::shared_ptr<std::vector<T>> data;
```

Type T is type like the others so you can use it as you want, in T, T & T*. All combinations are possible.

Member functions of class templates
Member functions can be defined in the header or in the body. If it is outside the header, specify template<T> and the class name followed by:: and the method name.
Example:
In the header:

```
    MyPtr& operator=(MyPtr<T> &ptr);
In the cpp:

template<typename T>
MyPtr<T>& MyPtr<T>::operator=(MyPtr<T> &ptr)
{
    if (m_ptr!= nullptr)
            delete m_ptr;
    m_ptr = ptr.m_ptr;
    m_count++;
    return *this;
}
```

In the MyPtr<T> template, we distinguish several subtleties. The operators * and -> have been redefined for transparent use of the smart pointer mechanism (smart pointers).

Static members and templates
It is possible to put static members in class templates.

```
template <typename T> class Foo {
public:
  static std::size_t count() { return ctr; }
private:
  static std::size_t ctr;
};
```

All Foo<T> objects share the same static data.

```
// limb instantiation static Foo<string>::ctr and Foo<string>::count Foo<string> fs;
// all 3 objects share members
Foo<int>::ctr and Foo<int>::count Foo<int> fi, fi2, fi3;
```

Default Templates and Arguments
It is possible to pass default types for template type parameters.

```
template <typename T, typename F = less<T>>
int compare(const T &v1, const T &v2, F f = F())
```

```
{
    if (f(v1, v2)) return -1;
    if (f(v2, v1)) return 1;
    return 0;
}
```

Here the second parameter of the template is by default less<T>. The less function of the STL takes two parameters (x and y) and returns x<y.

Specialization of template

In certain specific cases, we are obliged to ask for a specific function of the template for a specific parameter type. Let's take an example:

```
template <typename T>
struct wrap
{
        typename typedef T type;
        static const T& MakeWrap(const T& t)
        {
                return t;
        }
        static const T& Unwrap(const T& t)
        {
                return t;
        }
};
```

This Wrap<T> template represents a universal wrapper. By default MakeWrap and Unwrap returns T and the typedef type also returns a T. For all simple types, this wrapper works but for HSTRING types and pointers, you have to wrap it differently. This development is specific to Windows 8.

```
template <>
struct wrap<HSTRING>
{
        typedef HStringHelper type;
        static HStringHelper MakeWrap(const HSTRING& t)
        {
                HStringHelper str;
                str.Set(t);
                return str;
        }
        static HSTRING Unwrap(const HStringHelper& t)
        {
                HSTRING str;
                t.CopyTo(&str);
                return str;
```

```
                        }
                };

                template <typename T>
                struct wrap<T*>
                {
                        typename typedef ComPtr<T> type;
                        static ComPtr<T> MakeWrap(T* t)
                        {
                                ComPtr<T> ptr;
                                ptr. Attach(t);
                                return ptr;
                        }
                        static T* Unwrap(ComPtr<T> t)
                        {
                                ComPtr<T> ptr(t);
                                return t.Detach();
                        }
                };
```

The HSTRING type cannot be manipulated as it is like a HANDLE. This is why HSTRING is treated with a HStringHelper class and type becomes HStringHelper The same goes for pointers that need to be encapsulated in ComPtr<T> because they are COM components. The type is ComPtr<T> because the pointers are COM interfaces and must be encapsulated to use them. Yes it is Windows development but the main thing is to notice the specialization of the Wrap<T> template and its Wrap<HSTRING> and Wrap<T*> variants.

The key concept is that standard rules apply to specializations. To specialize a template, a statement of the original template must be accessible. The same applies to the specialized template before its use.

With ordinary classes or functions, missing statements are easy to find. For templates, it is often more complicated. Especially if the template specialization is not contained in the same header file as the main template. Templates and specialized templates must be declared in the same header file. First, we define the original template and then the specialized templates.

Reporting facilities in templates

In some cases, the typedef on a type will allow a better readability of the code. Example:

```
                template <class T>
                class Iterator : public RuntimeClass<IIterator<T>>
                {
                        InspectableClass(L"Library1.Iterator", BaseTrust)

                private:
                        typedef typename std::vector<typename Wrap<T>::type> WrappedVector;
                        typedef typename std::shared_ptr<WrappedVector> V;
                        typedef typename WrappedVector::iterator IT;

                        .. /.
```

Professional C++ - Philosophy and Principles

```
            private:
                V _v;
                IT _it;
                T _element;
                boolean _bElement = FALSE;
        };
```

This Iterator<T> template contains a WrappedVector that is a typedef on vector<typename Wrap<T>::type>. Using Wrap<T>::type does the magic of this template. For simple types, T is T and for HSTRING and T*, it will be HStringHelper and ComPtr<T>. This mechanism is very powerful.

In this example, the Iterator<T> template represents an iterator under Windows 8 in Windows Store mode. Yes I know it's Windows but it's the style that counts. Look at typedef, they use Wrap<T> in a vector<T> and the vector iterator is set to IT, easier to write.

The statement of V is a vector<T> shared_ptr with T that is Wrap<T>. This is quite complex but it means that it is a generic container of wrapped objects that can contain both simple types but also HSTRING and also T* interface pointers that will be managed as COM interface pointers so encapsulated with the Wrap<T*> specialization via ComPtr<T>.

Let's see how the GetCurrent method is defined for this iterator class.

```
            virtual HRESULT STDMETHODCALLTYPE get_Current(T *current)
            {
                try {
                        _LogInfo(L"Iterator::get_Current()...");
                    if (_it!= _v->end())
                    {
                        _bElement = TRUE;
                        _element = Wrap<T>::Unwrap(*_it);
                        *current = _element;
                    }
                    else
                    {
                        _bElement = FALSE;
                    }
                    return S_OK;
                _EXCEPTION_HANDLER(L"Iterator::get_Current()...");
            }
```

GetCurrent must return the current element; we check the iterator to see if we are at the end or not. We unwrap the element and return it in the function parameter. The _bElement boolean is positioned to have duplicate information on the position status of the iterator. It is useful for another method of the template to have if there is a current element.

You're gonna tell me, okay, we're declaring an iterator, but where's the class of the container that's using that iterator. This is the specific Vector<T> class for Windows 8 that allows you to manage a generic container by taking care of simple and complex types (HSTRING, COM interface pointers) with Wrap<T>.

```
template <typename T>
            class Vector: public RuntimeClass<IVector<T>,
```

```cpp
                        IIterable<T>,
                        IObservableVector<T>>
            {
                        InspectableClass(L"Library1.Vector", BaseTrust)

            private:
                        typedef typename std::vector<typename Wrap<T>::type>
WrappedVector;
                        typedef typename WrappedVector::const_iterator CIT;
                        typedef typename VectorChangedEventHandler<T> WFC_Handler;

            public:
                        Vector()
                        {
                                    _LogInfo(L"Vector::Vector()...");
                                    _v = std::make_shared<WrappedVector>();
                                    m_observed = false;
                        }
            public:
                        virtual HRESULT STDMETHODCALLTYPE GetAt(unsigned index, T
*item)
                        {
                                    _LogInfo(L"Vector::GetAt()...");
                                    *item = Wrap<T>::Unwrap((*_v)[index]);
                                    return S_OK;
                        }

                        ../.
                        virtual HRESULT STDMETHODCALLTYPE First(IIterator<T>
**first)
                        {
                                    _LogInfo(L"Vector::First()...");
                                    ComPtr<Iterator<T>> p = Make<Iterator<T>>();
                                    p->Init(_v);
                                    *first = p.Detach();
                                    return S_OK;
                        }
                        ../.
            private:
                        std::shared_ptr<WrappedVector> _v;
                        bool m_observed;
                        EventSource<VectorChangedEventHandler<T>> m_events;
            };
```

To simplify the understanding of this Vector<T> template, I have included only the GetAt method which allows to retrieve an element and the First method which returns an iterator on the Vector<T> via Iterator<T>, template which we discovered earlier. The Vector<T> template inherits several classes that are also templates.

Conclusion
Templates are classes or functions that generate classes. Their use requires a little practice but it is something apprehensive with a little effort. The power of templates lies in the possibility to define a generic class and to provide the necessary adaptations so that it can be used with the minimum of constraint. The partial specialization of templates is a great mechanism to correct the types a little limited or too painful to manage. In these operations, the typedef is your friend. We declare a T and then with its use we realize that T is too simple and that we need to wrap the T in some cases. This is cool. This article allows you to discover what templates are. This may seem complicated but with a little practice, you are completely sucked in and everything becomes clear. You must always put yourself in a situation with the template designer's hat and change from time to time as a template user. The discovery of the most complex compilation errors will be done via the usage code of the templates.

Professional C++

The Standard Template Library

We have a series of articles on the practice of C++ for you to get started. This month we are discussing the C++ standard library named STL: Standard Template Library.
The C language has its runtime and the C++ also has its runtime, called STL. In the Microsoft world, the C runtime is called MSVCRTxxx.dll and the C++ runtime is called MSVCPxxx.dll. However, the STL does not behave as a list of functions that can be called – fopen example in C. The STL consists of templatesThe STL is organized via header files.

The features offered by the standard library can be classified as follows:

- Support for the run-time of the language (for example, for allocation and run-time information).
- The standard C library (with really minor changes to minimize type system violation).
- Strings (with support for international character sets and localization).
- Support for regular expression matching.
- Input/output streams are an extensible framework for input and output to which users can add their own types, streams, buffering strategies, locales, and character sets.
- A framework of containers (like **vector and map**) and algorithms (like **find(), sort()**, and **merge()**). This framework, conventionally called STL, is extensible so that users can add their own containers and algorithms.
- Support for numerical computation (such as standard mathematical functions, complex numbers, vectors with arithmetic operations, and random number generators).
- Support for parallel programming, including **thread**s and locks. Parallel support is fundamental for users to be able to add support to new parallel models in libraries.
- Utility classes for supporting template-based meta programming (for example, trait type, generic programming with STL style (for example, **peer**), and general programming (for example, **clock**).
- 'Intelligent Pointers' for resource management (for example, **unique_ptr** and **shared_ptr**) and an interface for resource release.
- Special containers, such as **array, bitset**, and **tuple**.

The main criterion for including a class in the library was that:

- this could be useful to almost all C++ programmers (novices or experts)
- this could be provided in a general form that does not add significant overhead to a simplified version of the same functionality, and
- simple to use should be easy to learn (relative to the complexity of the task).

The C++ standard library essentially provides the most common basic data structures as well as the basic algorithms to be used with. We will sweep all or part of this exhaustive list.

Selecting standard library header files:	
<algorithm>	copy(), find(), sort()

Professional C++ - Philosophy and Principles

<array>	array
<chrono>	duration, time_point
<cmath>	sqrt(), pow()
<complex>	complex, sqrt(), pow()
<forward_list>	forward_list
<fstream>	fstream, ifstream, ofstream
<future>	future, promised
<ios>	hex,dec,scientific,fixed,defaultfloat
<iostream>	istream, ostream, cin, cost
<map>	map, multimap
<memory>	unique_ptr, shared_ptr, allocator
<random>	default_random_engine, normal_distribution
<regex>	regex, smatch
<string>	string, basic_string
<set>	set, multiset
<sstream>	istrstream, ostrstream
<stdexcept>	length_error, out_of_rang e, runtime_error
<thread>	thread
<unordered_map>	unordered_map, unordered_multimap
<utility>	move(), swap(), even
<vector>	vector

General concepts
The STL uses the namespace std. It is possible to do without it by using:

```
using namespace std;
```

The STL header files are named without the . h extension, example:

```
#include <iostream>
#include <sstream>
#include <fstream>
#include <string>
#include <vector>
#include <list>
#include <map>
#include <memory>
#include <array>
#include <utility>
#include <thread>
#include <algorithm>
using namespace std;
```

The string type

This type is defined in the <string> header file and is the type that links the char types of C to the string type of a higher level than the string type. The string type allows you to concatenate string between them. It's not a char pointer. It's a template.

```
typedef basic_string<char, char_traits<char>, allocator<char> >
    string;
```

It is possible to provide your own memory allocator. But who's going to use this? And yet it is planned... Remember in the article on classes when I was talking about the author's class cap and the user's class cap. We are exactly there except that it is a template class.

```
string msg = "Nutty is naughty!";
string msg2 = "Maggie is the queen of naughty girls!";
string s = msg + " " + msg2;
cout << s << endl;
string nutty = s.substr(0, 9);
cout << nutty << endl;
msg[3] = toupper(msg[3]);
cout << msg << endl;
string temp("VS 2019 v16.8.x is here!");
size_t t = temp.find_first_of("here");
cout << temp << " " << t << endl;
```

The string class contains many operations that avoid the path of the old C chains. To change from a string to a type C char *, use the c_str() function:

```
const char * psz = msg.c_str();
printf("String const char * = %s n", psz);
```

Regular expressions (regex)

Professional C++ - Philosophy and Principles

The regex functionality is available in the <regex> header file. The support is the same as in other languages; regex_match, regex_search, regex_replace, regex_iterator, regex_token_ietrator.

The IOs/Streams
The STL uses flows to manage I/O with buffers. The best known function is cout and its operator '<'.

```cpp
cout << "We're not just Mickeys!" << endl;
int i = 10;
float f = 2.5;
cout << i << ", " << f << endl;
```

The best friend of cout is cin. This allows to capture the inputs of the keyboard:

```cpp
int j = 0;
cout << "Give me a Int!" << endl;
cin >> j;
cout << "Thanks for " << j << endl;
```

In addition to managing standard types and string, it is possible to take advantage of the library to display other types. For example, consider the following type:

```cpp
struct CPersonne
{
    int age;
    string name;
};

ostream& operator<<(ostream& os, const CPersonne& p)
{
    return os << p.name << " " << p.age << " ans";
}

void TestIO()
{
    CPersonne p;
    p.age = 5;
    p.name = "Audrey Maggie";

    cout << "Lisa's sister is " << p << endl;
}
```

The << operator definition with the ostream type allows you to pass a CPersonne type at cost without forcing! Other aspects of the I/O library are formatting. To display types as does a printf function in C with %d, %f, %x and %s have their equivalent in the library.

```cpp
void TestFormating()
{
    float f = 2.50;
    cout << f << ";"
         << scientific << f << ";"
         << hexfloat << f << ";"
         << fixed << f << ";"
         << defaultfloat << f << endl;
```

}
```

File management is provided through the <fstream> header file:
- ifstream allows you to read a file
- ofstream allows you to write a file
- fstream allows you to read and write in a file

Example of file writing:
```
ofstream ofs("c:\\temp\\MyGirls.txt");
ofs << "Edith" << endl;
ofs << "Lisa" << endl;
ofs << "Maggie" << endl;
ofs.close();
```

It's really very simple. The I/O library allows you to manage buffers. The <sstream> header file allows you to manipulate strings:
- istringstream to play channels
- ostringstream to write channels
- stringstream for reading and writing channels

```
int i = 20;
float f = 5.75;
string s = "Maggie is too naughty!";
ostringstream oss;
oss << i << ", " << f << ", " << s;

string str = oss.str();
cout << str << endl;
```

The containers

The most commonly used container is vector<T>. It is available in the <vector> header file. It is a sequence of elements of a given type. Items are stored contiguously. To add elements to a vector, use the push_back() method. The path of a vector can be done with a range-for or by using an iterator. The STL containers are all accessible through an iterator. The functions begin(), end(), operator++, operator—m operator* allow you to manipulate an iterator. Example:

```
vector<CPersonne> v = { {12, "Edith"}, {9, "Lisa"}, {5, "Maggie"}};
CPersonne p;
p.age = 41;
p.name = "Papa";
v.push_back(p);
for (auto item: v)
{
        cout << item.age << " " << item.name << endl;
}
for (vector<CPersonne>::const_iterator it = begin(v); it!= end(v); ++it)
{
        CPersonne p = *it;
        cout << p.age << " " << p.name << endl;
}
```

Here is the list of main operations for vector<T>:
```

Professional C++ - Philosophy and Principles

Operation	Explanation
v.empty()	Returns true if v is empty. Otherwise returns false.
v.size()	Returns the number of elements in v.
v.push_back(t)	Adds a t-value element at the end of v.
v[n]	Returns a reference to the element in position n in v.
v1=v2	Replaces items in v1 with a copy of items in v2.
v1={a, b, c...}	Replaces the items in v1 with a copy of the list items.
v1==v2	v1 and v2 are equal if there are the same number of elements and value.
v1!= v2	opposite of v1==v2
<, <=, >, >=	Following the order of values returns a bool

There is a container that represents a double list linked through list. It is available through the <list> header file.

```
list<CPersonne> l = { { 12, "Edith" },{ 9, "Lisa" },{ 5, "Maggie" } };
CPersonne p = { 41, "Dad"};
1. push_front(p);
CPersonne p2 = { 40, "Mom"};
1. push_back(p2);
for (auto item : l)
{
        cout << item.age << " " << item.name << endl;
}
```

The container map<K,V> is very useful. It is available in the <map> header file. It is an associative container.

```
map<string, int> family = { { "Edith", 12 },{ "Lisa", 9 },{ "Maggie", 5 } };
        family["Papa"] = 41;
        for (map<string, int>::const_iterator it = begin(family); it!= end(family); ++it)
        {
                string name = it->first;
                int age = it->second;
                cout << name << " " << age << endl;
        }
```

There are other containers in the STL like the hashtable named unordered_map. The hashtable container and its derivatives (see table below) do not contain the term hashtable for naming purposes. There's probably existing code that made a class or template hashtable and that's to avoid name collision.

98

Professional C++

Containers available in the STL	
vector<T>	a vector of variable size
list<T>	a doubly-chained list
forward_list<T>	a linked list
deque<T>	a double ended queue
set<T>	a set (a map with an invalid key)
multiset<T>	a set that can be duplicated
map<K,V>	an associative table
multimap<K,V>	a map with a key that can be duplicated
unordered_map<K,V>	a map that uses a hashtable lookup
unordered_multimap<K,V>	a multimap that uses a hashtable lookup
unordered_set<K,V>	a set that uses a hashtable lookup
unordered_multiset<K,V>	a multiset that uses a hashtable lookup

The algorithms

The STL provides simple functions for browsing sets, making copies, insertions, deletions, simple or complex searches. The header file is <algorithm>. The strength of the algorithms lies in the fact that they take for the most part a start iterator and an end iterator in order to carry out the course on a finished set. It's a bit confusing at first and then finally, we realize that most of the proposed paths in this header file are well done. The iterators must be controlled: this is the only constraint. In the table below, b is begin() and e is end().

Selection of algorithms in the STL	
p=find(b,e ,x)	p is the first p in [b:e) so that p==x
p=find_if(b,e ,f)	p is the first p in [b:e) so that f(p)==true
n=count(b,e ,x)	n is the number of q elements in [b:e) so that q==x
n=count_if(b,e ,f)	n is the number of q elements in [b:e) in such a way that f(q,x)
replace(b,e ,v,v2)	Replaces the q elements in [b:e) so that q==v by v2
replace_if(b,e ,f,v2)	Replaces the q elements in [b:e) so that f(q) is v2

Professional C++ - Philosophy and Principles

p=copy(b,e ,out)	Copy [b:e) in [out:p)
p=copy_if(b,e ,out,f)	Copies the q elements of [b:e) in such a way that f(q) up to a [out:p)
p=move(b,e ,out)	Moves [b:e) to [out:p)
p=unique_copy(b,e ,out)	Copy [b:e) to [out:p); does not copy adjacent duplicates
lot(b,e)	Sort the elements of [b:e) using < as sort criteria
lot(b,e,f)	Sort the elements of [b:e) using the sort function f
(p1,p2)= equal_range(b,e ,v)	[p1:p2) is the sorting subsequence [b:e) with the value v; a binary search de v
p=merge(b,e ,b2,e2,out)	Merge two sequences [b:e) and [b2:e2) into [out:p)

Example with find:

```
vector<string> v = { "Edith", "Lisa", "Maggie" };

//auto res = find(begin(v), end(v), "Maggie");
vector<string>::iterator res = find(begin(v), end(v), "Maggie");

if (res == end(v))
{
    cout << "Not found!" << endl;
}
else
{
    cout << "Found! " << *res << endl;
}
```

The utility templates

Everything in the STL is not as simple as containers or the I/O stream library. There are template classes that allow you to take advantage of advanced features.
Considering resource management, there are two templates that are unique_ptr<T> and share_ptr<T>. unique_ptr<T> represents unique possession. shared_ptr<T> represents shared possession. Available in the <memory> header file, these «smart pointers» or intelligent pointers make it possible to no longer encode the delete, it is the template that takes care of it. The main advantage of using smart pointers is to avoid memory leakage.

```
unique_ptr<CPersonne> ptr(new CPersonne());
ptr->age = 41;
ptr->name = "Itchy";
// use ptr
// delete done automatically
```

Here is the list of common operations between unique_ptr<T> and shared_ptr<T>:

Operation	Explanation

shared_ptr<T> sp	Smart pointer null pointing to a T object
unique_ptr<T> up	Smart pointer null pointing to a T object
p	Uses p as a condition; true if p points to an object
*p	Dereference p to obtain the object on which p points
p->mem	Synonym for (*p). mem
p.get()	Returns the pointer in p.
swap(p,q)	Swap the pointers in p and q
p.swap(q)	Swap the pointers in p and q

The share_ptr<T> template has some subtleties:

Operation	Explanation
make_shared<T>(args)	Returns a shared_ptr on the allocated memory and initializes the object via args
shared_ptr<T> p(q)	p is a copy of q. Increment the internal reference counter
p=q	Increment the q reference counter
p.use_count()	Returns the number of objects shared with p
p.unique()	Returns true if p.use_count is 1 otherwise false

The array<T, C> template allows you to manage arrays as quickly as built-in arrays.

```cpp
array<string, 3> ar;
ar[0] = "Edith";
ar[1] = "Lisa";
ar[2] = "Audrey";
for (auto element : ar)
{
        cout << element << endl;
}
```

The pair<T, U> template represents two elements and is available in the <utility> header file. Use make_pair to fill in the pair object.

```cpp
pair<string, float> p;
p.first = "The C++ Object Model";
p.second = 50.0;
cout << p.first << " " << p.second << endl;
```

```cpp
pair<string, string> p2 = make_pair("Maggy", "you're a slut!");
cout << p2.first << " " << p2.second << endl;
```

The tuple<T...> template represents a sequence of different types and types. Use make_tuple to fill the tuple object.

```cpp
tuple<string, float, string> t;
t = make_tuple("C++ Primer", 50.0, "The best of all books!");
cout << get<0>(t) << ";" << get<1>(t) << ";" << get<2>(t) << endl;
```

Concurrency: the multithreading!

It is possible to run a task in parallel and wait for it to finish. We will use the thread class available in the <thread> header file. Simply pass a routine as argument to the thread class constructor. The join() method on the thread object allows you to wait for it to end.

```cpp
void ThreadFunc()
{
    // .. /.
}

void TestThread()
{
    t(ThreadFunc) thread;
    std::thread::id id = t.get_id();
    t.join();
    cout << "TestThread: TID:" << id << ", " << "Main:" << GetCurrentThreadId() << endl;
}
```

In the above example, the thread function does not take parameters. However, in some cases, we want to be able to pass parameters to the thread. Simply pass the parameters to the thread object constructor:

```cpp
class Param
{
public:
    string s;
    int i;
    float f;
};

void ThreadFunc2(Param param)
{
    cout << param.s << ", " << param.i << ", " << param.f << endl;
    // .. /.
}

void TestThreadWithParam()
{
    Param param = { "C++", 14, 50.0 };
    t(ThreadFunc2, param) thread;
    t.join();
}
```

Lock-like classes such as mutex or unique_lock<T> exist to protect access to shared data. You may notice that managing threads is quite simple to use.

Conclusion

We have scanned the different components of the standard library and the observation is the following: the source code of the STL is complex because it is an extensible framework; it has been seen on iostream and the passage of a cost structure; that you have to learn to master. From the simple examples in this chapter, you just have to get started. The most important aspect is the control of containers. Don't build your own list, hash_table or other structures anymore, use the STL! The use of vector<T> is the only way to get into the STL. You will have unrivalled performance.

Stop using delete and switch to smart pointers! unique_ptr<T> and shared_ptr<T> justify; as a vector<T>; a systematic use.

The end of memory leaks is another justification. A tip: leave the code a little old (legacy) with a dad style, and on the new code, unleash the underworld with STL everywhere...
 All this is to be taken with great moderation and wisdom but I am sure you understand me. The new code must be coded with all the fireworks of the C++ 11.
The code is more readable, the performances are there by default because of the Industry makes improvements on the STL.

You no longer have any excuses for not trying; It's up to you.
Like Herb Sutter (Chairman of the C++ ISO standard) says: it's "power & performance".

Professional C++ - Philosophy and Principles

C++ Language Features and Standard Library Components

Here is the language features and standard-library components that have been added to C++ for the C++11, C++14, C++17 and C++20 standards.

C++11 Language Features

[1] Uniform and general initialization using {}-lists
[2] Type deduction from initializer: **auto**
[3] Prevention of narrowing
[4] Generalized and guaranteed constant expressions: **constexpr**
[5] Range-**for**-statement
[6] Null pointer keyword: **nullptr**
[7] Scoped and strongly typed **enum**s: **enum class**
[8] Compile-time assertions: **static_assert**
[9] Language mapping of {}-list to **std::initializ er_list**
[10] Rvalue references, enabling move semantics
[11] Nested template arguments ending with >> (no space between the >s)
[12] Lambdas
[13] Variadic templates
[14] Type and template aliases
[15] Unicode characters
[16] **long long** integer type
[17] Alignment controls: **alignas** and **alignof**
[18] The ability to use the type of an expression as a type in a declaration: **decltype**
[19] Raw string literals
[20] Generalized POD (''Plain Old Data'')
[21] Generalized **union**s
[22] Local classes as template arguments
[23] Suffix return type syntax
[24] A syntax for attributes and two standard attributes: **[[carries_dependency]]** and **[[noreturn]]**
[25] Preventing exception propagation: the **noexcept** specifier
[26] Testing for the possibility of a **throw** in an expression: the **noexcept** operator.
[27] C99 features: extended integral types (i.e., rules for optional longer integer types); concatenation of narrow/wide strings; __STDC_HOSTED__; **_Pragma(X)**; vararg macros and empty macro arguments
[28] **__func__** as the name of a string holding the name of the current function
[29] **inline** namespaces
[30] Delegating constructors
[31] In-class member initializers
[32] Control of defaults: **default** and **delete**
[33] Explicit conversion operators

```
[34] User-defined literals
[35] More explicit control of **template** instantiation: **extern template**s
[36] Default template arguments for function templates
[37] Inheriting constructors
[38] Override controls: **override** and **final**
[39] A simpler and more general SFINAE (Substitution Failure Is Not An Error) rule
[40] Memory model
[41] Thread-local storage: **thread_local**
```

C++14 Language Features

```
[1] Function return-type deduction; §3.6.2
[2] Improved **constexpr** functions, e.g., **for**-loops allowed
[3] Variable templates
[4] Binary literals
[5] Digit separators
[6] Generic lambdas
[7] More general lambda capture
[8] **[[deprecated]]** attribute
[9] A few more minor extensions
```

C++17 Language Features

```
[1] Guaranteed copy elision
[2] Dynamic allocation of over-aligned types
[3] Stricter order of evaluation
[4] UTF-8 literals (**u8**)
[5] Hexadecimal floating-point literals
[6] Fold expressions
[7] Generic value template arguments (**auto** template parameters)
[8] Class template argument type deduction
[9] Compile-time **if**
[10] Selection statements with initializers
[11] **constexpr** lambdas
[12] **inline** variables
[13] Structured bindings
[14] New standard attributes: **[[fallthrough]]**, **[[nodiscard]]**, and **[[maybe_unused]]**
[15] **std::byte** type
[16] Initialization of an **enum** by a value of its underlying type
[17] A few more minor extensions
```

C++20 Language Features

```
[1] concepts, with terse syntax
[2] modules
```

Professional C++ - Philosophy and Principles

[3] designated initializers (based on the C99 feature, and common G++ extension)
[4] [=, this] as a lambda capture
[5] template parameter lists on lambdas
[6] three-way comparison using the "spaceship operator", operator <=>
[7] initialization of an additional variable within a range-based for statement
[8] lambdas in unevaluated contexts
[9] default constructible and assignable stateless lambdas
[10] allow pack expansions in lambda init-capture
[11] string literals as template parameters
[12] removing the need for typename in certain circumstances
[13] new standard attributes [[no_unique_address]],[[likely]] and [[unlikely]]
[14] conditional explicit, allowing the explicit modifier to be contingent on a boolean expression
[15] expanded constexpr: virtual functions, union, try and catch,[26] dynamic_cast and typeid,[27] std::pointer_traits
[16] immediate functions using the new consteval keyword
[17] signed integers are now defined to be represented using two's complement (signed integer overflow remains undefined behavior)
[18] a revised memory model
[19] various improvements to structured bindings (interaction with lambda captures, static and thread_local storage duration)
[20] coroutines
[21] using on scoped enums
[22] constinit keyword

C++11 Standard Library Components

The C++11 additions to the standard library come in two forms: new components (such as the regular expression matching library) and improvements to C++98 components (such as move constructors for containers).

[1] **initializ er_list** constructors for containers
[2] Move semantics for containers
[3] A singly-linked list: **forward_list**
[4] Hash containers: **unordered_map, unordered_multimap, unordered_set,** and **unordered_multiset**
[5] Resource management pointers: **unique_ptr, shared_ptr,** and **weak_ptr**
[6] Concurrency support: **thread,** mutexes, locks, and condition variables
[7] Higher-level concurrency support: **packaged_thread, future, promise,** and **async()**
[8] **tuple**s
[9] Regular expressions: **reg ex**
[10] Random numbers: distributions and engines
[11] Integer type names, such as **int16_t, uint32_t,** and **int_fast64_t**
[12] A fixed-sized contiguous sequence container: **array**
[13] Copying and rethrowing exceptions
[14] Error reporting using error codes: **system_error**
[15] **emplace()** operations for containers

```
[16] Wide use of constexpr functions
[17] Systematic use of noexcept functions
[18] Improved function adaptors: function and bind()
[19] string to numeric value conversions
[20] Scoped allocators
[21] Type traits, such as is_integral and is_base_of
[22] Time utilities: duration and time_point
[23] Compile-time rational arithmetic: ratio
[24] Abandoning a process: quick_exit
[25] More algorithms, such as move(), copy_if(), and is_sor ted()
[26] Garbage collection ABI
[27] Low-level concurrency support: atomics
```

C++14 Standard Library Components

```
[1] shared_mutex
[2] User-defined literals
[3] Tuple addressing by type
[4] Associative container heterogenous lookup
[5] Plus a few more minor features
```

C++17 Standard Library Components

```
[1] File system
[2] Parallel algorithms
[3] Mathematical special functions
[4] string_view
[5] any
[6] variant
[7] optional
[8] invoke()
[9] Elementary string conversions: to_chars and from_chars
[10] Polymorphic allocator
[11] A few more minor extensions
```

C++20 Standard Library Components

```
[1] ranges (The One Ranges Proposal)
[2] std::make_shared and std::allocate_shared for arrays
[3] atomic smart pointers (such as std::atomic<shared_ptr<T>> and []
std::atomic<weak_ptr<T>>)
[4] std::to_address to convert a pointer to a raw pointer
[5] calendar and time-zone additions to <chrono>
[6] std::span, providing a view to a contiguous array (analogous to
std::string_view but span can mutate the referenced sequence)
[7] <version> header
```

Professional C++ - Philosophy and Principles

[8] std::bit_cast<> for type casting of object representations, with less verbosity than memcpy() and more ability to exploit compiler internals
[9] feature test macros
[10] various constexpr library bits
[11] smart pointer creation with default initialization
[12] std::map::contains method
[13] bit operations, such as leading/trailing zero/one count,[49] and log2 operations

Professional C++

3. Modern C++ : C++ 11, 14, 17, C++20 and upcoming C++23

Modern C++

C++ is a living language. To prove this, while the ISO C++11 standard has been available since March 2011, the roadmap for future C++14, C++17 and C++20 and C++23 standards was recently announced by Herb Sutter, the ISO C++ language standardization secretary. The ISO committee decided to release new versions of the standard more quickly, both in terms of language extensions and the STL library (Standard Template Library). Here is the image Herb Sutter proposed to present the main features of C++11:

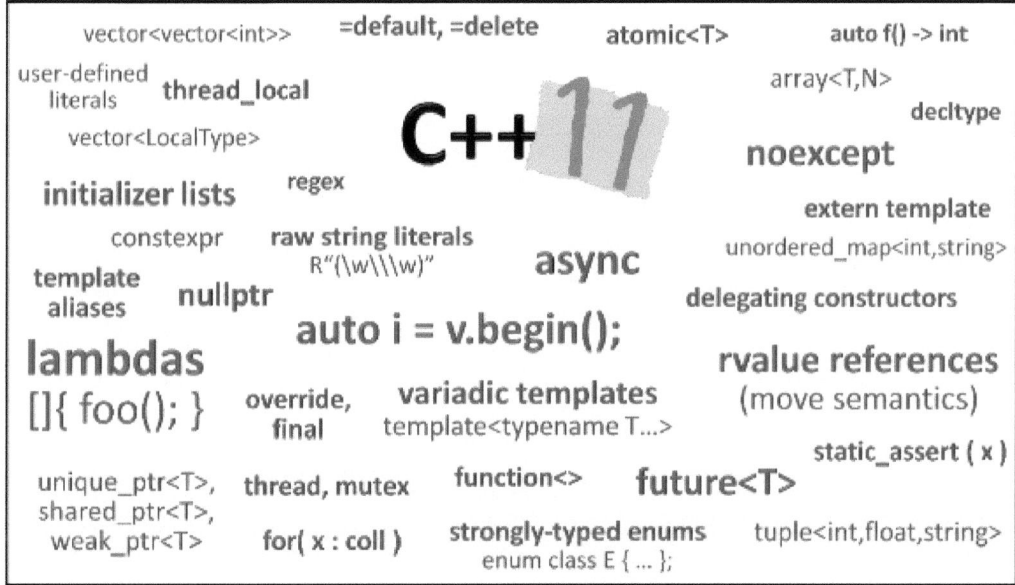

If you follow the evolution of C++, you know C++98, C++03, TR1 and C++0X which became C++11. In 2005, TR1 was inspired by many libraries available in the famous Boost project (www.boost.org).

Support for C++11 in compilers

Support for the C++11 by the main compilers on the market - GCC, CLang and Visual C++ - is now provided in full. The functionality was not implemented in one go; check the compliance support of your compiler if you are not using the latest version. C++11 includes both the C++ language and the STL library. The STL library exploits some new language features (e.g., displacement semantics).

Professional C++ - Philosophy and Principles

C++11 and STL

In modern C++ the use of the STL library is implicit because it provides, for example, string classes and «containers» like vector, list, set, map and support for hash tables. It is recognized that these collections are the most effective in practice. The STL also provides a set of algorithms for the path or transformation of datasets.

The lambdas in C++

The C++ now has the functionality of lambdas. A lambda is an anonymous function that can take arguments and has a function body and a return type. The default return type is void, but if you need to define another return type, you must specify this type with the syntax of the -> arrow. In addition to the arguments passed to the function, a lambda defines a capture list described between []. Here is a simple lambda function used with an operation for each:

```cpp
void Use_Lambda()
{
    vector<string> v;
    v.push_back("Edith");
    v.push_back("Lisa");
    v.push_back("Audrey Maggy");

    std::for_each(v.begin(), v.end(), [](string str) -> void {
        cout << str << endl;
    });
}
```

In this example, the capture list is empty. If [&] syntax is used, all local variables will be passed as references. Technically, a lambda function is defined in a class with operator overload ().

References RValue and *move constructor*

The C++11 introduces the concept of rvalue reference, identified by T&&. This notion makes it possible to implement the semantics of displacement (move semantic). The result is that we can freely move resources from one rvalue reference to another object. This moving mechanism is particularly useful to avoid copying variables passed by value which can be expensive in terms of performance. The best example is to return a vector created in a function. In C++03, the elements of the vector are copied behind each other. In C++11, the vector is moved. This operation is supported because the vector has a displacement constructor (move constructor) which takes as a parameter a rvalue reference to a vector.

```cpp
vector<string> Use_VectorReturn()
{
    vector<string> local_vector;
    local_vector.push_back("Edith");
    local_vector.push_back("Lisa");
    local_vector.push_back("Audrey Maggy");
```

```
        printf("local_vector=0x%08x n", local_vector);
        return local_vector;
}

int _tmain(int argc, _TCHAR* argv[])
{
        vector<string> v = Use_VectorReturn();
        printf("v=0x%08x n", v);
        return 0;
}
```

The output of this program proves that the address of the vector has been «stolen». In main, the vector points to the same address as the local variable of the Use_VectorReturn() function.

local_vector=0x00590a00

v=0x00590a00

In our example, the vector contains very few elements. In real life, a vector can contain a significant amount of elements and this mechanism that avoids local copies allows to gain performance. It should be noted that this displacement semantics is transparent for the user because the STL containers of the C++11 all have a displacement constructor, but also a displacement copy operator (move-assignment operator).

A displacement operation performs a "theft" of resources and does not allocate any resources. These travel operations are not intended to remove exceptions. For this, we need to specify it using the new noexcept keyword in both the h file and the cpp file.

The C++11 STL library introduces the function std::move() defined in the utility header file, which allows returning a rvalue reference.

Constant expression

The new constexpr keyword guarantees that a function or object construction is a constant operation guaranteed at compilation. The function body must contain exactly one return statement. The compiler replaces the call to a function directly constexpr by its value. The Visual C++ compiler does not support this feature.

Template marked extern

In important applications, instantiating the same template into multiple files can make compilation time important. To improve this, it is possible to refer to a template in different files without the compiler generating the code needed to instantiate it. You just have to prefix the definition of the template as extern.

Professional C++ - Philosophy and Principles

Initialization with {}

It is possible to initialize a variable or STL container as vector, list or map with the {} syntax as for C structures:

```
void Use_Initialization()
{
    int i = {0};
    vector<int> v = { 10, 20, 30, 40, 50 };
    list<string> mes_filles = { "Edith", "Lisa", "Audrey Maggy" };
}
```

Technically, list initialization is implemented using the class std::initializer_list.

Use of auto

The auto keyword is certainly the feature that will have the most success in terms of adoption. Using auto lets the compiler deduce the type of the declared variable.

```
void Use_auto()
{
    vector<int> v = { 10, 20, 30, 40, 50 };
    //for (vector<int>::iterator it = v.begin(); it!= v.end(); it++)
    for (auto it = v.begin(); it!= v.end(); it++)
    {
        int v = *it;
        cout << "value = " << v << endl;
    }
}
```

The auto keyword can be used with const and &.

Evolution of the for

The path of a data set with for is available since the C exists. C++11 introduces a variant for parsing sets through the use of the for keyword. The new syntax looks like this:

```
void Use_RangeFor()
{
    vector<string> mes_filles = { "Edith", "Lisa", "Audrey" };
    for (string s : mes_filles )
    {
        cout << s << endl;
    }
}
```

Evolution of the manufacturer

C++11 introduces the concept of manufacturer delegation. In C++03, a nontrivial constructor assigns values to member variables. If there are several constructors, we end up duplicating the code that assigns the default values to certain member variables. C++11 solves this problem like this:

```cpp
CPU class
{
public:
    CPU(string name, string company)
    {
        _name = name;
        _company = company;
    }
    CPU(string name, string company, double frequency): CPU(name, company)
    {
        _frequency = frequency;
    }
public:
    string _name;
    string _company;
    double _frequency;
};

void Use_CtorDelegation()
{
    cpu1 CPU("Pentium 4", "Intel");
    cpu2 CPU("Core I3", "Intel", 3.1);
}
```

In this example, there are two CPU manufacturers, and the second uses the first. So I don't have to duplicate code to initialize member variables.

Final marked class

If you define a class and do not want it to be derived, simply add the final keyword after your class name. If a class tries to derive from it, the compiler will err.

```cpp
class Bar final
{
};

// Illegal construction!!! Compilation error!!!
class DerivedBar: public Bar
```

Professional C++ - Philosophy and Principles

```
{
};
```

Null pointer constant

By convention and by compatibility with the C language, a null pointer is 0. The NULL preprocessor variable is used and is 0. The C++11 introduces the nullptr keyword to replace the use of null but is not 0!

Variadic template

A variadic template is a function or template class that takes a number of variable arguments. The syntax ... is used to define variable parameters.

String sequences

Handling complex character strings poses a problem in C or C++. Indeed, sequences with the '' character pose a problem. The '' character must be doubled in order not to conflict with sequences such as ' n', ' r', or 't'. In addition, you cannot declare a string on several lines. C++11 addresses this problem by providing support for «raw string literals». It is now possible to declare the contents of an XML document directly in the code. C++11 answers this with a sequence that looks like R" («content») ":

```
string strXML1 = R"(<DataApollo>
<Info>
<PriceUnit>euro</PriceUnit>
<VolumeUnit>TW0</VolumeUnit>
<RunCode>2012-03_00_avantEBO_V1_20130110</RunCode>
<RunOption>am</RunOption>
<GenerationDate>24-02-2014</GenerationDate>
<CoreVersion>2.3.3.894</CoreVersion>
<ReturnCode>0</ReturnCode>
</Info>
</DataApollo>
)";
```

The tuples

The STL library introduces the notion of tuple through the class std::tuple. This implementation is done using variadic templates. The std::tuple class takes a number of variable arguments.

```
void Use_Tuple()
```

```
{;
    tuple<string, string, int> maggy( "Maggy", "super naughty", 3);
    string str = get<1>(maggy);
    cout << str << endl;
}
```

The array type

The array class is defined in the array header file. This type allows to manage a sequence of elements of fixed size. It is like a standard array but with the support of the concept of iterator. This type is particularly suitable for embedded programming. It supports initialization as a list:

```
void Use_Array()
{
    array<int, 10> ar = { 0, 1, 2, 3, 4, 5, 6, 7, 8, 9};
    for (auto it = ar.begin(); it!= ar.end(); it++) {…}
    int a2 = ar[2]; int a3 = ar.at(3);
}
```

The hash tables

C++11 brings together a single notion of hash tables through the "unordered_set" and "unordered_map" header files. The old "hash_set" and "hash_map" files are obsolete.

The regular expressions

Support for regular expressions is provided through the "regex" header file. Regex can use the grammars of the following regular expressions: ECMAScript, standard POSIX, extended, awk, grep and egrep. The regex_match() and regex_search() functions determine whether a character sequence matches a given regex. The regex_replace() function allows you to find and replace a regular expression in a sequence. Regex also uses the notion of iterator through the regex_iterator class.

Intelligent pointers (smart pointers)

Support for "smart pointers" is provided through the "memory" header file. The most useful templates are shared_ptr<T>, unique_ptr<T> and weak_ptr<T>. The stated purpose of this intelligent pointer effort is to remove the use of delete and allow automatic release of memory. The memory management of objects can be entrusted to intelligent pointers. They will take care of the removal of objects on their own when the time comes. The shared_ptr<T> template works with all C++ types and requires no prior plumbing in the type that wants to take advantage of it. The shared_ptr<T> template also allows, for specific cases, to specify how to allocate or free the T-type. In short, it is possible to allocate or free any type of resources. To manage a smart pointer, simply encapsulate its T-type with the shared_ptr<T> template and use the make_shared<T>() function instead of new(). Access to type T is through the -> operator so type T is used as a standard pointer. Example:

Professional C++ - Philosophy and Principles

```
void Use_SharedPtr()
{
    shared_ptr<CPU> cpuPtr = make_shared<CPU>();
    cpuPtr->company = "Intel";
...
}
```

In this example, the delete function is not called, and the shared_ptr<T> will automatically delete it. It is possible to assign shared_ptr and their internal operation is based on the reference count. The counter is automatically incremented or decremented according to the use cases, and the managed object is released when the reference counter falls to 0.

Threads and mutex

Thread support is provided through the thread header file. The thread class encapsulates the thread and its associated processing routine. The thread class encapsulates the thread function of the operating system. The Linux and Windows APIs are different so the use of std::thread allows to standardize parallel programming. The lock management is performed through the mutex header file. A mutex is an object that represents exclusive access to a resource. It can be used to protect access to data and synchronize access to data shared across multiple threads. To start a thread, simply pass it the name of the routine that will be dedicated to processing and possibly a list of parameters to take as input to this routine. Declaring the thread immediately causes it to be launched and calling the join() method allows waiting for the end of processing.

```
void FnThread(vector<string> v)
{
    thread::id id = this_thread::get_id();
    for (string s: v) { cout << s << endl;         }
}

void Use_Thread()
{
    vector<string> mes_filles = { "Edith", "Lisa", "Audrey" };
    thread t(FnThread, mes_filles);
    t.join();
    cout << "Thread finished!" << endl;
}
```

It should be noted that the implementation of threads provided by the latest versions of Visual C++ uses the Concurrency Runtime (ConCRT) while the Boost library takes advantage of the PThreads system interfaces under Linux and the Win32 system APIs under Windows.

Meta programming and type traits

The type_traits header file contains everything you need to do meta programming. This topic goes beyond the scope of this article but deserves to be clarified.

C++14 and C++17

The C++ standard is evolving. C++14 will be a minor release. C++17 will integrate new libraries in the STL. These libraries are inspired by Boost like FileSystem or Network. There will also be support for parallel algorithms.

Books about C++11

Numerous reference works have been updated and republished to reflect the changes present with C++11. The most famous book is probably the one written by the inventor himself of the C++ language, namely Bjarne Stroustrup and his book «The C++ Programming Language», 4th edition. The second book is by Stanley B. Lippman, who worked with Bjarne Stroustrup, entitled "C++ Primer", 5th edition.

C++11 compilation environments

If you are running Linux or Mac, you can use GCC or CLang. For CLang, a 3.x version ensures maximum comfort. For GCC, a version 4.7 (released in March 2012) is very comfortable. GCC can be run on Windows via MinGW[33]. For Windows, Microsoft distributes Visual C++ in the latest version of Visual Studio 2013. I advise you to choose at least the Visual Studio 2012 version because the Visual Studio 2010 version offers only partial support. There is a free version of Visual Studio 2013 Express «for Desktop» running Windows 7 SP1 and above.

C++, The language of publishers

C++ is always at the forefront of technology and always THE reference language for many companies. Google, Apple, IBM, RedHat, Oracle, Intel and Microsoft are all C++ ambassadors. Never forget that compilers and other runtimes of Java or C# are all made in C++. Support for the latest processor architectures is done in C/C++. C++ offers power and performance.

---

[33] http://mingw-w64.org/doku.php

Professional C++ - Philosophy and Principles

Dynamic memory, vector<T> and smart pointers via shared_ptr<T>

Introduction

Since C++ exists, the vector<T> type is the king type of the standard STL library (Standard Template Library). Since the C++ 11 standard, we must force ourselves to use smart pointers because they make it easier to manage dynamic memory and especially because they avoid new and delete them.

The vector type of the standard STL library

A vector is a collection of objects of the same type. Each object in the collection has an index to access this object. A vector is often called a "container" because it contains other objects. To use a vector, you must make an appropriate #include. In our examples, we assume that a using std::vector is realized.

```
#include <vector>
using std::vector;
```

A vector is a template class. C++ has both template classes and templates functions. Templates are not classes or functions. This is a statement for the compiler to generate classes or functions. This is the instanciation phase. For a template class, you must specify the type to be managed via a series of <T>. In the case of the vector, here is how to declare it:

```
vector<int> ivec;         // vector de int
vector<Sales_item> Sales_vec; // Sales_items
vector<vector<string>> file object vector; // vector of vector of strings
```

In this example, the compiler generates 3 distinct types: vector<int>, vector<Sales_item>, and vector<vector<string>>.

We can define vectors to contain almost any type of data. It is possible to have a vector vector. It is possible.

The C++ 11 allows you to remove the space you used to write as vector<vector<int> and allows you to do this: vector<vector<int>>.

Initialization of the vector

An empty vector can be defined as follows:

```
vector<string> svec; // default initialization; svec has no elements.
```

It is possible to initialize a vector with values. It is possible to copy elements:

```
vector<int> ivec;               // empty
vector<int> ivec2(ivec);        // copy of ivec elements into ivec2
vector<int> ivec3 = ivec;       // copy of ivec elements in ivec3
vector<string> svec(ivec2);     // error: svec contains strings, not ints.
```

With the new C++ 11 standard, it is possible to initialize a vector with a list:

```
vector<string> articles = {"a", "an", "the"};
```
The vector has 3 elements: a, an, the.

```
vector<string> v1{"a", "an", "the"}; // list initialization
vector<string> v2("a", "an", "the"); // error
```

Other initialisations

It is possible to initialize a vector with a counter and a fill value.

```
vector<int> ivec(10, -1);    // 10 int elements, each initialized to -1 vector<string> svec(10, "hi!"); // 10 strings each
initialized to "hi"
```

You can only give the vector size and forget the default value. If the vector contains int, it will be initialized to 0. String elements will be automatically initialized.

```
vector<int> ivec(10);      // 10 elements, each set to 0
vector<string> svec(10);   // 10 elements, each initialized with an empty
string
```

Adding Elements to a Vector

How to add elements from 0 to 99? Use the push_back member of the vector. The push_back operation takes a value and pushes that value as the last element of the vector.

```
vector<int> v2;     // empty vector
for (int i = 0; i!= 100; ++i)
   v2.push_back(i);   // adding int to v2
// v2 contains 100 elements, values of 0.. 99.
```
Even though we know that we will have 100 elements, we declare v2 as empty.

The standard requires that vector implementations can add elements efficiently to the run-time.

Other operations on vector

Operation	Explanation
v.empty()	Returns true if v is empty. Otherwise returns false.
v.size()	Returns the number of elements in v.
v.push_back(t)	Adds a t-value element at the end of v.

Professional C++ - Philosophy and Principles

v[n]	Returns a reference to the item in position n in v.
v1=v2	Replaces items in v1 with a copy of items in v2.
v1={a, b, c...}	Replaces the items in v1 with a copy of the list items.
v1==v2	v1 and v2 are equal if there are the same number of elements and value.
v1!= v2	opposite of v1==v2
<, <=, >, >=	Following the order of values returns a bool

We have access to the elements of a vector in the same way that we have access to the characters of a string: via their position in the vector. For example, you can use a range-for to process elements of a vector:

```
vector<int> v{1,2,3,4,5,6,7,8,9};
for (auto &i: v)      // for each element in v (i is a reference)
     i *= i;
          for (auto i: v)     // for each element in v
cout << i << " "; // displays the cost element
<< endl;
```

The empty and size member correspond as in a string. Empty returns a boolean that indicates if the vector has elements and size returns the number of elements in the vector:

```
vector<int>::size_type // ok
vector::size_type   // error
```

Use of []

The [] operator can be used to fetch elements that exist:

```
vector<int> ivec;    // vector empty
cout << ivec[0];     // error: ivec has no

vector<int> ivec2(10) elements; // vector with 10 elements
cout << ivec2[10];   // error: ivec2 has elements 0 . . . 9
```

It is a mistake to fetch an element that does not exist.

The best way to avoid failure is to use a range as often as possible.

Vector Path

A vector can be scanned via an iterator. All containers in the standard library display iterators. Like pointers, iterators provide indirect access to an object. Members that provide access to iterators including begin() and end(). There are also members cbegin() and cend() to have an iterator const. It is even possible to have an iterator reverse via rbegin() and rend() and crbegin() and crend();

```
auto it = v.begin(); // auto allows to hide the type of the iterator.
```

An iterator is manipulated with the ++ increment operator. Access to the memory value is done with the use of *. In the case of the string vector, the iterator is written vector<string>::iterator it;

```
        vector<string> kids;
        kids.push_back("Edith");
        kids.push_back("Lisa");
        kids.push_back("Maggie");

        for (auto &it1 : kids)
        {
                cout << it1 << endl;
        }

        for (vector<string>::const_iterator it2 = kids.cbegin(); it2!=
kids.cend(); ++it2)
        {
                cout << *it2 << endl;
        }

        for (auto it3 = begin(kids); it3!= end(kids); ++it3)
        {
                cout << *it3 << endl;
        }
```

There is a convention since C++ 11 to do begin(kids) instead of kids.begin();

Introduction to Dynamic Memory

The programs we write use objects that have a well-defined duration. Global objects are allocated when the application starts and destroyed when the application ends. Local objects are created and destroyed at the beginning and end of the block. Static local objects are allocated before their first use and destroyed when the program ends. In addition to supporting automatic and static objects, C++ allows us to dynamically allocate objects. These dynamically allocated objects have a life cycle that is independent of when they were created; they exist until they are explicitly released.

Properly releasing dynamic objects often turns to fuel sources of errors. To make dynamic object allocation safer, the library defines two smart pointers that dynamically manages allocated objects. The smart pointers allow the automatic release of these objects in an appropriate way.

Our applications used only static or stack memory (on the stack). Static memory is used for static objects, for static class members, and for variables defined outside of functions. The stack memory (on the stack) is used for non-static objects defined in the functions. Objects allocated in static or stack memory are automatically created and destroyed by the

Professional C++ - Philosophy and Principles

compiler. Stack objects only exist in the block in which they are defined and that runs; static objects are allocated before use, and are destroyed when the application ends.

In addition to static or stack memory, an application can use a memory pool. This memory is called free store or heap (the heap). Applications use the heap for objects that are dynamically allocated – this means for objects that the application allocates to runtime. The application controls the life cycle of dynamic objects, but the code must explicitly destroy objects when no longer needed. It can be tricky (tricky☺)

Dynamic memory and smart pointers

In C++, dynamic memory is managed through new and delete operators. The new operator allocates and optionally initializes an object in memory and returns a pointer to that object. The delete operator, which takes a pointer to a dynamic object, destroys the object and frees the associated memory. Dynamic memory management is touchy because you have to free all the allocated memory otherwise you have a memory leak. The other error is to have pointers on an invalid memory area and there is application crash as soon as the pointer tries to be used. To make dynamic memory management easier, the new standard library provides 2 smart pointers that manage dynamic objects. A smart pointer is like a normal pointer with a notable difference that it automatically releases the object it points to. There are two types of smart pointers that differ in how they manage the life cycle of the object. The shared_ptr<T> allows multiple pointers to target the same object and unique_ptr<T> that has the object it points to. There is also weak_ptr<T> which is a weak reference on an object managed via shared_ptr<T>. All these smart pointers are templates defined in the memory header file.

Operations common to shared_ptr and unique_ptr

Operation	Explanation
shared_ptr<T> sp	Smart pointer null pointing to a T object
unique_ptr<T> up	Unique pointer null pointing to a T object
p	Uses p as a condition; true if p points to an object
*p	Dereference p to obtain the object on which p points
p->mem	Synonym for (*p). mem
p.get()	Returns the pointer in p.
swap(p,q)	Swap the pointers in p and q
p.swap(q)	Swap the pointers in p and q

Operations specific to shared_ptr

Operation	Explanation
make_shared<T>(args)	Returns a shared_ptr on the allocated memory and initializes the object via args
shared_ptr<T> p(q)	p is a copy of q. Increment the internal reference counter
p=q	Increment the q reference counter
p.use_count()	Returns the number of objects shared with p
p.unique()	Returns true if p.use_count is 1 otherwise false

The function make_shared<T>()

The safest way to allocate and use dynamic memory is to call the make_shared function of the library. This function allocates and initializes the object in dynamic memory and returns a shared_ptr that points to the object. When we call make_shared, we must specify the type of object we want to create. We do as with a template class except that it is a function.

```
// shared_ptr points to an int that is worth 42
shared_ptr<int> p3 = make_shared<int>(42);
// p4 points to a string with a value of 99999999
shared_ptr<string> p4 = make_shared<string>(10, '9');
// p5 points to an int that has a value initialized at 0
shared_ptr<int> p5 = make_shared<int>();
```

You can pass arguments to make_shared<T>(args) to make a desired call to the object constructor. The use of auto also makes the code more readable.

```
// p6 points to a dynamically allocated vector<string> and empty
auto p6 = make_shared<vector<string>>();
```

Automatic destruction of objects

When the last shared_ptr that points to an object is destroyed, the shared_ptr class automatically destroys the object it points to. This is achieved via the object destructor. The destructor or dtor releases the resource that the object has weighed down. In the case of the vector, there are several memory allocation operations to manage vector objects (the vector automatically grows). The shared_ptr destructor decreases its internal reference counter. As soon as it reaches 0, the destructor destroys the object pointed to by the shared_ptr and releases the memory used by that object.

Do not mix regular pointers and shared_ptr

A shared_ptr can only be destroyed with shared_ptr that are copied to itself. This is why you should use make_shared (which returns a shared_ptr) rather than new. In this way, we associate a shared_ptr with the object at the same time as its allocation. Consider the following code:

Professional C++ - Philosophy and Principles

```
// ptr is created and initialized when the function is called
void process(shared_ptr<int> ptr)
{
    // use ptr
} // ptr exits the scope and is destroyed
```

The process function parameter is passed by value so the process argument is copied to ptr. Copying a shared_ptr increments its reference counter. Therefore, inside the process the counter is at least 2. When the process ends, the ptr reference counter is decremented but cannot go to 0. The ptr local variable is destroyed but the memory on which ptr point will not be deleted. The correct method to use this function is to pass a shared_ptr.

```
shared_ptr<int> p(new int(42)); // reference count is 1
process(p); // copy p increment the counter; is 2 in process
int i = *p; // ok: reference count is 1
```

It is dangerous to use a standard pointer to access an object possessed by a smart pointer, because we do not know when the object will be destroyed and its memory freed.

The C++ Modern

The C++ ISO standard version C++11 introduces new features that upset the way we write C++. Lambdas, auto, range-for, shared_ptr<T>, initializer lists and so many other features make the new code have to adopt these new conventions and idioms. However, what should we do with the legacy code? The answer is simple: only the new code must be written in modern C++. The standard evolves in C++14 and C++17 but there will be no big revolutions compared to all that C++11 brings. C++11 was the rebirth of C++. It's a new way of writing, a new way of thinking about C++. Here is a reminder of everything that is introduced in C++11; this diagram is provided by Herb Sutter, chairman of the ISO C++ committee:

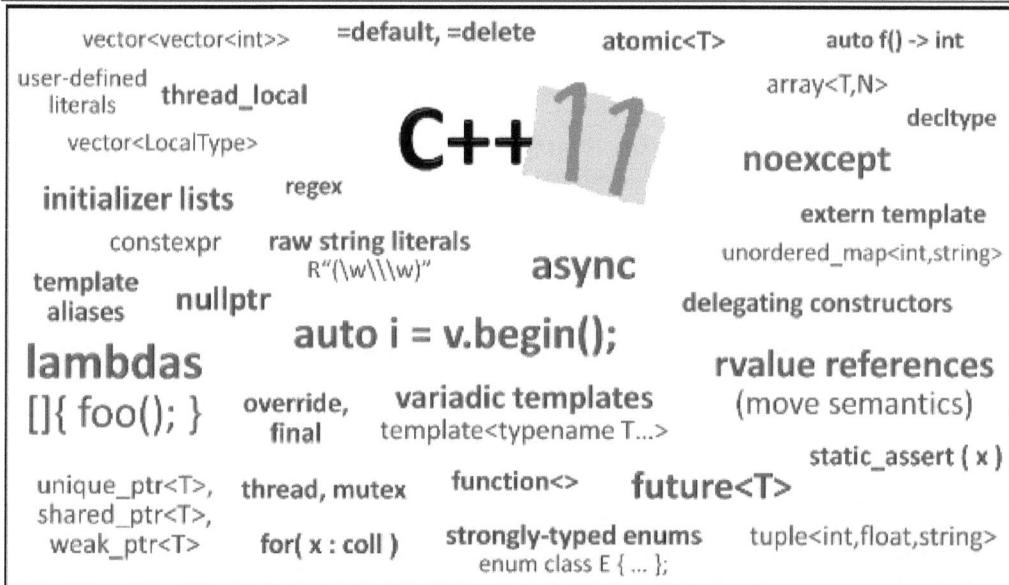

Conclusion

The memory can be manipulated easily and thanks to smart pointers, the writing of applications is very simple. Who knows that it is possible to make applications without new and delete. Now you know it! And yet, we don't need garbage collector like in .NET. Objects that are automatically freed in other languages such as C# leverage other systems to manage the life cycle of objects through different levels (GC generation). In C++, the rule is very simple. There is an internal counter for references and as soon as it drops to 0, POUM! The object is shot and the memory is released. The message of this article is simple: use the vector container and smart pointers; it's simple and effective and bug-free. C++ warriors have known this with Boost since 2001. The various implementations of Microsoft's C++ compiler are still behind GCC but now the situation is good. In short, use the conventions of C++ 11 and you will enter the world of modern C++.

Professional C++ - Philosophy and Principles

Latest Features from C++ 14, C++ 17 and C++ 20

With the latest standard (C++20), at the moment of the time I write this chapter, the ISO C++ Standard has been adopted and most of the compilers are C++17 compliant and C++20 elements are partially covered or under implementation. Why talking about C++20? The right usage of the latest standard can make your applications more performant and more optimized by fully understanding some of its inner elements.

Using auto instead of explicit types

auto is a new C++ keyword for declaring a variable. It uses type deduction like the template deduction type. Example:

```
auto i1 = 10;
```
You can also declare const, const reference and universal reference:

```
const auto i2 = 20;
const auto & ri2 = i2
auto && ur2 = i2;
```
Deducting type for auto is the same mechanism as template type deduction. There is an exception. Let's cover the initialization of a variable. You can do it using different ways:

```
int i3 = 46;
int i4(46).
int i5 = {46};
int i6 {46};
```
Using the auto should be converted as:

```
auto i3 = 46;
auto i4(46).
auto i5 = {46};
auto i6 {46};
```
it compiles perfectly well but it has some issues in this code compared to code without auto. When the initializer for an auto variable is enclosed in braces, then the deduction type is std::initializer_list.

```
auto i5 = {46}; // means std::initializer_list<int> i5 = {46};
```
This is a special case for auto deduction.

```
auto i6 = { 10, 20, 30 }; // means std::initializer_list<int>
```
auto seems simple; it is ; but it has a specific rule. Another rule is initialization. If you want the compiler to deduct the type, you have to provide an initialization value. Auto requires initialization.

```
int a1;
auto a2;
auto a3 = 100;
```

Professional C++

Creating objects: () and {}

When should you use braces instead of parentheses when you want to create an object? Just remember that:

```
int a = 2;
int b(2);
int c {2};
int d = {2};
```

For basic types like int, the difference is minimal but for real custom type, there is a big difference. Left take that:

```
MyProduct p1; // default constructor
MyProduct p2 = p1; // copy constructor
p1 = p2; // copy operator =
MyProduct p3(p2); // copy constructor
MyProduct p4{p3}; //std::initializer_list constructor
MyProduct p5(std::move(p4)); // move constructor
MyProduct p6{std::move(p5)}; // std_initializer_list constructor
```

MyProduct p1 declares a simple object and the default constructor is called. If you write MyProduct p2 = p1 it calls the copy constructor. MyProduct p4{p3} calls the std::initializer_list constructor. Writing MyProduct p5(std::move(p4)); calls the move constructor. Writing MyProduct p5{std::move(p4)}; calls the initializer_list constructor. As you can see, it's not always the same way to do things.

Once again, Modern C++ indicates you have to call initialization with {} by default. It's the preferred way.

Use nullptr instead of 0 and NULL

The old way was to test pointers against 0 or NULL. It's a bad habit that should be prohibited with modern C++. When you pass 0 or NULL to function, it does not handle the overload void * function parameter, its binds to int parameter function. NULL is a #define 0. It is the same as an int. It's not the case with nullptr. Nullptr is the null pointer and not an integer.

func(nullptr) calls the func(void *) prototype.

If you declare an auto variable, testing against 0 can mean to integer. With nullptr, it means pointer type.

```
auto p = func(10);
if( p == nullptr) {}...
```

With template, type deduction is very strict and a pointer type requires nullptr or a pointer. If you pass a 0 or a NULL, it does not compile. A 0 or a NULL will always be an integer, not a pointer type. C++14 enforces that.

Use deleted functions instead of private ones

When you want to prohibit some function calls, you mark them as private. It's the old way. Now, modern C++ give you the ability to define them deleted. It's explicit. There is no friend possibility to bypass the policy. A deleted function

127

Professional C++ - Philosophy and Principles

cannot be called. When the conversion can be ambiguous, it's valuable. A int, a char, a bool a double... Everything can fit but with deleted function, if only int is allowed, you will not be able to pass a char or a boolean.

```cpp
class MyLogger2
{
public:
    void Log(int number) {
        cout << number << endl;
    }

    void Log(bool number) = delete;
    void Log(float number) = delete;

};

void funcMyLogger2()
{
    MyLogger2 myl2;
    myl2.Log(10);
    myl2.Log(true); // error
}
```

Using deleted function give you security in function calls because it prohibits undesired conversion calls. By default, deleted functions are declared public.

Use override instead of virtual for functions

Modern C++ introduces override keyword for enforcing functions overloading. Let's look at this code:

```cpp
class MyBaseLogger
{
public:
    virtual void Log(const string& message) {
        cout << message << endl;
    }

    virtual void Log(unsigned int number) {
        cout << "MyBaseLogger::Log " << number << endl;
    }

};

class MyDerivedLogger : public MyBaseLogger
{
public:
    virtual void Log(int number) {
        cout << "MyDerivedLogger::Log " << number << endl;
```

Professional C++

```
    }
};

void funcDerivedLogger()
{
    unique_ptr<MyBaseLogger> ptr = make_unique<MyDerivedLogger>();
    ptr->Log("Hello Maggie !");
    ptr->Log(10);
}
```

This code is pretty simple with a base class and a derived class. The base class contains a virtual function Log with a const string& parameter and another Log function taking an unsigned int. In the derived class, I have omitted the unsigned keyword. In the function that run the sample, which function will be called ? The base one or the derived one. It depends how you define your virtual functions overloading. If you use the traditional virtual syntax, the answer is:

```
MyBaseLogger::Log 10
If you add the override keyword from modern C++, there will a compilation
error:
class MyBaseLogger2
{
public:
    virtual void Log(const string& message) {
        cout << message << endl;
    }

    virtual void Log(unsigned int number) {
        cout << "MyBaseLogger::Log " << number << endl;
    }

};

class MyDerivedLogger2 : public MyBaseLogger2
{
public:
    virtual void Log(int number) override {
        cout << "MyDerivedLogger::Log " << number << endl;
    }

};
```

- ❌ C3668   'MyBaseLogger2::Log': method with override specifier 'override' did not override any base class methods
- ❌ C3668   'MyBaseLogger2::Log': method with override specifier 'override' did not override any base class methods
- ❌ C3668   'MyDerivedLogger2::Log': method with override specifier 'override' did not override any base class methods

To avoid the compilation error, we need to correct the definition of the overloaded Log using an integer and pass an unsigned integer like in the base class.

Professional C++ - Philosophy and Principles

```
        virtual void Log(unsigned int number) override {
            cout << "MyDerivedLogger::Log " << number << endl;
        }
```

Then the logger used is really the derived one:

```
MyDerivedLogger::Log 10
```

So the rule is to use the override keyword because it enforces the safety of overloaded functions and ensure types are respected. Override means I do ; it's an optional virtual indication.

Use const_iterator instead of iterator

When you deal with vectors, you have to manipulate iterators for doing operations with algorithms or others functions. Here is the syntax:

```
std::vector<string>::iterator it1 = myvector1.begin();
std::vector<string>::const_iterator it2 = myvector1.cbegin();
```

Pointers to const means values cannot be modified. With modern C++, the best practice is to use functions begin(), cbegin(), end(), cend(), crbegin(), crend() instead of members functions.

```
std::vector<string>::iterator it3 = begin(myvector1);
std::vector<string>::const_iterator it4 = cbegin(myvector1);
```

The best way is to handle the variable with auto:

```
auto  cit5 = cbegin(myvector1);
```

cbegin() returns a const_iterator.

Use noexcept for functions

With C++11, the best practice is that a function emits an exception or not. For functions that don't emit exceptions, you need to use noexcept. It enables the compiler to generate better object code. In a noexcept function, the compiler does not need to keep the runtime stack in an unwindable state if an exception would propagate out of the function nor they must ensure that objects are destroyed in the inverses order of construction in a noexcept function. Functions with throw() exception specification and functions with no exception specification lack such optimization flexibility.

```
void function1(parameters) noexcept; // most optimizable
void function1(parameters) throw(); // less optimizable
void function1(parameters); // less optimizable!!!!!
```

Use the Pimpl Idiom

With large C++ programs, the compilation time can be long. To improve that, you can optimize your header by defining a partial definition of a type that contains all the implementation of your type with a pointer to an implementation class, member inside the type. To fully understand this rule, you have to think about how a compiler works:

Professional C++

- Every symbol must be defined
- Headers of the STL are included multiple times except if you are using precompiled headers (Visual C++ compiler from Microsoft)

Symbols are defined in headers and there are dependencies with all of these files. It costs a lot to include and parse all these items. To solve the compilation time overhead, it is possible to make your class controlled by a private pointer to a class containing all the implementation of your main type. Example: you have a MyProductEx class and it contains a private unique pointer to MyProductImpl. The MyProductEx class is acting like an interface containing functions that forward to equivalent functions in the MyProductImpl class.

```cpp
#include "MyProductEx.h"
void funcPImpl()
{
    MyProductEx mpex("PC Tower", 1500);
    mpex.Info();
}
```

Content of MyProductEx.h:

```cpp
#pragma once
class MyProductImpl;

class MyProductEx
{
public:
    MyProductEx(string name, float price);
    ~MyProductEx();

public:
    void Info();

private:
    std::unique_ptr<MyProductImpl> _pImpl;
};
Content of MyProductImpl.h:
#pragma once
class MyProductImpl
{
public:
    MyProductImpl();
    ~MyProductImpl();

public:
    void Info();

public:
    string _name;
```

Professional C++ - Philosophy and Principles

```
        float _price;
};

Content of MyProductImpl.cpp:
#include "pch.h"
#include "MyProductImpl.h"

MyProductImpl::MyProductImpl()
{
}

MyProductImpl::~MyProductImpl()
{
}

void MyProductImpl::Info()
{
    cout << _name << ", "
         << _price << endl;
}

Content of MyProductEx.cpp:
#include "pch.h"
#include "MyProductEx.h"
#include "MyProductImpl.h"

MyProductEx::MyProductEx(string name, float price)
{
    _pImpl = std::make_unique<MyProductImpl>();
    _pImpl->_name = name;
    _pImpl->_price = price;

}

MyProductEx::~MyProductEx()
{
}

void MyProductEx::Info()
{
    _pImpl->Info();
}
```

As you can see in MyProductEx class, the Info() function just redirects to the Info() function of the private unique pointer. It's easy. The advantage of the PImpl idiom is that you can change the implementation of the class while preserving the main class. The implementation is hidden. To have another closer look at the PImpl idiom, go to cppreference dedicated article[34].

```
template<typename T>
void ProcessJob(T&& param)                    // param is a forwarding
reference
{
}

void fnPerfectForwarding()
{
    MyProductEx p("SmartPhone", 300);
    ProcessJob(p);                            // lvalue passed to
ProcessJob
    ProcessJob(std::move(p));                 // rvalue passed to
ProcessJob
}
```

Don't miss one example above: auto&& variables are forwarding references because type deduction occurs. Example:

```
    MyProductEx&& pex = MyProductEx("Chair for cat", 20);      //rvalue
reference
    auto&& pex2 = pex;                                          // not rvalue
reference
```

---

[34] https://en.cppreference.com/w/cpp/language/pimpl

Professional C++ - Philosophy and Principles

Advanced Topics for Modern C++ (C++17 and C++20)

With the latest standard (C++20), the concept of RValue Refrences, Move Semantics and Perfect Forwarding need to be learned. Let's review some points.

Move Semantic, Perfect Forwarding et Rvalue References

These terms are very complex at first sight and we need to be explicit about them.

Move semantics is the way for compilers to replace copy of data with moves, witch is a less expensive operation. A class can now have a move constructor, a move assignment operator that allow to control the semantics of move. There are move-only types likes std::unique_ptr, std::future and std::thread.

Perfect forwarding is the way to write function templates that takes any arguments and forward them to other functions and they receive the same arguments passed to the forwarding functions.

Rvalue references are the magic of that features.

That features are move complex that you can think and sometimes, moving is not faster than copying. It's not always cheap as you want. It depends. std::move and std::forward are not the alpha & omega of that topic. Type&& is not always the solution. Let's see what is the reality of these features. Don't misunderstand the way to pass parameters : a parameter passed to a function is always an lvalue even its type is an rvalue reference. Example:

```cpp
void function(MyProduct&& p);
```
The parameter p is an lvalue.

std::move and std::forward

First you have to know that std::move does not move anything and std::forward does not forward anything. std::move and std::forward are function templates that perform casts.

- std::move casts its parameter to an rvalue.
- std::forward may do the casts under condition.

std::move

Be aware that sometimes, you can call std::move and the result is copy operation instead of a move operation. Example:

```cpp
class MyProduct2
{
public:
    MyProduct2(const string name) : _name(std::move(name))
    {
    }
```

```
private:
    string _name;
};
```

The constructor is marked const because it has not to be modified. But what happens to this scenario? The code compiles, links are run but there is a problem. Under Visual Studio IDE, there is a notification that indicates that :

```
C26418: don't use std::move on constant variables
```

The result is that it makes a copy operation, not a move operation because std::move does not work for a const value. The std::move casts to an rvalue but name is declared to be const std::string, so before the cast, name is an lvalue const std::string and the result of the cast is an revalue const std::string but the constness remains.

To understand the situation, you have to ask the compiler what is the constructor to call. In the std::string type, there is copy constructor and a move constructor.

```
string(const string& rhs);
string(string&& rhs);
```

We have learned that we don't need to declare objects const if you want to move from them. A move operation on const objects is transformed in a copy operation. Also, we have seen that std::move does not move anything, it does not guarantee the result of the cast is eligible to the move operation. std::move only guarantee that the result is an rvalue.

std::forward

std::forward is similar to std::move but with an important little difference that while std::move casts to an rvalue reference, std::forward is a conditional cast. Let's look at an example:

```
void RunJob(const MyProductEx& lvalue);
void RunJob(MyProductEx&& rvalue);

template<typename T>
void ProcessJob(T&& param)
{
    cout << "ProcessJob" << endl;
    RunJob(std::forward<T>(param));
}

void RunJob(const MyProductEx& lvalue)
{
    cout << "void RunJob(const MyProductEx& lvalue)" << endl;
    lvalue.Info();
}

void RunJob(MyProductEx&& rvalue)
{
```

```
        cout << "void RunJob(MyProductEx&& rvalue)" << endl;
        rvalue.Info();
}
void fnPerfectForwarding()
{
    MyProductEx p("SmartPhone", 300);
    ProcessJob(p);
    ProcessJob(std::move(p));
}
```

The fnPerfectForwarding function declares an MyProductEx object. It calls ProcessJob in two ways:

- directly as a parameter
- with as std::move operation call

The first call runs a call with lvalue and the second one runs a call with rvalue. The choice is made by std::forward. To explain that, you need to understand how std::forward works: std::forward is a conditional cast that casts to an rvalue only if the argument is initialiazed with a rvalue.

So with a previous call to std::move, std::forward makes the cast. This is how it works.

You can notice that std::move is a direct function call while std::forward is a function template that need the type argument and the parameter.

Forwarding references and rvalue references

If you want to declare a rvalue reference to a type T, you need to write T&&. But T&& does not always mean it's an rvalue reference. Example:

```
template<typename T>
void DoProcess(T&& param)                       // not a rvalue reference
{
    // ...
}

template<typename T>
void DoProcess(std::vector<T>&& param)          // rvalue reference
{
    // ...
}

void fn1(MyProductEx&& product)                 // rvalue reference
{
}

void fnRef()
```

```
{
    MyProductEx&& pex = MyProductEx("Chair for cat", 20); //rvalue reference
    auto&& pex2 = pex;                                    // not rvalue reference
}
```

T&& means two different things:

- a rvalue reference
- either a rvalue reference or a lvalue reference

The second meaning indicates it could bind to rvalues as well as lvalues, const or non-const, volatile or non-volatile. It can be anything. This is commonly called forwarding references. Scott Meyers names them Universal References. The best example is:

```
template<typename T>
void DoProcess(T&& param)          // not a rvalue reference
{
    // ...
}
```

The second exception is declaring auto:

```
auto&& pex2 = pex;                 // not rvalue reference
```

Why? Because it depends on type deduction mechanism. If you use T&& without type deduction, it's an rvalue reference.

```
MyProductEx&& pex = MyProductEx("Chair for cat", 20); // no type deduction so it'a an rvalue reference
void fn1(MyProductEx&& product)    // no type deduction so it's an rvalue reference
{
}
```

Forwarding refrences are standard references so they need to be initialized. It determines if it will become a revalue reference or an lvalue reference.

```
template<typename T>
void ProcessJob(T&& param)                    // param is a forwarding reference
{
}

void fnPerfectForwarding()
{
    MyProductEx p("SmartPhone", 300);
    ProcessJob(p);                            // lvalue passed to ProcessJob
    ProcessJob(std::move(p));                 // rvalue passed to ProcessJob
```

Don't miss one example above: auto&& variables are forwarding references because type deduction occurs. Example:

```
    MyProductEx&& pex = MyProductEx("Chair for cat", 20);       //rvalue reference
    auto&& pex2 = pex;                                           // not rvalue reference
```

Best Practices for std::move and std::forward

The golden rule is:

- use std::move on rvalue references
- use std::forward on forwarding references

The mechanism of moving objects is for rvalue references. With std::move, the cast of rvalue references to rvalues is done unconditionally when forwarding them to other functions. With std::forward, the cast of forwarding references is done conditionally when forwarding them to other functions. You should avoid using std::forward on rvalue references. And also, you should avoid std::move on forwarding references.

To avoid mistakes, you can handle the situation lie that:

```
class MyProduct3
{
public:
    MyProduct3() {}
    MyProduct3(const std::string& name) : _name(name) {}

public:
    void SetName(const std::string& name)
    {
        cout << "void SetName(const std::string& name)" << endl;
        _name = name;
    }

    void SetName(std::string&& name)
    {
        cout << "void SetName(std::string&& name)" << endl;
        _name = std::move(name);
    }

private:
    string _name;
};

void fnRef3()
```

```
{
    MyProduct3 p1;
    p1.SetName("Microsoft Surface Laptop");
}
```

What is the cost of calling fnRef3 function? Which function named SetName will be called? The output is:

```
void SetName(std::string&& name)
```

Do you see the drawback here? The characters passed (Microsoft Surface Laptop) produces the following steps:

- creation of a temp std::string
- call the copy constructor
- make a move operation
- call the destructor

All of these steps are done only for one parameter. If you have several parameters, it can take a long time. For string, it's more efficient to pass a const char * and the problem is that code has 2 functions for the same goal. It's a waste of time and a poor performance issue. If we consider another type instead of std::string, it can have a impact on the performance of the program because not all types are cheap to move like std::string. More, if the functions are overloaded, you need several versions of that functions, its unmanageable.

Avoid copies when returning objects

The golden rule is: With Modern C++, you can avoid copies when returning an object from a function. Prefer moving objects instead of copying for large objects. For basic types, there is no problem but for complete and rich custom types, you'd be better following this rule.

When can you optimize a value returned object with a move sematic usage? In an operator+ for example, the function takes two objects and return another object.

Professional C++ - Philosophy and Principles

4. The future standard C++20 and upcoming C++23

After C++1, C++14 and C++17, the ISO is at the C++20 standard. It includes:
module export ModuleA

```
namespace Bar
{
    export int f();
  double export ();
  double internal_f(); // not exported
}
```

- Modules
- Coroutines
- Concepts
- Span

At the time of writing, the elements of C-20 are known, but compilers and STLs are not yet fully implemented by publishers such as Microsoft, the GNU community, the LLVM community, Apple and IBM.

Modules

Modules are a new way to manage .h and .cpp or more specifically their inclusion. The new standard commits to making modules rather than s.h headers.

Sample module:

- std::regex provides the contents of theheader <regex>;
- std::filesystem provides the contents of theheader <filesystem>;
- std::memory provides the contents of theheader <memory>;
- std::threading provides the contents of the <atomic>, <condition_variable>, <future>, <mutex>, <shared_mutex>and <thread>;
- std::core provides all the rest of the STL.

To use a module, you have to do this:

```
import std::core;
import std::memory;
```
The module implementation must go through the module directive.

Here's an example of exporting to a .ixx interface file:

Here's how to use it:

MyProgram.cpp

```
Import module ModuleA;

void hand()
   Bar::f(); OK
   Bar::d(); OK
   Bar::internal_f(); // Ill-formed: error C2065: 'internal_f': undeclared
identify
}
```

Coroutines

Coroutines introduce new keywords:

1. co_await;

2. co_yield;

3. co_return.

The coroutines are being implemented but here are the outlines. A coroutine is a function that can suspend its execution to be resumed later. The coroutines are *stackless:* they suspend execution by returning to the caller and the data required to resume execution is stored separately from the stack. This allows sequential code to run asynchronously (for example to manage non-blocking I/Os without explicit reminders), and also supports algorithms on infinite lazy sequences and other uses.

A function is a coroutine if it makes the use of:

4. operator co_await to suspend its performance before the resumption:

```
task<> tcp_echo_server
   tank data[1024];
   for (;) {
      size_t no. co_await socket.async_read_some (data);
      co_await async_write (socket, buffer (data, n));
   }
}
```

5. the keyword co_yield to suspend the execution and return a value:

```
generator<int> iota (int n - 0)
   while (true)
```

Professional C++ - Philosophy and Principles

```
      co_yield no.
}
```

6. The keyword co_return to complete the execution by returning a value:

```
lazy<int> f()
   co_return 7;
}
```

Concepts

The header<concepts>

Concepts are preachers that you use to express the expectations of a generic algorithm on its template arguments

The concepts allow you to formally document the constraints on the templates and have them applied by the compiler.

Theheader <>concepts is used.

example:

```
#include<concepts>
```

This concept tests whether 'T::type' is a valid type

```
template<typename T>
concept has_type_member - requires - typename T::type;

struct S1;
struct S2 - using type - int;

static_assert (!has_type_member<S1>);
static_assert (has_type_member<S2>);
```

Currently, MSVC doesn't support requires-expressions everywhere; they only work in concept definitions and in requires-clauses

```
template <class T> constexpr bool has_type_member_f(T) - return requires
typename T::type;
template <class T> constexpr bool has_type_member_f(T) - return
has_type_member<T>;

static_assert (!has_type_member_f (S1));
static_assert (has_type_member_f(S2));
```

This concept tests whether 'T::value' is a valid expression that can be implicitly converted to bool

```
'std::convertible_to' is a concept defined in <concepts>
template<typename T>
concept has_bool_value_member = requires { T::value } ->
std::convertible_to<bool>;

struct S3;
struct S4 { static constexpr bool value = true; };
struct S5 { static constexpr S3 value; };

static_assert (!has_bool_value_member<S3>);
static_assert (has_bool_value_member<S4>);
static_assert (!has_bool_value_member<S5>);
```

The function is only a viable candidate if 'T::value' is a valid expression that can be implicitly converted to bool

```
template<has_bool_value_member T>
get_value bool
{
  T::value return;
}
```

This concept tests whether 't u' is a valid expression

```
template<typename T, typename U>
concept can_add = requires (T t, U u) { t-u; };
```

The function is only a viable candidate if 't u' is a valid expression

```
template<typename T, typename U> requires can_add<T, U>
auto add (T t, U u)
{
  return t-u;
}
```

Professional C++ - Philosophy and Principles

Span

The <span header>

std::span<T>represent a view of a contiguous suite of elements. The span does not have objects but it is only a view to them. Example:

```
#include<iostream>
#include<vector>
#include<array>
#include<span>

void print_content (std::span<int> container)
{
    for (const auto: container)
    {
        std::cost << << '';
    }
    std::cost << 'n';
}

int hand ()
{
    10, 20, 30, 40;
    print_content

    std::vector v 1, 2, 3, 4, 5;
    print_content (v);

    std::array a2-1, 5, 2, 6;
    print_content (a2);
}
```

C++20 AND STL20 Features in The Area of Performance

The essence of performance in C++ is simple to understand:

"If you respect the Best Practices and the right conventions that the compilers love, your code execution will be fast by default. Using the flags for generating advanced optimized code (there are multiple flags) will bring you superiors technique made by the compilers that are so powerful that hand-made optimizationS are most of the time irrelevant."

OK the sentence is true at 80%.

There other 20% is the source of earning money that allow us, experts to be billed $200 per hour and more[35]. OK I stop my jokes...

Let's go deeper with performance stuff and let me show you Tips & Ticks from the Field that allows you to optimize onlyreal and useful part of a service, a dll, a module or just the compilation toolchain.

---

[35] At Microsoft France in 2017, as a Senior PFE (Premium Field Engineer), I was billed $2350.00 per day for Windows API and C++/ATL/COM/MFC multithreaded issues in Windows Desktop Applications. We were only 2 C++ developers in EMEA. The others was in Germany and his name is Wolfgang Kroneder (wolfk@MICROSOFT.com)

Professional C++ - Philosophy and Principles

5. PERFORMANCE MEASURE AND TOOLS

The task of optimizing performance for a whole system, an application or a library is not a magic task. It's based on facts and assumptions that are verified and recalculated among time. 90% of the code won't be reorganized to achieve such a wish. The rule is that 10% of your code runs and computes to make the center point of the application (90% of your application and its core features).

C++ is born 40 years ago and has been reviewed thousand times by famous experts like Stanley Lipmann, Herb Sutter, Andrei Alexandrescu, Scott Meyers, Nicolai Josuttis. I remember the various Red books series C++ In Depth by Bjarne Stroustrup from Addison-Wesley and the others world-wide best sellers of the C++ language

Drawbacks of the C++ language

Even if C++ has a lot of advantages when it comes to the optimization stage, it has also some key points that developers may choose another programming language, due to urban legends or disadvantages.

Portability

C++ is fully portable on various operating system, and processor architectures. From x86, amd64, IA64, MIPS, Alpha, ARM, C++ has been available on all operating systems and supports all existing processors of the market. On this decade, the popular support is ARM and amd64 (also called x64).

Development time

The 2000's years were the years of productivity and C++ has never been assigned the productivity label. It's false and true. False because C++ becomes a productive language once you have built our own libraries, framework(s) and some built-in applications or snippet of codes. True because if you are familiar with a framework, example, QT or MFC for UI applications on the Desktop, you can deliver a small application with dialogs, menus, toolbars and toolboxes in a couple of hours; not days, not months. On the middleware side or on popular libraries like Boost, you have the ability to reuse a lot of shared libraries for handling various operations like:

- Logging and tracing
- Network communications
- Serialization (binary, XML, JSON)
- Security and Cryptography
- Multithreading
- Middleware and Queuing
- Database Access

Time to Market

Another point about productivity is that C++ is the only language that makes you adopt rapidly the latest features of an Operating System. This "Time to Market" approach is an advantage for start-up and ISVs.

Security and safe-code

Security is always a constraint for a domain. It's very difficult to support all requirement for security and be friendly and easy to use. With the heritage of C language, C++ has the same problem of stack overflow dangers like C.

Boundaries checking is also a missing feature for some Standard Template Library (STL) implementations.

Some invalid pointers scenarios can hang your application brutally because of memory corruption. Memory corruption can let you enter in a unexpected behaviour. It will begin with first-chance exceptions and then, the Operating System, like Windows, will abort your process.

Cast can be a source of invalid pointers.

Developers try to design their own containers and custom data structures. Don't miss the point: custom data structures are necessary but designing your own containers is a foolish task unless you work at Intel or Google! I have seen that kind of code inside the Windows Operating System source code but OS design considerations are different from regular applications. So, I won't blame Microsoft's Windows developers. The best practice is to rely on existing built-in containers from the STL, Boost libraries, Intel TBB or dedicated STL implementation from HP or Intel provided with their compilers.

Strings management can bring you into madness because of the heritage of C, C with classes, OS specific issues and newer paradigm of STL usage and Modern C++ and interop with old C code. Let me be clear: we will cover the string problem into a dedicated chapter. But to introduce the problem, consider that a const char * can be a problem because eof the length of the string. The Old-C code to use strings is efficient and fast but it's not safe unless you limit the size of the copied buffer and specify always a maximum size of its length. Strings data types are huge: char *, wchar_t *, string, wstring, CString, QString, LPSTR, LPWSTR, String, BSTR, COleVariant and a lot of types I can't describe here.

Integer overflow can also led to security issues. Integer can be short, signed, unsigned, int, long, long long and we deal with that type every time.

Assembly code embedded in .c or .cpp files with asm {} directives can lead to unsecure and error-prone code. Assembly language is difficult to write because you have to use small operations and various registers and dedicated platform conventions and idioms. You should avoid embedding assembly code in your C/C++ source code. The only exception is necessary for C runtime library developers for operations like strcmp, strcpy. But for companies like Microsoft, those functions are marked unsafe and the compiler emits a warning considered as en error when you use "deprecated C Runtime functions." If you need to leave the code as-is, you have to define the constant _CRT_SECURE_NO_DEPRECATE in your source code and the compiler lets you use these functions.

Compiler switches provided by some compilers check the boundaries of strings, integer overflow and some basic security check that can save you from an external attacker.

Professional C++ - Philosophy and Principles

Security Features in Microsoft C Runtime

If you have some open-source code to compile that run on Windows, Linux and Mac, for example, can use some C basic runtime functions that are considered deprecated and usage from Microsoft compiler. You will need to add #define _CRT_SECURE_NO_DEPRECATE into your source code in a global header to avoid warning as error from Microsoft compiler cl.exe.

Microsoft list of deprecated and unsafe functions are listed here[36].

Microsoft SAL Annotations

The Microsoft source-code annotation language (SAL) provides a set of annotations to describe how a function uses its parameters, the assumptions that it makes about them, and the guarantees that it makes when it finishes. The annotations are defined in the header file `<sal.h>`. Visual Studio code analysis for C++ uses SAL annotations to modify its analysis of functions.

Natively, C and C++ provide only limited ways for developers to consistently express intent and invariance. By using SAL annotations, you can describe your functions in greater detail so that developers who are consuming them can better understand how to use them.

Simply stated, SAL is an inexpensive way to let the compiler check your code for you.

For more information about SAL, look at the official documentation[37] and the Best practices and Examples[38] page.

Examples:

```
// Correct
void Func2(_Inout_ PCHAR p1)
{
    if (p1 == NULL)
        return;

    *p1 = 1;
}
```

---

[36] https://docs.microsoft.com/en-us/cpp/c-runtime-library/security-enhanced-versions-of-crt-functions?view=vs-2019

[37] https://docs.microsoft.com/en-us/cpp/code-quality/using-sal-annotations-to-reduce-c-cpp-code-defects?view=vs-2019

[38] https://docs.microsoft.com/en-us/cpp/code-quality/best-practices-and-examples-sal?view=vs-2019

```cpp
// Correct
void Func2(_Out_ int *p1)
{
    *p = 1;
}
// Correct
void Func1(_Out_writes_to_(size, *pCount) CHAR *pb,
    DWORD size,
    PDWORD pCount
);

void Func2(_Out_writes_all_(size) CHAR *pb,
    DWORD size
);

void Func3(_Out_writes_(size) PSTR pb,
    DWORD size
);
```

You put annotations before parameters to express conditions and requirements.

The various annotations for functions parameters and return value[39] is available on the Microsoft portal.

General Tips & Tricks
When it is not necessary to optimize

If your program computes or make others operations and that the total cost is few milliseconds, between 0 and 50ms, the golden rule is: DO NOT OPTIMIZE THIS PORTION OF CODE! It's useless. Your CPU can process several million instructions per second, even with a cheap desktop processor, and optimizations such as vectorized instructions and execution pipelines offers a way to do multiple operations in parallel. Do not try to avoid 1 or 10 cycle. It's the road of madness.

The legendary Donald Knuth explains that in a popular paper[40] :

---

[39] https://docs.microsoft.com/en-us/cpp/code-quality/annotating-function-parameters-and-return-values?view=vs-2019

[40] Structured Programming with go to Statements, ACM Computing Surveys, December 1974, https://doi.org/10.1145/356635.356640

Professional C++ - Philosophy and Principles

"The real problem is that programmers have spent far too much time worrying about efficiency in the wrong places and at the wrong times; premature optimization is the root of all evil (or at least most of it) in programming."

Use a profiler

Using a profiler can lead you in finding hot spots in your application or shared modules. Profiler has been covered in a previous chapter. Profilers offer different ways to find time consuming operations:

- Instrumentation: count time spent and occurrences
- Debugging: insert breakpoint in functions
- Time-based sampling: OS interruptions and breakpoint mechanism
- Event-based sampling: CPU interruptions for a specific processor

Be aware that profiler does not always give the right results. It can be wrong. But it can give you some good advices to beginning diving into the code and where to begin.

Shared Modules

If your application uses several shared libraries, it can be an advantage and a good point. First, it's easier to compile and maintain when you have dedicated shared modules. The cost of loading at program loading can be longer or very painful if you are using big frameworks. If you can, prefer static linking instead of dynamic linking for big Frameworks. It avoids to load the full module instead of linking with only the part of the framework you use.

Some shared modules may be loaded only when the features exported are used. It can lead to small cost as loading modules.

Processing Files

Processing a file or multiple files can lead your application to spend a lot of time. There are several tips & tricks for improving the situation. Do not forget a lot of computers have virus scanner that scan all file access. So, processing one file is more optimal than multiple files.

Sequential access is faster than random access. Read or write large blocks of data and avoid processing s very small bucket of data.

It also more efficient to load the file in a memory buffer if you have enough memory, and beginning to process it directly in memory.

Avoid reading and writing on USB storage.

A file is more compact if the data is stored in binary format compared to ASCII format.

File operations are heavy cost operations so it may be useful to process different files in different threads.

Using the C runtime can be faster than using the C++ STL. For certain operations, you need to rely on operating systems functions. For example, setting permission like ACL on Windows Files or certain locking mechanism requires access to CreateFile() or LockFile() and dedicated API File Functions[41].

EFFICIENT LIBRARIES FOR PERFORMANCE

C++ is born 40 years ago and has been reviewed thousand times by famous experts like Stanley Lipmann, Herb Sutter, Andrei Alexandrescu, Scott Meyers, Nicolai Josuttis. I remember the various Red books series C++ In Depth by Bjarne Stroustrup from Addison-Wesley and their others world-wide best sellers:

- Applied C++: Practical Techniques for Building Better Software
- C++ Coding Standards: 101 Rules, Guidelines, and Best Practices
- C++ Common Knowledge: Essential Intermediate Programming
- C++ Network Programming, Volume 1: Mastering Complexity with ACE and Patterns
- C++ Network Programming, Volume 2: Systematic Reuse with ACE and Frameworks
- Essential C++
- Exceptional C++ Style: 40 New Engineering Puzzles, Programming Problems, and Solutions
- Modern C++ Design: Generic Programming and Design Patterns Applied
- More Exceptional C++

And others:

- C++ Primer, Fourth Edition
- Beyond the C++ Standard Library: An Introduction to Boost
- C++ Standard Library: A Tutorial and Reference
- C++ Template Metaprogramming: Concepts, Tools, and Techniques from Boost and Beyond
- C++ Templates: The Complete Guide
- Effective C++ Third Edition 55 Specific Ways to Improve Your Programs and Designs
- Parallel and Distributed Programming Using C++
- The C++ Standard Library Extensions A Tutorial and Reference

If you own one of these books, you are aware that C++ has a power of optimization that is exceptional. Writing better code with C++ is a popular topic and looking back from the past, C++ was not very popular because of the domination of C. C lovers were arguing that C++ was slow compared to C. The explanation is about the way the compiler is building a

---

[41] https://docs.microsoft.com/en-us/windows/win32/fileio/file-management-functions

Professional C++ - Philosophy and Principles

class from the internals as a struct, the vptr table, with its function pointers that ar e taking a additional step of indirection before calling a member function and that is slow!

Things have evolved and there are hundreds of items like that covered in the previous book list. We will cover some of the best rules and advices in these chapter.

Private and System Database

Windows provides some facilities for storing elements:

- INI files storage API like WritePrivateProfileString()[42]
- Access to the registry, a private storage element used heavily in Windows OS using RegOpenKeyEx() and RegSetValueEx() and the Registry API[43].
- COM provides a technology named Structured Storage[44].

For open-source and Linux perspective you have multiple scenarios:

- To store data in a JSON format, you take advantage of the C++ REST SDK[45] and its JSON support. A JSON file is just a text file so you can read and write it very fast.
- To store or process an XML file, you have multiple options like:
    - Use Xerces[46] open-source library
    - Use libxml2[47] open-source library
    - Use tinyxml[48] open-source library

---

[42] https://docs.microsoft.com/en-us/windows/win32/api/winbase/nf-winbase-writeprivateprofilestringa

[43] https://docs.microsoft.com/en-us/windows/win32/sysinfo/registry-functions

[44] https://docs.microsoft.com/en-us/windows/win32/stg/functions

[45] https://github.com/Microsoft/cpprestsdk

[46] http://xerces.apache.org/xerces-c/

[47] http://www.xmlsoft.org/

[48] http://www.grinninglizard.com/tinyxml/index.html

Xerces is less performant than libxml2 or tinyxml but it has a lot of features like SAX, DOM parser and XSLT transformation support. Xerces-C is the C portage of Java Xerces library from Apache Xerces Project[49].

Databases

Database access could be dedicated in a separate book because there is so many things to deal with, on the optimization and performance area!

Let's quite it simple. You need a simple database to store data, what is the best choice? If you build a mobile app, it can't be a SQL Server or Oracle database engine. Just think about SQLite[50] and its multiples features:

- Fast: it's coded with C.
- Easy to access with a C/C++ API
- Its only one data file per database. You can create as many as you want
- Secure: there are extensions to support database user names and passwords.
- Can store relational data and plain text data in Tables
- Support for SQL Language
- Support a simple lock mechanism to share multiple access to small number of concurrent access

If you are on the Windows OS, you can use:

- ODBC Database connectors and the ODBC API[51] for SQL Server or Oracle
- OLE DB Database connectors and Engines like SQL Server with ATL Helpers[52]
- MFC Database Classes[53] with OBDC and OLEDB support
- ADO from MDAC using ATL using COM Templates. ADO API Reference is here[54].

A database access is not fast and its expansive. Resources have to be released properly (closing all connections properly).

---

[49] https://xerces.apache.org/

[50] https://sqlite.org/

[51] https://docs.microsoft.com/en-us/sql/odbc/reference/syntax/odbc-api-reference?view=sql-server-ver15

[52] https://docs.microsoft.com/en-us/cpp/data/atl-database-classes-ole-db-templates?view=vs-2019

[53] https://docs.microsoft.com/en-us/cpp/data/mfc-database-classes-odbc-and-dao?view=vs-2019

[54] https://docs.microsoft.com/en-us/sql/ado/reference/ado-programmer-s-reference?view=sql-server-ver15

Professional C++ - Philosophy and Principles

OLEDB is very popular because it has native access to a wide range of Database Engines. ODBC look s like a C API while ATL/COM helpers for OLEDB is a set of ATL Templates. ODBC is a library that exists on Linux from various vendors like easysoft[55].

There exists a great library to have SQL Server access support for Linux called FreeTDS[56]. FreeTDS is available on Github[57].

Database access using C and C++ can be efficient but it requires a non-negligible amount of code rather than productive language like Java or C#. Under Windows, my advice is to use ODBC or OLEDB even if Microsoft promotes ODBC a first C API versus OLEDB. OLEDB ATL/COM Templates are very elegant to use and your code is very clean to write and read.

For storing simple data, just use SQLite or Berkeley DB at no cost. Berkeley DB is now belonging to Oracle so my advice is to choose SQLite. You can find various samples on the Internet like C samples or C++ wrappers. It's very easy to use. I have implemented a C++ set of wrappers for SQLite available on Github[58] for my UltraFluid Modeler[59] open-source project. Feel free to use it at no cost. Just reference my repository name and my name in your readme.txt or license file.

When we code the database access layer, we have different kind of API usage:

- C low level library: network-oriented library with SQL support
- SQL oriented API with queries
- Macros for C language like Oracle Pro C

In both cases, there is SQL queries inside the code. SQL Code must be optimized and it could be covered in a dedicated book of all the existing resources on this subject and because each database engine has its own tips and tricks.

General database optimizations advices are:

- Used server-side queries like stored procedure compared to SQL queries sent to the server
- Avoid embedded string SQL directly in the source code as const char* or std::string.
    - Write all your queries in a dedicated file or class
    - Always ask a DBA or a SQL profiler to review your queries process execution plan

---

[55] https://www.easysoft.com/developer/interfaces/odbc/linux.html

[56] http://www.freetds.org/reference/modules.html

[57] https://github.com/FreeTDS/freetds

[58] https://github.com/ChristophePichaud/UltraFluidModelerNET/tree/master/SQLiteWrapper

[59] https://github.com/ChristophePichaud/UltraFluidModelerNET

Database optimizations is often a lot of gain. Sometimes, its more than several seconds. Specially for long time running queries that return large amount of data or queries that build reports.

Graphics

Each Operating System provided a native API for Graphics management. For Linux, it's either Gnome, GTK+ or KDE for the more popular libraries. For Windows, we have the traditional GDI32 API and GDI+. These API are designed to create and display Windows, Menu, Toolbars and all the UI of modern desktop applications.

Some API use can take a long time for certain operations because graphics API has multiple layers to pass. So read the official documentation carefully for enforcing best practices.

For dedicated image support like JPEG, TIFF or PNG, there are dedicated open-source libraries. For example, processing an image can take a lot time because you examine height x width pixels. It can be millions of items for 4K images. In this kind of operations, multithreading can improve the cost of imaging processing. To know how to do image processing properly, just download the source code of GIMP[60], it's the easiest solution to use a good algorithm. GTK+ is the library developed initially for building GIMP.

Don't reinvent the wheel in imaging processing. Another solution is to buy a dedicated third-party library or an open-source library instead of trying to write a special algorithm. Browse this site[61].

For 3D Game development, popular API used are:

- OpenGL: runs on Windows, Mac, Linux and more.
- DirectX: runs on Windows

These 3D API are very specialized and require a dedicate learning curve that can be long. But the performance is huge. It can support the video graphic card hardware via kernel drivers. 3D APIs have features like cache, mathematical routines and are oriented for performance, power and control. It's the perfect choice for game development.

Popular 3D prebuilt engine like Unreal Engine or Unity can also fit your needs.

Network, Middlewares and Brokers

Network access can cover the specific scenarios. Example:

- A connection to a remote file
- A connection to a remote database
- A socket on a dedicated application server

---

[60] https://www.gimp.org/

[61] https://cpp.libhunt.com/libs/graphics

Professional C++ - Philosophy and Principles

- An HTTP connection to a Web server
- A server-side software like a Web Server or a Web Service or a Web API
- A RPC application

For developing network software development, the way you can enhance your application performance and make optimizations depends the way you do it.

If you need file access, you use C file I/O like fopen() or open() functions or STL file streams. Under Windows, your file path contains \\servername\path-to-file and the Operating System make the network access for you. In this case, it's Windows Networking and it can causes timeout and failure if the remote server is not reachable. Also consider that frequent remote access is a heavy cost and you should process files locally if possible.

Under Linux, you can use NFS.

For socket usage, it's covered in a lot of dedicates books because there are multiple ways to use sockets.

If you need a simple way to do server-side code, just use the CPP Rest SDK for designing HTTP Web Servers and embedded Web API with JSON support and HTTP built-in support.

Another light-weight solution I have used in the past is an XML-RPC library called ulxmlrpcpp[62].

Others libraries used in the past are RPC or Corba Frameworks.

In the world of middleware products, the popular library is Redis[63]. There are a couple of optimizations you can make with Redis. Once again, Redis is a huge product and it can be explained in a dedicated book. Be aware there is a replication mechanism between Redis nodes.

Another popular special distributed database is OpenLDAP[64]. I have seen scenarios where it can hold the data and its inner replication and extensibility can bring superior execution time for data access. OpenLDAP is more a database than a middleware but it can be used like a middleware. OpenLDAP supports LDAP API.

---

[62] http://ulxmlrpcpp.sourceforge.net/

[63] https://redis.io/

[64] https://www.openldap.org/

Other popular middlewares are RabbitMQ[65] and ZeroMQ[66] which belong to asynchronous distributed Queuing systems supporting AMQP[67] aka Advanced Message Queuing Protocol. RabbitMQ is available on Github[68]. ZeroMQ is also available on GitHub[69]. Queuing systems are also called message broker systems.

Another popular asynchronous network library are libuv[70] and Boost.Asio[71]. Libuv is available on Github[72] and was developed to be used by NodeJS. Libuv is a fast and powerful library. It brings superior performance and it made the success of NodeJS by its inner performance.

Boost.Asio is also on Boost Libraries distributions[73] and also on Github[74]. Boost.Asio is very complete library and it can be very complicated to survive without samples.[75] Boost.Asio is a low level and asynchronous network library using the latest Modern C++ patterns (C++11? C++14 and C++17) and it will be incorporated later by the ISO C++ committee in the STL by the Networking working group. Boost.Asio is the best option for designing server-side software for the long term. It's powerful and you have control over all network events.

Others Performance Considerations

A performant software product is one that saves time to the user. It's a tool, a facility. With a slow software, we waste our time, it's difficult to use and you get nervous and angry rapidly. Let's cover some facts that make considerations on performance efficient and let's cover some aspects that can lead to poor performance:

---

[65] https://www.rabbitmq.com/

[66] https://zeromq.org/

[67] https://www.amqp.org/

[68] https://github.com/rabbitmq

[69] https://github.com/zeromq/libzmq

[70] http://libuv.org/

[71] https://www.boost.org/doc/libs/1_73_0/doc/html/boost_asio.html

[72] https://github.com/libuv/libuv

[73] https://www.boost.org/

[74] https://github.com/boostorg/asio

[75] https://www.boost.org/doc/libs/1_73_0/doc/html/boost_asio/examples.html

Professional C++ - Philosophy and Principles

- Big Frameworks

Java and NET provides a runtime execution engine a set of libraries called the Java Framework or the Microsoft NET Framework. It is shipped with dozen of shared libraries and it uses a lot of resources and brings its packets of compatibility issues, security issues and updates. It consumes a lot of memory and is CPU usage intensive. God saves us, the C++ ecosystem do not ship so many Big Frameworks. There are historical GUI Framework like QT or MFC but because it's native, you just redistribute few shared modules or you link your applications and modules statically to embedded the part of the library you use into your binary files. C++ is more efficient than those productive languages.

- Memory swapping

If your application allocates too much memory, more than the operating system can provide, then the Operating System provided a feature called memory swapping enable memory allocation by flushing some memory on disks or swapping from disk to memory and memory to disk. It's the role of the virtual memory manger.

- Installation Procedures

Installation and uninstall procedures should be done with the state of the art of the underlying operating system. Do not build your own system. Integrates your application fully on the OS. It can enable your application to use shared modules updated by the OS rather than shipping your copy of OS modules. Duplicated shared modules can lead to application failures and performance issues.

- Automatic Updates

Automatic updates of some applications or of the Operating System can show popups, notifications and disturb the current user. It can use huge amount of bandwidth network and your application can becoming slower until the updates are not finished.

- Compatibility Issues

Your application needs to be tested on different hardware, different Operating Systems and different access rights, different screen resolutions for UI desktop applications.

- Hardware Changes

Some intensives disk I/O operations can be cost effective and using modern SSD disk drives gives a totally different result versus standard disk drives. Use SSD disk drives !

- Security

Security requires additional programming steps with certificates, credentials, cryptography, secrets and clean code programming rules to be respected and applied. A good Microsoft Press book[76] on this subject exists.

- Background Services

Many services in the Operating System are unnecessary for the user. Mark them as manual start-up to let your system with lightweight and run fast. Services consumes memory and CPU usage when they wake up.

- Take User Feedback in account

You should take care of your customers feedback because they can give you a valuable source of information about the bugs, problems, wanted features and different other things. We build software for humans so let them remain in the first circle of our preoccupation.

The 90/10 Rule in Optimization

This rule is also called the 80/20 sometimes. 90% of your program runs in 10% of the code. This is a general rule that can be verified easily. An app has always some kind of plumbing and declarative parts. There is also wrappers and helpers to make the code cleaner and after all is done, the central part of the software is the main routine where data are computed, processed. You call it the name you want. It performs the job you have coded. This is this part of the code we need to upgrade and enhance its performance.

The Visual Rule

When you look at the code, you can segment the code your read into apartments:

- Startup, Initialization and Configuration
- Data acquisition
- Processing rules and tasks
- I/O operations
- Tracing and instrumentations
- Computation routines
- Database operations
- Network operations
- Multithreading operations

---

[76] Writing Secure Code for Windows Vista, by Michael Howard and David LeBlanc, Microsoft Press 2007

Professional C++ - Philosophy and Principles

Stop and Think. What is the most important part of the application ? Is it the data acquisition because you filter data or the processing rules that do the main job ? The visual rule is simple: you see what is important and you know what is to be done fast. Point it with comments in the code, write your function names on a papers and work on it.

The Logger is Your Best Friend

When your visual rule is enforced, you know what is essential to your application and now you have to verify your assumptions. You need to make measures with a logger. There is two part in the logger mechanism:

- The way to measure the time elapsed
- The way to log the information

Measuring time

In the standard library, we have date and time support in the <chrono> header. It's easy to use and it has supports for milliseconds operations ; exactly what we need.

```cpp
void funcTime()
{
    chrono::system_clock::time_point tpStart = chrono::system_clock::now();
    auto operation1 = []() {
        for (int i = 0; i < 10000; i++)
        {
            vector<int> v;
            v.push_back(i);
        }
    };
    operation1();
    chrono::system_clock::time_point tpStop = chrono::system_clock::now();

    chrono::duration<double> duration = tpStop - tpStart;
    cout << "Time: " << duration.count() << " s" << endl;
}
```

The useful function is system_clock::now(). It returns a system_clock::time_point type and the difference between two data of this type give a duration<double> type. The value is obtained by calling the count function.

Let's wrap the system_clock::now with a class we can use in any application. Let's design it as a header class.

```cpp
class MyWatch
{
public:
    MyWatch()
    {
        _elapsed = 0;
    };
```

160

Professional C++

```cpp
        virtual ~MyWatch() {};

public:
    void Start()
    {
        _start = chrono::system_clock::now();
    }

    void Stop()
    {
        _end = chrono::system_clock::now();
        chrono::duration<double> duration = _end - _start;
        _elapsed = duration.count();
    }

    double GetTime()
    {
        return _elapsed;
    }

protected:
    chrono::system_clock::time_point _start;
    chrono::system_clock::time_point _end;
    double _elapsed;
};
```

MyWatch is very simple to use once you have created an object:

- Call Start
- Call Stop
- Get the elapsed time with GetTime()

When the class is defined in a header, here is how to use it:

```cpp
void funcTime2()
{
    MyWatch watch;
    watch.Start();
    auto operation1 = []() {
        for (int i = 0; i < 10000; i++)
        {
            vector<int> v;
            v.push_back(i);
        }
    };
```

Professional C++ - Philosophy and Principles

```
    operation1();
    watch.Stop();
    cout << "Time: " << watch.GetTime() << " s" << endl;
}
```

Tracing operations

Once we have a little toolbox for measuring time for operations, we need to trace it. The basic stuff would consist of opening a file, seek to the =end an write a string. Yes it works and we have all done that in the past. But there is more elegant way to do: use a logger or a logging library. Here the basic features you can find into such a library:

- A configuration file containing the description of the loggers, the modes, the message, etc.
- Possibility to use multiple logger types (file, system log, network)
- Rolling file capabilities (by day, week, or by size)

List of Logging Libraries

Here is a list of popular logging library:

- Log4cxx : The Apache project comparable to Log4j
    - http://logging.apache.org/log4cxx
- Log4cpp : the most popular and historical logging library
    - http://log4cpp.sourceforge.net
- Log4cplus : another logging library
    - https://github.com/log4cplus/log4cplus
- Glog : Google logging library
    - https://github.com/google/glog
- Boost.Log : The log project from the Boost Libraries
    - https://www.boost.org/doc/libs/1_74_0/libs/log/doc/html/index.html

Overview of Log4cpp

Log4cpp is an old logging library adapted from log4j concepts. Here is a sample configuration file:

```
# a DailyRollingFileAppender test config

log4j.rootCategory=DEBUG, rootAppender
log4j.category.sub1=,DAILY, NCDAILY

log4j.appender.rootAppender=org.apache.log4j.ConsoleAppender
log4j.appender.rootAppender.layout=org.apache.log4j.BasicLayout

log4cpp.appender.DAILY=DailyRollingFileAppender
log4cpp.appender.DAILY.fileName=dailyrolling.log
log4cpp.appender.DAILY.maxDaysKeep=1
```

```
log4cpp.appender.DAILY.layout=PatternLayout
log4cpp.appender.DAILY.layout.ConversionPattern=%d [%p] The message %m at
time %d{%H:%M}%n

log4cpp.appender.NCDAILY=DailyRollingFileAppender
log4cpp.appender.NCDAILY.fileName=nesteddir/dailyrolling.log
log4cpp.appender.NCDAILY.maxDaysKeep=1
log4cpp.appender.NCDAILY.layout=PatternLayout
log4cpp.appender.NCDAILY.layout.ConversionPattern=%d [%p] The message %m at
time %d{%H:%M}%n
```

Here is how to use the rolling file appender:

```
int TestConfigDailyRollingFileAppender()
{
    std::string initFileName;
    initFileName = "./testConfig.log4cpp.dailyroll.nt.properties";
    log4cpp::PropertyConfigurator::configure(initFileName);

    log4cpp::Category& root = log4cpp::Category::getRoot();

    log4cpp::Category& sub1 =
        log4cpp::Category::getInstance(std::string("sub1"));

    root.error("root error");
    root.warn("root warn");
    sub1.error("sub1 error");
    sub1.warn("sub1 warn");

    log4cpp::Category::shutdown();
    return 0;
}
```

The useful functions are error, warn or info.

If the popular logger does not fit your needs, you can build your own logger. The logger is basically a class that looks like that:

```
class MyLogger
{
public:
    MyLogger() {}
    virtual ~MyLogger() {}

public:
    void Info(const string& message);
    void Debug(const string& message);
    void Error(const string& message);
```

```
};
```
You can provide a database connection string, a file name or some properties and implement your own logging library but it's useless most of the times if you deal with simple text files. If you have a database, OK build your own classes, but most of the time, choosing an open-source provides the necessary features to achieve our goals.

Logging Usage

Now we have a logger, we have to use it wisely. The rule is not to trace all the instructions you have in the code nor the time elapsed for all the functions existing in the source code. The basic usage is to make traces in useful locations:

- The start of the program
- The end of the program
- The main functions of the applications

This is a case study for every application. Applications are unique in the way they work. The best practice is to create a daily file logging appender and in this scenario, there will be one file per day. The other choice is segmenting the file by its size. You put in configuration that, for example, 10 MB is the maximum size of a file. The goal is not to produce a GB trace file per day because it won't be easy to analyze. By design, you can have a verbose logging strategy. You can trace a lot of stuff for debugging purposes in DEBUG mode and when the application is bug-free, you change your configuration to switch to INFO mode and then, you logging traces produced at this time will be only INFO and ERROR. If the application produces a strange behavior one day, you can active the appender in DEBUG mode and then your traces appear again. For a critical application, you can trace the following elements:

- The function names
- The value of the parameters
- The running steps
- Exception handler's information

This kind of tracing strategy should be enforced from the beginning of the development of the application. It's not when something goes bad that you put instrumentation in the code. When your are in production mode after the bug free experience, your log file should only trace the startup and shutdown entries. Eventually, the main routine of the application to show something happened but it's even not necessary. Once again, I see to many applications that don't use the switching flag DEBUG/INFO and that are producing thousand lines of logging traces per minute; others are also tracing the SQL queries for example. It's completely unnecessary. Don't forget that you produce traces from the code to give information that matters. Just put in the traces the necessary information and be always explicit. Don't trace something like: i= 10. It's useless.

Build Your Own Tracing GUI Tool

Another approach, for banking systems for example, is to trace business information for the record. In this case, the traces need to be put in a database. Sometimes, you have to trace the changes of data values. In this case, you trace the UserId, the DateTime, the business process name, and the old and new value.

For a banking company, I had a series of complexes operations running from 00:00 AM to 06:00 AM from multiple threads with chained workflows. In this situation, the workflows steps were traced with a GUID and registered in the database logging tables with a current GUID and a parent GUID. Then I used a GUI front end to display the various steps of the workflows and the support users were able to click on a step and see its associated log portion. If your application is critical, provide your own logging support GUI tool.

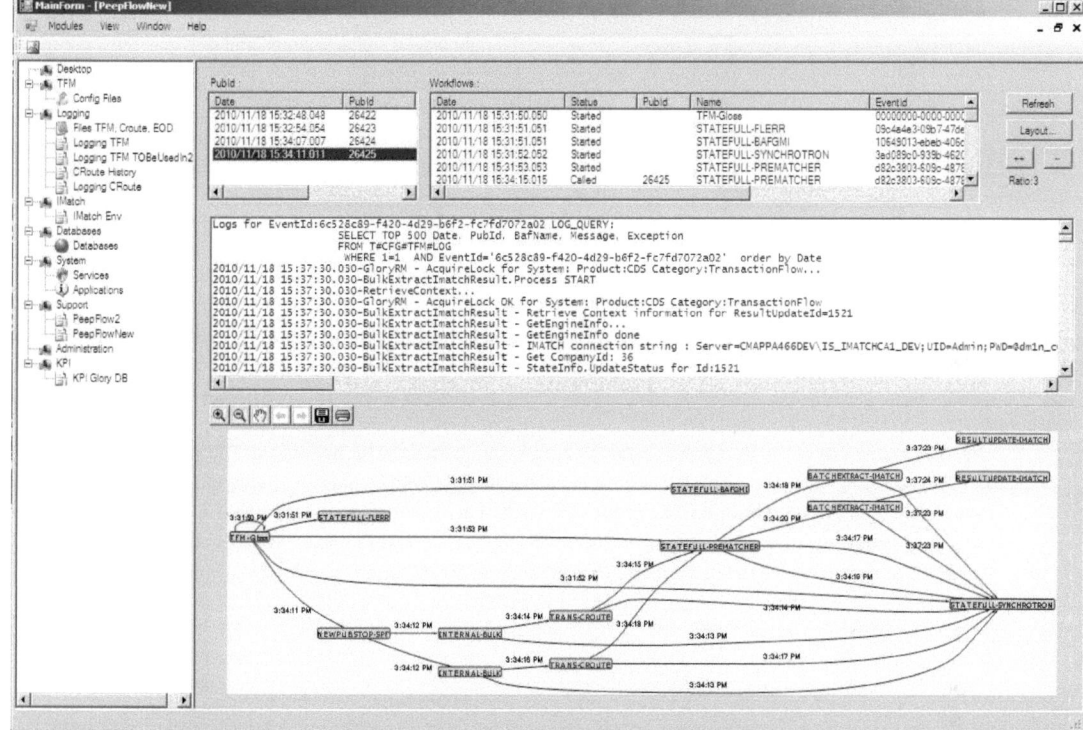

Before I fixed the application and developed the GUI tool, the company was paying a developer to read the logging files from home in the middle of the nigh to see whatever thread crashed! The house of mad men. The developer was so tired in the morning that he was importing bugs in the day and was debugging in the middle of the night. Sometimes, in big companies, it's hard to believe...

In my example, the logic of the workflow is presented with a diagram and when you click on an item, the GUID of the item allows the tracing app to get the associated logs.

The GUI tools was containing multiple windows:

- Configuration files viewer

Professional C++ - Philosophy and Principles

- Remote application start/stop
- Logging basic search with criteria in the whole database
- GUI enhanced logging view

Creating a tool that display the configuration files content is easy and can save you time and energy when it's time to check a configuration. You run the tools, open the right window and it's done. Compared to terminal ssh login or remote RDP connection, its' priceless. In my application, when the mouse passes over an item, a popup displays the XML input information sent to the workflow. If every s processed the right way, it's blue or green and if an exception occurred, the item is red. Colors allows to check rapidly the status of a whole processing.

If you want to display such a layout, you can use Microsoft Automatic Graph Layout available here: https://www.microsoft.com/en-us/research/project/microsoft-automatic-graph-layout

Other third-party libraries like Telerik, SyncFusion and Infragistics, offer GUI features like that but it's not free.

Another feature that is extremely useful in support mode in tools is the ability to open multiple windows with MDI mode. In my example, the tool id developed with Windows Forms technology using the Microsoft .NET Framework. MDI implementation is very easy to achieve. You create forms with the MDI property set to true, you store the form object in a collection and when you select an item in the central view of the left pane, you create or activate a MDI child window. That's all.

Another example of GUI tools is a basic logging trace viewer I have done for newspaper. The log files were dedicated to an ETL processing application. This is a customized application log with commands, status and client name. The GUI tool allows to filter on client, date and status of the commands. For support users, the first operation was to filter of status searching for failures. They were clicking on Search and that's all. In this example, the application is a single dialog using an ODBC connection string to the database. The various lines are displayed in a list view in report mode provided by Windows.

Professional C++

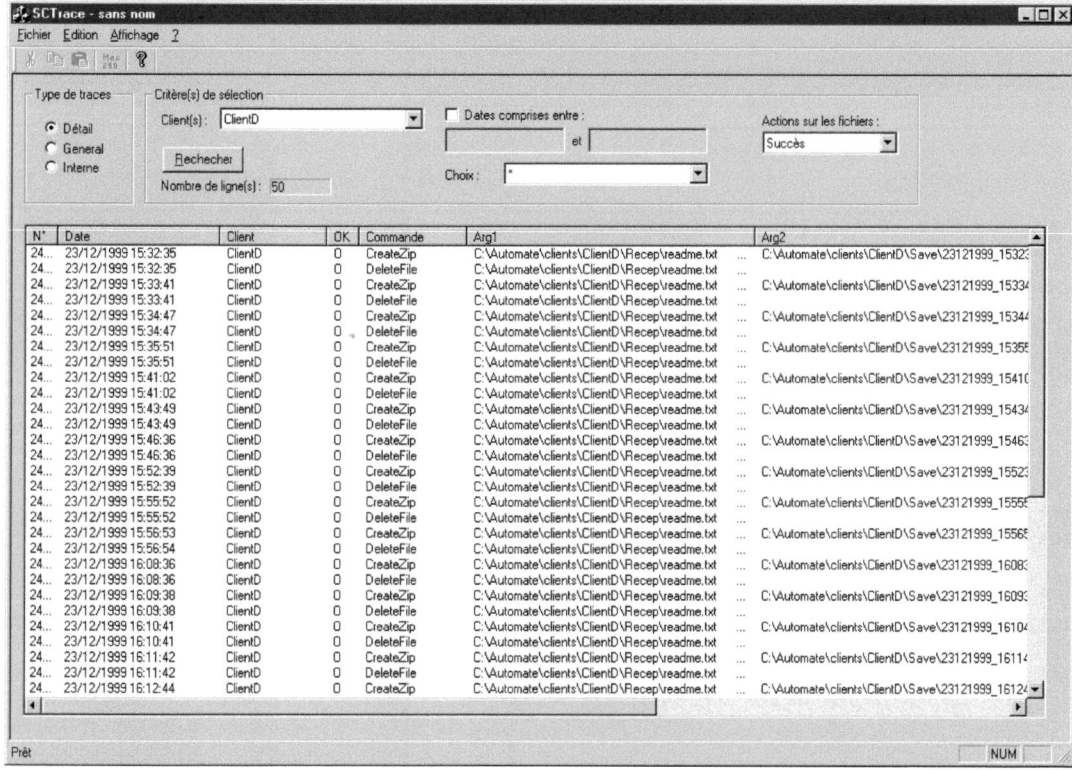

The rule is that we produce traces under development for debugging but also for the support Team that will live with it. A custom tool is better than notepad or notepad++ !

Excellence in Tracing

The rule is simple. If the support team or the development team need to activate the DEBUG mode also called the verbose mode under configuration file, your application needs to dump useful information. If the application uses multiple threads, the message must include the thread Id to follow and join the operation for a same thread. If your application processes commands for example, you have to include a custom field in the message called command. A trace message is not just a const string &. It's built using data fields, so you have to put all the essentials ones.

The Compiler Code Profiler

Every compiler has a switch for code profiling. It allows to instrument all the functions of the code. Example of the book's source code:

167

Professional C++ - Philosophy and Principles

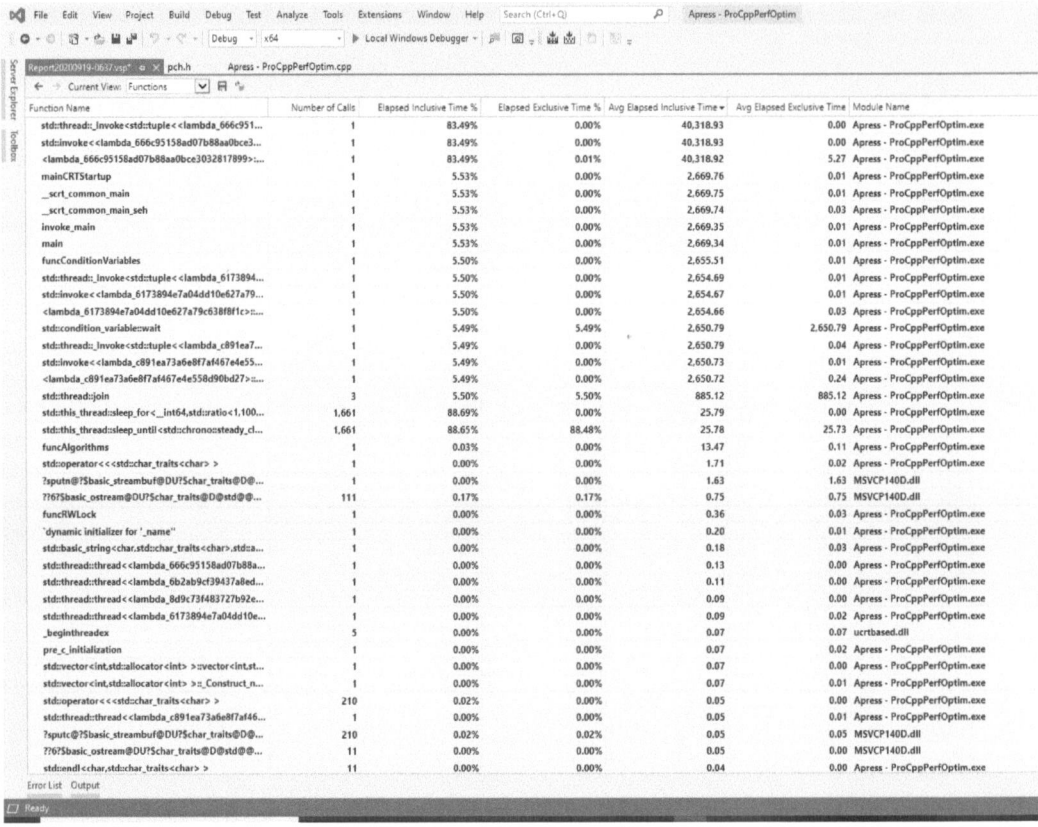

To produce such a report, you need to make a specific build of the application and run it. For each function, we have the information like:

- Function name
- Number of calls
- The elapsed time %
- The elapsed time milliseconds

The information is very low level because it's only source code information: functions, lambdas, etc. It gives an overview of a run. With a profiler, you have the big picture where the application spends most of its time. It's priceless for optimization work.

There is also a module view:

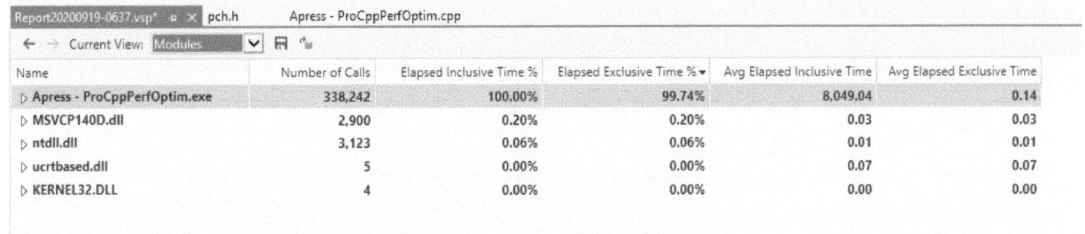

In this case, there was 338K calls in the console process (exe) and 2900 calls in the standard library (MSVCP140D.dll) and 3123 calls to the operating system (ntdll.dll). It's important to see where the code spends most of its time. Be aware of some standard library usage.

All the various reports can be exported as CSV. Load it in Excel or make reports and you are encouraged to compare those data on regular time.

Unit Tests and DevOps

On modern stage of development, we all use a SCM (Source Control Management) and we a minimal build server or a full CI/CD platform. Nowadays, it's essentials to have unit tests that is covering the major part of the source code. Some SCM have policies and the unit tests are run on every check-in to verify that the build pipeline with unit tests are not broken. Unit Tests allow you to test the various part of your application on a clean infrastructure dedicated to this step. Your unit tests can produce logs of time measurement and sophisticated scenarios and you can keep record of this logs.

Between two sprints, you can compare the performance of your function's calls. I suggest you to create dedicated performance tests additionally to regular unit tests. Performance tests should use the MyWatch class presented earlier in this chapter. You can use either system_clock::now() or GetTickCount64 to measure time, it's not a problem but put the chrono on. You need to measure the time and have an idea of how it performs.

Just like profiling, when you have a large base of code and thousands functions and objects, you need to make a choice: what piece of code do I need to enhance? You can't do it with a finger asking you were is the wind? A technical process named the *"doigt mouillé"* in french ; translated in the "wet finger". It has to be scientific.

You should create these kind of performance tests:

- Loading configuration files
- Data input acquisition
- Doing a full business processing with data acquisition
- Split the business processes in various steps
- Rendering data processed to the desired output

For each test, you do it for one item, for 10, for 100. It may not be linear.

Professional C++ - Philosophy and Principles

List of Unit Tests Library

Unit tests is not new for C++. The historical library CPPUnit started in 2000 from a port of JUnit. It passes tests as suite tests. Here is a list of popular Tests Frameworks:

- CPPUnit: the historical library
    - https://freedesktop.org/wiki/Software/cppunit
- Google Test: the Google toolkit integrated with Visual Studio
    - https://github.com/google/googletest
- Boost.Test: the Test library from Boost Libraries
    - https://www.boost.org/doc/libs/1_74_0/libs/test/doc/html/index.html

Overview of CPPUnit

CPPUnit is very easy to use. You create one or more classes derived from TestFixture and you implement test functions into the class. You have multiple CPPUNIT_ASSERT handlers to create your assertions. Into such a class, you can define a setup function that is executed first to initiate the test. This is where, for example, you make data acquisition.

To run a series of tests with CPPUnit, you need to link your unit test project with CPPUnit.lib. It's a small library. A test project is just a console application that invokes the CPPUnit engine.

CPPUnit example of a test case, file ExampleTestCase.h:

```cpp
#ifndef CPP_UNIT_EXAMPLETESTCASE_H
#define CPP_UNIT_EXAMPLETESTCASE_H

#include <cppunit/extensions/HelperMacros.h>

/*
 * A test case that is designed to produce
 * example errors and failures
 *
 */
class ExampleTestCase : public CPPUNIT_NS::TestFixture
{
  CPPUNIT_TEST_SUITE( ExampleTestCase );
  CPPUNIT_TEST( example );
  CPPUNIT_TEST( anotherExample );
  CPPUNIT_TEST( testAdd );
  CPPUNIT_TEST( testEquals );
  CPPUNIT_TEST_SUITE_END();

protected:
  double m_value1;
  double m_value2;
```

```
public:
  void setUp();

protected:
  void example();
  void anotherExample();
  void testAdd();
  void testEquals();
};


#endif
```

File ExampleTestCase.cpp:

```
#include <cppunit/config/SourcePrefix.h>
#include "ExampleTestCase.h"

CPPUNIT_TEST_SUITE_REGISTRATION( ExampleTestCase );

void ExampleTestCase::example()
{
  CPPUNIT_ASSERT_DOUBLES_EQUAL( 1.0, 1.1, 0.05 );
  CPPUNIT_ASSERT( 1 == 0 );
  CPPUNIT_ASSERT( 1 == 1 );
}


void ExampleTestCase::anotherExample()
{
  CPPUNIT_ASSERT (1 == 2);
}

void ExampleTestCase::setUp()
{
  m_value1 = 2.0;
  m_value2 = 3.0;
}

void ExampleTestCase::testAdd()
{
  double result = m_value1 + m_value2;
  CPPUNIT_ASSERT( result == 6.0 );
}
```

Professional C++ - Philosophy and Principles

```cpp
void ExampleTestCase::testEquals()
{
  long* l1 = new long(12);
  long* l2 = new long(12);

  CPPUNIT_ASSERT_EQUAL( 12, 12 );
  CPPUNIT_ASSERT_EQUAL( 12L, 12L );
  CPPUNIT_ASSERT_EQUAL( *l1, *l2 );

  delete l1;
  delete l2;

  CPPUNIT_ASSERT( 12L == 12L );
  CPPUNIT_ASSERT_EQUAL( 12, 13 );
  CPPUNIT_ASSERT_DOUBLES_EQUAL( 12.0, 11.99, 0.5 );
}

class FixtureTest : public CPPUNIT_NS::TestFixture
{
};

CPPUNIT_TEST_FIXTURE(FixtureTest, testEquals)
{
  CPPUNIT_ASSERT_EQUAL( 12, 12 );
}

CPPUNIT_TEST_FIXTURE(FixtureTest, testAdd)
{
  double result = 2.0 + 2.0;
  CPPUNIT_ASSERT( result == 4.0 );
}
```

Running the sample test cases simple gives that output:

```
testAdd::TestBody : OK
D:\Dev\cpp\cppunit-1.15.1\examples\simple\ExampleTestCase.cpp(8) : error :
Assertion
Test name: ExampleTestCase::example
double equality assertion failed
- Expected: 1
- Actual  : 1.1
- Delta   : 0.05
```

```
D:\Dev\cpp\cppunit-1.15.1\examples\simple\ExampleTestCase.cpp(16) : error :
Assertion
Test name: ExampleTestCase::anotherExample
assertion failed
- Expression: 1 == 2

D:\Dev\cpp\cppunit-1.15.1\examples\simple\ExampleTestCase.cpp(28) : error :
Assertion
Test name: ExampleTestCase::testAdd
assertion failed
- Expression: result == 6.0

D:\Dev\cpp\cppunit-1.15.1\examples\simple\ExampleTestCase.cpp(45) : error :
Assertion
Test name: ExampleTestCase::testEquals
equality assertion failed
- Expected: 12
- Actual   : 13

Failures !!!
Run: 6   Failure total: 4   Failures: 4   Errors: 0
```

Anatomy of a test application

Here is a brief description how you can handle your unit tests. First, define as many test functions there are business routines. Then you add test routines for each step of each business rules. Sometimes, you will test internal functions or plumbing. It is very important to test that kind of code to ensure it will always work whatever change will occur in the source code. A test application is just a console application that returns an exit code.

Can I make my own test application without a test framework? Yes, but you are not in a modern era. Every test framework allows you to build extensions. Take this option if you need more than basic ASSERT macros. Remember that test functions ensure that everything works well. All indicators should be passed (green color) OK. It ensures the various part of the applications have no regression. This is what we want to test.

Conclusion

Coupling unit tests and logging can make your application more testable and you can have measures on various part of the software even in the plumbing. Most of the time, plumbing can play a huge role in the waiting tasks. It's important to beware that you use a third library for example and that's not your primary code who is busy but the third library.

Once again, measures are the only way to know exactly where the long operations occurred. It's not magic. You can't achieve these tasks just by looking at the source code, you need evidences. Play it like the FBI. Be a cop. An elite cop. You track your enemies. You put traps (logging areas and timing measures), you play again and again the unit tests with various context and data inputs. Sometimes, long running operations depend on the volumetry of the input data to process. Tracing is the best option you have to begin an investigation. Next, you track the guilty functions. Do not make assumptions too early. I know that some impressions can become an obsession and you can dive very deep without

Professional C++ - Philosophy and Principles

seeing the light because you follow an option. Don't' be fool. Avoid the madness step. Be pragmatic, analyze the profiler report, put traces and understand it like an FBI agent. Most of the time, the goal is to enhance the primary bottleneck not the small stuff that exists everywhere in the source code.

6. Containers

You need to store data in a various container. By default, in C++, you have to use the STL containers because of various factors. In the beginning of the 90's there was a lot of STL vendors and each compiler had some difficulties in some part of the STL.

It was very difficult to share code from various compilers because of the instability of some components of the STL. There were some problems whether it was Loki, Intel's one, Microsoft's one, Borland's one or other vendors.

In the 2000's, it became more professional and a lot of compilers were very stable with there shipped STL with compilers.

At first sight, when you discover and learn the STL, it is not easy to choose which data structure or container (it's called container in the STL) to choose. Should I write myself or rely on an existing one?

The answer is : "NEVER build you own data structure unless the existing one do not really fit your needs or any extension or if your product is so deeply requiring an OVNI stuff, ok make it on your own but for 99% of the average and daily programming tasks, STL is enough."

In fact, the Data structures is the half part of the answer. The other part is the algorithm you will use to process your data from your data structures.

Containers are data structures for storing collections of items. Containers and algorithms work together and the interaction between the two are iterators.

Hardware and Memory

The memory is provided by Memory kits like 8GB Kit (2x8GB). The Operating System handles the management of the memory. In Windows, it's provided by the kernel (ke) in the mm submodules which means Memory Management.

The header <iterator>

Iterators

An iterator is the way to list the elements of a container. There are three types of access for iterators:

- The Forward (F)
- The Bidirectionals (B)
- Random Access (R)

There are several operations on iterators:

Professional C++ - Philosophy and Principles

operation	description
`T a, T()`, `T b(a), b`	Default builder, destroyer, copy builder, copy operator.
`a 'b', a!'`	Operator of equality and difference
`A, a->m, 'a' t,` `'a' t`	Deferral.
`'a', 'a', 'a'`	Increment operators.
`--a, a--`[77]	Decrement operators.
`a[n]`[78]	Access via index.
`a 'n', 'no',` `a - n, a 'n 'n',` `a - no.`[79]	Arithmetic operators. Move forward or backward an iterator.
`a - b`[80]	Calculate the distance between two iterators.
`a <b, a > b,` `a < b, a > b`[81]	Other operators.

---

[77] Not available for F

[78] Available only for R

[79] Available only for R

[80] Available only for R

[81] Available only for R

Access features

To get an iterator, you have to use functions on a container:

Non-member function	description
begin (end)	Returns an iterator to the first item or after the last item
cbegin(// ash ()	Const versions of begin (and end)
rbegin (/ renders ()	/	Returns a reverse iterator from the last to before the first item
crbegin (/ crend ()	/	Const version of rbegin () and renders ()

There are other features:

- std::d istance (iter1, iter2) : Turns the distance between two iterators.
- std::advance (iter, dist) : Advance the iterator from a given distance.
- std::next (iter, dist-1) : Equivalent to advance (iter, dist) and return iter.
- std::p rev (iter, dist-1) : Equivalent to advance (iter, -dist) and return iter.

The header <vector>

std::vector

A vector is a vector that stores the elements in an adjoining way. To add an element to a vector, the push_back function is used.

```
vector<int>v1;
    v1.push_back(10);
    v1.push_back(20);
```

It is also possible to use the insert function:

```
v1.insert (v1.begin) - 1, 15);
```

It is possible to take advantage of the semantics of displacement with the function emplace_back().

A vector also has size(or capacity) functions that contain the size of the vector and its capacity. The reallocation of memory is done via the reserve function.) The decreasing function of a vector is resize.)

The removal of an item is done via pop_back() or by erase():

- **erase** (iter): removes the element from the iterator

- **erase (first, last):** remove a range of items

To remove items, it is recommended to use std::remove() or std::remove_if().

The header <array>

std::array

A array type is a fixed-size container known for compiling as a template. It supports the operator [] and random access iterators.

```
std::array<int,10> arr1;
std::array<int,3> arr2, 2, 3;
```

Insertion is not possible. Neither is the deletion.

The headers <list> et <forward_list>

std::list and std::forward_list

The std::list type stores items as a double chained list while std::forward_list stores them as a single chained list. The operator [] is not supported.

The insertion and removal operations are very fast because there are few operations to be carried out.

Here is the list of operations supported for a list (L) and a forward_list (F):

operation	description
merge ()	Merges two sorted lists. The list that is merged is emptied.
remove ()	Deletes items from a list for a given value.
remove_if	Deletes items from a list for a given predicted.
reverse ()	Reverses the contents of a list.
fate ()	Sort the elements.
splice ()[82]	Moves items from a list before a given position.
splice_after[83]	Moves items from a list after a given position.
unique ()	Replaces consecutive duplicate items with a single value.

Here's how to use std::list:

```
std::mylist list  100, 20, 300, 40, 500, 20 .100;
    mylist.sort();
    mylist.unique();
```

Container operations

The operations supported by vectors (V), deque (D), array (A), list (L) and forward_list (F) are described below.

Iterators

operation	description
begin ()	Returns an iterator to the first item or after the last item
end ()	

---

[82] Not available for F

[83] Nn available for L

cbegin cend ()	Const versions of begin(and end)
rbegin renders ()[84]	Returns a reverse iterator from the last to before the first item
crbegin() crend ()[85]	Const version of rbegin() and renders ()
before_begin[86]	Returns an iterator to the item before the item returned by begin()
cbefore_begin[87]	Const version of before_begin()

---

[84] Not available for F

[85] Not available for F

[86] Available only for F

[87] Available only for F

Size and capacity

operation	description
`size ()` [88]	Turns the number of items
`max_size`	Returns the maximum number of items that can be stored in the container
`resize()` [89]	Resizes the container
`empty ()`	Returns true if the container is empty, false if not
`capacity ()` [90]	Turns the container's current capacity
`reserve ()` [91]	Capacity Reserve
`shrink_to_fit` [92]	Reduces container capacity to size

---

[88] Not available for F

[89] Not available for A

[90] Available only for V

[91] Available only for V

[92] Available only for V and D

Professional C++ - Philosophy and Principles

access

operation	description
operator[] [93]	Returns a reference to the item at a given position.
at () [94]	Returns a reference to the item at a given position. Can lift the exception std::out_of_range.
data () [95]	Return a pointer to the data.
front ()	Returns a reference to the first item.
back () [96]	Returns a reference to the last item.

---

[93] Not available for L and F

[94] Not available for L and F

[95] Not available for D, L and F

[96] Not available for F

Changes

operation	description
assign ()	Replaces the contents of the container with values of a given item, or a range, or a initializer_list.
clear ()[97]	Destroys all the elements.
emplace ()[98]	Builds a new value before the position of the iterator.
emplace_back[99]	Built a new element at the end.
emplace_after[100]	Builds a new element after an existing item.
emplace_front[101]	Built a new element at the beginning.
erase ()[102]	Clears the elements.
erase_after[103]	Clears the items after the position of the iterator.
fill (fill)[104]	Fills the container with a given item.

[97] Not available for A

[98] Not available for A and F

[99] Not available for A and F

[100] Available only for F

[101] Not available for V and A

[102] Not available for A and F

[103] Available only for F

[104] Available only for A

Professional C++ - Philosophy and Principles

`insert ()`[105]	Insert one or more elements before the item pointed by an iterator.
`insert_after`[106]	Inserts one or more items after the item pointed by an iterator.
`push_back` `pop_back`[107]	Adds an item at the end, removes the last item.
`push_front` `pop_front`[108]	Adds an item at the beginning, removes the first item.
`swap ()`	Swap the contents of two containers.

Non-member functions

operation	description
`'<, <, >, >'`	Comparisons
`std::swap ()`	Swaps the contents of two containers
`std::size ()`	Turns the number of items.
`std::empty ()`	Return if the container is empty.
`std::d ata`	As the function member of `ata()`.

---

[105] Not available for A and F

[106] Available only for F

[107] Not available for A and F

[108] Not available for V and A

The header <bitset>

std::bitset

A bitset type is a container to store a fixed number of bits.

```
    std::bitset<10> bit1;
std::bitset<4> bit2 ("1010");
```

access

operation	description
All () Any () none ()	Returns true if all, at least one or none of the bits is reported.
count ()	Returns the number of bits reported.
operator[]	Access a bit from an index.
test ()	Access a bit from an index. Can lift the exception std::out_of_range.
==, !=	Return true whether tied or not.
size ()	Returns the number of bits that can be contained in the bitset.
to_string to_ulong to_ullong	Conversion of bitset into thong, unsigned long, or unsigned long.

Operations

operation	description
flip ()	Flippe the values of all bits
reset()	Positions all bits or a specific bit to false
set ()	Positions all bits to true or a specific bit to a value

Professional C++ - Philosophy and Principles

The bitset type supports bit operations such as: '" ' " " " " ' ' | | <<, <<, >>, and >>.

The header<queue>

std::tail

A std type::queue represents a FIFO container *(first in, first out)*. The main functions are back(), front(), push_back(), pop_front().

std::p riority-tail

A std::p riority-tail type can only modify the container from the back, not the forehead. So the functions supported are front(), push_back() and pop_back().

std::stack

A std::stack type represents a LIFO container *(last in, first out)*. The main functions are back(), front(), push_back(),

references

operation	description
`emplace ()`	*Tail:* Builds a new item at the end. *Priority*tail: Builds a new element in place. *Stack:* Builds a new element above.
`empty ()`	Return true if it's empty.
`front ()` `back ()`	*Tail:* Returns a reference to the first or last item. *Priority*tail: n/a *Stack:* n/a
`pop ()`	*Tail:* Removes the first element from the tail. *Priority*tail: Removes the highest priority item. *Stack:* Remove the point from the top.
`push ()`	*Tail:* Inserts a new element at the end of the tail. *Priority*tail: Inserts a new element. *Stack:* Inserts a new element above.
`size ()`	Turns the number of items.
`swap ()`	Swap the contents of two tails or stack.
`top ()`	*Tail:* n/a *Priority*tail: Returns a reference to the higher priority item.

Stack: Returns a reference to the top element.

The header <map>

std::map

A std::map type is a data structure that stores key/value elements. The keys must be unique. Here's an example:

```
std::map<int, Product>map1
Product (1, "Item 1")
Product (10, "Item 2")
    };
map1[3] - Product(30, "Item 3");
for (std::pair<int, Product>elt: map1)
    {
cost <<  elt.first  <<";
cost <<  elt.second.price  <<"
<< elt.second.name  endl <<;
    }
```

std::multimap

A std type::multimap is like a map but allows duplicates at the key level.

The header <set>

std::map and std::multiset

A std::set type is like a map except it only stores the keys. A std::multiset type allows duplicated keys.

Search operations

The search for a key in an association container is done with:

- find : : Returns an iterator to the found item or end iterator if the key is not found.
- count () : Returns the number of keys that match.
- lower_bound(), upper_bound() : Flips an iterator that points to the item that is < or > to a given key.
- equal_range() : Returns a std::pair of two iterators: lower_bound() and upper_bound.

Moving knots

Use of map functions::extract() and map::insert() with std ::move().

Professional C++ - Philosophy and Principles

```
map<int, string> girls '9', 'Audrey','13' and 'Lisa',
16, "Edith";
auto nh - girls.extract(13);
nh.key() - 14; // Anniv on Nov 10
girls.insert (std::move (nh));
"Audrey," "Lisa," "16," "Edith"
```

The extract function allows you to remove a knot and insert allows it to be inserted.

Container merger

To merge a container, the std function is used.

example:

```
std::vector<int>vi1, 2, 5, 10, 15, 20;
std::vector<int>vi2 1, 3, 7, 12, 18, 23;
std::sort (vi1.begin(), vi1.end());
std::sort (vi2.begin(), vi2.end());
std::vector<int>dest;
std::merge (vi1.begin(), vi1.end(),
    vi2.begin(), vi2.end(),
    std::back_inserter (dest));
output
std::cout << "dest:";
std::copy (dest.begin(), dest.end(),
std::ostream_iterator<int>(std::cout, "));
std::cost << std::endl;
```

The output is as follows:

```
dest: 1 1 2 3 5 7 10 12 15 18 20 23
```

reference

We will list the operations supported by maps (M), multimap (MM), set (S) and multiset (MS)

Iterators

Access to iterators is made with: `begin()`, `end()`, `cbegin()`, `cend()`, `rbegin()`, renders, `crbegin()` and `crend()`.

waist

operation	description
empty ()	Returns true if the container is empty if not false
max_size	Returns the maximum number of items that can be stored

188

`size ()`	Turns the number of items

Access and Search

operation	description
`at ()` [109]	Returns a reference to the item for a given key. Can lift the exception `std::out_of_range`.
`operator[]` [110]	Returns a reference to the item for a given key.
`count ()`	Turns back the number of items that match a given key.
`find ()`	Find an item for a given key.
`lower_bound`	Returns an iterator to the first item for a key < a given key.
`upper_bound`	Returns an iterator to the first item for a key > a given key.
`equal_range`	Flip a row for a given key. Equivalent to a `lower_bound` call() and `upper_bound(`

---

[109] Available only for M

[110] Available only for M

Professional C++ - Philosophy and Principles

Changes

operation	description
clear ()	Empty the container.
emplace ()	Builds a new element.
emplace_hint	As an emplace() but faster.
erase ()	Deletes an item at a given position, a range of items, or all items for a given key.
extract ()	Extracts a knot for insertion into another container.
insert ()	Insert new items or nodes extracted from another container.
merge ()	Merge a container into a container.
swap ()	Swap the contents of two containers.

operation	Description
insert_or_assign	Insert a new item or crush a value.
try_emplace	Builds a new key-value peer in place.

Non-member functions

You can use the operators , , <, <, >, > and functions std::swap(), std::size(), and std::empty().

The headers <unordered_map> and <unordered_set>

Hash Map

The unordered_map, unordered_multimap, unordered_set and unordered_multiset types are *hash*tables. These are containers that are very efficiently stored.

190

references

Observers

operation	description
hash_function	Returns hash function used for key hashing
key_eq	Returns the function used to achieve equality on the keys

Interface Bucket

operation	description
begin (int) end (int) cbegin (int) cend (int)	Returns an iterator to the first or last for a given index.
bucket (key)	Flips the bucket index for a given key
bucket_count	Turns the bucket number
bucket_size (int)	Returns the number of items in the bucket for a given index
max_bucket_count	Returns the maximum number of buckets that can be created

Hash Policy

operation	description
load_factor	Returns the average number of items in a bucket.
max_load_factor	Returns or positions the maximum load factor.
rehash ()	Positions the number of buckets for a specific value and makes a rehash of all the items.
reserve ()	Reserve a number of buckets.

Non-member functions

Supported functions are `operator`, `operator`, `std::swap()`, `std::size()` and `std::empty()`.

7. Algorithms

To process data, the standard library provides algorithms. Algorithms work with iterators to provide a row of elements on which the algorithm will apply.

The header <algorithm>

for_each

The for_each function is defined as:

```
Function for_each (InIt first, InIt last, Function function)
```

It calls for a function for each element of the row (first, last.

example:

```
vector<string>girls " Edith", "Lisa", "Audrey" -
std::for_each (girls), end (girls),
[](thong str)
    {
            cost << str << endl;
    }
);
```

Transform

The std::trasnform() function transforms all the elements in the row (first1, last1) and the operation is called on each of the values. The resultis placed in the output iterator (target).

```
auto it1 - std::transform (begin (girls), end (girls), begin (girls),
[](thong str)
    {
            return str - ": love!" ;
    }
);
for (thong str: girls)
{
    cost << str << endl;
}
```

In this example, each channel is given a "love!"

Check for items

The following functions return true if all or none or at least one of the elements in the row (first, last) satisfies the predicate:

- std::all_of

Professional C++ - Philosophy and Principles

- std::none_of
- std::any_of

example:

```
bool res1 - std::all_of (begin(girls), end (girls), [](thong   str)
        {
                if (str.find ('e')- string::npos)
                        falsereturn;
                Else
                        returntrue;
        }
);
```

Find items

The following features search for the first item in a row of items (first, last):

- std::find
- std::find_if
- std::find_if_not

example:

```
vector<int>v1, 20, 30, 40, 50, 1, 2, 3, 4, 5, 100, 101, 102;
auto it - find_if (begin(v1), end (v1), [](int   i)
        {
                return(i.e.,3) - 0;
        }
);
```

If you want to get more than one item, you have to use std::copy_if(). Example:

```
std::vector<int>viA 1, 2, 5, 10, 15, 20;
std::vector<int>destA (viA.size));
auto itA - std::copy_if (viA.begin(), viA.end(),
destA.begin(),[int   ii)
return (ii% 2 -0);
        });
shrink container to new size
destA.resize (std::d istance (destA.begin));
output
std::cout <<  "copy_if dest:";
std::copy (destA.begin(), destA.end(),
std::ostream_iterator<int>(std::cout,  "));
std::cost <<   std::endl;
```

There are also:

- std::find_first_of
- std::adjacent_find

Find Min/Max items

The following functions search for the minimum, maximum or min/max pair in a row of items:

- std::min_element
- std::max_element
- std::minmax_element

example:

```
std::vector<int>viB 1, 2, 5, 10, 15, 20;
int a10 - std::rand();
int b10 - std::rand();
int resmin10 - std::min (a10, b10);
int resmax10 - std::max (a10, b10);
std::cout <<   a10   <<," "<<   b10
<<": min:"  <<   resmin10
<<": max:"  <<   resmax10   <<  endl;
```

Binary search

To find an item in a row (first, last),there are:

- std::binary_search

Example:

```
std::vector<int>viC 1, 2, 5, 10, 15, 20;
iC int - 10;
if (std::binary_search (viC.begin(), viC.end(), iC))
{
cost <<   found!"   <<  endl;
}
```

There is alsoa version that gives the low, high limit and both:

- std::equal_ranger
- std::lower_bound
- std::upper_bound

Search other

Other search features include:

Professional C++ - Philosophy and Principles

- std::search
- std::find_end
- std::search_n

The search() function looks for a seque que of consecutive elements between two containers. Example:

```
std::vector<int>viD 1, 2, 5, 10, 15, 20;
std::vector<int>siD 5, 10, 15;
auto itD - std::search (viD.begin(), viD.end(),
    siD.begin(), siD.end());
if (itD!  viD.end))
{
cost <<  "found!" <<  endl;
}
```

The head <functional> provides the following types of research:

- std::d efault-searcher : linear algorithm (like std::search))
- std::boyer_moore_searcher
- std::boyer_moore_horspool_searcher

Comparison sequences

Here are some comparison features:

- std::equal
- std::mismatch

Example:

```
std::vector<int>viE 5, 10, 15;
std::vector<int>viF 5, 10, 15;
if (std::equal (viE.begin(), viE.end(), viF.begin())
{
cost <<  "equal!" <<  endl;
}
```

Generation sequences

Here are some generation features:

- std::fill
- std::fill_n

- std::generate
- std::generate_n
- std::iota

Example of filling a vector with 0:

```
std::vector<int>viG 1, 2, 4, 5, 10, 15;
std::fill (viG.begin(), viG.end(), 0);
output
std::cout <<  "dest:";
std::copy (viG.begin(), viG.end(),
std::ostream_iterator<int>(std::cout,  "));
std::cost <<   std::endl;
```

exit:

```
dest: 0 0 0 0 0 0 0
```

Copy, Move, Exchange

Other features include:

- std::copy
- std::copy_if
- std::copy_backward
- std::copy_n
- std::move
- std::move_backward
- std::iter_swap

Sample copy of items:

```
std::vector<int>viH 1, 2, 5, 10, 15, 20;
std::vector<int>viI 50, 100, 150;
std::copy (viI.begin(), viI.end(),
   std::back_inserter (viH));
output
std::cout <<   "copy dest:";
std::copy (viH.begin(), viH.end(),
std::ostream_iterator<int>(std::cout,  "));
std::cost <<   std::endl;
```

exit:

```
copy dest: 1 2 5 10 15 20 50 100 150
```

Professional C++ - Philosophy and Principles

Delete and Replace

Other features include:

- std::remove
- std::remove_if
- std::unique
- std::replace
- std::replace_if
- std::remove_copy
- std::unique_copy
- std::replace_copy
- std::replace_copy_if

example:

```
vector<int> v2 - 1.2,2,3,3,4.5.5
auto it2 - std::unique (begin(v2), end (v2));
v2.erase (it2, end(v2));
```

Reversal and Rotations

Other features include:

- std::reverse
- std::rotate
- std::rotate_copy

Example of element reversal:

```
std::vector<int>viJ 1, 2, 5, 10, 15, 20;
std::reverse (viJ.begin(), viJ.end());
output
std::cost <<  "reverse dest:";
std::copy (viJ.begin(), viJ.end(),
std::ostream_iterator<int>(std::cout,  "));
std::cost <<   std::endl;
```

exit:

```
reverse dest: 20 15 10 5 2 1
```

Partying

Other features include:

- std::is_partioned
- std::p artition
- std::stable_partition
- std::p artition-copy
- std::p artition-point

Example of partitioning:

```
std::vector<int>viK 1, 2, 3, 4, 5, 6, 7, 8, 9, 10-
auto itK - std::p artition (viK.begin(), viK.end(),
[](int  ii)
return (ii%  2 -0);
      });
output
std::cout <<  "partition dest:";
std::copy (viK.begin)), itK,
std::ostream_iterator<int>(std::cout,  "));
std::cost <<  "O";
std::copy (itK, viK.end),
std::ostream_iterator<int>(std::cout,  "));
std::cost <<   std::endl;
```

exit:

```
partition dest: 10 2 8 4 6 - 5 7 3 9 1
```

sort

Other features include:

- std::out
- std::stable_sort
- std::p artial-sort
- std::p artial-sort-copy
- std::is_sorted
- std::is_sorted_until
- std::lexicographical_compare

Professional C++ - Philosophy and Principles

- std::nth_element

Example of sorting:

```
std::vector<int>viL 10, 2, 50, 1, 150, 20, -5, 40;
std::sort (viL.begin(), viL.end());
output
std::cost <<  "sort dest:";
std::copy (viL.begin(), viL.end(),
std::ostream_iterator<int>(std::cout,  "));
std::cost <<   std::endl;
```

exit:

```
fate dest: -5 1 2 10 20 40 50 150
```

Sampling and Shuffling

Other features include:

- std:sample
- std::shuffle

Operations on sorted rows

Other features include:

- std::includes
- std::merge
- std::inplace_merge
- std::union
- std::set_intersection
- std::set_difference
- std::set_difference
- std::set_symetric_difference

Example of searching for non-consecutive items:

```
std::vector<int>viM 1, 2, 5, 10, 15, 20, 65;
std::vector<int>viN 10, 65;
if (std::includes (viM.begin(), viM.end(),
    viN.begin(), viN.end()))
{
cost <<  "includes!" <<  endl;
}
```

permutation

Other features include:

- std::is_permutation
- std::next_permutation
- std::p rev-permutation

Example of permutation:

```
std::vector<int>vi0 1, 2, 5;
std::sort (vi0.begin(), vi0.end());
do
{
    output
std::cost << "vi0:";
    std::copy (vi0.begin(), vi0.end(),
std::ostream_iterator<int>(std::cout, "));
std::cost << std::endl;
}
while (std::next_permutation (vi0.begin(),
    vi0.end()));
```

exit:

```
vi0: 1 2 5
vi0: 1 5 2
vi0: 2 1 5
vi0: 2 5 1
vi0: 5 1 2
vi0: 5 2 1
```

Heaps

Other features include:

- std::make_heap
- std::p ush-heap
- std::p op-heap
- std::sort_heap
- std::is_heap
- std::is_heap_until

Professional C++ - Philosophy and Principles

The header <numeric>

Reductions

Other features include:

- std::accumulated
- std::reduce
- std::transform_reduce

scalar product

Other features include:

- std::inner_product
- std::transform_reduce

Amounts and differences

Other features include:

- std::p artial-sum
- std::inclusive_scan
- std::exclusive_scan
- std::transform_inclusive
- std::transform_exclusive_scan
- std::adjacent_difference

The header <memory>

Memory algorithms

Other features include:

- std::uninitialized_default_construct
- std::uninitialized_value_construct
- std::uninitialized_value_construct_n
- std::uninitialized_copy
- std::uninitialized_copy_n
- std::uninitialized_move

- std::uninitialized_move_n
- std::uninitialized_fill
- std::uninitialized_fill_n
- std::d estroy
- std::d estroyon

The head <execution>

Parallel algorithms

All algorithms can run in parallel. Just put *a policy* first.

object	type	description
seq	`sequenced_policy`	The execution is not parallelized.
by	`parallel_policy`	The execution can be parallelized.
par_unseq	`parallel_unsequenced_policy`	The execution can be parallelized. To facilitate vectoring, function algorithm invocations are done on the same thread.

Sample code:

```
sequential
fate (v.begin(v.end));
sequential (same as the default)
fate(seq,v.begin(),v.end());
Parallel
fate (para,v.begin(),v.end());
parallel and/or vectorized
(par_unseq,v.begin(),v.end());
```

The header <iterator>

Iterator adapters

The standard library provides 5 iterator adapters:

- move_iterator
- reverse_iterator
- back_insert_iterator

203

- front_insert_iterator
- insert_iterator

To create the last three adapters, there are three functions:

- std::back_inserter()
- front_inserter
- insert ()

8. Memory Managment

Every application allocates memory. It's done either statically or dynamically. C++ provides the keyword new to make dynamic allocation. Modern C++ (C++11) and the standard library provides smart pointers that free memory automatically and developers can avoid usage of new!

Basic usage

When you need an object, you declare a class like:

```
MyClass mc;
mc.FunctionX();
```

It's very simple. Then you use your object's members directly. The problem with that is that you use plan old object and when you pass objects to functions, you make copy of the objects. It is not good practice. You should avoid copy of objects.

If you want to make dynamic allocation of memory, you can use the new keyword:

```
MyClass* pmc = new MyClass();
pmc->FunctionX();
```

In this case, you can pass the pointer among functions and everybody has access to the memory location of the object. It's better but its old school like C++03. We can do better and safer.

Prefer passing pointers or reference

If copying object is a mess, the way to follow is using pointers. If you want to address the address of the object, you use the & operator. In this case, you use one object at a time, it's always the same memory location that is accessed. When objects don't need to be modified, just pass a const ref &.

Pass Objects by Reference

The standard library provides std::ref() function to pass an object by reference.

Smart Pointers

Modern C++ provides unique_ptr<T> and shared_ptr<T> to bringing superior features compared to basic and raw pointers. With Modern C++, you can avoid new and delete usage. The <memory> header provides class templates that allow the developer to manage shared (shared_ptr) and non-shared pointers (unique_ptr). Shared pointers can be passed to functions but unique pointers don't because the = operator is deleted. To create a smart pointer, you have to call functions from the standard library:

Professional C++ - Philosophy and Principles

- make_unique for unique_ptr<T>
- make_shared for shared_ptr<T>

With smart pointers, the resources are freed when it out of the scope or when there is no more usage of it. Unique_ptr<T> is releasing resources when the object gets out of the scope block. For a shared_ptr<T>, there is a static usage counter inside and when the object is shared (shared ownership), the counter is incremented. The destructor makes a decrement of the counter and when its value is zero, the resources are freed. Those two templates are very sophisticated. They also allow to provide an allocator.

A closer look at shared_ptr

Some people think that C++ is a painful language because it does not have a garbage collector (GC) for managing automatic deletion of allocated resource. Sorry guys, we have the RIIA idiom. We rely on destructors and we have some modern patterns that are more efficient than GC and that does not cost some background threads that can freeze the whole system. Smart pointers and the dedicated shared_ptr is the best of the both world:

- automatic release of shared dynamic memory allocation of resources
- relying on destructors

The shared_ptr<T> template is a safe and secure way to handle automatic memory management facility. shared_ptr relies on a reference count that is incremented in ctor and decremented in dtor. It has the following attributes:

- std::shared_ptr has the double size of a raw pointer
- memory is allocated dynamically
- the reference count is incremented or decremented in a atomic way

shared_ptr handles move semantics. In this case; the reference counter is not incremented. Like std::unique_pointer, std::shared_ptr uses delete as its default resource destruction mech<<<<<<<anism but is also supports custom deleters. std::shared_ptr can be passed to functions but std::unique_ptr can't because the operator= is deleted for std::unique_ptr.

Using smart pointers

Shared_ptr has the get() function to return the raw pointer. The best practice is to not share shared_ptr on functions but use the * and get() function on the smart pointer to get a reference. Example:

```
class MyProduct
{
public:
    MyProduct(string name, float price)
        : _name(name), _price(price)
    {}
    ~MyProduct() {}
```

```cpp
        void Info() {
            cout << _name << ", "
                << _price << endl;
        }

    public:
        string _name;
        float _price;
};

void fn1(shared_ptr<MyProduct> product)
{
    product->_price += 10;
}

void fn2(MyProduct& product)
{
    product._price += 10;
}

void fn3(const MyProduct& product)
{
    cout << "fn3 price:"
        << product._price
        << endl;
}

void funcSmartPtr()
{
    unique_ptr<MyProduct> p1 = make_unique<MyProduct>("TV", 500);
    p1->Info();

    shared_ptr<MyProduct> ps1 = make_shared<MyProduct>("Dell XPS13", 1300);
    ps1->Info();
    fn1(ps1); // taking a shared_ptr
    ps1->Info();
    fn2(*ps1.get()); //taking an object or reference
    ps1->Info();
    fn3(*ps1.get()); // taking a const ref on MyProduct
    ps1->Info();
}
```

Look at fn1, fn2 and fn3 above. Each function has a different way to handle parameters:

- fn1 takes a shared pointer: shared_ptr<MyProduct>
- fn2 takes a reference: MyProduct&
- fn3 takes a const reference: const MyProduct&

Professional C++ - Philosophy and Principles

When I was a beginner with smart pointers, I used to share shared_ptr on functions. It's a not an elegant style. Prefer sharing reference or const references. It's more readable and the functions in class headers won't require shared_ptr annotations with types. It will be standard C++.

Prefer make_unique and make_shared instead of new

It is possible to write something like that:

```
unique_ptr<MyProduct> p0(new MyProduct("Android 9", 300));
p0->Info();
shared_ptr<MyProduct> ps0(new MyProduct("Microsoft Wireless Mouse", 25));
ps0->Info();
```

It works but's not the right way. It's not because new is used you have to delete your object. The smart pointer works! No need to use delete with smart pointers, either you allocate the object using new, make_unique or make_shared.

Use modern C++ ensure to not duplicate code. Example:

```
auto ptr1 = make_unique<MyProduct>("TV", 400);
auto ptr2 = make_shared<MyProduct>("ChromeBook", 250);
```

With auto, you don't have to duplicate the name of the class to create:

- in the type declaration name of the variable
- in the make_unique or make_shared

Using make_shared or make_unique lets the compiler generate smaller and faster code than a constructor with memory allocation done using new keyword.

The C routines alternative

When you need to allocate a lot of memory in a dynamic way, you should also make some experimentations with the C functions founded in the C Runtime like:

- malloc : allocate some memory
- calloc : allocate multiple blocks of memory
- free : free allocated memory

calloc means contiguous allocation. It allocates multiple blocks of memory in a dynamic way and it is used to allocate complex data structures or arrays.

malloc is used to allocate a single block of memory.

While those two functions are used to allocate memory space, the difference between malloc and calloc it that calloc can allocate multiple blocks at a single time, is most efficient and can allocate larger memory space and that the resulting memory is initialized to zero while malloc contains a garbage value.

```
int *ptr = (int *)calloc(10, sizeof(int));
free(ptr);
```

Under certain circumstance, you may want to reallocate memory. In this case, you can use realloc() function. realloc can expand or reduce the quantity of allocated memory.

Game Development and Embedded Devices Specific Cases

For game development and embedded devices, there are some specific issue and particulary in memory management rules. It's more than best Practices. It's the Law Tables, a series of golden rules you have to follow. If you don't follow these rules, your application will failed under certain context like, devices powered with few memory, low cpu, old compilers, etc.

On an embedded device or military project for example or industrial project, your hardware is not a traditional server with multiple GB. On embedded devices, hardware is restricted on resources and you can write source code like a traditional application with assumption like "we have all the memory we want, its' available!". You need to allocate memory on startup and you can't allocate dynamic memory during the execution of your application. We can't rely on a hypothetical memory routine to fail and abort the program. Imagine an automatic car driving system. It needs to run, always. We can stand for an error in a middle of a trip. So you need to minimize some error trap. Dynamic memory allocation is prohibited. You do it on startup by allocation a large amount of memory you need and the, you play with it.

It's a common pattern for industrial system, embedded devices (portable ones, not heavy machines) and game development.

Game Development

Game development is a big business. It's earning more money than the cinema (movie) industry. There are multiple platforms and multiple operating system. It a common situation to found a game on PC, Xbox, PS4, Android, iOS. So, what does it implies ? You have to make most of your code portable and have some limited specific platform code dependent to make the development phase easier. You will use different compilers and if you use the C++ Standard Template Library, you can face difficulties because of the various implementations of the STL based on the version of the C++ compilers can produces some different behaviors.

Writing platform dependent code is a problem but it is necessary. How does it works ? You have to include code with #ifdef directives. Example:

```
#if _WINDOWS
    // make specific Windows API calls
#else if _MACOS
    // make specific Mac OS calls
#else if _LINUX
    // make specific Linux calls
#endif
```

Professional C++ - Philosophy and Principles

Portable Development and Memory Allocation

On the Windows Operating System, also called Win32 API, there are several ways to allocated memory and it can be very efficient. Sometimes, it faster than STL and you can find function that offers features not covered in the STL. In this case, it's platform specific.

Windows Specific Development

For Windows development coding, you have to follow the Windows API documentation[111] step by step. It's not very complex but it's harder that C runtime or STL.

The Microsoft Press Windows API Reference Book

If you need to cover memory allocation on the Windows platform, you can find useful information in the popular Microsoft Press programming book[112] from Jeffrey Richter and Christophe Nasarre. Windows via C/C++ is the new name in its 5th Edition but the original name of the book is *Programming Applications for Microsoft Windows*. The Part III is covering Memory Management : The Windows Memory Architecture, The Virtual Memory and all you need to allocate and use virtual Memory. Under Windows, allocating memory for an application means, most of the times, allocating virtual memory.

Win32 Virtual Memory Functions – [EXTRACT FROM MICROSOFT.COM]

The virtual memory functions enable a process to manipulate or determine the status of pages in its virtual address space. They can perform the following operations:

- Reserve a range of a process's virtual address space. Reserving address space does not allocate any physical storage, but it prevents other allocation operations from using the specified range. It does not affect the virtual address spaces of other processes. Reserving pages prevents needless consumption of physical storage, while enabling a process to reserve a range of its address space into which a dynamic data structure can grow. The process can allocate physical storage for this space, as needed.
- Commit a range of reserved pages in a process's virtual address space so that physical storage (either in RAM or on disk) is accessible only to the allocating process.
- Specify read/write, read-only, or no access for a range of committed pages. This differs from the standard allocation functions that always allocate pages with read/write access.
- Free a range of reserved pages, making the range of virtual addresses available for subsequent allocation operations by the calling process.

---

[111] https://docs.microsoft.com/en-us/windows/win32/api/

[112] Windows via C/C++ 5th Edition, Microsoft Press, 2007

- Decommit a range of committed pages, releasing their physical storage and making it available for subsequent allocation by any process.
- Lock one or more pages of committed memory into physical memory (RAM) so that the system cannot swap the pages out to the paging file.
- Obtain information about a range of pages in the virtual address space of the calling process or a specified process.
- Change the access protection for a specified range of committed pages in the virtual address space of the calling process or a specified process.

Win32 VirtualAlloc Reference API Documentation

Under the Win32 API, the main API to allocate and set flags on memory is VirtualAlloc[113]:

```
PVOID VirtualAlloc(
    PVOID pvAddress,
    SIZE_T dwSize,
    DWORD fdwAllocationType,
    DWORD fdwProtect);
```

The Microsoft Docs gives the following description:

Reserves, commits, or changes the state of a region of pages in the virtual address space of the calling process. Memory allocated by this function is automatically initialized to zero.

Remarks:

Each page has an associated page state. The VirtualAlloc function can perform the following operations:

- Commit a region of reserved pages
- Reserve a region of free pages
- Simultaneously reserve and commit a region of free pages

VirtualAlloc cannot reserve a reserved page. It can commit a page that is already committed. This means you can commit a range of pages, regardless of whether they have already been committed, and the function will not fail.

You can use VirtualAlloc to reserve a block of pages and then make additional calls to VirtualAlloc to commit individual pages from the reserved block. This enables a process to reserve a range of its virtual address space without consuming physical storage until it is needed.

If the lpAddress parameter is not NULL, the function uses the lpAddress and dwSize parameters to compute the region of pages to be allocated. The current state of the entire range of pages must be compatible with the type of allocation

---

[113] https://docs.microsoft.com/en-us/windows/win32/api/memoryapi/nf-memoryapi-virtualalloc

specified by the flAllocationType parameter. Otherwise, the function fails and none of the pages are allocated. This compatibility requirement does not preclude committing an already committed page, as mentioned previously.

To execute dynamically generated code, use VirtualAlloc to allocate memory and the VirtualProtect function to grant PAGE_EXECUTE access.

The VirtualAlloc function can be used to reserve an Address Windowing Extensions (AWE) region of memory within the virtual address space of a specified process. This region of memory can then be used to map physical pages into and out of virtual memory as required by the application. The MEM_PHYSICAL and MEM_RESERVE values must be set in the AllocationType parameter. The MEM_COMMIT value must not be set. The page protection must be set to PAGE_READWRITE.

The VirtualFree function can decommit a committed page, releasing the page's storage, or it can simultaneously decommit and release a committed page. It can also release a reserved page, making it a free page.

When creating a region that will be executable, the calling program bears responsibility for ensuring cache coherency via an appropriate call to FlushInstructionCache once the code has been set in place. Otherwise attempts to execute code out of the newly executable region may produce unpredictable results.

If you want to find all the memory management functions for the Win32, please refer to the Microsoft Docs documentation[114]. There are multiple categories:

- General memory functions
- Data execution prevention functions
- File mapping functions
- AWE functions
- Heap functions
- Virtual memory functions
- Global and local functions
- Bad memory functions
- Enclave functions
- ATL thunk functions
- Obsolete functions

Comparing Memory Allocation Methods by Microsoft

The following is a brief comparison of the various memory allocation methods:

- CoTaskMemAlloc
- GlobalAlloc
- HeapAlloc

---

[114] https://docs.microsoft.com/en-us/windows/win32/memory/memory-management-functions

- LocalAlloc
- malloc
- new
- VirtualAlloc

Although the GlobalAlloc, LocalAlloc, and HeapAlloc functions ultimately allocate memory from the same heap, each provides a slightly different set of functionality. For example, HeapAlloc can be instructed to raise an exception if memory could not be allocated, a capability not available with LocalAlloc. LocalAlloc supports allocation of handles which permit the underlying memory to be moved by a reallocation without changing the handle value, a capability not available with HeapAlloc.

Starting with 32-bit Windows, GlobalAlloc and LocalAlloc are implemented as wrapper functions that call HeapAlloc using a handle to the process's default heap. Therefore, GlobalAlloc and LocalAlloc have greater overhead than HeapAlloc.

Because the different heap allocators provide distinctive functionality by using different mechanisms, you must free memory with the correct function. For example, memory allocated with HeapAlloc must be freed with HeapFree and not LocalFree or GlobalFree. Memory allocated with GlobalAlloc or LocalAlloc must be queried, validated, and released with the corresponding global or local function.

The VirtualAlloc function allows you to specify additional options for memory allocation. However, its allocations use a page granularity, so using VirtualAlloc can result in higher memory usage.

The malloc function has the disadvantage of being run-time dependent. The new operator has the disadvantage of being compiler dependent and language dependent.

The CoTaskMemAlloc function has the advantage of working well in either C, C++, or Visual Basic. It is also the only way to share memory in a COM-based application, since MIDL uses CoTaskMemAlloc and CoTaskMemFree to marshal memory.

Linux Development

Instead of Windows Operating System, Linux makes the promotion of the C Runtime instead of proprietary functions in most of its source code applications. You rely on calloc, malloc, realloc and free.

Professional C++ - Philosophy and Principles

There are some specific API from the kernel in the core API[115] like kmalloc[116] and vmalloc[117].

All the memory management functions API list is available here[118].

---

[115] https://www.kernel.org/doc/html/latest/core-api/memory-allocation.html

[116] https://www.kernel.org/doc/htmldocs/kernel-api/API-kmalloc.html

[117] https://www.kernel.org/doc/htmldocs/kernel-api/API-vmalloc.html

[118] https://www.kernel.org/doc/htmldocs/kernel-api/ch04s03.html

9. EASTL study

EASTL means Electronic Arts Standard Template Library

The case study is Electronic Arts and the study is based on an electronic paper called EASTL – Electronic Arts Standard Template Library[119] published on 2007-04-27 by Paul Pedriana. The document abstract is telling that:

Gaming platforms and game designs place requirements on game software which differ from requirements of other platforms. Most significantly, game software requires large amounts of memory but has a limited amount to work with. Gaming software is also faced with other limitations such as weaker processor caches, weaker CPUs, and non-default memory alignment requirements. A result of this is that game software needs to be careful with its use of memory and the CPU. The C++ standard library's containers, iterators, and algorithms are potentially useful for a variety of game programming needs. However, weaknesses and omissions of the standard library prevent it from being ideal for high performance game software. Foremost among these weaknesses is the allocator model. An extended and partially redesigned replacement (EASTL) for the C++ standard library was implemented at Electronic Arts in order to resolve these weaknesses in a portable and consistent way. This paper describes game software development issues, perceived weaknesses of the current C++ standard, and the design of EASTL as a partial solution for these weaknesses.

The EASTL project is available on Github[120]. EASTL is covered in the next chapter with a lot of details AS EXACTLY IT IS PRESENTED IN GITHUB MD FILES[121].

Credits And Maintainers

EASTL was created by Paul Pedriana and he maintained the project for roughly 10 years.

EASTL was subsequently maintained by Roberto Parolin for more than 8 years. He was the driver and proponent for getting EASTL opensourced. Rob was a mentor to all members of the team and taught us everything we ever wanted to know about C++ spookyness.

After Rob, maintenance of EASTL passed to Max Winkler for roughly a year, until landing with its current maintainer Liam Mitchell.

Significant EASTL contributions were made by (in alphabetical order):

- Avery Lee
- Colin Andrews

---

[119] http://www.open-std.org/jtc1/sc22/wg21/docs/papers/2007/n2271.html

[120] https://github.com/electronicarts/EASTL

[121] https://github.com/electronicarts/EASTL/tree/master/doc/html

Professional C++ - Philosophy and Principles

- JP Flouret
- Liam Mitchell
- Matt Newport
- Max Winkler
- Paul Pedriana
- Roberto Parolin

License

Modified BSD License (3-Clause BSD license)

EASTL Modules

Module List

As you can read, it looks like a standard STL shipped by any C++ compiler.

Module	Description
config	Configuration header. Allows for changing some compile-time options.
slist fixed_slist	Singly-linked list. fixed_slist is a version which is implemented via a fixed block of contiguous memory.
list fixed_list	Doubly-linked list.
intrusive_list intrusive_slist	List whereby the contained item provides the node implementation.
array	Wrapper for a C-style array which extends it to act like an STL container.
vector fixed_vector	Resizable array container.
vector_set vector_multiset	Set implemented via a vector instead of a tree. Speed and memory use is improved but resizing is slower.
vector_map vector_multimap	Map implemented via a vector instead of a tree. Speed and memory use is improved but resizing is slower.
deque	Double-ended queue, but also with random access. Acts like a vector but insertions and removals are efficient.
bit_vector	Implements a vector of bool, but the actual storage is done with one bit per bool. Not the same thing as a bitset.
bitset	Implements an efficient arbitrarily-sized bitfield. Note that this is not strictly the same thing as a vector of bool (bit_vector), as it is optimized to act like an arbitrary set of flags and not to be a generic container which can be iterated, inserted, removed, etc.

Professional C++ - Philosophy and Principles

set multiset fixed_set fixed_multiset	A set is a sorted unique collection, multiset is sorted but non-unique collection.
map multimap fixed_map fixed_multimap	A map is a sorted associative collection implemented via a tree. It is also known as dictionary.
hash_map hash_multimap fixed_hash_map fixed_hash_multimap	Map implemented via a hash table.
intrusive_hash_map intrusive_hash_multimap intrusive_hash_set intrusive_hash_multiset	hash_map whereby the contained item provides the node implementation, much like intrusive_list.
hash_set hash_multiset fixed_hash_set fixed_hash_map	Set implemented via a hash table.
basic_string fixed_string fixed_substring	basic_string is a character string/array. fixed_substring is a string which is a reference to a range within another string or character array. cow_string is a string which implements copy-on-write.
algorithm	min/max, find, binary_search, random_shuffle, reverse, etc.
sort	Sorting functionality, including functionality not in STL. quick_sort, heap_sort, merge_sort, shell_sort, insertion_sort, etc.
numeric	Numeric algorithms: accumulate, inner_product, partial_sum, adjacent_difference, etc.
heap	Heap structure functionality: make_heap, push_heap, pop_heap, sort_heap, is_heap, remove_heap, etc.

stack	Adapts any container into a stack.	
queue	Adapts any container into a queue.	
priority_queue	Implements a conventional priority queue via a heap structure.	
type_traits	Type information, useful for writing optimized and robust code. Also used for implementing optimized containers and algorithms.	
utility	pair, make_pair, rel_ops, etc.	
functional	Function objects.	
iterator	Iteration for containers and algorithms.	
smart_ptr	Smart pointers: shared_ptr, shared_array, weak_ptr, scoped_ptr, scoped_array, linked_ptr, linked_array, intrusive_ptr.	

Module Behaviour

The overhead sizes listed here refer to an optimized release build; debug builds may add some additional overhead. Some of the overhead sizes may be off by a little bit (usually at most 4 bytes). This is because the values reported here are those that refer to when EASTL's container optimizations have been complete. These optimizations may not have been completed as you are reading this.

Xxx

Professional C++ - Philosophy and Principles

Container	Stores	Container Overhead (32 bit)	Container Overhead (64 bit)	Node Overhead (32 bit)	Node Overhead (64 bit)	Iterator category	size() efficiency	operator[] efficiency	Insert efficiency	Erase via Iterator efficiency	Find efficiency	Sort effici
slist	T	8	16	4	8	f	n	-	1	1	n	n-
list	T	12	24	8	16	b	n	-	1	1	n	n log
intrusive_slist	T	4	8	4	8	f	n	-	1	1	n	n-
intrusive_list	T	8	16	8	16	b	n	-	1	1	n	n log
array	T	0	0	0	0	r	1	1	-	-	n	n log
vector	T	16	32	0	0	r	1	1	1 at end, else n	1 at end, else n	n	n log
vector_set	T	16	32	0	0	r	1	1	1 at end, else n	1 at end, else n	log(n)	1
vector_multiset	T	16	32	0	0	r	1	1	1 at end, else n	1 at end, else n	log(n)	1
vector_map	Key, T	16	32	0	0	r	1	1	1 at end, else n	1 at end, else n	log(n)	1
vector_multimap	Key, T	16	32	0	0	r	1	1	1 at end, else n	1 at end, else n	log(n)	1
deque	T	44	84	0	0	r	1	1	1 at begin or end, else n / 2	1 at begin or end, else n / 2	n	n log
bit_vector	bool	8	16	0	0	r	1	1	1 at end, else n	1 at end, else n	n	n log
string (all types)	T	16	32	0	0	r	1	1	1 at end, else n	1 at end, else n	n	n log
set	T	24	44	16	28	b	1	-	log(n)	log(n)	log(n)	1
multiset	T	24	44	16	28	b	1	-	log(n)	log(n)	log(n)	1
map	Key, T	24	44	16	28	b	1	log(n)	log(n)	log(n)	log(n)	1
multimap	Key, T	24	44	16	28	b	1	-	log(n)	log(n)	log(n)	1
hash_set	T	16	20	4	8	b	1	-	1	1	1	-
hash_multiset	T	16	20	4	8	b	1	-	1	1	1	-
hash_map	Key, T	16	20	4	8	b	1	-	1	1	1	-
hash_multimap	Key, T	16	20	4	8	b	1	-	1	1	1	-
intrusive_hash_set	T	16	20	4	8	b	1	-	1	1	1	-
intrusive_hash_multiset	T	16	20	4	8	b	1	-	1	1	1	-
intrusive_hash_map	T (Key == T)	16	20	4	8	b	1	-	1	1	1	-
intrusive_hash_multimap	T (Key == T)	16	20	4	8	b	1	-	1	1	1	-

Notes:
- - means that the operation does not exist.
- 1 means amortized constant time. Also known as O(1)
- n means time proportional to the container size. Also known as O(n)
- log(n) means time proportional to the natural logarithm of the container size. Also known as O(log(n))
- n log(n) means time proportional to log(n) times the size of the container. Also known as O(n log(n))
- n+ means that the time is at least n, and possibly higher.
- Iterator meanings are: f = forward iterator; b = bidirectional iterator, r = random iterator.
- Overhead indicates approximate per-element overhead memory required in bytes. Overhead doesn't include possible additional overhead that may be imposed by the memory heap used to allocate nodes. General heaps tend to have between 4 and 16 bytes of overhead per allocation, depending on the heap.
- Some overhead values are dependent on the structure alignment characteristics in effect. The values reported here are those that would be in effect for a system that requires pointers to be aligned on boundaries of their size and allocations with a minimum of 4 bytes (thus one byte values get rounded up to 4).
- Some overhead values are dependent on the size_type used by containers. size_type defaults to size_t, but it is possible to force it to be 4 bytes for 64 bit machines by defining EASTL_SIZE_T_32BIT.
- Inserting at the end of a vector may cause the vector to be resized; resizing a vector is O(n). However, the amortized time complexity for vector insertions at the end is constant.
- Sort assumes the usage of the best possible sort for a large container of random data. Some sort algorithms (e.g. quick_sort) require random access iterators and so the sorting of some containers requires a different sort algorithm. We do not include bucket or radix sorts, as they are always O(n).

Some containers (e.g. deque, hash*) have unusual data structures that make per-container and per-node overhead calculations not quite account for all memory.

Glossary for the STL

The STL supports support a lot of features. Here is a Glossary from the EASTL:

adapter	An adapter is something that encapsulates a component to provide another interface, such as a C++ class which makes a stack out of a list.
algorithm	Algorithms are standalone functions which manipulate data which usually but not necessarily comes from a container. Some algorithms change the data while others don't. Examples are reverse, sort, find, and remove.
associative container	An associative container is a variable-sized container that supports efficient retrieval of elements (values) based on keys. It supports insertion and removal of elements, but differs from a sequence in that it does not provide a mechanism for inserting an element at a specific position. Associative containers include map, multimap, set, multiset, hash_map, hash_multimap, hash_set, hash_multiset.
array	An array is a C++ container which directly implements a C-style fixed array but which adds STL container semantics to it.
basic_string	A templated string class which is usually used to store char or wchar_t strings.
begin	The function used by all conventional containers to return the first item in the container.
BidirectionalIterator	An input iterator which is like ForwardIterator except it can be read in a backward direction as well.
BinaryOperation	A function which takes two arguments and returns a value (which will usually be assigned to a third object).
BinaryPredicate	A function which takes two arguments and returns true if some criteria is met (e.g. they are equal).

Professional C++ - Philosophy and Principles

binder1st, binder2nd	These are function objects which convert one function object into another. In particular they implement a binary function whereby you can specify one of the arguments. This is somewhat abstract concept but has its uses.
bit vector	A specialized container that acts like vector<bool> but is implemented via one bit per er STL vector<bool> is usually implemented as a bit vector but EASTL avoids this in favor of specific bit vector container.
bitset	An extensible yet efficient implementation of bit flags. Not strictly a conventional STL container and not the same thing as vector<bool> or a bit_vector, both of which are for iterate-able containers.
capacity	Refers to the amount of total storage available in an array-based container such as vecte string, and array. Capacity is always >= container size and is > size in order to provide ex space for a container to grow into.
const_iterator	An iterator whose iterated items are cannot be modified. A const_iterator is akin to a cc pointer such as 'const char*'.
container	A container is an object that stores other objects (its elements), and that has methods fe accessing its elements. In particular, every type that is a model of container has an assoc iterator type that can be used to iterate through the container's elements.
copy constructor	A constructor for a type which takes another object of that type as its argument. For a hypothetical Widget class, the copy constructor is of the form Widget(const Widget& sr
Compare	A function which takes two arguments and returns the lesser of the two.
deque	The name deque is pronounced "deck" and stands for "double-ended queue."

		A deque is very much like a vector: like vector, it is a sequence that supports random access to elements, constant time insertion and removal of elements at the end of the sequence, and linear time insertion and removal of elements in the middle.
		The main way in which deque differs from vector is that deque also supports constant time insertion and removal of elements at the beginning of the sequence. Additionally, deque does not have any member functions analogous to vector's capacity() and reserve(), and does not provide the guarantees on iterator validity that are associated with those member functions.
difference_type		The typedef'd type used by all conventional containers and iterators to define the distance between two iterators. It is usually the same thing as the C/C++ ptrdiff_t data type.
empty		The function used by all conventional containers to tell if a container has a size of zero. In many cases empty is more efficient than checking for size() == 0.
element		An element refers to a member of a container.
end		The function used by all conventional containers to return one-past the last item in the container.
equal_range		equal_range is a version of binary search: it attempts to find the element value in an ordered range [first, last). The value returned by equal_range is essentially a combination of the values returned by lower_bound and upper_bound: it returns a pair of iterators i and j such that i is the first position where value could be inserted without violating the ordering and j is the last position where value could be inserted without violating the ordering. It follows that every element in the range [i, j) is equivalent to value, and that [i, j) is the largest subrange of [first, last) that has this property.

Professional C++ - Philosophy and Principles

explicit instantiation	Explicit instantiation lets you create an instantiation of a templated class or function with actually using it in your code. Since this is useful when you are creating library files that u templates for distribution, uninstantiated template definitions are not put into object files. An example of the syntax for explicit instantiation is:	
	template class vector<char>;	
	template void min<int>(int, int);	
	template void min(int, int);	
ForwardIterator	An input iterator which is like InputIterator except it can be reset back to the beginning.	
Function	A function which takes one argument and applies some operation to the target.	
function object, functor	A function object or functor is a class that has the function-call operator (operator()) defi	
Generator	A function which takes no arguments and returns a value (which will usually be assigned an object).	
hash_map, hash_multimap, hash_set, hash_multiset	The hash containers are implementations of map, multimap, set, and multiset via a hash instead of via a tree. Searches are O(1) (fast) but the container is not sorted.	
Heap	A heap is a data structure which is not necessarily sorted but is organized such that the highest priority item is at the top. A heap is synonymous with a priority queue and has numerous applications in computer science.	
InputIterator	An input iterator (iterator you read from) which allows reading each element only once a only in a forward direction.	

intrusive_list, intrusive_hash_map, etc.	Intrusive containers are containers which don't allocate memory but instead use their contained object to manage the container's memory. While list allocates nodes (with mpPrev/mpNext pointers) that contain the list items, intrusive_list doesn't allocate nodes but instead the container items have the mpPrev/mpNext pointers.
intrusive_ptr	intrusive_ptr is a smart pointer which doesn't allocate memory but instead uses the contained object to manage lifetime via addref and release functions.
Iterator	An iterator is the fundamental entity of reading and enumerating values in a container. Much like a pointer can be used to walk through a character array, an iterator is used to walk through a linked list.
iterator category	An iterator category defines the functionality the iterator provides. The conventional iterator categories are InputIterator, ForwardIterator, BidirectionalIterator, RandomAccessIterator, and OutputIterator. See the definitions of each of these for more information. Iterator category is synonymous with *iterator_tag*.
iterator_tag	See *iterator category*.
key_type, Key	A Key or key_type is the identifier used by associative (a.k.a. dictionary) containers (e.g. map, hash_map) to identify the type used to index the mapped_type. If you have a dictionary of strings that you access by an integer id, the ids are the keys and the strings are the mapped types.
lexicographical compare	A lexicographical compare is a comparison of two containers that compares them element by element, much like the C strcmp function compares two strings.

Professional C++ - Philosophy and Principles

linked_ptr	A linked_ptr is a shared smart pointer which implements object lifetime via a linked list of linked_ptrs that are referencing the object. linked_ptr, like intrusive_ptr, is a non-memory allocating alternative to shared_ptr.
list	A list is a doubly linked list. It is a sequence that supports both forward and backward traversal, and (amortized) constant time insertion and removal of elements at the beginning or the end, or in the middle. Lists have the important property that insertion and splicing not invalidate iterators to list elements, and that even removal invalidates only the iterators that point to the elements that are removed. The ordering of iterators may be changed (that is, list<T>::iterator might have a different predecessor or successor after a list operation it did before), but the iterators themselves will not be invalidated or made to point to different elements unless that invalidation or mutation is explicit.
lower_bound	lower_bound is a version of binary search: it attempts to find the element value in an ordered range [first, last). Specifically, it returns the first position where value could be inserted without violating the ordering.
map	Map is a sorted associative container that associates objects of type Key with objects of T. Map is a pair associative container, meaning that its value type is pair<const Key, T>. It is also a unique associative container, meaning that no two elements have the same key. Map is implemented with a tree structure.
mapped_type	A mapped_type is a typedef used by associative containers to identify the container object which is accessed by a key. If you have a dictionary of strings that you access by an integer, the ids are the keys and the strings are the mapped types.

member template	A member template is a templated function of a templated class. Thus with a member template function there are two levels of templating -- the class and the function.
multimap,	Multimap is a sorted associative container that associates objects of type Key with objects of type T. multimap is a pair associative container, meaning that its value type is pair<const Key, T>. It is also a multiple associative container, meaning that there is no limit on the number of elements with the same key. It is implemented with a tree structure.
multiset	Multiset is a sorted associative container that stores objects of type Key. Its value type, as well as its key type, is Key. It is also a multiple associative container, meaning that two or more elements may be identical. It is implemented with a tree structure.
node	A node is a little holder class used by many containers to hold the contained items. A linked-list, for example, defines a node which has three members: mpPrev, mpNext, and T (the contained object).
npos	npos is used by the string class to identify a non-existent index. Some string functions return npos to indicate that the function failed.
rel_ops	rel_ops refers to "relational operators" and is a set of templated functions which provide operator!= for classes that have only operator== and provide operator > for classes that have only operator <, etc. Unfortunately, rel_ops have a habit of polluting the global operator space and creating conflicts. They must be used with discretion.

Professional C++ - Philosophy and Principles

reverse_iterator	A reverse_iterator is an iterator which wraps a bidirectional or random access iterator and allows the iterator to be read in reverse direction. The difference between using reverse_iterators and just decrementing regular iterators is that reverse_iterators use operator++ to move backwards and thus work in any algorithm that calls ++ to move through a container.
OutputIterator	An output iterator (iterator you write to) which allows writing each element only once in in a forward direction.
POD	POD means Plain Old Data. It refers to C++ classes which act like built-in types and C structs. These are useful to distinguish because some algorithms can be made more efficient when they can detect that they are working with PODs instead of regular classes.
Predicate	A function which takes one argument returns true if the argument meets some criteria.
priority_queue	A priority_queue is an adapter container which implements a heap via a random access container such as vector or deque.
queue	A queue is an adapter container which implements a FIFO (first-in, first-out) container with which you can add items to the back and get items from the front.
RandomAccessIterator	An input iterator which can be addressed like an array. It is a superset of all other input iterators.
red-black tree	A red-black tree is a binary tree which has the property of being always balanced. The colors red and black are somewhat arbitrarily named monikers for nodes used to measure the balance of the tree. Red-black trees are considered the best all-around data structure for sorted containers.
scalar	A scalar is a data type which is implemented via a numerical value. In C++ this means integers, floating point values, enumerations, and pointers.

scoped_ptr	A scoped_ptr is a smart pointer which is the same as C++ auto_ptr except that it cannot be copied.
set	Set is a sorted associative container that stores objects of type Key. Its value type, as well as its key type, is Key. It is also a unique associative container, meaning that no two elements are the same. It is implemented with a tree structure.
sequence	A sequence is a variable-sized container whose elements are arranged in a strict linear (though not necessarily contiguous) order. It supports insertion and removal of elements. Sequence containers include vector, deque, array, list, slist.
size	All conventional containers have a size member function which returns the count of elements in the container. The efficiency of the size function differs between containers.
size_type	The type that a container uses to define its size and counts. This is similar to the C/C++ size_t type but may be specialized for the container. It defaults to size_t, but it is possible to force it to be 4 bytes for 64 bit machines by defining EASTL_SIZE_T_32BIT.
skip list	A skip-list is a type of container which is an alternative to a binary tree for finding data.
shared_ptr	A shared_ptr is a smart pointer which allows multiple references (via multiple shared_ptrs) to the same object. When the last shared_ptr goes away, the pointer is freed. shared_ptr is implemented via a shared count between all instances.
Slist	An slist is like a list but is singly-linked instead of doubly-linked. It can only be iterated in a forward-direction.
smart pointer	Smart pointer is a term that identifies a family of utility classes which store pointers and free them when the class instance goes out of scope. Examples of smart pointers are shared_ptr, linked_ptr, intrusive_ptr, and scoped_ptr.

Professional C++ - Philosophy and Principles

Splice	Splicing refers to the moving of a subsequence of one Sequence into another Sequence.
Stack	A stack is a adapter container which implements LIFO (last-in, first, out) access via another container such as a list or deque.
STL	Standard Template Library.
StrictWeakOrdering	A BinaryPredicate that compares two objects, returning true if the first precedes the second. Like Compare but has additional requirements. Used for sorting routines.
	This predicate must satisfy the standard mathematical definition of a strict weak ordering. StrictWeakOrdering has to behave the way that "less than" behaves: if a is less than b then b is not less than a, if a is less than b and b is less than c then a is less than c, and so on.
String	See basic_string.
T	T is the template parameter name used by most containers to identify the contained element type.
template parameter	A template parameter is the templated type used to define a template function or class. the declaration 'template <typename T> class vector{ },' T is a template parameter.
template specialization	A template specialization is a custom version of a template which overrides the default version and provides alternative functionality, often for the purpose of providing improved or specialized functionality.
treap	A tree-like structure implemented via a heap. This is an alternative to a binary tree (e.g. black tree), skip-list, and sorted array as a mechanism for a fast-access sorted container

type traits	Type traits are properties of types. If you have a templated type T and you want to know if it is a pointer, you would use the is_pointer type trait. If you want to know if the type is a POD, you would use the is_pod type trait. Type traits are very useful for allowing the implementation of optimized generic algorithms and for asserting that types have properties expected by the function or class contract. For example, you can use type_traits to tell if a type can be copied via memcpy instead of a slower element-by-element copy.
typename	Typename is a C++ keyword used in templated function implementations which identifies to the compiler that the following expression is a type and not a value. It is used extensively in EASTL, particularly in the algorithms.
UnaryOperation	A function which takes one argument and returns a value (which will usually be assigned to second object).
upper_bound	upper_bound is a version of binary search: it attempts to find the element value in an ordered range [first, last). Specifically, it returns the last position where value could be inserted without violating the ordering.
value_type, Value	A value_type is a typedef used by all containers to identify the elements they contain. In most cases value_type is simply the same thing as the user-supplied T template parameter. The primary exception is the associative containers whereby value_type is the pair of key_type and mapped_type.
vector	A vector is a Sequence that supports random access to elements, constant time insertion and removal of elements at the end, and linear time insertion and removal of elements at the beginning or in the middle. The number of elements in a vector may vary dynamically; memory management is automatic. Vector is the simplest of the container classes, and in many cases the most efficient.

Professional C++ - Philosophy and Principles

vector_map, vector_multimap, vector_set, vector_multiset	These are containers that implement the functionality of map, multimap, set, and multiset via a vector or deque instead of a tree. They use less memory and find items faster, but are slower to modify and modification invalidates iterators.
weak_ptr	A weak_ptr is an adjunct to shared_ptr which doesn't increment the reference on the contained object but can safely tell you if the object still exists and access it if so. It has use in preventing circular references in shared_ptrs.

You can see that some items in the glossary are not usual STL items.

A High Performance STL

Each option taken in EASTL is made for a defined goal: the performance of the STL for each target platform, for each compiler and so there are some things to avoid and prohibit.

Design of the EASTL

EASTL (EA Standard Template Library) is designed to be a template library which encompasses and extends the functionality of standard C++ STL while improving it in various ways useful to game development. Much of EASTL's design is identical to standard STL, as the large majority of the STL is well-designed for many uses. The primary areas where EASTL deviates from standard STL implementations are essentially the following:
- EASTL has a simplified and more flexible custom allocation scheme.
- EASTL has significantly easier to read code.
- EASTL has extension containers and algorithms.
- EASTL has optimizations designed for game development.

Of the above items, the only one which is an incompatible difference with STL is the case of memory allocation. The method for defining a custom allocator for EASTL is slightly different than that of standard STL, though they are 90% similar. The 10% difference, however, is what makes EASTL generally easier and more powerful to work with than standard STL. Containers without custom allocators act identically between EASTL and standard STL.

Motivations

Our motivations for making EASTL drive the design of EASTL. As identified in the EASTL RFC (Request for Comment), the primary reasons for implementing a custom version of the STL are:

- Some STL implementations (especially Microsoft STL) have inferior performance characteristics that make them unsuitable for game development. EASTL is faster than all existing STL implementations.
- The STL is sometimes hard to debug, as most STL implementations use cryptic variable names and unusual data structures.

- STL allocators are sometimes painful to work with, as they have many requirements and cannot be modified once bound to a container.
- The STL includes excess functionality that can lead to larger code than desirable. It's not very easy to tell programmers they shouldn't use that functionality.
- The STL is implemented with very deep function calls. This results is unacceptable performance in non-optimized builds and sometimes in optimized builds as well.
- The STL doesn't support alignment of contained objects.
- STL containers won't let you insert an entry into a container without supplying an entry to copy from. This can be inefficient.
- Useful STL extensions (e.g. slist, hash_map, shared_ptr) found in existing STL implementations such as STLPort are not portable because they don't exist in other versions of STL or aren't consistent between STL versions.
- The STL lacks useful extensions that game programmers find useful (e.g. intrusive_list) but which could be best optimized in a portable STL environment.
- The STL has specifications that limit our ability to use it efficiently. For example, STL vectors are not guaranteed to use contiguous memory and so cannot be safely used as an array.
- The STL puts an emphasis on correctness before performance, whereas sometimes you can get significant performance gains by making things less academcially pure.
- STL containers have private implementations that don't allow you to work with their data in a portable way, yet sometimes this is an important thing to be able to do (e.g. node pools).
- All existing versions of STL allocate memory in empty versions of at least some of their containers. This is not ideal and prevents optimizations such as container memory resets that can greatly increase performance in some situations.
- The STL is slow to compile, as most modern STL implementations are very large.
- There are legal issues that make it hard for us to freely use portable STL implementations such as STLPort.
- We have no say in the design and implementation of the STL and so are unable to change it to work for our needs.

Prime Directives

The implementation of EASTL is guided foremost by the following directives which are listed in order of importance.

- Efficiency (speed and memory usage)
- Correctness
- Portability
- Readability

Note that unlike commercial STL implementations which must put correctness above all, we put a higher value on efficiency. As a result, some functionality may have some usage limitation that is not present in other similar systems but which allows for more efficient operation, especially on the platforms of significance to us.

Portability is significant, but not critical. Yes, EASTL must compile and run on all platforms that we will ship games for. But we don't take that to mean under all compilers that could be conceivably used for such platforms. For example, Microsoft VC6 can be used to compile Windows programs, but VC6's C++ support is too weak for EASTL and so you simply cannot use EASTL under VC6.

Readability is something that EASTL achieves better than many other templated libraries, particularly Microsoft STL and STLPort. We make every attempt to make EASTL code clean and sensible. Sometimes our need to provide optimizations (particularly related to type_traits and iterator types) results in less simple code, but efficiency happens to be our prime directive and so it overrides all other considerations.

Professional C++ - Philosophy and Principles

Thread Safety

It's not simple enough to simply say that EASTL is thread-safe or thread-unsafe. However, we can say that with respect to thread safety that EASTL does the right thing.

Individual EASTL containers are not thread-safe. That is, access to an instance of a container from multiple threads at the same time is unsafe if any of those accesses are modifying operations. A given container can be read from multiple threads simultaneously as well as any other standalone data structure. If a user wants to be able to have modifying access an instance of a container from multiple threads, it is up to the user to ensure that proper thread synchronization occurs. This usually means using a mutex.

EASTL classes other than containers are the same as containers with respect to thread safety. EASTL functions (e.g. algorithms) are inherently thread-safe as they have no instance data and operate entirely on the stack. As of this writing, no EASTL function allocates memory and thus doesn't bring thread safety issues via that means.

The user may well need to be concerned about thread safety with respect to memory allocation. If the user modifies containers from multiple threads, then allocators are going to be accessed from multiple threads. If an allocator is shared across multiple container instances (of the same type of container or not), then mutexes (as discussed above) the user uses to protect access to indivudual instances will not suffice to provide thread safety for allocators used across multiple instances. The conventional solution here is to use a mutex within the allocator if it is exected to be used by multiple threads.

EASTL uses neither static nor global variables and thus there are no inter-instance dependencies that would make thread safety difficult for the user to implement.

EASTL Design

EASTL (EA Standard Template Library) is designed to be a template library which encompasses and extends the functionality of standard C++ STL while improving it in various ways useful to game development. Much of EASTL's design is identical to standard STL, as the large majority of the STL is well-designed for many uses. The primary areas where EASTL deviates from standard STL implementations are essentially the following:

- EASTL has a simplified and more flexible custom allocation scheme.
- EASTL has significantly easier to read code.
- EASTL has extension containers and algorithms.
- EASTL has optimizations designed for game development.

Of the above items, the only one which is an incompatible difference with STL is the case of memory allocation. The method for defining a custom allocator for EASTL is slightly different than that of standard STL, though they are 90% similar. The 10% difference, however, is what makes EASTL generally easier and more powerful to work with than standard STL. Containers without custom allocators act identically between EASTL and standard STL.

Motivations

Our motifications for making EASTL drive the design of EASTL. As identified in the EASTL RFC (Request for Comment), the primary reasons for implementing a custom version of the STL are:

- Some STL implementations (especially Microsoft STL) have inferior performance characteristics that make them unsuitable for game development. EASTL is faster than all existing STL implementations.
- The STL is sometimes hard to debug, as most STL implementations use cryptic variable names and unusual data structures.
- STL allocators are sometimes painful to work with, as they have many requirements and cannot be modified once bound to a container.
- The STL includes excess functionality that can lead to larger code than desirable. It's not very easy to tell programmers they shouldn't use that functionality.
- The STL is implemented with very deep function calls. This results is unacceptable performance in non-optimized builds and sometimes in optimized builds as well.
- The STL doesn't support alignment of contained objects.
- STL containers won't let you insert an entry into a container without supplying an entry to copy from. This can be inefficient.
- Useful STL extensions (e.g. slist, hash_map, shared_ptr) found in existing STL implementations such as STLPort are not portable because they don't exist in other versions of STL or aren't consistent between STL versions.
- The STL lacks useful extensions that game programmers find useful (e.g. intrusive_list) but which could be best optimized in a portable STL environment.
- The STL has specifications that limit our ability to use it efficiently. For example, STL vectors are not guaranteed to use contiguous memory and so cannot be safely used as an array.
- The STL puts an emphasis on correctness before performance, whereas sometimes you can get significant performance gains by making things less academcially pure.
- STL containers have private implementations that don't allow you to work with their data in a portable way, yet sometimes this is an important thing to be able to do (e.g. node pools).
- All existing versions of STL allocate memory in empty versions of at least some of their containers. This is not ideal and prevents optimizations such as container memory resets that can greatly increase performance in some situations.
- The STL is slow to compile, as most modern STL implementations are very large.
- There are legal issues that make it hard for us to freely use portable STL implementations such as STLPort.
- We have no say in the design and implementation of the STL and so are unable to change it to work for our needs.

Prime Directives

The implementation of EASTL is guided foremost by the following directives which are listed in order of importance.

1. Efficiency (speed and memory usage)
2. Correctness
3. Portability
4. Readability

Note that unlike commercial STL implementations which must put correctness above all, we put a higher value on efficiency. As a result, some functionality may have some usage limitation that is not present in other similar systems but which allows for more efficient operation, especially on the platforms of significance to us.

Portability is significant, but not critical. Yes, EASTL must compile and run on all platforms that we will ship games for. But we don't take that to mean under all compilers that could be conceivably used for such platforms. For example, Microsoft VC6 can be used to compile Windows programs, but VC6's C++ support is too weak for EASTL and so you simply cannot use EASTL under VC6.

Professional C++ - Philosophy and Principles

Readability is something that EASTL achieves better than many other templated libraries, particularly Microsoft STL and STLPort. We make every attempt to make EASTL code clean and sensible. Sometimes our need to provide optimizations (particularly related to type_traits and iterator types) results in less simple code, but efficiency happens to be our prime directive and so it overrides all other considerations.

Thread Safety

It's not simple enough to simply say that EASTL is thread-safe or thread-unsafe. However, we can say that with respect to thread safety that EASTL does the right thing.

Individual EASTL containers are not thread-safe. That is, access to an instance of a container from multiple threads at the same time is unsafe if any of those accesses are modifying operations. A given container can be read from multiple threads simultaneously as well as any other standalone data structure. If a user wants to be able to have modifying access an instance of a container from multiple threads, it is up to the user to ensure that proper thread synchronization occurs. This usually means using a mutex.

EASTL classes other than containers are the same as containers with respect to thread safety. EASTL functions (e.g. algorithms) are inherently thread-safe as they have no instance data and operate entirely on the stack. As of this writing, no EASTL function allocates memory and thus doesn't bring thread safety issues via that means.

The user may well need to be concerned about thread safety with respect to memory allocation. If the user modifies containers from multiple threads, then allocators are going to be accessed from multiple threads. If an allocator is shared across multiple container instances (of the same type of container or not), then mutexes (as discussed above) the user uses to protect access to indivudual instances will not suffice to provide thread safety for allocators used across multiple instances. The conventional solution here is to use a mutex within the allocator if it is excted to be used by multiple threads.

EASTL uses neither static nor global variables and thus there are no inter-instance dependencies that would make thread safety difficult for the user to implement.

Containers Efficiencies

Container	empty() efficiency	size() efficiency	operator[] efficiency	insert() efficiency	erase() efficiency	find() efficiency	sort efficiency
slist	1	O(n)	-	O(1)	O(1)	O(n)	O(n+)
list	1	n	-	1	1	n	n log(n)
intrusive_slist	1	n	-	1	1	1	n+
intrusive_list	1	n	-	1	1	1	n log(n)
array	1	1	1	-	-	n	n log(n)
vector	1	1^a	1	1 at end, else n	1 at end, else n	n	n log(n)
vector_set	1	1^a	1	1 at end, else n	1 at end, else n	log(n)	1
vector_multiset	1	1^a	1	1 at end, else n	1 at end, else n	log(n)	1
vector_map	1	1^a	1	1 at end, else n	1 at end, else n	log(n)	1
vector_multimap	1	1^a	1	1 at end, else n	1 at end, else n	log(n)	1
deque	1	1^a	1	1 at begin or end, else n / 2	1 at begin or end, else n / 2	n	n log(n)
bit_vector	1	1^a	1	1 at end, else n	1 at end, else n	n	n log(n)
string, cow_string	1	1^a	1	1 at end, else n	1 at end, else n	n	n log(n)
set	1	1	-	log(n)	log(n)	log(n)	1
multiset	1	1	-	log(n)	log(n)	log(n)	1
map	1	1	log(n)	log(n)	log(n)	log(n)	1
multimap	1	1	-	log(n)	log(n)	log(n)	1
hash_set	1	1	-	1	1	1	-
hash_multiset	1	1	-	1	1	1	-
hash_map	1	1	-	1	1	1	-
hash_multimap	1	1	-	1	1	1	-
intrusive_hash_set	1	1	-	1	1	1	-
intrusive_hash_multiset	1	1	-	1	1	1	-
intrusive_hash_map	1	1	-	1	1	1	-
intrusive_hash_multimap	1	1	-	1	1	1	-

Notes:
- - means that the operation does not exist.
- 1 means amortized constant time. Also known as O(1)
- n means time proportional to the container size. Also known as O(n)
- log(n) means time proportional to the natural logarithm of the container size. Also known as O(log(n))
- n log(n) means time proportional to log(n) times the size of the container. Also known as O(n log(n))
- n+ means that the time is at least n, and possibly higher.
- Inserting at the end of a vector may cause the vector to be resized; resizing a vector is O(n). However, the amortized time complexity for vector insertions at the end is constant.
- Sort assumes the usage of the best possible sort for a large container of random data. Some sort algorithms (e.g. quick_sort) require random access iterators and so the sorting of some containers requires a different sort algorithm. We do not include bucket or radix sorts, as they are always O(n).
- a vector, deque, string size is O(1) but involves pointer subtraction and thus integer division and so is not as efficient as containers that store the size directly.

Professional C++ - Philosophy and Principles

Algorithms Better Implementation

EASTL algorithms provide a variety of optimized implementations of fundamental algorithms. Many of the EASTL algorithms are the same as the STL algorithm set, though EASTL adds additional algorithms and additional optimizations not found in STL implementations such as Microsoft's. The copy algorithm, for example, will memcpy data types that have the has_trivial_relocate type trait instead of doing an element-by-element copy.

The classifications we use here are not exactly the same as found in the C++ standard; they have been modified to be a little more intuitive. Not all the functions listed here may be yet available in EASTL as you read this. If you want some function then send a request to the maintainer. Detailed documentation for each algorithm is found in algorithm.h or the otherwise corresponding header file for the algorithm.

Search

- find, find_if
- find_end
- find_first_of
- adjacent_find
- binary_search
- search, search_n
- lower_bound
- upper_bound
- equal_range

Sort

- is_sorted
- quick_sort
- insertion_sort
- shell_sort
- heap_sort
- merge_sort, merge_sort_buffer
- merge
- inplace_merge
- partial_sort
- stable_sort
- partial_sort_copy
- <other sort functions found in the EASTL bonus directories>

Modifying

- fill, fill_n
- generate, generate_n
- random_shuffle

- swap
- iter_swap
- swap_ranges
- remove, remove_if
- remove_copy, remove_copy_if
- replace, replace_if
- replace_copy, replace_copy_if
- reverse
- reverse_copy
- rotate
- rotate_copy
- partition
- stable_partition
- transform
- next_permutation
- prev_permutation
- unique
- unique_copy

Non-Modifying

- for_each
- copy
- copy_backward
- count, count_if
- equal
- mismatch
- min
- max
- min_element
- max_element
- lexicographical_compare
- nth_element

Heap

- is_heap
- make_heap
- push_heap
- pop_heap
- change_heap
- sort_heap

- remove_heap

Set

- includes
- set_difference
- set_symmetric_difference
- set_intersection
- set_union

Professional C++

10. Applied Optimizations in EASTL using ISO C++

The world of multithreading brings capabilities to your application by running code in the

EASTL Best Practices

List all the others items

In this chapter, we discuss best practices for using EASTL. The primary emphasis is on performance with a secondary emphasis on correctness and maintainability. Some best practices apply only to some situations, and these will be pointed out as we go along. In order to be easily digestible, we present these practices as a list of items in the tone of the Effective C++ series of books.

Summary

The descriptions here are intentionally terse; this is to make them easier to visually scan.

- Consider intrusive containers.
- Consider fixed-size containers.
- Consider custom allocators.
- Consider hash tables instead of maps.
- Consider a vector_map (a.k.a. sorted vector) for unchanging data.
- Consider slist instead of list.
- Avoid redundant end() and size() in loops.
- Iterate containers instead of using operator[].
- Learn to use the string class appropriately.
- Cache list size if you want size() to be O(1).
- Use empty() instead of size() when possible.
- Know your container efficiencies.
- Use vector::reserve.
- Use vector::set_capacity to trim memory usage.
- Use swap() instead of a manually implemented version.
- Consider storing pointers instead of objects.
- Consider smart pointers instead of raw pointers.
- Use iterator pre-increment instead of post-increment.
- Make temporary references so the code can be traced/debugged.
- Consider bitvector or bitset instead of vector<bool>.
- Vectors can be treated as contiguous memory.
- Search hash_map<string> via find_as() instead of find().
- Take advantage of type_traits (e.g. EASTL_DECLARE_TRIVIAL_RELOCATE).
- Name containers to track memory usage.

Professional C++ - Philosophy and Principles

- Learn the algorithms.
- Pass and return containers by reference instead of value.
- Consider using reset_lose_memory() for fast container teardown.
- Consider using fixed_substring instead of copying strings.
- Consider using vector::push_back(void).

Consider intrusive containers.

Intrusive containers (such as intrusive_list) differ from regular containers (such as list) in that they use the stored objects to manage the linked list instead of using nodes allocated from a memory heap. The result is better usage of memory. Additionally intrusive_list objects can be removed from their list without knowing what list they belong to. To make an intrusive_list of Widgets, you have Widget inherit from intrusive_list_node or simply have mpPrev/mpNext member variables.

To create an intrusive_list container, you can use the following code:

```
class Widget : public intrusive_list_node
{ };
intrusive_list<Widget> widgetList;
widgetList.push_back(someWidget);
```

Consider fixed-size containers.

Fixed-size containers (such as fixed_list) are variations of regular containers (such as list) in that they allocate from a fixed block of local memory instead of allocating from a generic heap. The result is better usage of memory due to reduced fragmentation, better cache behavior, and faster allocation/deallocation. The presence of fixed-size containers negate the most common complaint that people have about STL: that it fragments the heap or "allocates all over the place."

EASTL fixed containers include:

- fixed_list
- fixed_slist
- fixed_vector
- fixed_string
- fixed_map
- fixed_multimap
- fixed_set
- fixed_multiset
- fixed_hash_map
- fixed_hash_multimap

- fixed_hash_set
- fixed_hash_multiset

To create a fixed_set, you can use the following code:

```
fixed_set<int, 25> intSet; // Create a set capable of holding 25 elements.
intSet.push_back(37);
```

Consider custom allocators.

While EASTL provides fixed-size containers in order to control container memory usage, EASTL lets you assign a custom allocator to any container. This lets you define your own memory pool. EASTL has a more flexible and powerful mechanism of doing this that standard STL, as EASTL understands object alignment requirements, allows for debug naming, allows for sharing allocators across containers, and allows dynamic allocator assignment.

To create a list container that uses your custom allocator and uses block naming, you can use the following code:

list<int> intList(pSomeAllocator, "graphics/intList");

intList.push_back(37);

Consider hash tables instead of maps.

Hash containers (such as hash_map) provide the same interface as associative containers (such as map) but have faster lookup and use less memory. The primary disadvantage relative to associative containers is that hash containers are not sorted.

To make a hash_map (dictionary) of integers to strings, you can use the following code:

```
hash_map<int, const char*> stringTable;
stringTable[37] = "hello";
```

Consider a vector_map (a.k.a. sorted vector) for unchanging data.

You can improve speed, memory usage, and cache behavior by using a vector_map instead of a map (or vector_set instead of set, etc.). The primary disadvantage of vector_map is that insertions and removal of elements is O(n) instead of O(1). However, if your associative container is not going to be changing much or at all, you can benefit from using a vector_map. Consider calling reserve on the vector_map in order to set the desired capacity up front.

To make a vector_set, you can use the following code:

Professional C++ - Philosophy and Principles

```
vector_set<int> intSet(16); // Create a vector_set with an initial capacity of
16.
intSet.insert(37);
```

Note that you can use containers other than vector to implement vector_set. Here's how you do it with deque:

```
vector_set<int, less<int>, EASTLAllocatorType, deque<int> > intSet;
intSet.insert(37);
```

Consider slist instead of list.

An slist is a singly-linked list; it is much like a list except that it can only be traversed in a forward direction and not a backward direction. The benefit is that each node is 4 bytes instead of 8 bytes. This is a small improvement, but if you don't need reverse iteration then it can be an improvement. There's also intrusive_slist as an option.

To make an slist, you can use the following code:

```
slist<int> intSlist;
intSlist.push_front(37);
```

Avoid redundant end() and size() in loops.

Instead of writing code like this:

```
for(deque<int>::iterator it = d.begin(); it != d.end(); ++it)
    ...
```

write code like this:

```
for(deque<int>::iterator it = d.begin(), itEnd = d.end(); it != itEnd; ++it)
    ...
```

The latter avoids a function call and return of an object (which in deque's case happens to be more than just a pointer). The above only works when the container is unchanged or for containers that have a constant end value. By "constant end value" we mean containers which can be modified but end always remains the same.

Iterate containers instead of using operator[].

It's faster to iterate random access containers via iterators than via operator[], though operator[] usage may look simpler.

Instead of doing this:

```
for(unsigned i = 0, iEnd = intVector.size(); i != iEnd; ++i)
```

```
    intVector[i] = 37;
```

you can execute more efficiently by doing this:

```
for(vector<int>::iterator it = intVector.begin(), itEnd = intVector.end(); it != itEnd; ++it)
    *it = 37;
```

Learn to use the string class appropriately.

Oddly enough, the most mis-used STL container is easily the string class. The tales of string abuse could rival the 1001 Arabian Nights. Most of the abuses involve doing things in a harder way than need be. In examining the historical mis-uses of string, it is clear that many of the problems stem from the user thinking in terms of C-style string operations instead of object-oriented strings. This explains why statements such as strlen(s.c_str()) are so common, whereas the user could just use s.length() instead and be both clearer and more efficient.

Here we provide a table of actual collected examples of things done and how they could have been done instead. Here we provide a table of actual collected examples of things done and how they could have been done instead.

What was written	What could have been written
s = s.Left(i) + '+' + s.Right(s.length() - i - 1);	s[i] = '+';
string s(""); // This is the most commonly found misuse.	string s;
s = "";	s.clear();
s.c_str()[0] = 'u';	s[0] = 'u';
len = strlen(s.c_str());	len = s.length();
s = string("u");	s = "u";

Professional C++ - Philosophy and Principles

puts(s + string("u"));	puts(s + "u");
string s(" "); puts(s.c_str());	puts(" ");
s.sprintf("u");	s = "u";

char array[32];
sprintf(array, "%d", 10);
s = string(array);
	s.sprintf("%d", 10);

The chances are that if you want to do something with a string, there is a very basic way to do it. You don't want your code to appear in a future version of the above table.

Cache list size if you want list::size() to be O(1).

EASTL's list, slist, intrusive_list, and intrusive_slist containers have a size() implementation which is O(n). That is, these containers don't keep a count (cache) of the current list size and when you call the size() function they iterate the list. This is by design and the reasoning behind it has been deeply debated and considered (and is discussed in the FAQ and the list header file). In summary, list doesn't cache its size because the only function that would benefit is the size function while many others would be negatively impacted and the memory footprint would be negatively impacted, yet list::size is not a very frequently called function in well-designed code. At the same time, nothing prevents the user from caching the size himself, though admittedly it adds some tedium and risk to the code writing process.

Here's an example of caching the list size manually:

```
list<int> intList;
   size_t   n = 0;
   intList.push_back(37);
   ++n;
   intList.pop_front();
   --n;
```

Use empty() instead of size() when possible.

All conventional containers have both an empty function and a size function. For all containers empty() executes with O(1) (constant time) efficiency. However, this is not so for size(), as some containers need to calculate the size and others need to do pointer subtraction (which may involve integer division) to find the size.

Use vector::reserve.

You can prevent vectors (and strings) from reallocating as you add items by specifying up front how many items you will be requiring. You can do this in the constructor or by calling the reserve function at any time. The capacity function returns the amount of space which is currently reserved.

Here's how you could specify reserved capacity in a vector:

```
vector<Widget> v(37);    // Reserve space to hold up to 37 items.
    or
vector<Widget> v;        // This empty construction causes to
                         // memory to be allocated or reserved.
v.reserve(37);
```

The EASTL vector (and string) implementation looks like this:

```
template <typename T>
  class vector {
    T* mpBegin;      // Beginning of used element memory.
    T* mpEnd;        // End of used element memory.
    T* mpCapacity;   // End of storage capacity. Is >= mpEnd
    }
```

Another approach to being efficient with vector memory usage is to use fixed_vector.

Use vector::set_capacity to trim memory usage.

A commonly asked question about vectors and strings is, "How do I reduce the capacity of a vector?" The conventional solution for std STL is to use the somewhat non-obvious trick of using vector<Widget>(v).swap(v). EASTL provides the same functionality via a member function called set_capacity() which is present in both the vector and string classes.

An example of reducing a vector is the following:

```
vector<Widget> v;
...
v.set_capacity();
```

An example of resizing to zero and completely freeing the memory of a vector is the following:

```
vector<Widget> v;
...
v.set_capacity(0);
```

Professional C++ - Philosophy and Principles

Use swap() instead of a manually implemented version.

The generic swap algorithm provides a basic version for any kind of object. However, each EASTL container provides a specialization of swap which is optimized for that container. For example, the list container implements swap by simply swapping the internal member pointers and not by moving individual elements.

Consider storing pointers instead of objects.

There are times when storing pointers to objects is more efficient or useful than storing objects directly in containers. It can be more efficient to store pointers when the objects are big and the container may need to construct, copy, and destruct objects during sorting or resizing. Moving pointers is usually faster than moving objects. It can be useful to store pointers instead of objects when somebody else owns the objects or the objects are in another container. It might be useful for a Widget to be in a list and in a hash table at the same time.

Consider smart pointers instead of raw pointers.

If you take the above recommendation and store objects as pointers instead of as objects, you may want to consider storing them as smart pointers instead of as regular pointers. This is particularly useful for when you want to delete the object when it is removed from the container. Smart pointers will automatically delete the pointed-to object when the smart pointer is destroyed. Otherwise, you will have to be careful about how you work with the list so that you don't generate memory leaks. Smart pointers implement a shared reference count on the stored pointer, as so any operation you do on a smart pointer container will do the right thing. Any pointer can be stored in a smart pointer, and custom new/delete mechanisms can work with smart pointers. The primary smart pointer is shared_ptr.

Here is an example of creating and using a shared_ptr:

```
typedef shared_ptr<Widget> WPtr;
list<WPtr> wList;
wList.push_back(WPtr(new Widget)); // The user may have operator new/delete
overrides.
wList.pop_back();                  // Implicitly deletes the Widget.
```

Here is an example of creating and using a shared_ptr that uses a custom allocation and deallocation mechanism:

```
typedef shared_ptr<Widget, EASTLAllocatorType, WidgetDelete> WPtr; //
WidgetDelete is a custom destroyer.
list<WPtr> wList;
wList.push_back(WPtr(WidgetCreate(Widget))); // WidgetCreate is a custom
allocator.
wList.pop_back();          // Implicitly calls WidgetDelete.
```

Professional C++

Use iterator pre-increment instead of post-increment.

Pre-increment (e.g. ++x) of iterators is better than post-increment (x++) when the latter is not specifically needed. It is common to find code that uses post-incrementing when it could instead use pre-incrementing; presumably this is due to post-increment looking a little better visually. The problem is that the latter constructs a temporary object before doing the increment. With built-in types such as pointers and integers, the compiler will recognize that the object is a trivial built-in type and that the temporary is not needed, but the compiler cannot do this for other types, even if the compiler sees that the temporary is not used; this is because the constructor may have important side effects and the compiler would be broken if it didn't construct the temporary object.

EASTL iterators are usually not trivial types and so it's best not to hope the compiler will do the best thing. Thus you should always play it safe an use pre-increment of iterators whenever post-increment is not required.

Here is an example of using iterator pre-increment; for loops like this should always use pre-increment:

```
for(set<int>::iterator it(intSet.begin()), itEnd(intSet.end()); it != itEnd;
++it)
        *it = 37;
```

Make temporary references so the code can be traced/debugged.

Users want to be able to inspect or modify variables which are referenced by iterators. While EASTL containers and iterators are designed to make this easier than other STL implementations, it makes things very easy if the code explicitly declares a reference to the iterated element. In addition to making the variable easier to debug, it also makes code easier to read and makes the debug (and possibly release) version of the application run more efficiently.

Instead of doing this:

```
for(list<Widget>::iterator it = wl.begin(), itEnd = wl.end(); it != itEnd; ++it)
{
        (*it).x = 37;
        (*it).y = 38;
        (*it).z = 39;
}
```

Consider doing this:

```
for(list<Widget>::iterator it = wl.begin(), itEnd = wl.end(); it != itEnd; ++it)
{
        Widget& w = *it; // The user can easily inspect or modify w here.
        w.x = 37;
        w.y = 38;
        w.z = 39;
}
```

Professional C++ - Philosophy and Principles

Consider bitvector or bitset instead of vector<bool>.

In EASTL, a vector of bool is exactly that. It intentionally does not attempt to make a specialization which implements a packed bit array. The bitvector class is specifically designed for this purpose. There are arguments either way, but if vector<bool> were allowed to be something other than an array of bool, it would go against user expectations and prevent users from making a true array of bool. There's a mechanism for specifically getting the bit packing, and it is bitvector.

Additionally there is bitset, which is not a conventional iterateable container but instead acts like bit flags. bitset may better suit your needs than bitvector if you need to do flag/bit operations instead of array operations. bitset does have an operator[], though.

Vectors can be treated as contiguous memory.

EASTL vectors (and strings) guarantee that elements are present in a linear contiguous array. This means that you can use a vector as you would a C-style array by using the vector data() member function or by using &v[0].

To use a vector as a pointer to an array, you can use the following code:

```
struct Widget {
      uint32_t x;
      uint32_t y;
   };
vector<Widget> v;
quick_sort((uint64_t*)v.data(), (uint64_t*)(v.data() + v.size()));
```

Search hash_map<string> via find_as() instead of find().

EASTL hash tables offer a bonus function called find_as when lets you search a hash table by something other than the container type. This is particularly useful for hash tables of string objects that you want to search for by string literals (e.g. "hello") or char pointers. If you search for a string via the find function, your string literal will necessarily be converted to a temporary string object, which is inefficient.

To use find_as, you can use the following code:

```
hash_map<string, int> hashMap;
  hash_map<string, int>::iterator it = hashMap.find_as("hello"); // Using default
hash and compare.
```

Take advantage of type_traits (e.g. EASTL_DECLARE_TRIVIAL_RELOCATE).

EASTL includes a fairly serious type traits library that is on par with the one found in Boost but offers some additional performance-enhancing help as well. The type_traits library provides information about class types, as opposed to class instances. For example, the is_integral type trait tells if a type is one of int, short, long, char, uint64_t, etc.

There are three primary uses of type traits:

- Allowing for optimized operations on some data types.
- Allowing for different logic pathways based on data types.
- Allowing for compile-type assertions about data type expectations.

Most of the type traits are automatically detected and implemented by the compiler. However, EASTL allows for the user to explicitly give the compiler hints about type traits that the compiler cannot know, via the EASTL_DECLARE declarations. If the user has a class that is relocatable (i.e. can safely use memcpy to copy values), the user can use the EASTL_DECLARE_TRIVIAL_RELOCATE declaration to tell the compiler that the class can be copied via memcpy. This will automatically significantly speed up some containers and algorithms that use that class.

Here is an example of using type traits to tell if a value is a floating point value or not:

```
template <typename T>
  DoSomething(T t) {
    assert(is_floating_point<T>::value);
  }
```

Here is an example of declaring a class as relocatable and using it in a vector.

```
EASTL_DECLARE_TRIVIAL_RELOCATE(Widget);   // Usually you put this at the Widget
class declaration.
vector<Widget> wVector;
wVector.erase(wVector.begin());           // This operation will be optimized via
using memcpy.
```

The following is a full list of the currently recognized type traits. Most of these are implemented as of this writing, but if there is one that is missing, feel free to contact the maintainer of this library and request that it be completed.

- is_void
- is_integral
- is_floating_point
- is_arithmetic
- is_fundamental
- is_const
- is_volatile
- is_abstract
- is_signed
- is_unsigned
- is_array
- is_pointer
- is_reference

- is_member_object_pointer
- is_member_function_pointer
- is_member_pointer
- is_enum
- is_union
- is_class
- is_polymorphic
- is_function
- is_object
- is_scalar
- is_compound
- is_same
- is_convertible
- is_base_of
- is_empty
- is_pod
- is_aligned
- has_trivial_constructor
- has_trivial_copy
- has_trivial_assign
- has_trivial_destructor
- has_trivial_relocate[1]
- has_nothrow_constructor
- has_nothrow_copy
- has_nothrow_assign
- has_virtual_destructor
- alignment_of
- rank
- extent

1 has_trivial_relocate is not found in Boost nor the C++ standard update proposal. However, it is very useful in allowing for the generation of optimized object moving operations. It is similar to the is_pod type trait, but goes further and allows non-pod classes to be categorized as relocatable. Such categorization is something that no compiler can do, as only the user can know if it is such. Thus EASTL_DECLARE_TRIVIAL_RELOCATE is provided to allow the user to give the compiler a hint.

Name containers to track memory usage.

All EASTL containers which allocate memory have a built-in function called set_name and have a constructor argument that lets you specify the container name. This name is used in memory tracking and allows for the categorization and measurement of memory usage. You merely need to supply a name for your container to use and it does the rest.

Here is an example of creating a list and naming it "collision list":

```
list<CollisionData> collisionList(allocator("collision list"));
```

or

```
list<CollisionData> collisionList;
collisionList.get_allocator().set_name("collision list");
```

Note that EASTL containers do not copy the name contents but merely copy the name pointer. This is done for simplicity and efficiency. A user can get around this limitation by creating a persistently present string table. Additionally, the user can get around this by declaring static but non-const strings and modifying them at runtime.

Learn the algorithms.

EASTL algorithms provide a variety of optimized implementations of fundamental algorithms. Many of the EASTL algorithms are the same as the STL algorithm set, though EASTL adds additional algorithms and additional optimizations not found in STL implementations such as Microsoft's. The copy algorithm, for example, will memcpy data types that have the has_trivial_relocate type trait instead of doing an element-by-element copy.

The classifications we use here are not exactly the same as found in the C++ standard; they have been modified to be a little more intuitive. Not all the functions listed here may be yet available in EASTL as you read this. If you want some function then send a request to the maintainer. Detailed documentation for each algorithm is found in algorithm.h or the otherwise corresponding header file for the algorithm.

Search

- find, find_if
- find_end
- find_first_of
- adjacent_find
- binary_search
- search, search_n
- lower_bound
- upper_bound
- equal_range

Sort

- is_sorted
- quick_sort
- insertion_sort
- shell_sort
- heap_sort

Professional C++ - Philosophy and Principles

- merge_sort, merge_sort_buffer
- merge
- inplace_merge
- partial_sort
- stable_sort
- partial_sort_copy
- <other sort functions found in the EASTL bonus directories>

Modifying

- fill, fill_n
- generate, generate_n
- random_shuffle
- swap
- iter_swap
- swap_ranges
- remove, remove_if
- remove_copy, remove_copy_if
- replace, replace_if
- replace_copy, replace_copy_if
- reverse
- reverse_copy
- rotate
- rotate_copy
- partition
- stable_partition
- transform
- next_permutation
- prev_permutation
- unique
- unique_copy

Non-Modifying

- for_each
- copy
- copy_backward
- count, count_if
- equal
- mismatch
- min
- max
- min_element
- max_element
- lexicographical_compare

- nth_element

Heap

- is_heap
- make_heap
- push_heap
- pop_heap
- change_heap
- sort_heap
- remove_heap

Set

- includes
- set_difference
- set_symmetric_difference
- set_intersection
- set_union

Pass and return containers by reference instead of value.

If you aren't paying attention you might accidentally write code like this:

```
void DoSomething(list<Widget> widgetList) {
       ...
}
```

The problem with the above is that widgetList is passed by value and not by reference. Thus the a copy of the container is made and passed instead of a reference of the container being passed. This may seem obvious to some but this happens periodically and the compiler gives no warning and the code will often execute properly, but inefficiently. Of course there are some occasions where you really do want to pass values instead of references.

Consider using reset_lose_memory() for fast container teardown.

EASTL containers have a reset function which unilaterally resets the container to a newly constructed state. The contents of the container are forgotten; no destructors are called and no memory is freed. This is a risky but power function for the purpose of implementing very fast temporary containers. There are numerous cases in high performance programming when you want to create a temporary container out of a scratch buffer area, use the container, and then just "vaporize" it, as it would be waste of time to go through the trouble of clearing the container and destroying and freeing the objects. Such functionality is often used with hash tables or maps and with a stack allocator (a.k.a. linear allocator).

Here's an example of usage of the reset function and a PPMalloc-like StackAllocator:

Professional C++ - Philosophy and Principles

```
pStackAllocator->push_bookmark();
 hash_set<Widget, less<Widget>, StackAllocator> wSet(pStackAllocator);
<use wSet>
wSet.reset_lose_memory();
pStackAllocator->pop_bookmark();
```

Consider using fixed_substring instead of copying strings.

EASTL provides a fixed_substring class which uses a reference to a character segment instead of allocating its own string memory. This can be a more efficient way to work with strings under some circumstances.

Here's an example of usage of fixed_substring:

```
basic_string<char> str("hello world");
fixed_substring<char> sub(str, 6, 5); // sub == "world"
fixed_substring can refer to any character array and not just one that derives
from a string object.
```

Consider using vector::push_back(void).

EASTL provides an alternative way to insert elements into containers that avoids copy construction and/or the creation of temporaries. Consider the following code:

vector<Widget> widgetArray;

widgetArray.push_back(Widget());

The standard vector push_back function requires you to supply an object to copy from. This incurs the cost of the creation of a temporary and for some types of classes or situations this cost may be undesirable. It additionally requires that your contained class support copy-construction whereas you may not be able to support copy construction. As an alternative, EASTL provides a push_back(void) function which requires nothing to copy from but instead constructs the object in place in the container. So you can do this:

```
vector<Widget> widgetArray;
widgetArray.push_back();
widgetArray.back().x = 0; // Example of how to reference the new object.
```

Other containers with such copy-less functions include:

```
vector::push_back()
deque::push_back()
deque::push_front()
list::push_back()
```

```
list::push_front()
slist::push_front()
map::insert(const key_type& key)
multimap::insert(const key_type& key)
hash_map::insert(const key_type& key)
hash_multimap::insert(const key_type& key)
```

Note that the map functions above allow you to insert a default value specified by key alone and not a value_type like with the other map insert functions.

11. Multithreading using ISO C++

The world of multithreading brings capabilities to your application by running code in the background. To support this kind of operations, the operating system lets you create a thread. What is a thread? It's a function that is scheduled by the operating system to run continuously. The Windows operating system schedules threads while the Linux operating system schedules processes. But each operating system supports threads. Under Linux it's called pthread.

Basics of threads

The STL supports threads in the <thread> header. To create a thread, you have multiple choices. The easiest way is to declare a function and pass it to the thread's constructor. The function join blocks the execution of the program until the thread is finished. Example:

```
void MonitoringServer()
{
    // ...
    cout << "Monitoring Server..." << endl;
}

void Routine1()
{
    for (int i = 0; i < 1024; ++i)
    {
        MonitoringServer("SERVER01");
        this_thread::sleep_for(60s);
    }
}
```

Professional C++ - Philosophy and Principles

```cpp
int main()
{
    thread t1(Routine1);
    t1.join();
    return 0;
}
```

Passing arguments to a thread

To pass one or more argument to a thread, just pass it after the function name in the thread's constructor. Example:

```cpp
void MonitoringServer(const string& server)
{
    // ...
    cout << "Monitoring Server..." << server << endl;
}

void Routine2(const vector<string>& servers)
{
    for_each(servers.begin(), servers.end(), [](const string& name) {
        MonitoringServer(name);
        this_thread::sleep_for(1s);
    });
}

int main()
{
    vector<string> servers{ "SERVER01", "SERVER02", "SERVER03", "SERVER04", "SERVER05", "SERVER06" };
    thread t2(Routine2, ref(servers));
    t2.join();

    return 0;
}
```

In this example, the vector of server names is passed to the thread. You can see that servers variable is passed using ref to tell the compiler it's by reference else it would be passed by value. It's easy to create and call threads.

Returning result from a thread

To return result from a thread, we have to create the infrastructure. By default, a thread is just a function unit that processes instructions and it's not designed to return data. To enable this feature, we have to build some code. We create a class and we will wrap the routine not only in a function but within a whole class. The function will be called using the () operator. Example:

Professional C++

```cpp
class BackgroundTask
{
public:
    BackgroundTask(const std::string& name, const int& age) : _name(name),
_age(age) {}

    double GetResult() const
    {
        return _res;
    }

    void operator()()
    {
        std::cout << "Name:" << _name
            << ", Age:" << _age << std::endl;
        _res = _age * 10.52;
    }

private:
    std::string _name;
    int _age = 0;
    double _res = 0.0;
};

int main()
{
    BackgroundTask task("Lisa", 14);
    std::thread t3(ref(task));
    t3.join();
    std::cout << "Result: " << task.GetResult() << endl;

    return 0;
}
```

In this example, we declare a BackgroundTask object and it's passed by reference to the thread's constructor. Doing this, it will call the () operator to run the function. The function modifies one or more members and when the thread is finished, you use your object to retrieve the member.

Sharing Data

A thread is a function but a real application will create multiple threads and will need to share some data. Sharing data needs to be synchronized to allow one only thread to access to the data at a time. It means you need to lock the data, access it and unlock the data. There are multiple locks; some are heavy and some are light. Let's look at the various locks.

Professional C++ - Philosophy and Principles

Mutexes

The header <mutex> contains a simple object to use: the mutual exclusion object alias the mutex. To use it, you declare it globally and you use the functions lock/unlock to access and release the data. Example:

```
int _counter = 0;
string _name = "";
mutex _mutex;

void RoutineModifyMembers()
{
    for (int i = 0; i < 10000; ++i)
    {
        _mutex.lock();
        ++_counter;
        _name += to_string(i);
        _mutex.unlock();
        this_thread::sleep_for(chrono::milliseconds(10));

    }
}

void RoutinePrintMembers()
{
    for (int i = 0; i < 10000; ++i)
    {
        _mutex.lock();
        //cout << "Name: " << _name << ", Counter: " << _counter << endl;
        cout << "Counter: " << _counter << endl;
        _mutex.unlock();
        this_thread::sleep_for(chrono::milliseconds(5));

    }
}

int main()
{
    thread t4(RoutineModifyMembers);
    thread t5(RoutinePrintMembers);
    t4.join();
    t5.join();
    return 0;
}
```

You can see that both threads makes some pause of few milliseconds using the this_thread::sleep function and using chrono specifications. Every access to the variables must be synchronized. If not, a race condition can happen. The utilization of the mutex object can be simplified by using the scoped_lock object. Instead of making a lock/unlock, you declare a scoped_lock and it acts like a smart pointer, the unlock is called when it leaves the current scope. Example of modifications for the two functions:

```cpp
void RoutineModifyMembers2()
{
    for (int i = 0; i < 10000; ++i)
    {
        std::scoped_lock lock(_mutex);

        ++_counter;
        _name += to_string(i);

        this_thread::sleep_for(chrono::milliseconds(10));

    }
}


void RoutinePrintMembers2()
{
    for (int i = 0; i < 10000; ++i)
    {
        std::scoped_lock lock(_mutex);

        cout << "Counter: " << _counter << endl;

        this_thread::sleep_for(chrono::milliseconds(5));

    }
}
```

If the lock needs to be passed to a function, we need to change scoped_lock to unique_lock because scoped_lock cannot be copied. Another way to make the application better is to shared the mutex instead of creating new ones. The object is named shared_mutex and is located in the <shared_mutex> header. Example:

```cpp
shared_mutex _smutex;
void RoutineModifyMembers3()
{
    for (int i = 0; i < 10000; ++i)
    {
        _smutex.lock_shared();
        ++_counter;
        _name += to_string(i);
        _smutex.unlock_shared();
        this_thread::sleep_for(chrono::milliseconds(10));

    }
```

```cpp
}

void RoutinePrintMembers3()
{
    for (int i = 0; i < 10000; ++i)
    {
        _smutex.lock_shared();
        cout << "Counter: " << _counter << endl;
        _smutex.unlock_shared();
        this_thread::sleep_for(chrono::milliseconds(5));

    }
}
```

We use the methods lock_shared and unlock_shared of the shared_mutex class.

Tasks

A task is a high-level object that use the underlying technology of threads. It's provided by the standard library and it's very useful.

future and promise

The point to understand is that future and promise enable the transfer of a value between two tasks without explicit use of a lock. When a task wants to pass a value to another, the value is put into a promise. The value appears in the corresponding future where you can read it. On a future, you call the get function and it blocks until it arrives. The promise and its function set_value provide the put operation. Promise and future are defined in the <future> header.

async

To launch a task to run asynchronously, we can use the async function. The async function returns a future so you concentrate your code of the task and you use the returned future to get the result. It is very comfortable. Example:

```cpp
void funcAsync()
{
    future<int> f1 = async([]() {
        int data = 0;
        for (int i = 0; i < 100; ++i)
        {
            data += i;
        }
        return data;
    });

    int data = f1.get();
    cout << "Task returned : " << data << endl;
```

```
    }
```

In the async function, we put a lambda expression that computes an int. We declare the future, link it with the async function and use the get function to retrieve the result of the task.

Optimization of Locks

Some locks are useful and some are useless. If you need to just increment or decrement a value, exchange some value or make a small operation, you need to call the atomic operations defined in the <atomic> header. Atomic operations do not need to be protected by a lock. There exist typedefs for the atomic<T> template:

- std::atomic_schar (signed char)
- std::atomic_uchar (unsigned char)
- std::atomic_ushort
- std::atomic_uint
- std::atomic_ulong
- std::atomic_llong
- std::atomic_ullong

Example:

```
atomic_int _count = 0;

void funcAtomic()
{
    thread t1([=]() { for (int i = 0; i < 10000; ++i) {
        _count = _count + 1;
        this_thread::sleep_for(chrono::milliseconds(25));
    }
    });

    thread t2([=]() { for (int i = 0; i < 10000; ++i) {
        _count = _count + 10;
        this_thread::sleep_for(chrono::milliseconds(25));
    }
    });

    thread t3([=]() { for (int i = 0; i < 10000; ++i) {
        cout << "Count: " << _count << endl;
        this_thread::sleep_for(chrono::milliseconds(25));
    }
    });

    t1.join();
    t2.join();
```

Professional C++ - Philosophy and Principles

```
    t3.join();
}
```

Read/Write Lock

Sophisticated locks are a combination of multiple locks. The single write/multiple readers lock is a perfect example. Here is how to implement it. Example:

```
typedef std::shared_mutex Lock;
typedef std::unique_lock<Lock>  WriterLock;
typedef std::shared_lock<Lock>  ReaderLock;
Lock myLock;

void funcRWLock()
{
    thread t1([=]() { for (int i = 0; i < 10000; ++i) {
        WriterLock w_lock(myLock);
        _count = _count + 1;
        this_thread::sleep_for(chrono::milliseconds(25));
    }
    });

    thread t2([=]() { for (int i = 0; i < 10000; ++i) {
        WriterLock w_lock(myLock);
        _count = _count + 10;
        this_thread::sleep_for(chrono::milliseconds(25));
    }
    });

    thread t3([=]() { for (int i = 0; i < 10000; ++i) {
        ReaderLock r_lock(myLock);
        cout << "Count: " << _count << endl;
        this_thread::sleep_for(chrono::milliseconds(25));
    }
    });

    t1.join();
    t2.join();
    t3.join();
}
```

We use a shared_mutex and two locks: a unique_lock for writing operations and a shared_lock for reading operations.

Condition Variable

The <condition_variable> header provided features like waiting and emitting notifications. Condition variables permit concurrent invocation of the wait, wait_for_all, wait_until, notify_one, notify_all member functions. Condition variables work with a unqiue_lock and when the modification on a synchronized data is done, the wait function is blocked and become unblocked when notify_one function is called. Example:

```cpp
condition_variable _cv;
mutex _mutex1;
int _counter2 = 0;

void funcConditionVariables()
{
    thread t1([=]() {
        unique_lock<mutex> lock(_mutex1);
        _cv.wait(lock);
        cout << "Counter: " << _counter2 << endl;
    });

    thread t2([=]() {
        unique_lock<mutex> lock(_mutex1);
        for (int i = 0; i < 100; ++i) {
            _counter2 = _counter2 + 10;
            cout << i;
            this_thread::sleep_for(chrono::milliseconds(25));
    }
        lock.unlock();
        _cv.notify_one();
    });

    t1.join();
    t2.join();
}
```

As you can see, the use of the standard library offers a wide range of capabilities for concurrency tasks.

Parallel Algorithms

The standard library provides the capability to execute algorithms in parallel on each data item. There are multiple possibilities for the execution:

- seq : sequential execution
- par : parallel execution
- par_unseq : parallel and/or unsequenced execution (vectorized)

When your algorithms run in parallel mode, be sure to avoid data races and deadlock.

Professional C++ - Philosophy and Principles

Windows API and specific issues

Some years ago, before C++11, there was no standard about all of this. The code needed to be platform specific. Under Windows, there are multiple locks and atomic operations:

- critical sections
- mutexes
- events
- semaphore
- SingleWriterMultipleReaders[122] (SWMR)
- Interlocked operations

The criticial section and interlocked operations are not kernel object. A kernel object is a HANDLE and need to be released by calling CloseHandle function. Wait operations on a kernel object are done with WaitForSingleObject and WaitForMultipleObjects functions.

Using various lock implies various performances:

Table 1: Comparison of Windows synchronization mechanism performance

Threads	Volatile read	Volatile write	Interlock increment	Critical Section	SRWLock shared	SRWLock exclusive	Mutex
1	8	8	35	66	66	67	1060
2	8	76	153	268	134	148	11082
4	9	145	361	768	244	307	23785

The Table 1 contains the elapsed time in milliseconds between the start of the thread doing 1000000 operations and the end of the thread for the following tasks:

- Read a volatile long value:

```
LONG lValue = g_value;
```

- Write into a volatile value:

```
g_value = 10;
```

---

[122] From Jeffrey Richter's book, Programming Applications for Microsoft Windows, from Microsoft Press

- Using InterlockIncrement:

```
InterlockIncrement(&g_value);
```

- Using a critical section:

```
EnterCriticalSection(g_cs);
g_value = 10;
LeaveCriticalSection(&g_cs);
```

- Using a SRWLock:

```
AcquireSRWLockShared/Exclusive(&g_srwLock);
g_value = 100;
ReleaseSRWLockShared/Exclusive(&g_srwLock);
```

- Using a kernel object (mutex):

```
WaitForSingleObject(g_Mutex, INFINITE);
g_value = 100;
ReleaseMutex(g_Mutex);
```

Optimizing Concurrency – Tips and Tricks

In a multithreading application, events occur and the execution context is never the same because there are synchronzation, locks and contexte switching from the operating system. Each run can become different ; When it fails, it's never the same context.

Modern hardware architecture contains multiple CPU core, multiple Core on the graphic card, a network card, audio processors, disk controllers and memory. Everything run in parallel. In the IT history, CPU have been built using a single core and in the 2000's, hardwares became shipped with multicore microsprocessors. The operating systems provided API for creating and handling threads with C. Later with C++, the standard library incorporated threads in <thread> header.

Concurrency improves performance by permItting operations to run while others and pending, waiting for synchronization objects (locks, mutexes, events, etc).

Optimizing multithreaded C++ applications can be very complex, first because it's very complex to make it runnning well without pain. Shared members should be (must be) synchronized with leight-weigth locks like SWMR (Single Writer Multiple Readers) locks instead of basic and ugly lock/unlock.

Avoid ctor and dtor

When you have designed classes into your application, you naturally design constructors and destrtuctors for various classes. In parallel mode, it's not a good idea. Implement a couple of Init/Uninit member functions instead. When a class is being used, you can explicitly use the Init function. Why ? It's easier to fix typesafety types and it's always a good idea to not be faulty I a constructor or a destructor. Throwing exceptions in ctor/dtor is not also a good practice. So, avoid code in ctor and dtor.

Always use a multithreaded logger

Your logger should write the runnning thread ID. It will allows you to parse your log file for a lot of concurrent operations running at the same time. Adopt a logger like log4cpp or log4cxx, its well designed and easy to use. See Chapter 2.

Create async tasks instead of threads

std::async is better than creating operating threads with std::thread. Creating a thread is easier than creating a process but it consumes more resources compared to std::async.

Implement a thread pool mechanism

A thread pool is a data structure that contains a fixed size of long running threads and a task queue. In a task oriented programming, the thread pool run tasks using threads in the pool. When a tread become available, it fetches a task from the queue. When the thread finishes the task, it does not terminate, it waits or takes anothers task to be executed in the task queue. Treading pool eliminates the creation of threads for short operations.

Create as many threads as Cores

Your hardware owns multiple cores : use them ! It's free. If you need to server multiple clients, size your pool to manage as many threads there are cores on your system at the minimum. Most of the times, a threal pool with 20 or 25 active threads can serve thousands of clients.

Make a wall between compute and I/O

When you design a multithreaded application, you make apartments with components needed to interact together. Try to separated the threads that make acquisition of data, from others who process data and others that do I/O operations. It scales better. A compute routine can be optimized by the compiler but if it's mixed with I/O operation sin the middle, the compiler can't group operations into a compute pipeline or a vectorized task.

Use or implement a middleware or a messaging pipeline

Messaging is the alternative to threading. You subscribe to on or multiple events, and you routine is executed by the thread pool.

Enhance your locks

You have to keep the scope of your lock very small, it's better between reading and writing operations.

The thread pool can server the whole earth

Remember that with 20 threads, you can server multiple (thousands) requests sper seconds.

You have to limit the number of threads to he strict minimum.

Resources need to be managed carefully

Your resources (mémory, CPU, disks) are precious. Use them wisley and do not waste them.

Avoid memory leaks by keeping a good memory allocator wrapper. The perfect candidate is the usage of smart pointers like std::unique_ptr and std::shared_ptr.

Avoid infinite wait

Prefer time guarded locks insetad of infinite time wait. It's easier to debug multithreaded applications using this kind of locks because if the ttimeout is reached, you cn do an exit failed operation !

Don't create your own lock types

This is a "boy scout" rule but tdon't design your own lock types. You waste your time. Try to adopt Boost.Lockfree or Intel TBB, it would be more suitable and it can save your applications.

Concurrency Libraries

We have an overview of Boost and Intel TBB in previous paragraphs. There are also many open-source projects that give you enhancements to the Standard Template Library for supporting thread and tasks. In the Windows eco-system, Microsoft shipped PPL (Parallel Patterns Library) and its embedded into an initiative called **Concurrency Runtime**.

Write lock-free applications

Third-party libraries like Boost[123] and Intel TBB (Thread Building Blocks) contain lock-free containers.

---

[123] https://www.boost.org/

Professional C++ - Philosophy and Principles

Boost and Lock-free Mecanism

Boost is a set of popular libraries in the C++ community. Boost is available on Github[124]. Current version is 1.74. Inside Boost, it exists a library called Boost.Lockfree[125]. Here is some data structures you can look at:

`boost.lockfree` implements three lock-free data structures:

- `boost::lockfree::queue`: a lock-free multi-producer/multi-consumer queue
- `boost::lockfree::stack`: a lock-free multi-producer/multi-consumer stack
- `boost::lockfree::spsc_queue`: a wait-free single-producer/single-consumer queue (commonly known as ringbuffer)

This is a powerful set of classes to use in your applications.

The term **non-blocking** denotes concurrent data structures, which do not use traditional synchronization primitives like guards to ensure thread-safety. Let's distinguish 3 types of non-blocking data structures, each having different properties:

data structures are **wait-free**, if every concurrent operation is guaranteed to be finished in a finite number of steps. It is therefore possible to give worst-case guarantees for the number of operations.

data structures are **lock-free**, if some concurrent operations are guaranteed to be finished in a finite number of steps. While it is in theory possible that some operations never make any progress, it is very unlikely to happen in practical applications.

data structures are **obstruction-free**, if a concurrent operation is guaranteed to be finished in a finite number of steps, unless another concurrent operation interferes.

Some data structures can only be implemented in a lock-free manner, if they are used under certain restrictions. The relevant aspects for the implementation of `boost.lockfree` are the number of producer and consumer threads. **Single-producer (sp)** or **multiple producer (mp)** means that only a single thread or multiple concurrent threads are allowed to add data to a data structure. **Single-consumer (sc)** or **Multiple-consumer (mc)** denote the equivalent for the removal of data from the data structure.

---

[124] https://github.com/boostorg

[125] https://www.boost.org/doc/libs/1_74_0/doc/html/lockfree.html

Properties of Non-Blocking Data Structures

Non-blocking data structures do not rely on locks and mutexes to ensure thread-safety. The synchronization is done completely in user-space without any direct interaction with the operating system[126]. This implies that they are not prone to issues like priority inversion (a low-priority thread needs to wait for a high-priority thread).

Instead of relying on guards, non-blocking data structures require **atomic operations** (specific CPU instructions executed without interruption). This means that any thread either sees the state before or after the operation, but no intermediate state can be observed. Not all hardware supports the same set of atomic instructions. If it is not available in hardware, it can be emulated in software using guards. However this has the obvious drawback of losing the lock-free property.

Performance of Non-Blocking Data Structures

When discussing the performance of non-blocking data structures, one has to distinguish between **amortized** and **worst-case** costs. The definition of 'lock-free' and 'wait-free' only mention the upper bound of an operation. Therefore lock-free data structures are not necessarily the best choice for every use case. In order to maximise the throughput of an application one should consider high-performance concurrent data structures[127].

Lock-free data structures will be a better choice in order to optimize the latency of a system or to avoid priority inversion, which may be necessary in real-time applications. In general we advise to consider if lock-free data structures are necessary or if concurrent data structures are sufficient. In any case we advice to perform benchmarks with different data structures for a specific workload.

Introduction to Intel TBB

Intel TBB is an open-source library developed by Intel and now available on Github[128].

Intel® Threading Building Blocks (Intel® TBB) is a library that supports scalable parallel programming using standard ISO C++ code. It does not require special languages or compilers. It is designed to promote scalable data parallel programming. Additionally, it fully supports nested parallelism, so you can build larger parallel components from smaller parallel components. To use the library, you specify tasks, not threads, and let the library map tasks onto threads in an efficient manner.

---

[126] Spinlocks do not directly interact with the operating system either. However it is possible that the owning thread is preempted by the operating system, which violates the lock-free property.

[127] Intel's Thread Building Blocks library provides many efficient concurrent data structures, which are not necessarily lock-free.

[128] https://github.com/oneapi-src/oneTBB

Professional C++ - Philosophy and Principles

Many of the library interfaces employ generic programming, in which interfaces are defined by requirements on types and not specific types. The C++ Standard Template Library (STL) is an example of generic programming. Generic programming enables Intel TBB to be flexible yet efficient. The generic interfaces enable you to customize components to your specific needs.

The net result is that Intel TBB enables you to specify parallelism far more conveniently than using raw threads, and at the same time can improve performance.

Here is a sample code:

```
/*
    Copyright (c) 2005-2020 Intel Corporation

    Licensed under the Apache License, Version 2.0 (the "License");
    you may not use this file except in compliance with the License.
    You may obtain a copy of the License at

        http://www.apache.org/licenses/LICENSE-2.0

    Unless required by applicable law or agreed to in writing, software
    distributed under the License is distributed on an "AS IS" BASIS,
    WITHOUT WARRANTIES OR CONDITIONS OF ANY KIND, either express or implied.
    See the License for the specific language governing permissions and
    limitations under the License.
*/

// Workaround for ICC 11.0 not finding __sync_fetch_and_add_4 on some of the Linux platforms.
#if __linux__ && defined(__INTEL_COMPILER)
#define __sync_fetch_and_add(ptr,addend) _InterlockedExchangeAdd(const_cast<void*>(reinterpret_cast<volatile void*>(ptr)), addend)
#endif
#include <string>
#include <cstring>
#include <cctype>
#include <cstdlib>
#include <cstdio>
#include "tbb/concurrent_hash_map.h"
#include "tbb/blocked_range.h"
#include "tbb/parallel_for.h"
#include "tbb/tick_count.h"
#include "tbb/tbb_allocator.h"
#include "tbb/global_control.h"
#include "../../common/utility/utility.h"
#include "../../common/utility/get_default_num_threads.h"

//! String type with scalable allocator.
/** On platforms with non-scalable default memory allocators, the example scales
    better if the string allocator is changed to tbb::tbb_allocator<char>. */
```

```cpp
typedef std::basic_string<char,std::char_traits<char>,tbb::tbb_allocator<char> >
MyString;

using namespace tbb;
using namespace std;

//! Set to true to counts.
static bool verbose = false;
static bool silent = false;
//! Problem size
long N = 1000000;
const int size_factor = 2;

//! A concurrent hash table that maps strings to ints.
typedef concurrent_hash_map<MyString,int> StringTable;

//! Function object for counting occurrences of strings.
struct Tally {
    StringTable& table;
    Tally( StringTable& table_ ) : table(table_) {}
    void operator()( const blocked_range<MyString*> range ) const {
        for( MyString* p=range.begin(); p!=range.end(); ++p ) {
            StringTable::accessor a;
            table.insert( a, *p );
            a->second += 1;
        }
    }
};

static MyString* Data;

static void CountOccurrences(int nthreads) {
    StringTable table;

    tick_count t0 = tick_count::now();
    parallel_for( blocked_range<MyString*>( Data, Data+N, 1000 ), Tally(table) );
    tick_count t1 = tick_count::now();

    int n = 0;
    for( StringTable::iterator i=table.begin(); i!=table.end(); ++i ) {
        if( verbose && nthreads )
            printf("%s %d\n",i->first.c_str(),i->second);
        n += i->second;
    }

    if ( !silent ) printf("total = %d  unique = %u  time = %g\n", n, unsigned(table.size()), (t1-t0).seconds());
}
```

Professional C++ - Philosophy and Principles

```cpp
/// Generator of random words

struct Sound {
    const char *chars;
    int rates[3];// beginning, middle, ending
};
Sound Vowels[] = {
    {"e", {445,6220,1762}}, {"a", {704,5262,514}}, {"i", {402,5224,162}}, {"o", {248,3726,191}},
    {"u", {155,1669,23}}, {"y", {4,400,989}}, {"io", {5,512,18}}, {"ia", {1,329,111}},
    {"ea", {21,370,16}}, {"ou", {32,298,4}}, {"ie", {0,177,140}}, {"ee", {2,183,57}},
    {"ai", {17,206,7}}, {"oo", {1,215,7}}, {"au", {40,111,2}}, {"ua", {0,102,4}},
    {"ui", {0,104,1}}, {"ei", {6,94,3}}, {"ue", {0,67,28}}, {"ay", {1,42,52}},
    {"ey", {1,14,80}}, {"oa", {5,84,3}}, {"oi", {2,81,1}}, {"eo", {1,71,5}},
    {"iou", {0,61,0}}, {"oe", {2,46,9}}, {"eu", {12,43,0}}, {"iu", {0,45,0}},
    {"ya", {12,19,5}}, {"ae", {7,18,10}}, {"oy", {0,10,13}}, {"ye", {8,7,7}},
    {"ion", {0,0,20}}, {"ing", {0,0,20}}, {"ium", {0,0,10}}, {"er", {0,0,20}}
};
Sound Consonants[] = {
    {"r", {483,1414,1110}}, {"n", {312,1548,1114}}, {"t", {363,1653,251}}, {"l", {424,1341,489}},
    {"c", {734,735,260}}, {"m", {732,785,161}}, {"d", {558,612,389}}, {"s", {574,570,405}},
    {"p", {519,361,98}}, {"b", {528,356,30}}, {"v", {197,598,16}}, {"ss", {3,191,567}},
    {"g", {285,430,42}}, {"st", {142,323,180}}, {"h", {470,89,30}}, {"nt", {0,350,231}},
    {"ng", {0,117,442}}, {"f", {319,194,19}}, {"ll", {1,414,83}}, {"w", {249,131,64}},
    {"k", {154,179,47}}, {"nd", {0,279,92}}, {"bl", {62,235,0}}, {"z", {35,223,16}},
    {"sh", {112,69,79}}, {"ch", {139,95,25}}, {"th", {70,143,39}}, {"tt", {0,219,19}},
    {"tr", {131,104,0}}, {"pr", {186,41,0}}, {"nc", {0,223,2}}, {"j", {184,32,1}},
    {"nn", {0,188,20}}, {"rt", {0,148,51}}, {"ct", {0,160,29}}, {"rr", {0,182,3}},
    {"gr", {98,87,0}}, {"ck", {0,92,86}}, {"rd", {0,81,88}}, {"x", {8,102,48}},
    {"ph", {47,101,10}}, {"br", {115,43,0}}, {"cr", {92,60,0}}, {"rm", {0,131,18}},
    {"ns", {0,124,18}}, {"sp", {81,55,4}}, {"sm", {25,29,85}}, {"sc", {53,83,1}},
    {"rn", {0,100,30}}, {"cl", {78,42,0}}, {"mm", {0,116,0}}, {"pp", {0,114,2}},
    {"mp", {0,99,14}}, {"rs", {0,96,16}}, /*{"q", {52,57,1}},*/ {"rl", {0,97,7}},
    {"rg", {0,81,15}}, {"pl", {56,39,0}}, {"sn", {32,62,1}}, {"str", {38,56,0}},
    {"dr", {47,44,0}}, {"fl", {77,13,1}}, {"fr", {77,11,0}}, {"ld", {0,47,38}},
    {"ff", {0,62,20}}, {"lt", {0,61,19}}, {"rb", {0,75,4}}, {"mb", {0,72,7}},
    {"rc", {0,76,1}}, {"gg", {0,74,1}}, {"pt", {1,56,10}}, {"bb", {0,64,1}},
```

```cpp
    {"sl", {48,17,0}}, {"dd", {0,59,2}}, {"gn", {3,50,4}}, {"rk", {0,30,28}},
    {"nk", {0,35,20}}, {"gl", {40,14,0}}, {"wh", {45,6,0}}, {"ntr", {0,50,0}},
    {"rv", {0,47,1}}, {"ght", {0,19,29}}, {"sk", {23,17,5}}, {"nf", {0,46,0}},
    {"cc", {0,45,0}}, {"ln", {0,41,0}}, {"sw", {36,4,0}}, {"rp", {0,36,4}},
    {"dn", {0,38,0}}, {"ps", {14,19,5}}, {"nv", {0,38,0}}, {"tch", {0,21,16}},
    {"nch", {0,26,11}}, {"lv", {0,35,0}}, {"wn", {0,14,21}}, {"rf", {0,32,3}},
    {"lm", {0,30,5}}, {"dg", {0,34,0}}, {"ft", {0,18,15}}, {"scr", {23,10,0}},
    {"rch", {0,24,6}}, {"rth", {0,23,7}}, {"rh", {13,15,0}}, {"mpl", {0,29,0}},
    {"cs", {0,1,27}}, {"gh", {4,10,13}}, {"ls", {0,23,3}}, {"ndr", {0,25,0}},
    {"tl", {0,23,1}}, {"ngl", {0,25,0}}, {"lk", {0,15,9}}, {"rw", {0,23,0}},
    {"lb", {0,23,1}}, {"tw", {15,8,0}}, /*{"sq", {15,8,0}},*/ {"chr", {18,4,0}},
    {"dl", {0,23,0}}, {"ctr", {0,22,0}}, {"nst", {0,21,0}}, {"lc", {0,22,0}},
    {"sch", {16,4,0}}, {"ths", {0,1,20}}, {"nl", {0,21,0}}, {"lf", {0,15,6}},
    {"ssn", {0,20,0}}, {"xt", {0,18,1}}, {"xp", {0,20,0}}, {"rst", {0,15,5}},
    {"nh", {0,19,0}}, {"wr", {14,5,0}}
};
const int VowelsNumber = sizeof(Vowels)/sizeof(Sound);
const int ConsonantsNumber = sizeof(Consonants)/sizeof(Sound);
int VowelsRatesSum[3] = {0,0,0}, ConsonantsRatesSum[3] = {0,0,0};

int CountRateSum(Sound sounds[], const int num, const int part)
{
    int sum = 0;
    for(int i = 0; i < num; i++)
        sum += sounds[i].rates[part];
    return sum;
}

const char *GetLetters(int type, const int part)
{
    Sound *sounds; int rate, i = 0;
    if(type & 1)
        sounds = Vowels, rate = rand() % VowelsRatesSum[part];
    else
        sounds = Consonants, rate = rand() % ConsonantsRatesSum[part];
    do {
        rate -= sounds[i++].rates[part];
    } while(rate > 0);
    return sounds[--i].chars;
}

static void CreateData() {
    for(int i = 0; i < 3; i++) {
        ConsonantsRatesSum[i] = CountRateSum(Consonants, ConsonantsNumber, i);
        VowelsRatesSum[i] = CountRateSum(Vowels, VowelsNumber, i);
    }
    for( int i=0; i<N; ++i ) {
        int type = rand();
        Data[i] = GetLetters(type++, 0);
```

```cpp
        for( int j = 0; j < type%size_factor; ++j )
            Data[i] += GetLetters(type++, 1);
        Data[i] += GetLetters(type, 2);
    }
    MyString planet = Data[12]; planet[0] = toupper(planet[0]);
    MyString helloworld = Data[0]; helloworld[0] = toupper(helloworld[0]);
    helloworld += ", "+Data[1]+" "+Data[2]+" "+Data[3]+" "+Data[4]+" "+Data[5];
    if ( !silent ) printf("Message from planet '%s': %s!\nAnalyzing whole text...\n", planet.c_str(), helloworld.c_str());
}

int main( int argc, char* argv[] ) {
    try {
        tbb::tick_count mainStartTime = tbb::tick_count::now();
        srand(2);

        //! Working threads count
        // The 1st argument is the function to obtain 'auto' value; the 2nd is the default value
        // The example interprets 0 threads as "run serially, then fully subscribed"
        utility::thread_number_range threads(utility::get_default_num_threads,0);

        utility::parse_cli_arguments(argc,argv,
            utility::cli_argument_pack()
            //"-h" option for displaying help is present implicitly
            .positional_arg(threads,"n-of-threads",utility::thread_number_range_desc)
            .positional_arg(N,"n-of-strings","number of strings")
            .arg(verbose,"verbose","verbose mode")
            .arg(silent,"silent","no output except elapsed time")
        );

        if ( silent ) verbose = false;

        Data = new MyString[N];
        CreateData();

        if ( threads.first ) {
            for(int p = threads.first;  p <= threads.last; p = threads.step(p)) {
                if ( !silent ) printf("threads = %d  ", p );
                global_control c(tbb::global_control::max_allowed_parallelism, p);
                CountOccurrences( p );
            }
        } else { // Number of threads wasn't set explicitly. Run serial and parallel version
            { // serial run
                if ( !silent ) printf("serial run    ");
```

```
                global_control c(tbb::global_control::max_allowed_parallelism, 1)
;
                CountOccurrences(1);
            }
            { // parallel run (number of threads is selected automatically)
                if ( !silent ) printf("parallel run ");
                global_control c(tbb::global_control::max_allowed_parallelism, ut
ility::get_default_num_threads());
                CountOccurrences(0);
            }
        }

        delete[] Data;

        utility::report_elapsed_time((tbb::tick_count::now() - mainStartTime).sec
onds());

        return 0;
    } catch(std::exception& e) {
        std::cerr<<"error occurred. error text is :\"" <<e.what()<<"\"\n";
    }
}
```

There is no complexity in this sample.

Introduction to Microsoft Concurrency Runtime

The Concurrency Runtime is divided into four components: the Parallel Patterns Library (PPL), the Asynchronous Agents Library, the Task Scheduler, and the Resource Manager. These components reside between the operating system and applications. The following illustration shows how the Concurrency Runtime components interact among the operating system and applications:

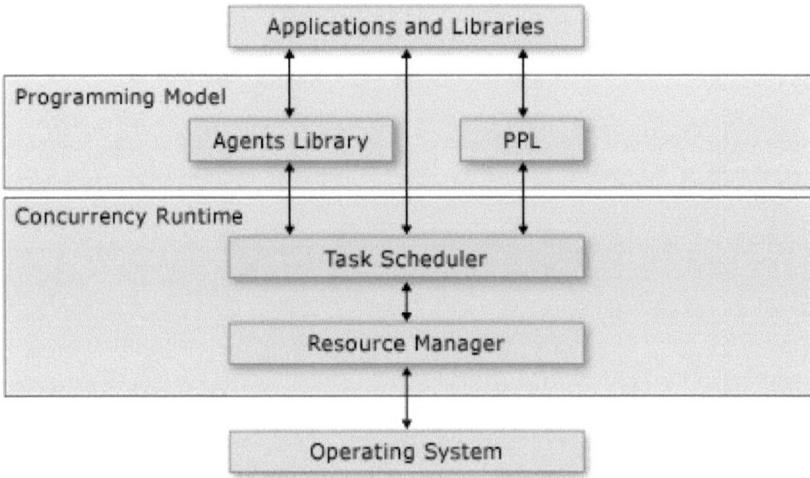

Introduction to Parallel Patterns Library

The Parallel Patterns Library (PPL) provides general-purpose containers and algorithms for performing fine-grained parallelism. The PPL enables *imperative data parallelism* by providing parallel algorithms that distribute computations on collections or on sets of data across computing resources. It also enables *task parallelism* by providing task objects that distribute multiple independent operations across computing resources.

Use the Parallel Patterns Library when you have a local computation that can benefit from parallel execution. For example, you can use the concurrency::parallel_for[129] algorithm to transform an existing **for** loop to act in parallel.

---

[129] https://docs.microsoft.com/en-us/cpp/parallel/concrt/reference/concurrency-namespace-functions?view=vs-2019#parallel_for

Professional C++

For more information about the Parallel Patterns Library, see the official documentation[130].

Example of PPL code

The PPL provides a programming model that resembles the C++ Standard Library. The following example demonstrates many features of the PPL. It computes several Fibonacci numbers serially and in parallel. Both computations act on a std::array object. The example also prints to the console the time that is required to perform both computations.

The serial version uses the C++ Standard Library std::for_each algorithm to traverse the array and stores the results in a std::vector object. The parallel version performs the same task, but uses the PPL concurrency::parallel_for_each algorithm and stores the results in a concurrency::concurrent_vector object. The concurrent_vector class enables each loop iteration to concurrently add elements without the requirement to synchronize write access to the container.

Because parallel_for_each acts concurrently, the parallel version of this example must sort the concurrent_vector object to produce the same results as the serial version.

Note that the example uses a naïve method to compute the Fibonacci numbers; however, this method illustrates how the Concurrency Runtime can improve the performance of long computations.

```
// parallel-fibonacci.cpp
// compile with: /EHsc
#include <windows.h>
#include <ppl.h>
#include <concurrent_vector.h>
#include <array>
#include <vector>
#include <tuple>
#include <algorithm>
#include <iostream>

using namespace concurrency;
using namespace std;

// Calls the provided work function and returns the number of milliseconds
// that it takes to call that function.
template <class Function>
__int64 time_call(Function&& f)
{
    __int64 begin = GetTickCount();
    f();
```

[130] https://docs.microsoft.com/en-us/cpp/parallel/concrt/parallel-patterns-library-ppl?view=vs-2019

```cpp
    return GetTickCount() - begin;
}

// Computes the nth Fibonacci number.
int fibonacci(int n)
{
    if(n < 2)
        return n;
    return fibonacci(n-1) + fibonacci(n-2);
}

int wmain()
{
    __int64 elapsed;

    // An array of Fibonacci numbers to compute.
    array<int, 4> a = { 24, 26, 41, 42 };

    // The results of the serial computation.
    vector<tuple<int,int>> results1;

    // The results of the parallel computation.
    concurrent_vector<tuple<int,int>> results2;

    // Use the for_each algorithm to compute the results serially.
    elapsed = time_call([&]
    {
        for_each (begin(a), end(a), [&](int n) {
            results1.push_back(make_tuple(n, fibonacci(n)));
        });
    });
    wcout << L"serial time: " << elapsed << L" ms" << endl;

    // Use the parallel_for_each algorithm to perform the same task.
    elapsed = time_call([&]
    {
        parallel_for_each (begin(a), end(a), [&](int n) {
            results2.push_back(make_tuple(n, fibonacci(n)));
        });

        // Because parallel_for_each acts concurrently, the results do not
        // have a pre-determined order. Sort the concurrent_vector object
        // so that the results match the serial version.
        sort(begin(results2), end(results2));
    });
    wcout << L"parallel time: " << elapsed << L" ms" << endl << endl;
```

```cpp
    // Print the results.
    for_each (begin(results2), end(results2), [](tuple<int,int>& pair) {
        wcout << L"fib(" << get<0>(pair) << L"): " << get<1>(pair) << endl;
    });
}
```

Others PPL Topics

There are others facilities in the PPL library:

- Task Parallelism[131]: Describes the role of tasks and task groups in the PPL.
- Parallel Algorithms[132]: Describes how to use parallel algorithms such as parallel_for and parallel_for_each.
- Parallel Containers and Objects[133]: Describes the various parallel containers and objects that are provided by the PPL.
- Cancellation in the PPL[134]:   Explains how to cancel the work that is being performed by a parallel algorithm.
- Concurrency Runtime[135]: Describes the Concurrency Runtime, which simplifies parallel programming, and contains links to related topics.

General considerations on PPL

Microsoft made the asynchronous task patterns available in the open source C++ REST SDK[136]. This library is actively maintained and is truly cross-platform. It includes some of the PPL library as a PPLX subset, so if that's what you want the PPL for, then it's a reasonable choice.

The C++ REST SDK is presented in another chapter called Web Services and Server Side Components later in this book.

---

[131] https://docs.microsoft.com/en-us/cpp/parallel/concrt/task-parallelism-concurrency-runtime?view=vs-2019

[132] https://docs.microsoft.com/en-us/cpp/parallel/concrt/parallel-algorithms?view=vs-2019

[133] https://docs.microsoft.com/en-us/cpp/parallel/concrt/parallel-containers-and-objects?view=vs-2019

[134] https://docs.microsoft.com/en-us/cpp/parallel/concrt/cancellation-in-the-ppl?view=vs-2019

[135] https://docs.microsoft.com/en-us/cpp/parallel/concrt/concurrency-runtime?view=vs-2019

[136] https://github.com/Microsoft/cpprestsdk

Professional C++ - Philosophy and Principles

Advice

Using concurrency can improve the performance of your application.

Consider using tasks rather than threads.

Don't mix Operating System calls and standard library calls. Make a choice.

Standard library types are type safe.

Prefer the use of parallel algorithm to direct use of thread/tasks.

Avoid sharing data when you can.

Use scoped_lock, unique_lock and shared_lock by default.

Release the locks as soon as possible.

Use future and promise.

Take a look at Boost, Intel TBB and Microsoft PPL.

12. Multithreading on Windows

Here we do some specific Windows but note that everything that has been written compiles also on Windows because we used the STL of C++ and that it is portable at source level. The C++ is ISO and multiplatform.

Introduction

Under Windows in the 1990s where Windows was booming, system programming was described in Charles Petzold's book, «Programming Windows». This book that many developers have devoured describes the use of Windows APIs and one of the chapters in the section «Advanced Topics» is multithreading. The other successful author was Jeffrey Richter and his book only on the Win32 system. For those interested, Jeffrey Richter's book became Windows via C/C++...

Let's go back to the front of Win32. Before Windows 95 and Windows NT, the only way to do background operations was to use a Timer object. The number of objects was limited but this already allowed to realize things of good quality. With Win32, the system has the notion of threads. The founder and architect of Windows NT, Dave Cutler, created the system like the Digital OS of the time with the notion of security at the level of Kernel objects. I explain: A thread is a Kernel object. It is not like a GDI window. It is identified by a HANDLE type and it must be managed properly otherwise we degrade the system. A HANDLE is obtained with the primitive CreateThread and it must be released via CloseHandle. This primitive is defined in Windows. h:

```
HANDLE WINAPI CreateThread(
  _In_opt_    LPSECURITY_ATTRIBUTES  lpThreadAttributes,
  _In_        SIZE_T                 dwStackSize,
  _In_        LPTHREAD_START_ROUTINE lpStartAddress,
  _In_opt_    LPVOID                 lpParameter,
  _In_        DWORD dwCreationFlags,
  _Out_opt_   LPDWORD                lpThreadId
);
```

Professional C++ - Philosophy and Principles

A thread is an operation (a function alias a C routine) launched in the background and scheduled by the operating system.

At first glance, you will tell me, CreateThread is not easy to use... In fact a good sample will do the trick to understand. The first parameter is a security descriptor structure and can be NULL. The second is the size of the stack. If it is set to 0, we will have the default size. The third is the function of the thread. The fourth is the pointer to the parameters to pass to the thread. The fifth is a set of flags to tell if the thread is suspended or started immediately: 0 or CREATE_SUSPENDED. The last parameter returns the thread id. Finally, the function returns the HANDLE of the thread if the function has passed otherwise it is null. A sample?

```
#include <Windows. h>

DWORD WINAPI MyThreadProc(LPVOID lpParam)
{
    for (int i = 0; i < 10000; i++)
    {
        printf(".");
    }

    printf("\n");
    return 0;
}


int main()
{
    DWORD dwThreadId = 0;
    HANDLE hThread = CreateThread(NULL, 0, &MyThreadProc, NULL, 0, &dwThreadId);
    WaitForSingleObject(hThread, INFINITE);
    CloseHandle(hThread);
    return 0;
}
```

As you can see, there is a bit of glue to wait for the end of the thread via the primitive WaitForSingleObject... This type of code works from Windows NT and Win95 and will still work. System APIs are never marked *deprecated!*

A variant in Runtime C

There is a variant to CreateThread in the C runtime, the CRT. It is via the functions _beginthread and _beginthreadex. Here is the variant with _beginthread:

```
#include <stdio. h>
#include <process. h>
#include <Windows. h>
```

```
void MyThreadProc3(void* pArguments)
{
    for (int i = 0; i < 10000; i++)
    {
        printf(".");
    }

    printf("\n");
}

int main()
{
    unsigned int threadID = 0;
    HANDLE hThread3 = (HANDLE)_beginthread(&MyThreadProc3, 0, NULL);
    WaitForSingleObject(hThread3, INFINITE);
    CloseHandle(hThread3);

    return 0;
}
```

The _beginthreadex variant is of very little interest because it is exactly modeled on CreateThread:

```
unsigned int threadID = 0;
HANDLE hThread2 = (HANDLE)_beginthreadex(NULL, 0, &MyThreadProc2, NULL, 0,
&threadID);
WaitForSingleObject(hThread2, INFINITE);
CloseHandle(hThread2);
```

If a routine wants to hold or hand over other threads, just call the Sleep(xxx ms) function;

```
DWORD WINAPI MyThreadProc(LPVOID lpParam)
{
    for (int i = 0; i < 100; i++)
    {
        printf(".");
        Sleep(50);
    }

    printf("\n");
    return 0;
}
```

This allows to control the execution speed of the thread.

Professional C++ - Philosophy and Principles

The termination of a thread

A thread ends in several ways:
- The function ends with a return code
- The thread kills itself via ExitThread
- A thread in the same process or another calls TerminateThread
- The process that contains the thread ends

Suspending or summarizing a thread

The ResumeThread(HANDLE hThread) routine resumes a thread.
The SuspendThread(HANDLE hThread) routine allows you to suspend a thread.

The priority of a thread

It is possible to increase the priority of a thread via SetThreadPriority. Careful, you have to experiment with this function before using it in production!

Thread Priority	Symbolic Constant
Time-critical	THREAD_PRIORITY_TIME_CRITICAL
Highest	THREAD_PRIORITY_HIGHEST
Above normal	THREAD_PRIORITY_ABOVE_NORMAL
Normal	THREAD_PRIORITY_NORMAL
Below normal	THREAD_PRIORITY_BELOW_NORMAL
Lowest	THREAD_PRIORITY_LOWEST
Idle	THREAD_PRIORITY_IDLE

The interlocked routines

There are routines to do ATOMIC operations. Example: to increment, decrement a variable. This is the Interlocked_FUNCTION_NAME series like InterlockedIncrement, InterlockedDecrement, InterlockedExchange, etc

Threads synchronization in User mode

To synchronize threads, one can go through boolean for example but provided to protect them. Critical sections serve this through routines:
- InitializeCriticalSection
- EnterCriticalSection
- LeaveCriticalSection

```
long _x = 0;
long _y = 0;
CRITICAL_SECTION _cs1;

DWORD WINAPI MyThreadP1(LPVOID lpParam)
{
      InitializeCriticalSection(&_cs1);

      for (int i = 0; i < 10000; i++)
      {
            EnterCriticalSection(&_cs1);
            _x++;
            _y++;
            printf("%d/%d.", _x, _y);
            LeaveCriticalSection(&_cs1);
      }
```

```
        printf("\n");
        return 0;
}

int main()
{
    DWORD dwThreadId1 = 0;
    HANDLE hThread1 = CreateThread(NULL, 0, &MyThreadP1, NULL, 0,
&dwThreadId1);
    DWORD dwThreadId2 = 0;
    HANDLE hThread2 = CreateThread(NULL, 0, &MyThreadP1, NULL, 0,
&dwThreadId2);
    DWORD dwThreadId3 = 0;
    HANDLE hThread3 = CreateThread(NULL, 0, &MyThreadP1, NULL, 0,
&dwThreadId3);
    HANDLE hTab[3] = { hThread1, hThread2, hThread3 };
    WaitForMultipleObjects(3, hTab, TRUE, INFINITE);
    CloseHandle(hThread1);
    CloseHandle(hThread2);
    CloseHandle(hThread3);

    return 0;
}
```

You will notice that variables are protected in writing but also in reading!

Threads synchronization in Kernel mode

There are mechanisms more powerful than critical sections and they are Kernel objects. The best known being the mutex. These objects are reportable; here is the comparison table between a mutex and a critical section:

Characteristic	Mutex	Critical Section
Performance	Slow	Fast
Can be used across process boundaries	Yes	No
Declaration	`HANDLE hmtx;`	`CRITICAL_SECTION cs;`
Initialization	`hmtx = CreateMutex (NULL, FALSE, NULL);`	`InitializeCriticalSection(&cs);`
Cleanup	`CloseHandle(hmtx);`	`DeleteCriticalSection(&cs);`
Infinite wait	`WaitForSingleObject (hmtx, INFINITE);`	`EnterCriticalSection(&cs);`
0 wait	`WaitForSingleObject (hmtx, 0);`	`TryEnterCriticalSection(&cs);`
Arbitrary wait	`WaitForSingleObject (hmtx, dwMilliseconds);`	Not possible
Release	`ReleaseMutex(hmtx);`	`LeaveCriticalSection(&cs);`
Can be waited on with other kernel objects	Yes (use `WaitForMultipleObjects` or similar function)	No

Professional C++

The Concurrency Runtime alias ConcRT

In 2011, Microsoft released a C++ library to fully exploit processor threads: the Concurrency Runtime:

Parallel Patterns Library
PPL provides collections classes (containers) and algorithms to perform parallel operations and distributed operations on datasets or collections. PPL also allows parallelism of tasks by providing Task objects distributed over hardware resources.

Asynchronous Agents Library
Agents Library makes it possible to communicate different elements of a program through interfaces and implements an advanced pipeline.

The Task Scheduler manages and coordinates the execution tasks. The Task Scheduler is cooperative.

Resource Manager
The role of the Resource Manager is to manage memory and processor resources.

The following header files are required to take advantage of the different parts of CR:

Component	Header file
Parallel Patternshhhhh Library (PPL)	ppl.h ppltasks.h concurrent_queue.h concurrent_vector.h
Asynchronous Agents Library	agents.h
Task Scheduler	concrt.h
Resource Manager	concrtrm.h

All ConcRT classes and templates are incorporated into the Concurrency namespace.

The cooperative blockage
With cooperative blocking, a task can suspend its execution and hand over to the Task Scheduler to reuse resources and thus optimize the use of these resources to perform other tasks. Unlike the low-level primitives of the operating system (Windows), processor resources are optimized. Cooperative blocking improves the performance of parallel applications by making full use of CPU resources. The main synchronization objects are single lock (critical_section class), SWMR type lock alias Single Writer Multiple Readers (reader_writer_lock class), manual event (event class).

List of cooperative blocking operations:

Cooperative blocking operations	Description
task_group::wait	waits for completion of a task or task group

Professional C++ - Philosophy and Principles

critical_section::lock	acquisition of a critical section type lock
critical_section::scope_lock	exception safe version
reader_writer_lock::lock	acquisition of a reader/writer type lock in writing
reader_writer_lock::scope_lock	exception safe version
reader_writer_lock::lock_read	acquisition of a read reader/writer lock
reader_writer_lock::scope_lock_read	exception safe version
event::wait	equivalent to a reset event manual
agent::wait	waits for the end of the agent
agent::wait_for_all, wait_for_one	waits for the end of one or more agents
Concurrency::wait	blockage during an interval
Context::Block	internal to CR
Context::Yield	gives a hand to another execution context
parallel_for, parallel_for_each, parallel_invoke	functions for parallel algorithms
send, asend	message data transmission functions
receive	message reception function

Tasks and threads

When a task has to be executed, the Task Scheduler calls the task routine in a thread of its choice. The task does not change thread. This is a guarantee for code that has been refined with a thread or a use for example of TLS (Thread Local Storage). Creating a task is a less costly operation than explicitly creating a thread. It is possible for an application to create hundreds or thousands of tasks while running efficiently. This is not possible with explicit threads. Designing a task-based application is less complicated than designing a threaded application.

Creating Tasks

Job creation can be done with lambdas or simple function pointers. The task_group class can be used in different ways. For a detailed statement, the task_group class uses the overloaded run() method which takes a task_handle parameter in which the name of the function to be used is explicitly specified. The modern syntax of the C++ style allows the use of the auto keyword to hide the type returned by the make_task function. The new C++ standard introduces template classes for the management of function pointers and it is possible to write all these forms in the same function. However, the functions to be used must have a void function(void) signature.

```
void DoSimpleTask(void)
{
    Logger::LogDebug("Enter DoSimpleTask...");
    wait(1000);
    Logger::LogDebug("Leave DoSimpleTask...");
}

void Call_Task_Group_Run()
```

```
{
    // Statement by the Task Group
    task_group g;
    // With an explicit statement of task_handle and prototype
    task_handle<void (*)(void)> t1 = make_task(&DoSimpleTask);
    // With auto
    auto t2 = make_task(&DoSimpleTask);
    // With std::tr1::function
    std::function<void (void)> f3 = &DoSimpleTask;
    auto t3 = make_task(f3);
    // Creating Tasks
    g.run(t1);
    g.run(t2);
    g.run(t3);
    g.run( &DoSimpleTask );
    g.wait();
}
```

The pppltasks header file. h introduces new templates and classes to manage tasks. Thus, we find the template of the task class<> which takes as parameter in its constructor an object of type std::function. The function passed to the task class can also return a given type and thus resemble a classic thread that returns, usually 0 if successful:

```
int DoSimpleTask_Random()
{
    Logger::LogDebug("Enter DoSimpleTask_Random...");
    wait(1000);
    // Generation of a random number of 1.. 1000
    unsigned int r = 0;
    srand(1); rand_s(&r);
    r = (unsigned int) ((double)r / ((double) UINT_MAX + 1 ) * 1000.0) + 1;
    Logger::LogDebug("Leave DoSimpleTask_Random...");
    return r;
}

void Call_Task_Group_Run_Extras()
{
    std::function<int (void)> f1 = &DoSimpleTask_Random;
    task<int> t1(f1);
    t1.wait();
    int ret = t1.get();
    printf("Tasks t1 returns %d n", ret);

    std::function<void (void)> f2 = &DoSimpleTask;
    task<void> t2(f2);
    t2.wait();
}
```

Professional C++ - Philosophy and Principles

The ConcRT sample pack introduces operators that make the syntax more elegant. To create two tasks and wait for them to finish, just use the &&operator.

```
void Call_Task_Group_Run_Extras_WithOperator()
{
    std::function<int (void)> f1 = &DoSimpleTask_Random;
    task<int> t1(f1);
    std::function<int (void)> f2 = &DoSimpleTask_Random;
    task<int> t2(f2);
    (t1 && t2).wait();
    printf("Tasks t1 returns %d \n", t1.get());
    printf("Tasks t2 returns %d \n", t2.get());
}
```

To sequence the creation of a task once the first two tasks are complete, use the then() method:

```
void Call_Task_Group_Run_Extras_WithOperator2()
{
    std::function<void (void)> f1 = &DoSimpleTask;
    task<void> t1(f1);
    std::function<void (void)> f2 = &DoSimpleTask;
    task<void> t2(f2);
    std::tr1::function<void (void)> f3 = &DoSimpleTask;
    auto t3 = (t1 && t2).then(f3);
    t3.wait();
}
```

Managing the Task Scheduler

It is possible to choose how the ConcRT will handle tasks through the use of threads. The SchedulerPolicy class specifies the minimum and maximum number of CPU resources (virtual processors) via the MinConcurrency and MaxConcurrency properties. The SchedulerKing properties allows you to choose the type of threads: Win32 or UMS. UMS or User-mode scheduling is a lightweight thread management mechanism available in 64-bit versions of Windows 10 and Windows Server 2019.

```
SchedulerPolicy policy(2,
        MinConcurrency, 1,
        MaxConcurrency, 2);
CurrentScheduler::Create(policy);
```

It is also possible to finely control the way tasks are distributed by creating a scheduler group via the Scheduler and ScheduleGroup classes. The ScheduleTask() method can also be used to create light-weight tasks (light-weight task). The Agents library makes intensive use of this method. ConcRT does not handle and does not capture exceptions generated by light tasks. In addition, the termination of a light task is not reported by the ConcRT runtime.

Conclusion

Managing threads in Win32 may seem complex but APIs are relatively simple to use. The problem does not come from system primitives but from the complexity of multithreads applications and data sharing and the resulting bugs in the event of unprotection. And it is in this case that the Concurrency Runtime takes its place because simpler, more practical. It's up to you!

Professional C++ - Philosophy and Principles

13. Multithreading with Linux

Let's talk about the Linux platform. We will explain what is and how to do multithreading in C++ under Linux. To do this we will take as support the STL (Standard Template Library) of C++ which provides everything you need.

An integrated environment: VSCode
Microsoft provides a free and lightweight IDE which is VSCode. This IDE is available on Windows, Mac and Linux. My post is under Ubuntu and VSCode is nice to use.

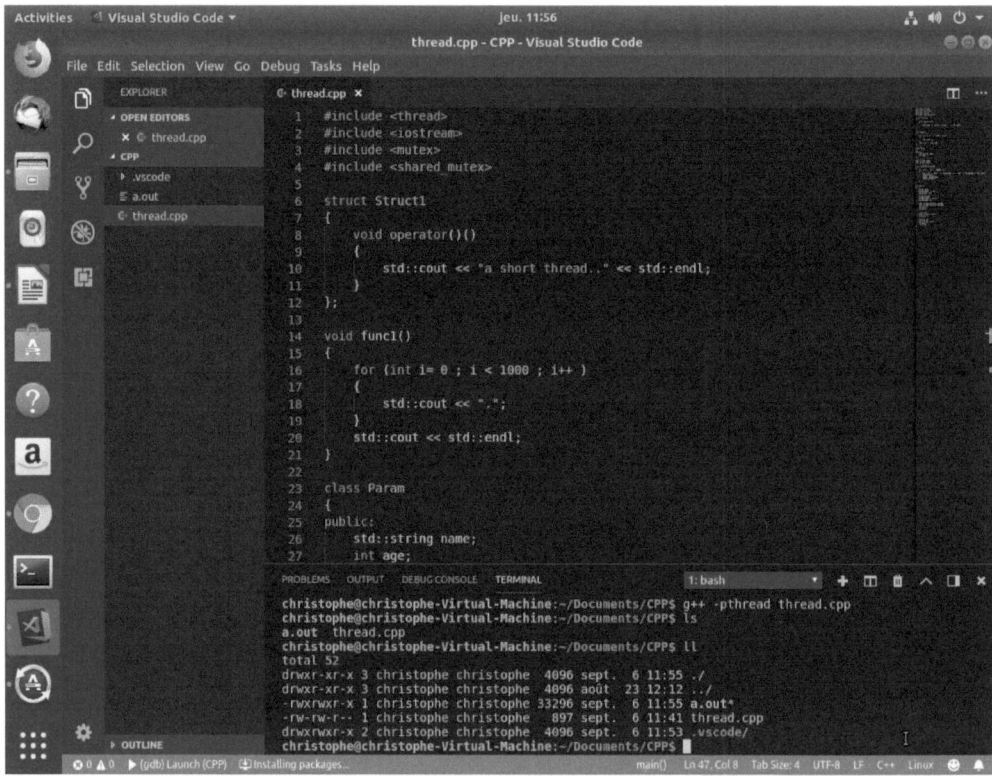

As you can see on the screen photo, VSCode contains a terminal to start the compilation.

Linux
My environment is a Ubuntu Desktop 18.04.

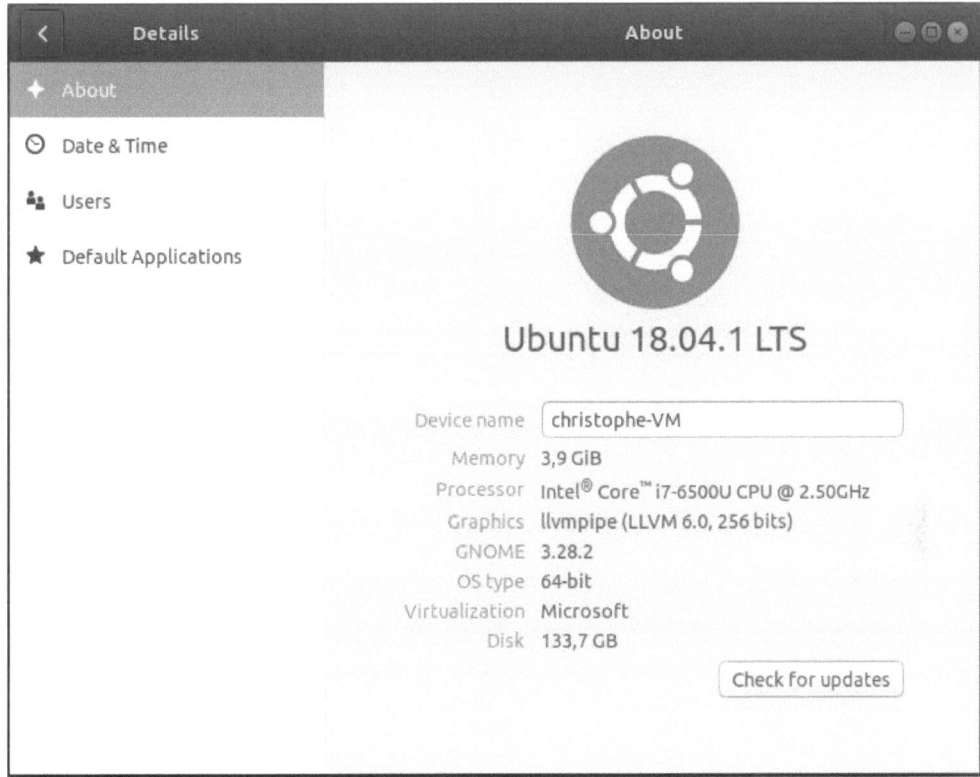

Now that we have a Linux system and an IDE, we have to choose a compiler: GCC. That is the historical standard. You don't change a winning team! With a g++ –v, I'm in GCC version 7.3. It supports C++11 and C++14 and C++17: that's the main thing.

What is multithreading and threads?
A thread is a routine that runs in the background. It is the operating system that handles threads. Under Windows, the operating system orders threads, under Linux, the operating system orders processes. The thread is a lightweight mechanism. The thread provides access to resources and to avoid access conflicts, these resources must be protected. Example: If a global variable is used in two threads that run, there may be memory corruption. The first thread does an assignment operation, it is preempted (it becomes inactive) and the second thread becomes active and in turn modifies the variable. In this case, there is memory corruption because the memory location is changed at the same time...
    To avoid this, we will put a blocker of type mutex, semaphore or barrier.

The STL or the system APIs?
To create a thread, we have two solutions. Either we use the API of the operating system so in our case the pthread library or we use the STL and its header file <thread>. The advantage of using STL is that the code is portable or cross-platform. Using pthread directly, my code will only run on Linux... It's the same on Windows, if I use the Win32 CreateThread routine, my code is locked for Windows...

My first thread

Professional C++ - Philosophy and Principles

The <thread> header file of the STL allows to create threads. A thread is created by instantiating the thread class and passing it as a parameter either a structure, a class or a function. The join() method allows you to wait until the thread runs out.

```cpp
#include <thread>
#include <iostream>

struct Struct1
{
    void operator()()
    {
        std::cout << "a short thread.." << std::endl;
    }
};

void func1()
{
    for (int i= 0; i < 1000; i++ )
    {
        std::cout << "." ;
    }
    std::cout << std::endl;
}

int main()
{
    std::thread t(func1);
    t.join();

    Struct1 s1;
    std::thread t2(s1);
    t2.join();
    return 0;
}
```

Note that to be used with a structure or class, a thread uses the operator () override to execute. The simplest form is if not to provide a simple routine. Threads run in the same memory space and can communicate through shared objects. Such communications are protected by locks to avoid access competition that causes application crashes as there is memory corruption in case of competing access on the same data.

Compilation with g++
The compilation suite is that of GCC and more specifically g++ which is the c++ compiler. To compile a program that uses threads, specify the –pthread option; we use the standard C++17 via –std:c++17:

```
$ g++ -pthread -std=c++17 thread.cpp -o thread
```

This produces an executable thread file that can be run via ./thread.

Professional C++

Passage of arguments
To be able to perform its job, a thread needs parameter(s). Just pass them as arguments to the thread class constructor:

```cpp
class Param
{
public:
     std::string name;
     int age;
};

void func3(Param param)
{
     std::cout << "Name:" << param.name << ", Age:" << param.age << std::endl;
}

int main()
{
     Param param;
     param.name = "Lisa";
     param.age = 12;
     std::thread t3(func3, param);
     t3.join();
}
```

In this example, the func3 routine takes a Param class as a parameter.

Return of value
It is possible for a thread to return elements, a value, fields, etc.

```cpp
struct Struct2
{
public:
     Struct2(Param param, double * result)
     {
          _param = param;
          _res = result;
     }

public:
     void operator()()
     {
          std::cout << "Name:" << _param.name
                    << ", Age:" << _param.age << std::endl;
          *_res = 10;
     }

private:
     double * _res;
```

297

```
        Param _param;
};

int main()
{
        Param param;
        param.name = "Lisa";
        param.age = 12;

        double d = 0;
        Struct2 s2(param, &d);
        std::thread t4(s2);
        t4.join();
        std::cout << "ret d=" << d << std::endl;
}
```

In this example, we pass the address of a double to the constructor of the structure in addition to the Param class. This member is pointed to the address of a member variable and then the thread changes the member value. That is all!

Data Sharing
Data sharing is sometimes necessary. In this case, access to the data must be protected. The simplest object to achieve this is the mutex: *mutual exclusion object*. This object is usually declared as global or in the class and is used to protect a block of data.

```
std::string _name;
std::mutex _mutex;

void func5(Param param)
{
        for (int i = 0; i < 100; i++)
        {
                std::cout << "Name:" << param.name << ", Age:" << age param.age << std::endl;
                _mutex.lock();
                _name = param.name;
                _mutex.unlock();
        }
}

int main()
{
        Param param;
        param.name = "Lisa";
        param.age = 12;

        Param param2;
        param2.name = "Audrey";
```

```cpp
        param2.age = 8;

        std::thread t5(func5, param);
        std::thread t6(func5, param2);
        t5.join();
        t6.join();
}
```

The best way to break into a thread is to use the sleep_for() routine, which restores the other threads. Here's how to make a 250 millisecond wait:

```cpp
std::this_thread::sleep_for(std::chrono::milliseconds(250));
```

It is also possible to use a lighter lock which is the shared_mutex:

```cpp
std::shared_mutex _smutex;

void func6(Param param)
{
    for (int i = 0; i < 10000; i++)
    {
        _smutex.lock();
        _name = param.name;
        _smutex.unlock();

        _smutex.lock_shared();
        std::cout << "Name:" << _name << std::endl;
        _smutex.unlock_shared();
    }
}

int main()
{
    Param param;
    param.name = "Lisa";
    param.age = 12;

    Param param2;
    param2.name = "Audrey";
    param2.age = 8;

    std::thread t5(func6, param);
    std::thread t6(func6, param2);
    t5.join();
    t6.join();
}
```

In this case, the lock_shared() method is used for read access and the lock() method is used for write access.

Professional C++ - Philosophy and Principles

Tasks: Future and Promised

There is a higher level mechanism than threads and mutex: these are the classes available in the <future> header. When a transfer value between two tasks can be done without locks, we implement futures and promises all being managed by tasks rather than threads. When a task wants to pass a value to another task, it positions the value in the promise; the mechanics make that the value is readable in the future. The call is made this way if we have a future<X> fx:

X x = fx.get();

Example of a future:

```cpp
int MySum(int i, int j)
{
    return i + j;
}
void ft()
{
    std::packaged_task<int(int, int)> task(MySum); // wrap the function
    std::future<int> f1 = task.get_future();       // get a future
    std::thread t(std::move(task), 10, 20); // launch on a thread
    f1.wait();
    std::cout << "Done! result: " << f1.get() << std::endl;
    t.join();
}
```

It is also possible to do this with a promise by setting the value via a set_value:

```cpp
void ft3()
{
    // future from a promise
    std::promise<int> p;
    std::future<int> f3 = p.get_future();
    std::thread([&p] { p.set_value_at_thread_exit(9); }).detach();

    std::cout << "Waiting..." << std::flush;
    f3.wait();
    std::cout << "Done! result: " << f3.get() << std::endl;
}
```

The simplest remaining use of async:

```cpp
void ft2()
{
    // future from an async()
    std::future<int> f2 = std::async(std::launch::async, [] { return 8; });
    f2.wait();
    std::cout << "Done! result: " << f2.get() << std::endl;
}
```

Conclusion
The use of threads is not very complicated. Just take care to protect the shared data well and set up the mutex that go well. For higher-level use, note that async may be easy to use too. The C++ is ISO and multiplatform so what is valid on Linux is also valid on other platforms like Android, iOS, Mac or Windows via the STL (Standard Template Library) of C++.

Professional C++ - Philosophy and Principles

14. Web Services and Web API using Modern C++

The Microsoft REST SDK CPP

Imagine that you can develop the back-end of your software solution on a server with the king of languages that is C++? On Linux: yes. On Windows: yes. One cell phone code? Yes. The whole without delirious complexity just with classes and methods of treatment... And we return from the JSON for a front-end in JS? Chiche! Follow me, I'll explain...

Casablanca alias C++ REST SDK

To develop an API Web, many of us only know about ASP.NET and C#... Since MFC ISAPI and ATL Server, Visual C++ no longer provides project templates for server developments. A SDK takes up the torch: the REST SDK, code name «Casablanca». This SDK written in modern C++ (C++ 11) proposes to create server and client code using the latest patterns namely http and JSON support.
Available on Github at https://github.com/Microsoft/cpprestsdk . This SDK also offers sample code to get started smoothly.

A simple REST http server

Let's look at the minimum code to create an API web server that returns JSON. First, you need to define a class that contains an **http_listener.**

```cpp
using namespace web;
using namespace http;
using namespace utility;
using namespace http::experimental::listener;

class MyServer
{
public:
    MyServer() {}
    MyServer(utility::string_t url);

    pplx::task<void> open() { return m_listener.open(); }
    pplx::task<void> close() { return m_listener.close(); }

private:

    static void handle_get(http_request message);
    static void handle_put(http_request message);
    static void handle_post(http_request message);
    static void handle_delete(http_request message);

    http_listener m_listener;
};
```

Next, you have to configure this listener by providing it with a URI on which you listen as well as the handlers for GET, PUT, POST and DELETE operations. But first of all, declare the server as a global variable as follows:

```cpp
std::unique_ptr<MyServer> g_http;
```

Then, you have to prepare the essential elements for the server, namely its listening URI:

```cpp
    utility::string_t port = U("34568");
    utility::string_t address = U("http://localhost:");
    address.append(port);

    uri_builder uri(port);
    uri.append_path(U("MyServer/Action/"));

    auto addr = uri.to_uri().to_string();
    g_http = std::unique_ptr<MyServer>(new MyServer(addr));
    g_http->open().wait();
```

Professional C++ - Philosophy and Principles

```
        ucout << utility::string_t(U("Listening for requests at: ")) << addr <<
std::endl;
```

The call to open() activates listening. We still have to discover the MyServer class's constructor code because we have to save the handlers on the HTTP methods:

CE f

```
MyServer::MyServer(utility::string_t url) : m_listener(url)
{
    std::function<void(http_request)> fnGet = &MyServer::handle_get;
    m_listener.support(methods::GET, fnGet);

    std::function<void(http_request)> fnPut = &MyServer::handle_put;
    m_listener.support(methods::PUT, fnPut);

    std::function<void(http_request)> fnPost = &MyServer::handle_post;
    m_listener.support(methods::POST, fnPost);

    std::function<void(http_request)> fnDel = &MyServer::handle_delete;
    m_listener.support(methods::DEL, fnDel);

}
```

OK the http server body is there... Let's look at the HTTP method body. We're going to code only one, but the system is simple.

304

```cpp
void MyServer::handle_post(http_request message)
{
    ucout << message.to_string() << endl;
    message.reply(status_codes::OK);
};

void MyServer::handle_delete(http_request message)
{
    ucout << message.to_string() << endl;
    message.reply(status_codes::OK);
}

void MyServer::handle_put(http_request message)
{
    ucout << message.to_string() << endl;
    message.reply(status_codes::OK);
};
```

These methods are not implemented but patience, here is what we will code. On the GET method if we are sent «get_developers» then we dump a data structure in JSON.

The body of the GET handler

The returned JSON data structure is defined as follows:

{"job":"Developers","people":[{"age":25,"name":"Franck"},{"age":20,"name":"Joe"}]}

Let's see the body of this GET method:

```cpp
void MyServer::handle_get(http_request message)

{
    ucout << U("Message") << U(" ")
          << message.to_string() << endl;

    ucout << U("Relative URI") << U(" ")
          << message.relative_uri().to_string() << endl;

    auto paths = uri::split_path(uri::decode(message.relative_uri().path()));
```

```cpp
        for (auto it1 = paths.begin(); it1!= paths.end(); it1++)
        {
            ucout << U("Path") << U(" ")
                  << *it1 << endl;
        }

        auto query =
   uri::split_query(uri::decode(message.relative_uri().query()));
        for (auto it2 = query.begin(); it2!= query.end(); it2++)
        {
            ucout << U("Query") << U(" ")
                  << it2->first << U(" ") << it2->second << endl;
        }

        auto queryItr = query.find(U("request"));
        utility::string_t request = queryItr->second;
        ucout << U("Request") << U(" ") << request << endl;

        if (request == U("get_developers"))
        {
            Data data;
            data.job = U("Developers");
            People p1;
            p1.age = 25;
            p1.name = U("Franck");
            data.peoples.push_back(p1);
            People p2;
            p2.age = 20;
            p2.name = U("Joe");
            data.peoples.push_back(p2);

            utility::string_t response = data.AsJSON().serialize();
            ucout << response << endl;

            message.reply(status_codes::OK, data.AsJSON());
            return;
        }

        message.reply(status_codes::OK);
};
```

Should we start by dumper the input received? The request, the requested url and the parameters are displayed. You will notice that `uri::split_query` returns a string map to retrieve the query parameters. If the request is "get_developers", then a data structure is declared and JSON is generated.

Professional C++

```
C:\WINDOWS\system32\cmd.exe - MyServer

D:\Dev\cpp\MyCpp\MyRestSample\Debug>MyServer
Listening for requests at: http://localhost:34568/MyServer/Action/
Press ENTER to exit.
Message GET /MyServer/Action/?request=get_developers&city=Paris HTTP/1.1
Connection: Keep-Alive
Host: localhost:34568
User-Agent: cpprestsdk/2.9.0

Relative URI /?request=get_developers&city=Paris
Query city Paris
Query request get_developers
Request get_developers
{"job":"Developers","people":[{"age":25,"name":"Franck"},{"age":20,"name":"Joe"}]}
```

Generation of the JSON

Let's look at the code that generates JSON from a data structure. There is nothing magical, look:

```cpp
struct People
{
    utility::string_t name;
    double age;

    static People FromJSON(const web::json::object & object)
    {
        People result;
        result.name = object.at(U("name")).as_string();
        result.age = object.at(U("age")).as_integer();
        return result;
    }

    web::json::value AsJSON() const
    {
        web::json::value result = web::json::value::object();
        result[U("name")] = web::json::value::string(name);
        result[U("age")] = web::json::value::number(age);
        return result;
    }
};
```

Professional C++ - Philosophy and Principles

This structure represents a developer. There are 2 properties: name and age. The string transformation mechanism is done with the `object.at().as_string()` and `web::json::value::string()` methods. For an integer, this is with `object.at(). as_integer()` and `web::json::value::number()`. It is quite simple. For the following structure, which implements an array (vector), other methods must be used:

```
struct Data
{
    std::vector<People> peoples;
    utility::string_t job;

    Data() {}

    void Clear() { peoples.clear(); }

    static Data FromJSON(const web::json::object &object)
    {
        Data res;

        web::json::value job = object.at(U("job"));
        res.job = job.as_string();

        web::json::value p = object.at(U("people"));
        for (auto iter = p.as_array().begin(); iter!= p.as_array().end(); ++iter)
        {
            if (!iter->is_null())
            {
                People people;
                people = People::FromJSON(iter->as_object());
                res.peoples.push_back(people);
            }
        }

        return res;
    }

    web::json::value AsJSON() const
    {
        web::json::value res = web::json::value::object();
        res[U("job")] = web::json::value::string(job);

        web::json::value jPeoples = web::json::value::array(peoples.size());

        int idx = 0;
        for (auto iter = peoples.begin(); iter!= peoples.end(); iter++)
        {
```

```
                    jPeoples[idx++] = iter->AsJSON();
            }

            res[U("people")] = jPeoples;
            return res;
        }
};
```

To generate a JSON array, use the `web::json::value::array` function. Then we iterate on the vector to associate the elements of the array one by one.

The client part

The client side can be developed with any technology as long as it is allowed to trigger http requests and read JSON. Here, the client is also written in C++ to show you how easy it is to use the REST SDK:

```
#ifdef _WIN32
#  define iequals(x, y) (_stricmp((x), (y))==0)
#else
#  define iequals(x, y) boost::iequals((x), (y))
#endif

int wmain(int argc, wchar_t *argv[])
{
    utility::string_t port = U("34568");
    if(argc == 2)
    {
        port = argv[1];
    }

    utility::string_t address = U("http://localhost:");
    address.append(port);
    http::uri uri = http::uri(address);

    http_client client(http::uri_builder(uri)
            .append_path(U("/MyServer/Action/")).to_uri();

    while (true)
    {
        std::string method;
        ucout << "Enter method:";
        cin >> method;

        http_response response;
```

```cpp
                if (iequals(method.c_str(), "get_developers"))
                {
                        utility::ostringstream_t buf;
                        buf << U("?request=")
                                << utility::conversions::to_string_t(method)
                                << U("&city=Paris");

                        response = client.request(methods::GET, buf.str()).get();

                        ucout << U("Response") << response.to_string() << endl;

                        json::value jdata = json::value::array();
                        jdata = response.extract_json().get();
                        Data data = Data::FromJSON(jdata.as_object());
                }
    else
        {
            ucout << utility::conversions::to_string_t(method)
                            << ": not understood n";
}
}

    return 0;
}
```

Web API in C++ with the CPP Rest SDK

Imagine that you can develop the back-end of your software solution on a server with the king of languages that is C++? On Linux: yes. On Windows: yes. One cell phone code? Yes. The whole without delirious complexity just with classes and methods of treatment... And we return from the JSON for a front-end in JS? Chiche! Follow me, I'll explain...

A simple REST http server

Let's look at the minimum code to create an API web server that returns JSON. First, you need to define a class that contains an **http_listener**.

```cpp
using namespace web;
using namespace http;
using namespace utility;
using namespace http::experimental::listener;

class MyServer
{
public:
    MyServer() {}
    MyServer(utility::string_t url);

    pplx::task<void> open() { return m_listener.open(); }
    pplx::task<void> close() { return m_listener.close(); }

private:

    static void handle_get(http_request message);
    static void handle_put(http_request message);
    static void handle_post(http_request message);
    static void handle_delete(http_request message);

    http_listener m_listener;
};
```

Next, you have to configure this listener by providing it with a URI on which you listen as well as the handlers for GET, PUT, POST and DELETE operations. But first of all, declare the server as a global variable as follows:

Professional C++ - Philosophy and Principles

```cpp
std::unique_ptr<MyServer> g_http;
```

Then, you have to prepare the essential elements for the server, namely its listening URI:

```cpp
    utility::string_t port = U("34568");
    utility::string_t address = U("http://localhost:");
address.append(port);

    uri_builder uri(port);
    uri.append_path(U("MyServer/Action/"));

    auto addr = uri.to_uri().to_string();
    g_http = std::unique_ptr<MyServer>(new MyServer(addr));
    g_http->open().wait();

    ucout << utility::string_t(U("Listening for requests at: ")) << addr << std::endl;
```

The call to open() activates listening. We still have to discover the MyServer class's constructor code because we have to save the handlers on the HTTP methods:

OK the http server body is there... Let's look at the HTTP method:

```cpp
MyServer::MyServer(utility::string_t url) : m_listener(url)
{
    std::function<void(http_request)> fnGet = &MyServer::handle_get;
    m_listener.support(methods::GET, fnGet);

    std::function<void(http_request)> fnPut = &MyServer::handle_put;
    m_listener.support(methods::PUT, fnPut);

    std::function<void(http_request)> fnPost = &MyServer::handle_post;
    m_listener.support(methods::POST, fnPost);

    std::function<void(http_request)> fnDel = &MyServer::handle_delete;
    m_listener.support(methods::DEL, fnDel);
}
```

Method body. We're going to code only one, but the system is simple.

```cpp
void MyServer::handle_post(http_request message)
{
    ucout <<  message.to_string() << endl;
    message.reply(status_codes::OK);
};

void MyServer::handle_delete(http_request message)
{
    ucout << message.to_string() << endl;
    message.reply(status_codes::OK);
}

void MyServer::handle_put(http_request message)
{
    ucout << message.to_string() << endl;
    message.reply(status_codes::OK);
};
```

These methods are not implemented but patience, here is what we will code. On the GET method if we are sent «get_developers» then we dump a data structure in JSON.

The body of the GET handler

The returned JSON data structure is defined as follows:

{"job":"Developers","people":[{"age":25,"name":"Franck"},{"age":20,"name":"Joe"}]}

Let's see the body of this GET method:

```cpp
void MyServer::handle_get(http_request message)
{
    ucout << U("Message") << U(" ")
            << message.to_string() << endl;

    ucout << U("Relative URI") << U(" ")
            << message.relative_uri().to_string() << endl;

    auto paths = uri::split_path(uri::decode(message.relative_uri().path()));
    for (auto it1 = paths.begin(); it1!= paths.end(); it1++)
```

```
        {
                ucout << U("Path") << U(" ")
                        << *it1 << endl;
        }

        auto query =
uri::split_query(uri::decode(message.relative_uri().query()));
        for (auto it2 = query.begin(); it2!= query.end(); it2++)
        {
                ucout << U("Query") << U(" ")
                        << it2->first << U(" ") << it2->second << endl;
        }

        auto queryItr = query.find(U("request"));
        utility::string_t request = queryItr->second;
        ucout << U("Request") << U(" ") << request << endl;

        if (request == U("get_developers"))
        {
                Data data;
                data.job = U("Developers");
                People p1;
                p1.age = 25;
                p1.name = U("Franck");
                data.peoples.push_back(p1);
                People p2;
                p2.age = 20;
                p2.name = U("Joe");
                data.peoples.push_back(p2);

                utility::string_t response = data.AsJSON(). serialize();
                ucout << response << endl;

                message.reply(status_codes::OK, data.AsJSON());
                return;
        }

        message.reply(status_codes::OK);
};
```

Should we start by dumper the input received? The request, the requested url and the parameters are displayed. You will notice that `uri::split_query` returns a string map to retrieve the query parameters. If the request is "get_developers", then a data structure is declared and JSON is generated.

Professional C++

```
D:\Dev\cpp\MyCpp\MyRestSample\Debug>MyServer
Listening for requests at: http://localhost:34568/MyServer/Action/
Press ENTER to exit.
Message GET /MyServer/Action/?request=get_developers&city=Paris HTTP/1.1
Connection: Keep-Alive
Host: localhost:34568
User-Agent: cpprestsdk/2.9.0

Relative URI /?request=get_developers&city=Paris
Query city Paris
Query request get_developers
Request get_developers
{"job":"Developers","people":[{"age":25,"name":"Franck"},{"age":20,"name":"Joe"}]}
```

Generation of the JSON

Let's look at the code that generates JSON from a data structure. There is nothing magical, look:

```cpp
struct People
{
    utility::string_t name;
    double age;

    static People FromJSON(const web::json::object & object)
    {
        People result;
        result.name = object.at(U("name")).as_string();
        result.age = object.at(U("age")).as_integer();
        return result;
    }

    web::json::value AsJSON() const
    {
        web::json::value result = web::json::value::object();
        result[U("name")] = web::json::value::string(name);
        result[U("age")] = web::json::value::number(age);
        return result;
    }
};
```

315

Professional C++ - Philosophy and Principles

This structure represents a developer. There are 2 properties: name and age. The string transformation mechanism is done with the `object.at()`. `as_string()` and `web::json::value::string()` methods. For an integer, this is with `object.at()`. `as_integer()` and `web::json::value::number()`. It is quite simple. For the following structure, which implements an array (vector), other methods must be used:

```
struct Data
{
    std::vector<People> peoples;
    utility::string_t job;

    Data() {}

    void Clear() { peoples.clear(); }

    static Data FromJSON(const web::json::object &object)
    {
        Data res;

        web::json::value job = object.at(U("job"));
        res.job = job.as_string();

        web::json::value p = object.at(U("people"));
        for (auto iter = p.as_array().begin(); iter!= p.as_array().end(); ++iter)
        {
            if (!iter->is_null())
            {
                People people;
                people = People::FromJSON(iter->as_object());
                res.peoples.push_back(people);
            }
        }

        return res;
    }

    web::json::value AsJSON() const
    {
        web::json::value res = web::json::value::object();
        res[U("job")] = web::json::value::string(job);

        web::json::value jPeoples = web::json::value::array(peoples.size());

        int idx = 0;
        for (auto iter = peoples.begin(); iter!= peoples.end(); iter++)
        {
```

```
                        jPeoples[idx++] = iter->AsJSON();
                }

                res[U("people")] = jPeoples;
                return res;
        }
};
```

To generate a JSON array, use the `web::json::value::array` function. Then we iterate on the vector to associate the elements of the array one by one.

The client party

The client side can be developed with any technology as long as it is allowed to trigger http requests and read JSON. Here, the client is also written in C++ to show you how easy it is to use the REST SDK:

```
#ifdef _WIN32
# define iequals(x, y) (_stricmp((x), (y))==0)
#else
# define iequals(x, y) boost::iequals((x), (y))
#endif

int wmain(int argc, wchar_t *argv[])
{
    utility::string_t port = U("34568");
    if(argc == 2)
    {
        port = argv[1];
    }

    utility::string_t address = U("http://localhost:");
    address.append(port);
    http::uri uri = http::uri(address);

    http_client client(http::uri_builder(uri)
            .append_path(U("/MyServer/Action/")).to_uri();

    while (true)
    {
        std::string method;
        ucout << "Enter method:";
        cin >> method;

            http_response response;

            if (iequals(method.c_str(), "get_developers"))
```

Professional C++ - Philosophy and Principles

```cpp
                {
                        utility::ostringstream_t buf;
                        buf << U("?request=")
                                << utility::conversions::to_string_t(method)
                                << U("&city=Paris");

                        response = client.request(methods::GET, buf.str()).get();

                        ucout << U("Response") << response.to_string() << endl;

                        json::value jdata = json::value::array();
                        jdata = response.extract_json().get();
                        Data data = Data::FromJSON(jdata.as_object());
                }
        else
                {
                    ucout << utility::conversions::to_string_t(method)
                            << ": not understood n";
                }
        }
        }

            return 0;
}
```

What is the Performance & Optimization point to remember?

The C++ REST SDK is easy to implement and allows to have server features without any particular difficulties. The support of the JSON is not too painful. Operations are simple and performance is standard. The advantage of the proposed solution is that it does not depend on IIS. The server module is *stand-alone*. To finalize the application, you have to add a layer of Windows service and there, it's a party!

The C++ REST SDK allows for developer to build upon an independent stack and layers of libraries that are no linked in any form to Oracle, Google to Microsoft. There are lot of partnerships to enhance the library and it's a huge asset to be able to deploy Web API or Web Service without IIS, Apache or NGINX, just on the Operating System.

Under the hood, CPP Rest SDK is Built with Boost Libraries and particularly with Boost.Asio... above on the libuv stuff?

15. Introduction to The Boost C++ Libraries

Boost is a community of C++ programmers whose goal is to push their libraries towards C++ standardization. Boost is a portable C++ library. You can use it with Visual C++ on Windows and GCC or CLang on Linux. Boost libraries are the place to be for every C++ developers who wants to contribute to the ISO C++ ecosystem. Most of their libraries are published as Boost Libraries and 3, 5 or 10 years later, there are incorporated into the standard STL packages and optimized (if it's still possible...) by each compiler's vendors.

How do I get Boost?

Very simply by going to the download section of the site and you are and you download a zip of 120 MB or a targz of 80 MB. You unpack your archive and you're almost ready. Decompression gives you a 430 MB tree structure. There is a lot of HTML documentation, which is why the file size is so large.

Build Boost

Although Boost is mostly a set of templates and inline functions so just the header files are enough, there are some libraries that need to be compiled.
The first thing to do is to start the compilation of the library. This is done in two stages. First, you have to compile the Boost custom Make which is called bjam. You have to run bootstrap.bat. Now that bjam is compiled, we'll build the library with our particular build string for a platform. I work with Visual Studio 2013 so here is my command line:

bjam toolset=msvc-12.0 variant=debug,release threading=multi link=shared

I do a compilation in debug and relay and indicating that I want a multi-thread and dynamic mode (DLL) library. The compilation takes a bit of time but let's say that in 15 minutes it's over.

Introduction to Boost.Serialization

Now that we have listed all the libraries available in Boost, we will move on to the code! Let's look at a very useful library that knows how to serialize and de-serialize classes in binary or XML format without forcing. This library allows to serialize containers which will avoid to browse our different collections to serialize simple elements. However, we must be careful about a name collision in the available namespace. Let me explain... Boost serializes boost::string, boost::vector & co... This means that we will have to transfer our objects written with the standard STL into compatible Boost objects unless our application is written completely with Boost. It's a choice of architecture!

Professional C++ - Philosophy and Principles

We're going to start with an app I wrote for my daughter in 2012. This is a drawing application where you have predefined elements on a page such as images, rectangles, circles, triangles, etc. This app allowed my 8 year old daughter at the time to know how to handle the mouse and play with the Ribbon to change the characteristics of objects (color, thickness of strokes, etc.).

The result of XML serialization

Let's start at the end… The drawing is as follows:

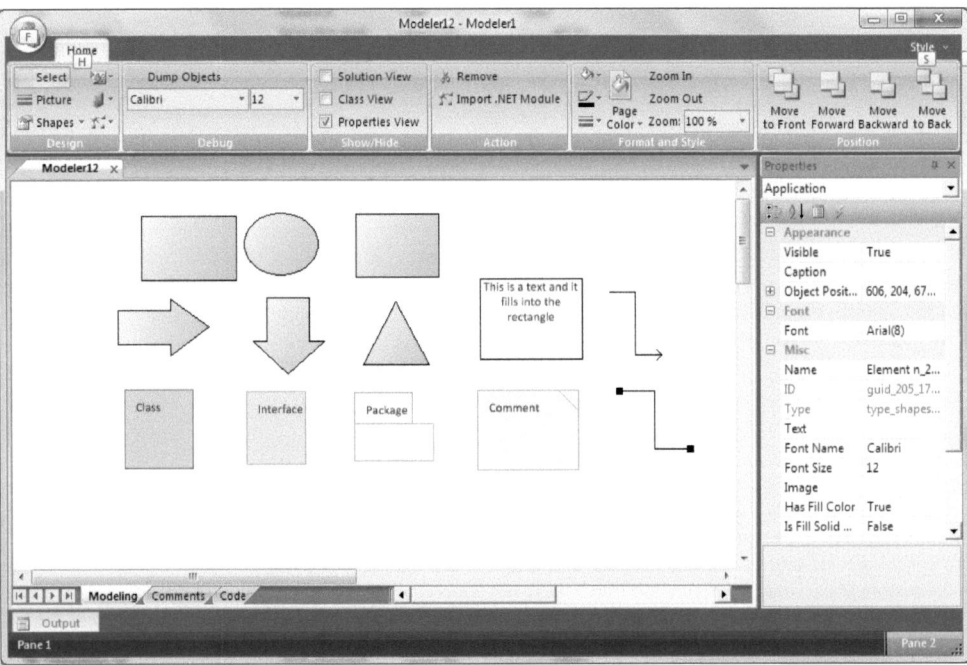

The goal of the game is to save this drawing as an XML document.

```xml
<?xml version="1.0" encoding="UTF-8" standalone="true"?>
<!DOCTYPE boost_serialization>
<boost_serialization version="12" signature="serialization::archive">
    <data version="1" tracking_level="0" class_id="0">
        <px version="1" tracking_level="1" class_id="1" object_id="_0">
            <m_shapes version="0" tracking_level="0" class_id="2">
                <count>21</count>
                <item_version>1</item_version>
                <item version="1" tracking_level="0" class_id="3">
                    <px version="1" tracking_level="1" class_id="4" object_id="_1">
                        <m_name>Element n_195</m_name>
                        <m_id>guid_195_115154_246_265837203</m_id>
                        <m_rect/>
                        <m_type>3</m_type>
                        <m_shapeType>50</m_shapeType>
                        <m_caption/>
                        <m_text/>
                        <m_x1>62</m_x1>
                        <m_y1>190</m_y1>
                        <m_x2>62</m_x2>
                        <m_y2>190</m_y2>
                        <m_colorFillR>154</m_colorFillR>
                        <m_colorFillG>200</m_colorFillG>
                        <m_colorFillB>249</m_colorFillB>
                        <m_colorLineR>0</m_colorLineR>
                        <m_colorLineG>0</m_colorLineG>
                        <m_colorLineB>0</m_colorLineB>
                        <m_bSolidColorFill>0</m_bSolidColorFill>
                        <m_bColorLine>0</m_bColorLine>
                        <m_bColorFill>1</m_bColorFill>
                    </px>
                </item>
                <item>
                    <px object_id="_2" class_id_reference="4">
                        <m_name>Element n_197</m_name>
                        <m_id>guid_197_115224_474_265867421</m_id>
                        <m_rect/>
                        <m_type>3</m_type>
                        <m_shapeType>50</m_shapeType>
                        <m_caption/>
                        <m_text/>
```

Let's open the Boost.Serialization documentation to take the thing on the right side and to arrive at the above result. If you have an eye, you will see that the application I propose to you is made with the Microsoft Foundation Classes (MFC) because it allows me to make a nice Ribbon and set up the Document/View support that allows me to make an application that loads/saves my data. Anyway, MFC rocks. I believe that we will redo a series I Practice C++ under Windows in 5 episodes so that you can also develop applications that rock! We'll see... let's get back to business. The XML. Boost.Serialization works with what we call an Archive in which we have access to data. We need to feed the archive with data. So I have a class of objects to draw and objects. The data model consists of 2 classes: CSimpleShape and CShapeCollection.

The CSimpleShape class
This class contains the following properties:
```
public:
    wstring m_name;
    wstring m_id;
    string m_rect;
```

Professional C++ - Philosophy and Principles

```
        long m_type;
        long m_shapeType;
        wstring m_caption;
        wstring m_text;
        long m_x1;
        long m_y1;
        long m_x2;
        long m_y2;
        int m_colorFillR;
        int m_colorFillG;
        int m_colorFillB;
        int m_colorLineR;
        int m_colorLineG;
        int m_colorLineB;
        bool m_bSolidColorFill;
        bool m_bColorLine;
        bool m_bColorFill;
};
```

```
BOOST_CLASS_VERSION(CSimpleShape, 1)
```

The CShapeCollection class
This class contains the list of elements:

```
public:
        vector<boost::shared_ptr<CSimpleShape> > m_shapes;
};
```

BOOST_CLASS_VERSION(CShapeCollection, 1)

It is a simple CSimpleShape vector... For these elements to be stored as a text, binary or XML file you need to specify a few things in the classes. This must be specified in private:

```
private:
        friend class boost::serialization::access;
        template<class Archive>
        void save(Archive & ar, const unsigned int version) const
        {
                ar & BOOST_SERIALIZATION_NVP(m_shapes);
        }

        template<class Archive>
        void load(Archive & ar, const unsigned int version)
        {
                ar & BOOST_SERIALIZATION_NVP(m_shapes);
        }
```

Professional C++

```
BOOST_SERIALIZATION_SPLIT_MEMBER()
```

This part of the code shows us the template to define. This is a template load and save function that works on an Archive. The syntax for embedding data in the archive is done through the &. operator. This part of code records the vector of elements. But for this to work, the CSimpleShape class must also save its elements in the archive.

```cpp
template<class Archive>
void save(Archive & ar, const unsigned int version) const
{
    // ar & name;
    // ar & id;
    ar & BOOST_SERIALIZATION_NVP(m_name);
    ar & BOOST_SERIALIZATION_NVP(m_id);
    ar & BOOST_SERIALIZATION_NVP(m_rect);
    ar & BOOST_SERIALIZATION_NVP(m_type);
    ar & BOOST_SERIALIZATION_NVP(m_shapeType);
    ar & BOOST_SERIALIZATION_NVP(m_caption);
    ar & BOOST_SERIALIZATION_NVP(m_text);
    ar & BOOST_SERIALIZATION_NVP(m_x1);
    ar & BOOST_SERIALIZATION_NVP(m_y1);
    ar & BOOST_SERIALIZATION_NVP(m_x2);
    ar & BOOST_SERIALIZATION_NVP(m_y2);
    ar & BOOST_SERIALIZATION_NVP(m_colorFillR);
    ar & BOOST_SERIALIZATION_NVP(m_colorFillG);
    ar & BOOST_SERIALIZATION_NVP(m_colorFillB);
    ar & BOOST_SERIALIZATION_NVP(m_colorLineR);
    ar & BOOST_SERIALIZATION_NVP(m_colorLineG);
    ar & BOOST_SERIALIZATION_NVP(m_colorLineB);
    ar & BOOST_SERIALIZATION_NVP(m_bSolidColorFill);
    ar & BOOST_SERIALIZATION_NVP(m_bColorLine);
    ar & BOOST_SERIALIZATION_NVP(m_bColorFill);
}
```

The load and save code is the same. The archive knows which way one works either in reading or in writing. Note that MFCs provide a similar infrastructure with << and >> operators; I think it's more legible to my liking but good. To compile this code, the following headers must be available:

```cpp
#define BOOST_SERIALIZATION_DYN_LINK TRUE
#define BOOST_ALL_DYN_LINK TRUE

#include <boost/smart_ptr/shared_ptr.hpp>
#include <boost/archive/tmpdir.hpp>
#include <boost/serialization/nvp.hpp>

#include <boost/archive/xml_iarchive.hpp>
#include <boost/archive/xml_oarchive.hpp>
#include <boost/archive/text_iarchive.hpp>
```

Professional C++ - Philosophy and Principles

```cpp
#include <boost/archive/text_oarchive.hpp>
#include <boost/serialization/shared_ptr.hpp>
#include <boost/serialization/base_object.hpp>
#include <boost/serialization/string.hpp>
#include <boost/serialization/list.hpp>
#include <boost/serialization/vector.hpp>
#include <boost/serialization/map.hpp>
#include <boost/serialization/utility.hpp>
#include <boost/serialization/assume_abstract.hpp>
using namespace boost;
```

Writing the data

Now that we have our classes that know how to use an Archive, let's see the code that gives the order to do Load or Save. You'll see, it's very simple:

```cpp
        boost::shared_ptr<CShapeCollection> data(new CShapeCollection());
        for( vector<std::shared_ptr<CElement>>::iterator i =
m_objects.m_objects.begin(); i!= m_objects.m_objects.end(); i++ )
        {
                std::shared_ptr<CElement> pElement = *i;
                boost::shared_ptr<CSimpleShape> pNewElement(new CSimpleShape());
                pNewElement->m_name = pElement->m_name;
                pNewElement->m_id = pElement->m_objectId;
                pNewElement->m_type = pElement->m_type;
                pNewElement->m_shapeType = pElement->m_shapeType;
                pNewElement->m_caption = pElement->m_caption;
                pNewElement->m_text = pElement->m_text;

                CPoint p1 = pElement->m_rect.TopLeft();
                CPoint p2 = pElement->m_rect.BottomRight();
                pNewElement->m_x1 = p1.x;
                pNewElement->m_y1 = p1.y;
                pNewElement->m_x2 = p2.x;
                pNewElement->m_y2 = p2.y;

                pNewElement->m_colorFillR = GetRValue(pElement->m_colorFill);
                pNewElement->m_colorFillG = GetGValue(pElement->m_colorFill);
                pNewElement->m_colorFillB = GetBValue(pElement->m_colorFill);
                pNewElement->m_colorLineR = GetRValue(pElement->m_colorLine);
                pNewElement->m_colorLineG = GetGValue(pElement->m_colorLine);
                pNewElement->m_colorLineB = GetBValue(pElement->m_colorLine);

                pNewElement->m_bSolidColorFill = pElement->m_bSolidColorFill;
                pNewElement->m_bColorLine = pElement->m_bColorLine;
                pNewElement->m_bColorFill = pElement->m_bColorFill;
```

```
                data->m_shapes.push_back(pNewElement);
    }

    std::ofstream xofs(filename.c_str());
    boost::archive::xml_oarchive xoa(xofs);
    xoa << BOOST_SERIALIZATION_NVP(data);
```

The filename variable is filled by opening a Common Dialog Windows SaveAs and all the magic is to declare an xml_archive and use the << operator to save all our data.

Reading the data

The reading of the data is modeled on the writing, the data is recovered and transferred into the collection that will be displayed on the screen:

```
    boost::shared_ptr<CShapeCollection> data(new CShapeCollection());
    // load an archive
    std::ifstream xifs(filename.c_str());
    assert(xifs.good());
    boost::archive::xml_iarchive xia(xifs);
    xia >> BOOST_SERIALIZATION_NVP(data);
    // Clear existing shapes
    m_objects.RemoveAll();

    for( vector<boost::shared_ptr<CSimpleShape> >::iterator i = data-
>m_shapes.begin(); i!= data->m_shapes.end(); i++ )
    {
            boost::shared_ptr<CSimpleShape> pElement = *i;
            //AfxMessageBox(pElement->m_name + " " + pElement->m_id);

            std::shared_ptr<CElement> pNewElement =
CFactory::CreateElementOfType((ElementType)pElement->m_type,


    (ShapeType)pElement->m_shapeType);
            pNewElement->m_name = pElement->m_name.c_str();
            pNewElement->m_objectId = pElement->m_id.c_str();
            pNewElement->m_caption = pElement->m_caption.c_str();
            pNewElement->m_text = pElement->m_text.c_str();
            pNewElement->m_pManager = this;
            pNewElement->m_pView = pView;

            CPoint p1;
            CPoint p2;
            p1.x = pElement->m_x1;
```

```cpp
                p1.y = pElement->m_y1;
                p2.x = pElement->m_x2;
                p2.y = pElement->m_y2;
                pNewElement->m_rect = CRect(p1, p2);

                int colorFillR = pElement->m_colorFillR;
                int colorFillG = pElement->m_colorFillG;
                int colorFillB = pElement->m_colorFillB;
                pNewElement->m_colorFill = RGB(colorFillR, colorFillG,
colorFillB);
                int colorLineR = pElement->m_colorLineR;
                int colorLineG = pElement->m_colorLineG;
                int colorLineB = pElement->m_colorLineB;
                pNewElement->m_colorLine = RGB(colorLineR, colorLineG,
colorLineB);

                pNewElement->m_bSolidColorFill = pElement->m_bSolidColorFill;
                pNewElement->m_bColorLine = pElement->m_bColorLine;
                pNewElement->m_bColorFill = pElement->m_bColorFill;

                m_objects.AddTail(pNewElement);
                pView->LogDebug(_T("object created ->") + pNewElement-
>ToString());
        }

        // Redraw the view
        Invalidate(pView);
```

Conclusion

The use of Boost and Boost.Serialization is rather simple to understand. The documentation provided is good and the examples are legion in the documentation. The advantage of Boost.Serialization is that archives are portable... So to make cross-platform, it's easy! The full drawing application code is available here: http://ultrafluid.codeplex.com .

Conclusion on the series «Je Pratique C++»
With this article, the series «I practice C++ » stops but I will find a deal with Programmez so that we always have C++ in Programmez. All Microsoft software is 90% C/C++ and it would not be normal not to talk about it. The C++ is not dead, far from it. With C++11, the C++ has been rejuvenated and the C++14 and C++17 standards bring their share of novelties. Stay tuned as the other would say and to Soon for new articles on C++.

16. I/O Async with Boost

Introduction

Multi-threading isn't the only way to optimize I/O performance.

Another way to do this is to use non-blocking operations (also called asynchronous), within the same execution thread.

Multi-threading + synchronous I/O

This model uses blocking operations (also called synchronous): The functions only return the hand to me when the I/O is complete, either with data if successful, or with an error code.

Advantage:
- Blocking operations follow one after the other, in the same order as the lines of source code. There is therefore no need to set up state data (progress of the various operations in progress, associated buffers for reading or writing).
- The code quite simple to develop for the designer, and just as simple to read by a maintainer.

Disadvantages:
- It is necessary to set up a synchronization of critical sections (e.g. mutex, semaphore) to ensure the integrity of the application state data in the face of potentially competing changes (due to the pre-emptive nature of multi-threading on most platforms).
- The system load can be quite heavy if the number of threads increases; however, this problem can be mitigated by using a thread pool: the model is no longer 1/1 (1 thread per client) but M/N (M threads for N clients, with M < N)

Sample pseudocode:
[@pic inspired by
https://www.boost.org/doc/libs/1_75_0/doc/html/boost_asio/example/cpp03/echo/blocking_tcp_echo_server.cpp]

```
Void echo_server(socket_ptr Sock)
{
  try
  {
    for (;;)
    {
      char data[max_length];
      error_code error;

      size_t length = sock->read_some(data), error);
      if (error == eof)
         station wagon; Connection closed cleanly by peer.
      else if (error)
         throw system_error(error); Some other error.
```

Professional C++ - Philosophy and Principles

```
            write(*sock,data, length));
        }
    }
    wrestling (std::exception& e)
    {
        std::cerr << "Exception in thread: " << e.what() << "\n";
    }
}
```

Single-threading + asynchronous I/O

This model uses non-blocking operations (also called asynchronous), within the same execution thread.
With each call, an additional parameter is passed to specify how to retrieve the result. The function immediately returns the hand to the caller by returning an "I/O in progress" code if all goes well, and the result can be retrieved thanks to the additional parameter. depending on the library chosen for I/O, this parameter can be a callback, a promise, a future.

Advantage:
- There is no need to worry about synchronization since there is no longer concurrent access to data.
- The system load is lighter, because there is no longer to allocate resources for different (potentially numerous) threads.

Disadvantages:
- The progress state of the different I/O must be maintained within the application
since all operations are distributed in different functions within the source code. It is therefore necessary to manage a kind of finite state automaton to manage the transitions (success/error results) between the different states (launches of asynchronous operations).
- The code is more difficult for the designer to develop, and even more difficult for a maintainer to read.

Sample pseudocode:
[@pic inspired by
https://www.boost.org/doc/libs/1_75_0/doc/html/boost_asio/example/cpp03/echo/async_tcp_echo_server.cpp]

```
Class echo_server
{
public:
   void start()
   {
      socket_.async_read(data_, max_length, handle_read)
   }

private:
   void handle_read(const error_code& error, size_t bytes_transferred)
   {
      if (!error)
      {
         async_write(socket_, data_, bytes_transferred, handle_write);
      }
```

```
        else
        {
            delete this;
        }
    }

    void handle_write(const error_code& error, size_t bytes_transferred)
    {
        if (!error)
        {
            socket_.async_read(data_, max_length, handle_read)
        }
        else
        {
            delete this;
        }
    }

    socket socket_;
    enum { max_length = 1024 };
    data_[max_length] tank;
};
```

Combining both synchronous and asynchronous models

The two models are not exclusive. They can be combined, and each thread then performs several asynchronous operations.

Benefits:
- We can take advantage of all the power of modern processors, which have a large number of cores, which would not be exploited in the single-threaded model.
- However, we limit the number of threads compared to the number of clients.

Disadvantages:
- The flow of execution is even more difficult to follow since we combine the respective complexities of multi-threading and asynchronicity.
- Data structures must be carefully developed to limit critical sections (necessary for multi-threading) so as not to restrict asynchronous I/O.

Choose an I/O model

There is no "best" model. It all depends on the particularities of the developed application or service.
On the server side, it is quite necessary to consider asynchronous I/O.

It should only be waived if I/O is relatively numerous, or if the complexity associated with asynchrony is explicitly considered undesirable.

On the client side, it is generally easier to encode synchronous I/O because there are fewer I/Os; but we can consider asynchronous I/O; In particular to minimize the total waiting time on several chains in case of large volume of data, or non-negligible probability of timeouts (timeouts add up).

The asynchronous model is the traditional model of UNIX platforms, which with some exceptions did not have multithreading before the introduction of the POSIX pthreads [**TODO: standard**] **standard,** for situations we did not want to use multi-processing (fork()/exec()).

The synchronous model is the model of Windows platforms. The Win32 API introduced asynchronous WriteFileEx() along with synchronous WriteFile() and multi-threading, but it was usually the synchronous+threading pair that stood out for its simplicity.

A traditional example to compare the two models is Apache/nginx:
Apache is based on a traditional multi-threading/processing model (with different variants e.g. pre-fork, thread pool). nginx, more recent, is entirely based on asynchronous I/O. The difference in performance has allowed nginx to continuously chip away at shares in the web server market.
Apache remains a very good software, however, with features not yet offered by nginx.
For example, it is common to see proxy configurations where all requests to static resources (images, scripts) are forwarded to nginx servers, and requests to dynamic resources to an application server with an Apache frontend.

Choose an implementation

Before standardization by ISO, there were different libraries, such as:
- ACE (Adaptive Communication Environment)
- libevent (used by memcached or Chromium), and its derivative libev
- libuv (used by NodeJS)

Asynchronous I/O was standardized by ISO in C++ in April 2018, in technical specification ISO/IEC TS 19216:2018 "Networking TS".

This specification is mainly based on the open source library Boost::Asio, from which it takes most of the data structures and APIs.

As often and on many evolutions of C++:
1. Boost initially serves as an incubator for proposals for new libraries, or extensions to existing libraries.
2. After maturation, ISO integrates the proposal into the standard, often with changes to the interface (simple renamings, new methods, moving a method to free function, etc.).
3. Boost integrates standard changes, while maintaining a compatibility layer for pre-standard code
4. Boost continues to evolve to stay at the forefront of technology, and the cycle resumes until the new version of the standard

Asio is therefore the best implementation so it is the one we will consider here [version 1.77 (August 11, 2021) https://www.boost.org/doc/libs/1_77_0/doc/html/boost_asio.html].

17. Boost ::Asio

Presentation

The Asio library allows you to:
1. Benefit from modern concepts about I/O and its management
2. Ignore the particularities of the OS or hardware platform
3. Minimize implementation differences between different types of I/O (network, files, serial port, etc.)
4. Use a unified interface for error handling
5. Use a unified interface for timeouts management
6. Benefit from a robust and efficient implementation

Benefit from modern concepts about I/O and its management

The ASIO API offers many concepts, including:

- io_context

- Endpoint

- socket

- Acceptor

- Resolver

Each of its concepts will be presented in the next section, along with its function.

This type of architecture corresponds to the state of the art, and is found in other modern languages, but Asio is certainly the best network library available in C++.

Ignore the particularities of the OS or hardware platform

There are considerable differences between the system services offered on different platforms; Like what:

- UNIX systems natively use the file descriptor (fd, integer type) to identify a resource, but Windows systems natively use the HANDLE (opaque type). The synchronization APIs are therefore totally different.

- On UNIX you can use Sockets with the select() API of the POSIX standard, but also the poll() API; each has a derived API (pselect, ppoll).

- Windows provides sockets compatibility, but compatibility is not complete (e.g. the SOCKET type is used instead of int for the fd). I/O synchronization can be complicated because the rest of the application uses the corresponding HANDLEs and APIs (WaitForSingleObject() / WaitForMultipleObjects())

Professional C++ - Philosophy and Principles

- Specific mechanisms exist on other systems: io_uring on Linux, IOCP on Windows, kqueue on BSD, /dev/poll on Solaris, etc. The direct use of these mechanisms maximizes I/O performance, but at the cost of code portability.

Minimize implementation differences between different types of I/O

I/O can concern different forms of support:

- network, with multiple protocols (TCP, UDP)
- Files
- device, e.g. serial port

Asio aims to hide these peculiarities as far as possible.

But the work is unfortunately not finished:

- The *platform-independent* part is totally portable and provides almost perfect encapsulation. It mainly concerns TCP and UDP network I/O.

- The *platform-specific* part is, as the name suggests, non-portable. Its different components are isolated in specific namespaces: boost::asio::windows, boost::asio::p osix.

Evolving your code to go for example from a TCP socket to a UDP socket will pose few problems: The overall architecture will not be disrupted, the vast majority of the code will be reusable. Obviously there will always be some adaptations to be made, but it will always represent much less work than the purely application changes necessary due to the change of connection mode.

But for other types of I/O, file or device, it is unfortunately still necessary to use platform-specific APIs.

Serial port I/O has been integrated. But file-based I/Os remains specific.

The interest in using ASIO persists, because the io_context allows to orchester all I/O.

But the dependency is regrettable, and we can only sincerely hope that a future version of ASIO corrects this lack.

Use a unified interface for error handling

Asio capitalizes on another library: Boost::System.

Boost::System provides the following classes:

- error_code: portable abstraction of an error code, allowing differences between systems, e.g. UNIX (which uses errno) and Windows (which uses GetLastError())

- system_error: An exception derived from std::runtime_error, which captures the error_code underlying the problem, and allows the error information in the application to be traced back to a catch block that will process it.

Benefit from utility classes for common operations

Asio offers utility classes for:

- I/O data buffer management. Classes mutable_buffer (for reading) and const_buffer (for writing) are used to securely manage data buffers (overflow protection)

- the definition and control of timers, in particular for the management of I/O deadlines (timeouts). For example, the steady_timer class is used to associate a timer with a io_context, and the expires_at() or expires_after() methods to define a delay.

- Managing concurrent access to data, when multi-threading is used in addition to I/O asynchronicity. The strand synchronization mechanism allows you to abstract the differences between systems (Mutex or critical section on Windows, semaphore or conditional variable on UNIX, etc.).

Use a robust and high-performance implementation

Asio is not only an API specification: it is also a freely licensed, quality implementation recognized worldwide by experts and all its users. It is available with its online documentation on https://www.boost.org/.

ASIO Main Concepts

io_context

The io_context[1] is the engine (a.k.a. runtime) that orchestrates the different I/O. It receives requests, blocks tasks waiting for the result, and unblocks them at the end by calling the callback associated with the IO.

The main ASIO objects always refer to a io_context, passed as a parameter of the constructor.

There can be several io_context in the same program: each manages its own I/O independently of the others. They can be associated with totally different resources (e.g. a TCP socket and a UDP socket, or 2 TCP sockets but one used for an HTPP protocol and the other for a WebSockets protocol, etc.).

io_context is therefore used to abstract calls like select()/poll()[2] on the 'BSD Sockets' API on UNIX, or WSAWaitForMultipleEvents ()[3] from the Winsock2 API on Windows.

There is always at least one io_context, whether on the server side or on the client side.

It is implemented in the boost::asio::io_context[4] class.

[1] io_service before renaming according to ISO standard

[2] https://pubs.opengroup.org/onlinepubs/9699919799/functions/select.html

https://pubs.opengroup.org/onlinepubs/9699919799/functions/poll.html

[3] https://docs.microsoft.com/en-us/windows/win32/api/winsock2/nf-winsock2-wsawaitformultipleevents

[4]

Professional C++ - Philosophy and Principles

Endpoint

The endpoint is used to define the type of network protocol and the resources on which the I/O will run.

An endpoint can be TCP (connected mode) or UDP (offline mode) for TCP/IP protocols (AF_INET family), but also for example a UNIX socket (AF_UNIX family) on systems that support it.

There is always at least one endpoint, whether on the server side or on the client side.

Endpoints allow:

- abstract calls like bind()([1]), htonl(), htons() of BSD Sockets / Winsock2 APIs

- simplify the resolution of domain names: a resolver (see § below) returns a list of endpoints (e.g. an IP address v4 and an IP address v6)

An endpoint serves as a parameter:

- a socket (see § below) on the client side to connect to the server

- an acceptor (see § below) on the server side, to wait for requests for connections from clients

Endpoints are implemented in classes

      - boost::asio::ip:: tcp::endpoint for TCP

      - boost::asio::ip:: udp::endpoint for UDP

socket

Sockets have methods to initiate I/O: async_read_some/async_write_some (asynchronous), read/write (synchronous; ASIO encourages asynchronous I/O but also allows synchronous mode to simplify certain use cases, such as a single request from a client to a server).

For client sockets:

- a connect()[2] method is used to connect to a server by specifying an endpoint

- The free function boost::asio::connect() allows you to connect to a server by specifying a list of endpoints. It iterates over endpoints until a successful connection occurs.

Sockets are implemented in classes

      - boost:: asio::ip::tcp::socket for TCP

      - boost::asio::ip:: udp::socket for UDP

Acceptor

The acceptor is specific to TCP servers.

The manufacturer receives as a parameter the associated io_context, and an endpoint (see § above).

The acceptor makes it possible to:

- Wait for requests for connections from clients

- accept connections on the endpoint

It is implemented in the boost::asio::ip:: tcp::acceptor class.

UDP servers do not require an acceptor, because UDP sockets have async_receive_from and async_send_to methods to communicate directly (offline mode a.k.a datagram).

Resolver

The resolver allows the resolution of domain names.

It takes as a parameter a triplet (protocol type, host, service) and returns a list of corresponding endpoints.

Protocol type: TCP, UDP, etc.

Host:

       - FQDN, e.g. www.apress.com

       - IPv4 address, e.g. 90.100.15.170

       - IPv6 address, e.g. 2A01:CB10:89B4:9300:6A3F:7DFF:FE17:5750

       - pseudo address, e.g. localhost (IPv4) or ::1 (IPv6)

Service:
       - a *Well-Known Service*[1] name, e.g. "SSH" or "HTTP"
       - a port number, e.g. 22 for SSH or 80 for HTTP

The resolver's resolve method returns a list of endpoints, because a host can be multi-homed: It can have multiple network interfaces alongside hardware, and each interface can have multiple addresses.

An endpoint can be used
- by a server-side acceptor to wait for connection requests.
- client-side by the connect() method of a socket, to connect to a server

The free function boost::asio::connect() allows you to connect to a server by providing a list of endpoints as returned by the resolver; She iterates through the list until she succeeds in a connection.

Professional C++ - Philosophy and Principles

ASIO Examples

Hello asynchronous TCP server

TODO

Hello Asynchronous TCP Client

TODO

TODO:

execution_context

steady_timer

Strand

third_party

Spawn

ASIO::Windows File I/O

spawn

asio::windows file i/o

Professional C++

18. C++ and Docker Containers on Azure

Introduction

For a Gold Partner with offices in Paris, I created an Azure technology showcase using Microsoft technologies. NET, C#, C++, LMDB, Win32 and Docker then the run of a Docker instance under Azure.

The story begins with the recovery of C++ sources under patent, the code of an unfinished database... This project was called the world's fastest database. OLAP cube engine and BI reporting were discussed to compete with SQL Server SSAS and Tableau Software... After investigating the source code for a month, I find that it is a nice project but it is not finished and that it will be difficult to achieve the missing part because the code is quite complex and especially under what conditions and for what result? In agreement with my boss, we decide to look for reusable components. The storage engine is getting my attention. But it happens to be an open-source library named OpenLDAP-LMDB that exists under Linux; it's a filesystem in memory... LMDB was covered in the March 2019 issue of Programmez. Search for the LMDBNet package on nuget: https://www.nuget.org/packages/LMDBNet

Software Architecture

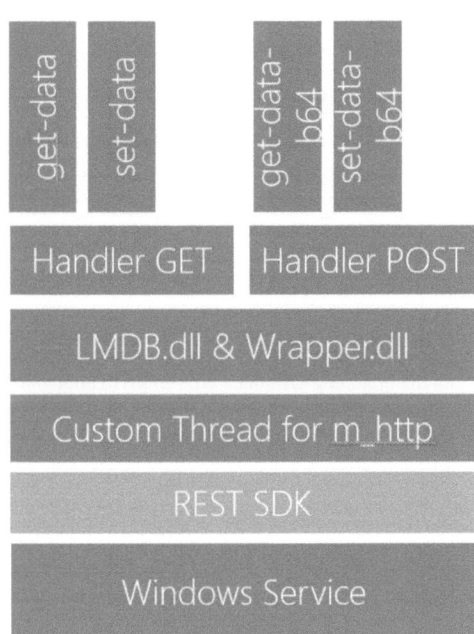

Here is the soft that will be built; it is a Windows service that embeds a stand-alone web server on which a Web Service REST API JSON has been added, all built in C++ with the Microsoft C++ REST SDK. The Web service publishes on port 7001. You have to be an administrator to be able to create the port.

It's a WinInet restriction.

337

Professional C++ - Philosophy and Principles

It is an embedded web server that exposes a web service REST API that allows to manage one or more NoSQL LMDB caches.

The project is a Windows Service x64 (LMDBService.exe) which loads several dll:
* cpprest141d_2_10.dll
* LMDBWindowsDllD64.dll
* LMDBWrapperD64.dll
* MySharedStuffD64.dll
* Msvcp140d.dll
* Vcruntime140d.dll
* Ucrtbased.dll

You will have noticed that the modules are in debug... This is to facilitate debugging.

Run in local

The Windows service starts via net start or in console mode... It consumes 2 MB of memory and the CPU is always at 0% or almost. This is the advantage of C++.
Console – launch demon: LMDBService.exe or net start LMDB Service.
Testing the embedded web server from Chrome: ip:7001

Implementation of Docker

First of all, you have to install Docker on Windows. It's not that complicated. We start the setup and it's over. The first problem is how to create an "application" for Docker. And here, it's a moment of solitude because the Docker documentation is very poorly done, it's a shame. Fortunately, I have a book called "Docker on Windows". A chance. The book explains that Docker is a virtualization system in which a blank image of the operating system is grafted components via a boot file (the dockerfile) and can run them as a VM and as soon as the container stops, we lose everything. We can start all over again.... In isolation.

The base: the DockerFile
A DockerFile is a boot file for the Docker image. We will tell him the operating system base on which to boot and the different application settings to add to it. Before mounting a docker container instance under Azure, you must first master its local operation with a docker in local, for example under Windows 10. This is my dockerfile using a Windows Sever 2016 LTSC (Long time support) image. The DockerFile is as follows:

FROM microsoft/iis:windowsservercore-ltsc2016
COPY *.* c:/
RUN sc sdset SCMANAGER D:(A;;CCLCRPRC;;AU)(A;;CCLCRPWPRC;;SY)(A;KA;;BA)S:(AU;FA;KA;;WD)(AU;OIIOFA;GA;;WD)
RUN sc create LMDBService start=auto binpath="C: LMDBService.exe"
EXPOSE 7001
RUN md c: temp

We start from an OS image provided by Microsoft that contains IIS...
The steps are as follows:
- Copy binaries to image
- Update of the administrative rights on the SCManager
- Creation of the service
- Opening of ports 80 and 7001

Local run under Docker

Next, build the Docker image:
docker image build –tag mydocker/myserver d: dev docker

Then, the container can be launched as a demon by opening the port 7001 created by the service:
docker run -d -p 7001:7001 -it mydocker/myserver

To be able to test the container, we need its IP address with its ID using:
docker ps –a

We take the first item on the list. Launch the following line with its id at the end:
docker inspect -f "{{ .NetworkSettings.Networks.nat.IPAddress }}" 543e57f54047

The answer is displayed => 172.26.255.203
It is now possible to test the container.

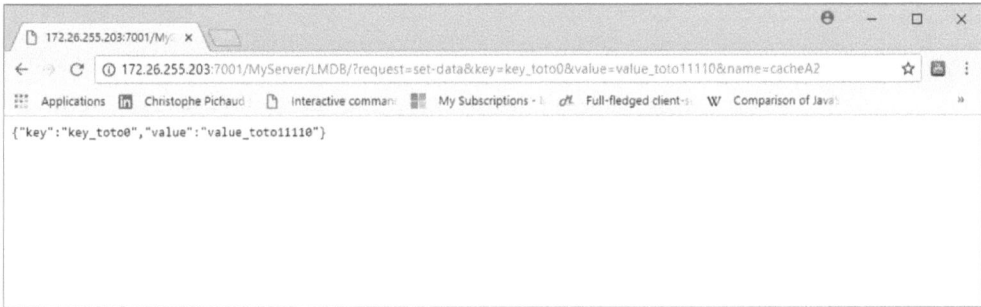

To stop the container, do:
docker -stop 543e57f54047

As you can see, Docker is almost painless and transparent. Docker allows anything that is not graphical to work. Communications services, daemons, Windows services are ideal candidates to run under Docker. Example: running a development SQL Server. It is a Windows service that uses port 1433. IIS which is a website that uses port 80.

Run in Azure

There, things get a little complicated…. First, to use Azure, you need a subscription. Then you have to create a registry. Indeed, a container can only be instantiated if there is a registry or is deposited the Docker image.

The first step is to create a repository in Azure Container Registry. Once created, this resource gives a user/pwd. Select the Access Keys item and retrieve the password from the clipboard: Connect to Azure Container Registry via its user/pwd from the docker console:
docker login lmdbreg2.azurecr.io -u lmdbreg2 -p V5nUpEG7Hu/V4KZ8kGy6hBT4r70tIeFl

Next, tag the registry for the Docker image:
docker tag myserver lmdbreg2.azurecr.io/lmdb

Professional C++ - Philosophy and Principles

Then it is possible to upload the docker image to ACR.
docker push lmdbws.azurecr.io/lmdb

The last command sends the image to ACR.

Create an instance of the container
Select Container Instances and set the registry information and credentials. Click OK. Select Open additional port and type 7001. Click OK.
Click OK. The container is deployed on Azure ACI in 3 or 4 minutes. Once deployed, we go to the portal to retrieve its IP address at the top right.

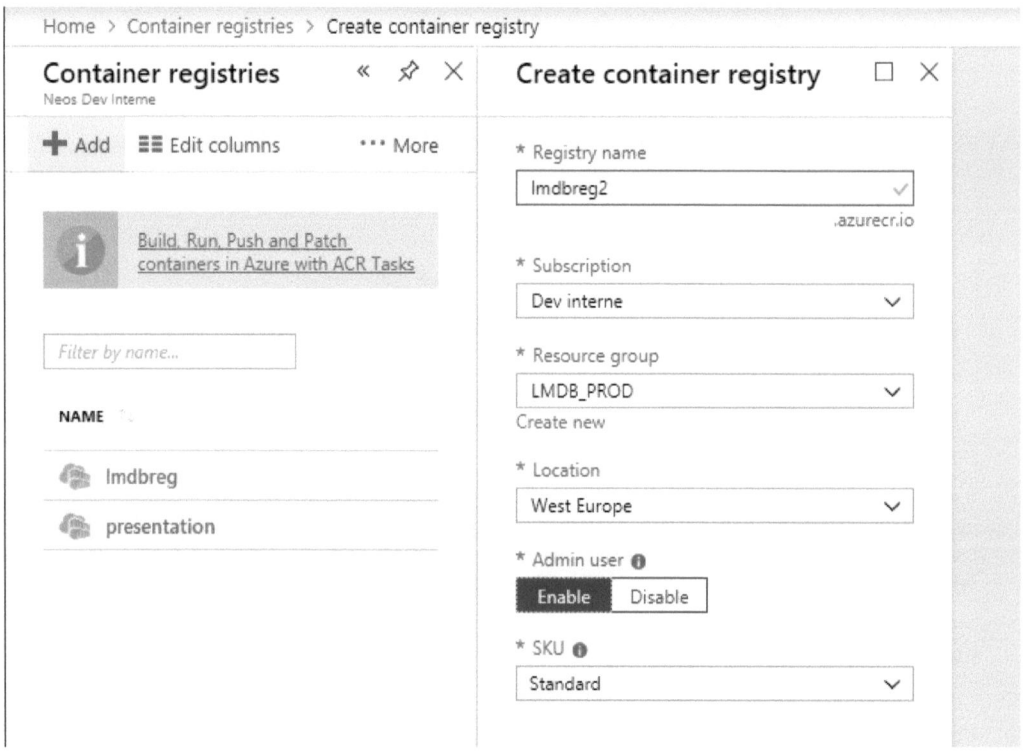

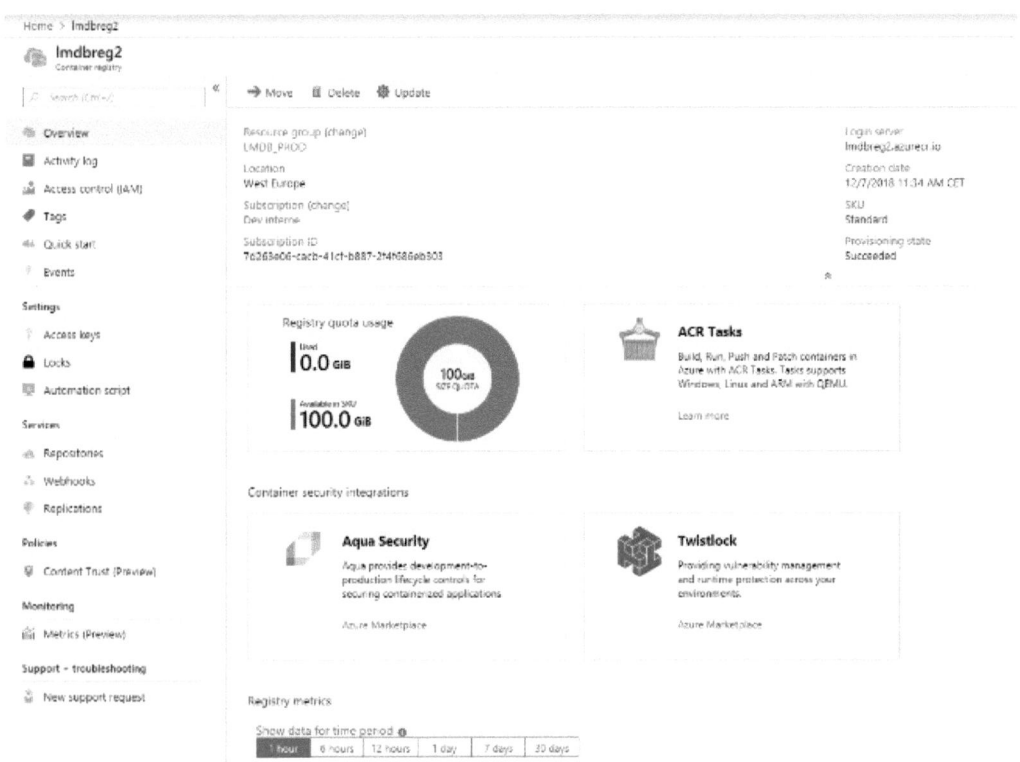

Professional C++ - Philosophy and Principles

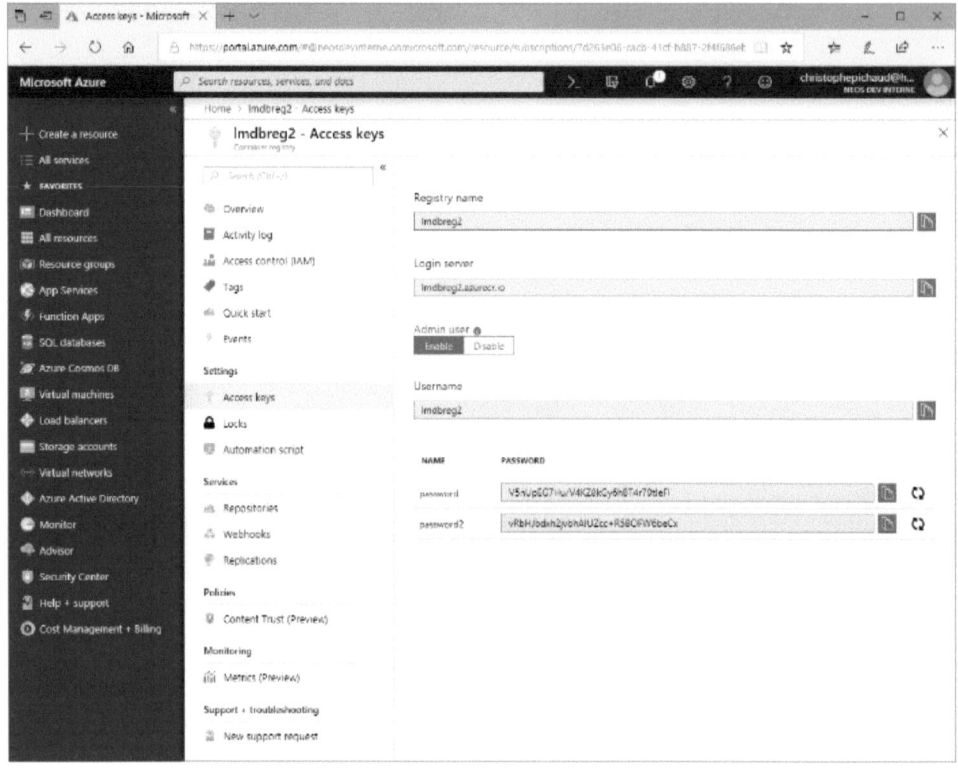

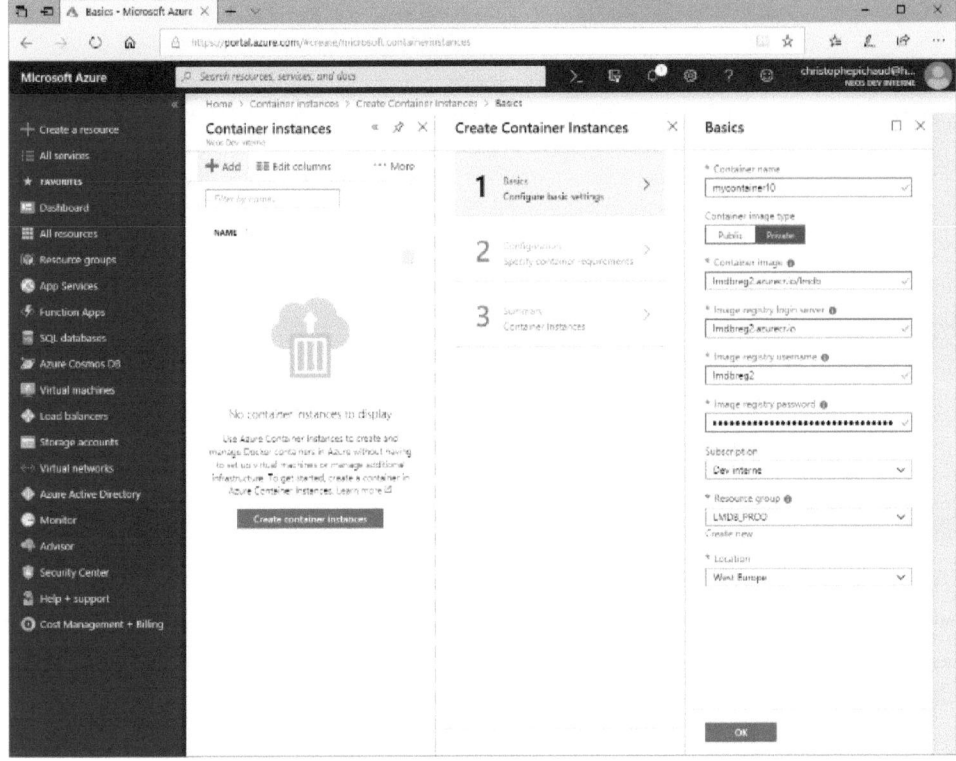

Professional C++ - Philosophy and Principles

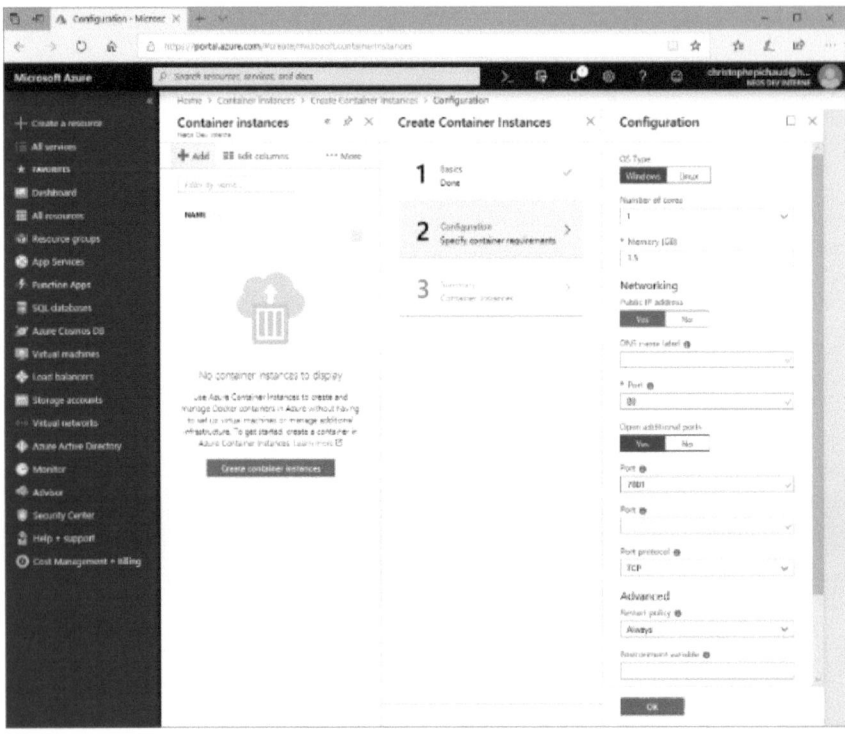

Professional C++

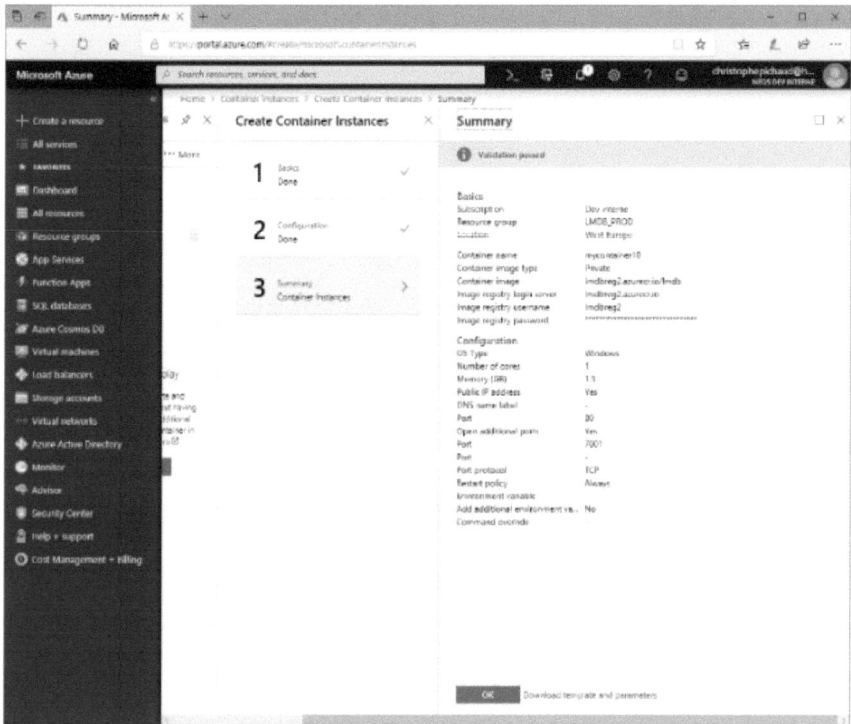

My Windows service contains an internal ping that returns its status: Let's test this ping software:
http://137.117.141. 0:7001/MyServer/LMDB/? request=ping

Let's also make a software About:
http://137.117.141. 0:7001/MyServer/LMDB/? request=about

345

Professional C++ - Philosophy and Principles

In an advanced version of the Windows service, I create a log file in c: temp logs and define my dockerfile with an image that contains IIS and I create a vdir on c: temp logs so, with port 80 from my browser, I can read my logs: http://137.117.141. 0/Logs/lmdb.txt

Network issue

During my first tests on Azure, I encountered difficulties in establishing the connection between the browser and my web service. Nothing was working out. I found information on the Web that said to list NICs (network maps). And indeed, there are several possibilities, either to create the services on all the network maps or on... the last one! Here is the code that iterates on the cards and keeps the last IP address in memory:

```
std::wstring ServerHelper::GetIP()
{
    //return L"127.0.0.1";
    //return L"0.0.0.0";

    // Init WinSock
    WSADATA wsa_Data;
    int wsa_ReturnCode = WSAStartup(MAKEWORD(2, 2), &wsa_Data);

    // Get the local hostname
    char szHostName[255];
    gethostname(szHostName, 255);

    struct hostent *remoteHost;
    struct in_addr addr;
    std::string ip;

    remoteHost = gethostbyname(szHostName);

    if (remoteHost->h_addrtype == AF_INET)
    {
        int i = 0;
        while (remoteHost->h_addr_list[i] != 0)
```

```
            {
                        addr.s_addr = *(u_long *)remoteHost->h_addr_list[i++];
                        printf(" tIPv4 Address #%d: %s n", i, inet_ntoa(addr));
                        ip = inet_ntoa(addr);
            }
      }

      WSACleanup();
      std::wstring ipw(ip.begin(), ip.end());
      return ipw;
}
```

This routine is used in the initialization procedure of the service that creates the web server and the REST service on port 7001:

```
DWORD AutomateThread(LPVOID pParam)
{
      try
      {
            g_Logger.WriteLog(_T("Running in console mode... Entering while()..."));
                  std::wstring port = Constants::MasterNodePort;
                  std::wstring host = ServerHelper::GetHostName();
                  std::wstring ip = ServerHelper::GetIP();
                  std::wstring url = ServerHelper::BuildURL(ip, port);
                  http::uri uri = http::uri(url);
                  std::wstring address = uri.to_string();
                  std::wstring name = _T("Master");

                  //
                  // Create the server instance
                  //

                  TCHAR sz[255];
                  _stprintf_s(sz, _T("IP: %s"), ip.c_str());
                  g_Logger.WriteLog(sz);

                  g_Logger.WriteLog(_T("Creating server ip/port..."));
                  TheServer client(address);
                  g_Logger.WriteLog(_T("Creating server ip/port ok"));
                  client._server = ip;
                  client._port = port;
                  client._name = name;
                  client.Init();

                  g_Logger.WriteLog(_T("Waiting..."));
                  while (TRUE)
```

Professional C++ - Philosophy and Principles

```
            {
                    if (_Module.m_bStop)
                    {
                            std::wcout << _T("Running in console mode.") << std::endl;
                            goto stop_service;
                            break;
                    }

                    //Sleep(200);
                    Sleep(5000);
                    g_Logger.WriteLog(_T("MainThread Sleep..."));

            } // Main loop
```

Comments on Docker

The advantage of container with C++ code is that the code is fast, we rarely heat the CPU, the RAM consumption is minimal so we pay almost nothing. The machines that run Docker containers are monsters and the example of my C++ code makes me 0% RAM and 0% CPU…. In short, to run good C++ communication code with different library versions, it is a good option.

What we have learned…

Using an application in Docker is not very complicated to implement. First, create a DockerFile with an OS image and copy its binaries. That is all! Then we open the communication ports and that's it.

19. Migrate your C++ code to 64 bits

Nowadays, Windows is installed in 64 bits: it is also called x64 mode or amd64 architecture. In the project files we are offered to manage this x64 target but there are many tips and tricks when passing through and it is not so automatic that just recompiling the sources of your applications and dll... We will scan the various elements with as much detail as possible. Objective: "Ça build!"

The necessary tools

When you install Visual Studio, you have a choice between multiple SDKs and multiple compilers. Currently, CL.EXE, the Microsoft compiler is available in 4 versions:
- cl.exe 32 bit for X86 / cl.exe 64 bit for X64
- cl.exe 32 bit and 64 bit for ARM

The big changes
The int and long type are 32-bit values. The size_t type is a 64-bit value. Here is the detail:

Scalar Type	C Data Type	Storage Size (in bytes)	Recommended Alignment
INT8	char	1	Byte
UINT8	unsigned char	1	Byte
INT16	short	2	Word
UINT16	unsigned short	2	Word
INT32	int, long	4	Doubleword
UINT32	unsigned int, unsigned long	4	Doubleword
INT64	__int64	8	Quadword
UINT64	unsigned __int64	8	Quadword
FP32 (single precision)	float	4	Doubleword
FP64 (double precision)	double	8	Quadword
POINTER	*	8	Quadword
__m64	struct __m64	8	Quadword
__m128	struct __m128	16	Octaword

Professional C++ - Philosophy and Principles

String management is more delicate. Let's remind you about Windows definitions. There are CHAR, WCHAR, LPSTR, LPCSTR, LPTSTR, LPCTSTR. Let's see the Windows definitions and their equivalents whether your project supports Unicode or not.

```
// Generic types

#ifdef UNICODE
    typedef wchar_t TCHAR;
#else
    typedef unsigned char TCHAR;
#endif

typedef TCHAR *LPTSTR, *LPTCH;

// 8-bit character specific

typedef unsigned char CHAR;
typedef CHAR *LPSTR, *LPCH;

// Unicode specific (wide characters)

typedef unsigned wchar_t WCHAR;
typedef WCHAR *LPWSTR, *LPWCH;
```

If the project supports Unicode, channel management is provided via wchar_t for CHAR. What we need to remember from these statements is that TCHAR is a useful ally. Indeed, TCHAR via tchar.h will allow us to make a generic code in string management. To declare a string, use the TCHAR definition:

TCHAR sz[255];

TCHAR will be either char or wchar_t. How do I know? It all depends if your project is Unicode! If you are in «Character Set» = «Use Unicode Character Set» then your project will define the UNICODE constant at the preprocessor level. Let's look at the properties of the project where this is defined:

Generic-Text Routine Mappings

TCHAR.H routine	_UNICODE & _MBCS not defined	_MBCS defined	_unicode defined
_tprintf	printf	printf	wprintf

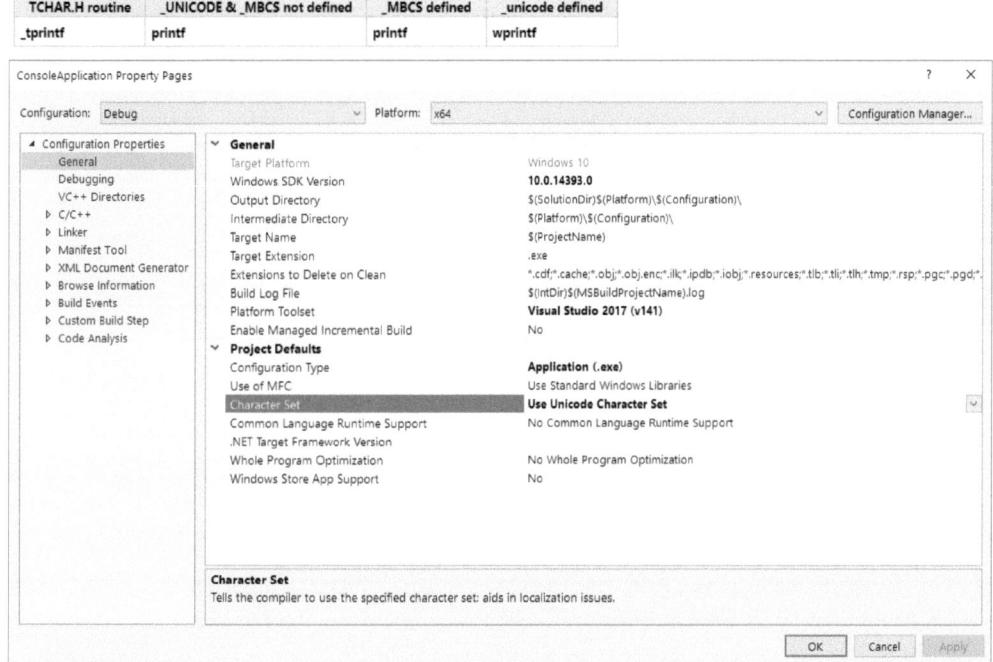

To be transparent, I urge you to code in a multiplatform manner. This requires a mapping table of C routines. https://msdn.microsoft.com/en-us/library/tsbaswba.aspx . Extract:

Professional C++ - Philosophy and Principles

Generic-text routine name	SBCS (_UNICODE & _MBCS not defined)	_MBCS defined	_UNICODE defined
_cgetts	_cgets	_cgets	_cgetws
_cgetts_s	_cgets_s	_cgets_s	_cgetws_s
_cputts	_cputs	_cputs	_cputws
_fgettc	fgetc	fgetc	fgetwc
_fgettchar	_fgetchar	_fgetchar	_fgetwchar
_fgetts	fgets	fgets	fgetws
_fputtc	fputc	fputc	fputwc
_fputtchar	_fputchar	_fputchar	_fputwchar
_fputts	fputs	fputs	fputws
_ftprintf	fprintf	fprintf	fwprintf

If you do TCHAR, you use the generic routine. And depending on whether UNICODE is defined or not, the function name is expanded to the desired name. Example of code to migrate:

```
char sz[255];
sprintf(sz, "Elapsed ms since Windows is up: %ld ms n", GetTickCount());
printf(sz);
```

In order for this code to compile in x86 and x64, precautions must be taken and the sprintf and printf correspondence in TCHAR mode must be obtained via tchar.h:

Generic-Text Routine Mappings

TCHAR.H routine	_UNICODE & _MBCS not defined	_MBCS defined	_UNICODE d
_stprintf	sprintf	sprintf	_swprintf
_stprintf_l	_sprintf_l	_sprintf_l	__swprintf_l

Thus, we know which function names should be used:

```
#include <tchar.h>

    TCHAR sz2[255];
    _stprintf(sz2, _T("Elapsed ms since Windows is up: %ld ms n"), GetTickCount());
```

```
_tprintf(sz2);
```

As you can see, strings are bordered by _T(" "). In Not Set or MBCS mode, _T is worthless whereas in UNICODE, it is worth L. This is how one designates a Unicode string.

Another ISO solution: STL
It is possible to manage the string type via the STL of C++: the Standard Template Library. Just do #include <string> and declare either std::string or std::wstring. These are either char or wchar_t strings. It depends on whether you want to code Windows or cross-platform. To be completely ISO, I promise you to use this solution based on STL. The ISO standard is language and STL. I want you to know that among experts, we don't all have the same point of view. My buddy Alain Z, from Redmond recommends to code in wchar_t. In fact, I see two modes. Next if you do a dll or next if you do an exe, next if you attack Windows APIs, next if you do Boost, a set of well-known C++ libraries available on Boost.org. If we do Boost, we will end up doing string or wstring on all floors (threads, filesystem, regexp, etc). Here's what it looks like with SSD:

```
#include <string>
#include <iostream>

        std::wstring sz3 = _T("hello world!");
        std::wcout << sz3 << std::endl;
```

The std::string & std::wstring conversions

If you use Windows APIs, you will need to use TCHAR. If you have external code, for example, that uses STL and std::wstring you will have to make matches. How do we do that? With STL it's not hard; you can return to the base type using the c_str() method:

```
        std::wstring s1 = L"UNICODE direct";
        const wchar_t * ws1 = s1.c_str();

        std::string s2 = "Hello world";
        const char * ss2 = s2.c_str();
```

Using the wstring ctor you can switch from a string to wstring easily and vice versa:

```
        std::string a1 = "A1";
        std::wstring u1 = _T("U1");

        std::wstring u2(a1.begin(), a1.end());
        std::wcout << u2 << std::endl;

        std::string a2(u1.begin(), u1.end());
        std::cout << a2 << std::endl;
```

These kinds of operations are not expensive. To live in a comfortable situation, I choose the STL and I go back and forth from time to time with the TCHAR when it is necessary to make calls with the Windows APIs. If I do a GUI in MFC, I use

Professional C++ - Philosophy and Principles

the CString classes. You're going to say to me, "What the hell, are we using everything???". You're right, but here's my explanation. Some APIs take types, and if you spend your time converting, you're better off... It is already quite complex for example when in COM we have to handle BSTR or VARIANTS... In short, use what is natural.

Alternate Windows solution via MFC and ATL/MFC

It is also possible to take a generic CString class managed by the common part ATL/MFC. This CString class exists in several variants: CStringT, CStringA, CStringW. Simple to understand if you will read the article from the start... In the middle of this code you can see the A2T and T2A functions that are handy. To use them, declare the USE_CONVERSION macro just behind the { entry in the function.

```
CString cs1 = sz;
CString cs2 = s1.c_str();
CString cs3 = A2T(s2.c_str());
CStringW cs4 = sz;
CStringW cs5 = s1.c_str();
CStringA cs6 = s2.c_str();
CStringA cs7 = T2A(s1.c_str());
```

There are variants:
- A2T and T2A
- W2T and T2W
- A2W and W2A

Compiler directive in effect	T becomes	OLE becomes
none	A	W
_UNICODE	W	W
OLE2ANSI	A	A
_UNICODE and OLE2ANSI	W	A

In the name of the macros, the source string type is left and the destination string type is right. A means LPSTR, T means LPTSTR and W means LPWSTR.

The C++ x64 project type

Everything happens in the project settings box. You must define an x64 platform via the Configuration Manager if it does not exist...

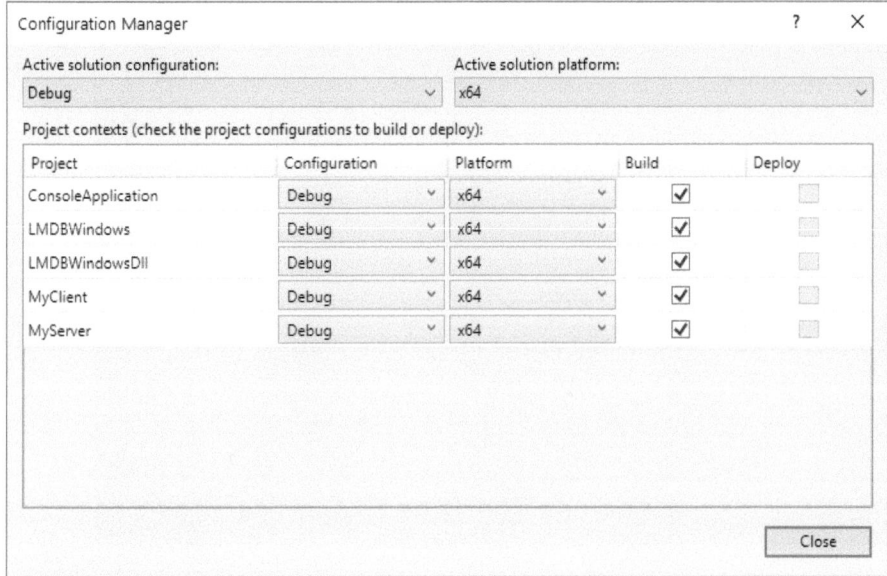

Naming of modules

There needs to be some rigour in the naming of modules. Boost is a model to follow.
We know the following information just in the name of the module:
- Is 32 bit or 64 bit
- Whether it is debug or not
- If it is shared or static
- The version of the Visual C++ with which it is compiled
- The version of the library

Professional C++ - Philosophy and Principles

```
x64 Native Tools Command Prompt for VS 2017
 Directory of D:\Dev\boost_1_66_0\stage\lib

02/01/2018  11:35 AM           518,144 boost_serialization-vc141-mt-gd-x32-1_66.dll
02/01/2018  11:35 AM           170,662 boost_serialization-vc141-mt-gd-x32-1_66.lib
02/01/2018  11:27 AM           694,272 boost_serialization-vc141-mt-gd-x64-1_66.dll
02/01/2018  11:27 AM           172,730 boost_serialization-vc141-mt-gd-x64-1_66.lib
02/01/2018  11:46 AM           198,144 boost_serialization-vc141-mt-x32-1_66.dll
02/01/2018  11:46 AM           169,884 boost_serialization-vc141-mt-x32-1_66.lib
02/01/2018  12:00 PM           257,024 boost_serialization-vc141-mt-x64-1_66.dll
02/01/2018  12:00 PM           171,924 boost_serialization-vc141-mt-x64-1_66.lib
02/01/2018  11:35 AM           317,440 boost_wserialization-vc141-mt-gd-x32-1_66.dll
02/01/2018  11:35 AM            69,068 boost_wserialization-vc141-mt-gd-x32-1_66.lib
02/01/2018  11:27 AM           431,104 boost_wserialization-vc141-mt-gd-x64-1_66.dll
02/01/2018  11:27 AM            69,784 boost_wserialization-vc141-mt-gd-x64-1_66.lib
02/01/2018  11:46 AM           135,680 boost_wserialization-vc141-mt-x32-1_66.dll
02/01/2018  11:46 AM            68,762 boost_wserialization-vc141-mt-x32-1_66.lib
02/01/2018  12:00 PM           169,472 boost_wserialization-vc141-mt-x64-1_66.dll
02/01/2018  12:00 PM            69,452 boost_wserialization-vc141-mt-x64-1_66.lib
02/06/2018  05:13 PM        31,175,838 libboost_serialization-vc141-mt-gd-x32-1_66.lib
02/06/2018  04:54 PM        36,351,756 libboost_serialization-vc141-mt-gd-x64-1_66.lib
02/06/2018  05:24 PM         9,677,960 libboost_serialization-vc141-mt-x32-1_66.lib
02/06/2018  05:05 PM        11,236,726 libboost_serialization-vc141-mt-x64-1_66.lib
02/06/2018  05:13 PM        20,356,362 libboost_wserialization-vc141-mt-gd-x32-1_66.lib
02/06/2018  04:54 PM        24,352,356 libboost_wserialization-vc141-mt-gd-x64-1_66.lib
02/06/2018  05:24 PM         7,427,836 libboost_wserialization-vc141-mt-x32-1_66.lib
02/06/2018  05:06 PM         8,566,804 libboost_wserialization-vc141-mt-x64-1_66.lib
              24 File(s)    152,829,184 bytes
               0 Dir(s)  21,538,459,648 bytes free

D:\Dev\boost_1_66_0\stage\lib>
```

Additionals Reminder

The modules must all be compiled in x64. We do not mix x86 and x64 otherwise it crashes! We build either in release or debug but we don't mix!

Command line compilation

The shortcut "x64 Native Tools Command Prompt for VS 2017" must be run and here it is:

```
x64 Native Tools Command Prompt for VS 2017
**********************************************************************
** Visual Studio 2017 Developer Command Prompt v15.6.1
** Copyright (c) 2017 Microsoft Corporation
**********************************************************************
[vcvarsall.bat] Environment initialized for: 'x64'

C:\Program Files (x86)\Microsoft Visual Studio\2017\Enterprise>
```

Conclusion

The 64-bit transition via the recompilation of the sources can be a costly and time-consuming work. It depends on the quality of the code. String management may be the obstacle to this passage. With the rules described in this chapter, we have the tips and tricks to get out of it without too much pain.

20. Tests in C++

The test tools for C++ are not recent and they have nothing to envy to those of managed languages. Of course, the concept of Reflection does not exist in C++ but the fundamentals have existed for almost 20 years; since 2000 exactly. To talk about testing, we will also talk about IDE because some tools are linked to Visual Studio, our favorite IDE.

CPPUnit

The pioneer, CPPUnit: this is the historical tool kit for C/C++. It has been forked several times and it is a safe bet. This is the port of JUnit, the tool made in Java.
It is available here: https://dev-www.libreoffice.org/src/cppunit/
CPPUnit is not integrated with Visual Studio, but it has the advantage of working on Linux and Windows. Its operation requires compiling it as lib or DLL and then running a Runner: a test runner of our tests! Compiling CPPUnit is not very difficult, just load the solution cppunit-1.13.2 src CppUnitLibraries2010.sln which is for Visual Studio 2010 and build on the cppunit and cppunit_dll projects. To see what a test program is, just include cppunit-1.13.2 simple examples simple.vcxproj in the solution. The solution requires cppunitd.lib to link and that's it. Let's see what running a series of C++ tests looks like:

```
Developer Command Prompt for VS 2017
D:\Dev\cppunit-1.13.2\examples\simple\Debug>simple
ExampleTestCase::example : assertion
ExampleTestCase::anotherExample : assertion
ExampleTestCase::testAdd : assertion
ExampleTestCase::testEquals : assertion
ExampleTestCase.cpp(8) : error : Assertion
Test name: ExampleTestCase::example
double equality assertion failed
- Expected: 1
- Actual   : 1.1
- Delta    : 0.05

ExampleTestCase.cpp(16) : error : Assertion
Test name: ExampleTestCase::anotherExample
assertion failed
- Expression: 1 == 2

ExampleTestCase.cpp(28) : error : Assertion
Test name: ExampleTestCase::testAdd
assertion failed
- Expression: result == 6.0

ExampleTestCase.cpp(45) : error : Assertion
Test name: ExampleTestCase::testEquals
equality assertion failed
- Expected: 12
- Actual   : 13

Failures !!!
Run: 4   Failure total: 4   Failures: 4   Errors: 0

D:\Dev\cppunit-1.13.2\examples\simple\Debug>
```

There are successes and failures. We also find the number of the line where the errors are. It is simple and effective. Now, let's look at the code level how we write tests in C++. We start by writing a test class:

```
#include <cppunit/extensions/HelperMacros.h>

class ExampleTestCase: public CPPUNIT_NS::TestFixture
{
  CPPUNIT_TEST_SUITE( ExampleTestCase );
  CPPUNIT_TEST( example );
  CPPUNIT_TEST( anotherExample );
```

Professional C++ - Philosophy and Principles

```
    CPPUNIT_TEST( testAdd );
    CPPUNIT_TEST( testEquals );
    CPPUNIT_TEST_SUITE_END();

  protected:
    double m_value1;
    double m_value2;

  public:
    void setUp();

  protected:
    void example();
    void anotherExample();
    void testAdd();
    void testEquals();
};
```

The setUp() routine is started at startup and here there is none, but the tearDown() method is executed at the end. That's the only subtlety of this class. For the rest, macros are used to define tests.

```
#include <cppunit/config/SourcePrefix.h>
#include "ExampleTestCase.h"

CPPUNIT_TEST_SUITE_REGISTRATION( ExampleTestCase );

void ExampleTestCase::example()
{
  CPPUNIT_ASSERT_DOUBLES_EQUAL( 1.0, 1.1, 0.05 );
  CPPUNIT_ASSERT( 1 == 0 );
  CPPUNIT_ASSERT( 1 == 1 );
}


void ExampleTestCase::anotherExample()
{
  CPPUNIT_ASSERT (1 == 2);
}

void ExampleTestCase::setUp()
{
  m_value1 = 2.0;
  m_value2 = 3.0;
}

void ExampleTestCase::testAdd()
```

```
{
  double result = m_value1 + m_value2;
  CPPUNIT_ASSERT( result == 6.0 );
}


void ExampleTestCase::testEquals()
{
  long* l1 = new long(12);
  long* l2 = new long(12);

  CPPUNIT_ASSERT_EQUAL( 12, 12 );
  CPPUNIT_ASSERT_EQUAL( 12L, 12L );
  CPPUNIT_ASSERT_EQUAL( *l1, *l2 );

  delete l1;
  delete l2;

  CPPUNIT_ASSERT( 12L == 12L );
  CPPUNIT_ASSERT_EQUAL( 12, 13 );
  CPPUNIT_ASSERT_DOUBLES_EQUAL( 12.0, 11.99, 0.5 );
}
```

As you can see from the source code, we use macros to declare what we're interested in. The mechanics is to use routines (macros) of type ASSERT with conditions to be fulfilled otherwise the test is in error. To run the test, you need a CPPUnit host, in the same module as your tests:

```
#include <cppunit/BriefTestProgressListener.h>
#include <cppunit/CompilerOutputter.h>
#include <cppunit/extensions/TestFactoryRegistry.h>
#include <cppunit/TestResult.h>
#include <cppunit/TestResultCollector.h>
#include <cppunit/TestRunner.h>


int main()
{
 // Create the event manager and test controller
  CPPUNIT_NS::TestResult controller;

 // Add a listener that colllects test result
  CPPUNIT_NS::TestResultCollector result;
 controller.addListener( &result );

 // Add a listener that print dots as test run.
  CPPUNIT_NS::BriefTestProgressListener progress;
 controller.addListener( &progress );
```

Professional C++ - Philosophy and Principles

```
   // Add the top suite to the test runner
   CPPUNIT_NS::TestRunner runner;
   runner.addTest( CPPUNIT_NS::TestFactoryRegistry::getRegistry().makeTest());
   runner.run( controller );

   // Print test in a compiler compatible format.
   CPPUNIT_NS::CompilerOutputter outputter( &result, CPPUNIT_NS::stdCOut());
   outputter.write();

   return result.wasSuccessful()? 0: 1;
}
```

The code is always the same so we make it a shared code and the trick is done... You will tell me that the result is a bit Spartan. Indeed, we use Visual Studio and it serves well that the tests can be viewed in the Visual Tests window... Let's look at another suite of tests.

Google Test Adapter

You're going to ticker... Google makes an add-in for VS? And yes, even it's open-source under GitHub. Here: https://github.com/csoltenborn/GoogleTestAdapter . It is also present on the Visual Studio marketplace. This add-in takes advantage of the «Test Explorer» window in Visual Studio. However, a solution must be compiled as follows. Open the googletest-master googletest msvc 2010 gtest.sln. There are several projects but the simplest way to understand the Google Tests philosophy is gtest_unittest-md. It contains a huge file with lots of test cases. To link to VS, compile the project and display the Test Explorer window. Here's what it looks like:

Professional C++

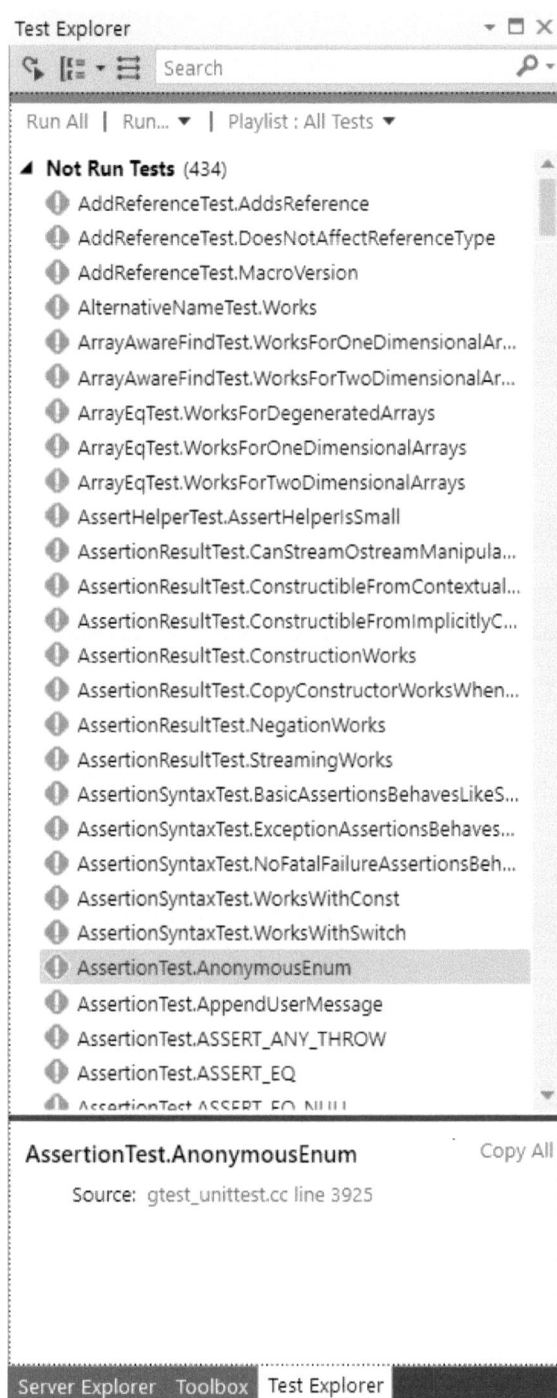

Professional C++ - Philosophy and Principles

At the code level, we will build one or more test sets as follows. The main file looks like this:

```cpp
#include "gtest/gtest.h"

int main(int argc, char **argv) {
    ::testing::InitGoogleTest(&argc, argv);
    return RUN_ALL_TESTS();
}
```

We add the gtest-all.cc file in our project like this, the project contains the hosting of Google Test. Let's create a test class in a MyTests file.h:

#pragma once

```cpp
#include "gtest/gtest.h"

class MyTests: public testing::Test
{
public:
    MyTests() {}
    ~MyTests() {}

public:
    int Add(int i, int j) { return i + j; }

    virtual void SetUp()
    {
        printf("SetUp()... \n");
    }

    virtual void TearDown()
    {
        printf("TearDown()... \n");
    }
};
```

In the MyTests.cpp file, there is this:
#include "MyTests.h"

TEST_F(MyTests, fn1) { printf("fn1 \n"); }
TEST_F(MyTests, fn2) { printf("fn2 \n"); }

TEST_F(MyTests, AddOK)
{
    EXPECT_EQ(10, Add(5, 5));
}

TEST_F(MyTests, AddFails)
{

```
        EXPECT_EQ(10, Add(15, 5));
}
```

You can see that the code is very simple. Two functions and two methods are being tested. Each time the SetUp() function is called and at the end the TearDown() function is also called.

If I compile this project and run it, the Test Explorer window of Visual Studio displays this:

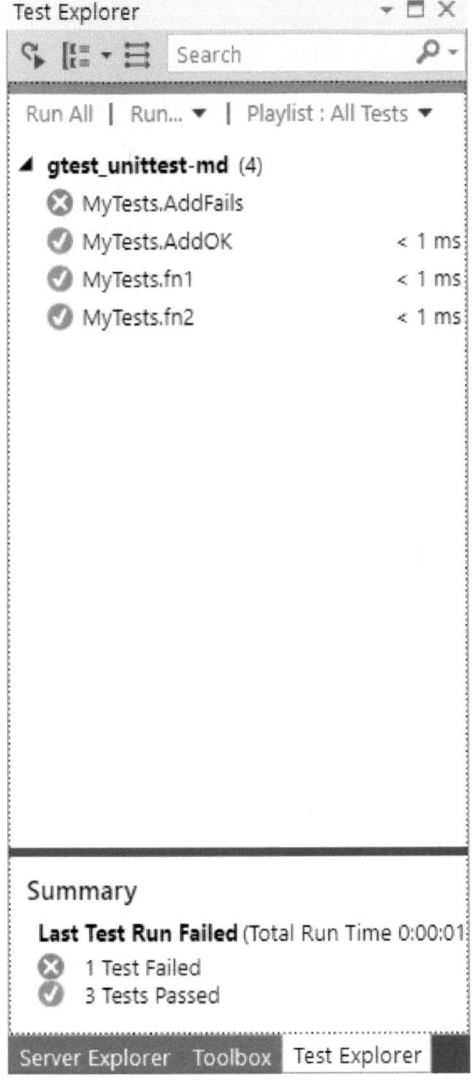

If you don't have Visual Studio, Google Test can launch online:

Professional C++ - Philosophy and Principles

```
Developer Command Prompt for VS 2017                                    —    □    ×

D:\Dev\Google Tests\googletest-master\googletest\msvc\2010\gtest-md\Win32-Debug>gtest_unittest.exe
[==========] Running 4 tests from 1 test case.
[----------] Global test environment set-up.
[----------] 4 tests from MyTests
[ RUN      ] MyTests.fn1
SetUp()...
fn1
TearDown()...
[       OK ] MyTests.fn1 (0 ms)
[ RUN      ] MyTests.fn2
SetUp()...
fn2
TearDown()...
[       OK ] MyTests.fn2 (1 ms)
[ RUN      ] MyTests.AddOK
SetUp()...
TearDown()...
[       OK ] MyTests.AddOK (0 ms)
[ RUN      ] MyTests.AddFails
SetUp()...
d:\dev\google tests\googletest-master\googletest\msvc\2010\mytests.cpp(22): error: Expected equality of these values:
  10
  Add(15, 5)
    Which is: 20
TearDown()...
[  FAILED  ] MyTests.AddFails (0 ms)
[----------] 4 tests from MyTests (6 ms total)

[----------] Global test environment tear-down
[==========] 4 tests from 1 test case ran. (7 ms total)
[  PASSED  ] 3 tests.
[  FAILED  ] 1 test, listed below:
[  FAILED  ] MyTests.AddFails

 1 FAILED TEST

D:\Dev\Google Tests\googletest-master\googletest\msvc\2010\gtest-md\Win32-Debug>
```

The gtest.cc file contains many tests and macros. It is possible to play with exceptions, input settings and many other things. It's a huge test suite.

Boost.Test

The Boost library is particularly well known in the C++ community. In addition, it has a lib called Test. The first thing to do is to build Boost and its libraries. Let's start at the beginning, we need to download Boost. Go to boost.org and download the 7z archive for Windows. Extract it locally and open a prompt VS command. Type bootstrap.bat. It will compile the build tool. Then type this:
bjam toolset=msvc-14.1 variant=debug,release threading=multi link=shared address-model=64
It takes a little bit of time and you're going to have all the libs in the stage lib directory.... The advantage of Boost is that it is well done and well documented. The libs test example directory contains test sets with different types of ASSERT. The principle is always the same, we do tests or follow-up tests. It is possible to perform test cases with or without parameters and on templates.
Here's how to do a minimum test with Boost.Test:

```
// ConsoleApplication1.cpp: Defines the entry point for the console
application.
```

```
//

#include "stdafx.h"
#include <boost/test/included/unit_test.hpp>
using namespace boost::unit_test;

void free_test_function()
{
    BOOST_TEST(true /* test assertion */);
}

test_suite* init_unit_test_suite(int /*argc*/, char* /*argv*/[])
{
    framework::master_test_suite().
        add(BOOST_TEST_CASE(&free_test_function));

    return 0;
}
```

The init_unit_test_suite function is required. Each Framework has its own hand, we have seen it. If we run this console program, we get this:

Continuous integration

Whether it's CPPUnit or Google Tests, console mode returns a code that lets you know if it's PASSED or FAILED. It is thus possible to rotate the unit tests in a chain of continuous integration.

Conclusion
Writing unit tests in C/C++ is very simple. We use the ASSERT macros of his favorite test framework and that's it. When you do unit tests, the intelligence is in tests and not in the framework of tests. There are other frameworks like wrestling, etc. But the principle is always the same. It's up to you!

Professional C++ - Philosophy and Principles

21. C++ Core Guidelines

The C++ Core Guidelines are available on GitHub[137] and on ISOCPP.ORG web site[138].
One implementation is available at GSL: Guidelines Support Library on GitHub[139].

"Within C++ is a smaller, simpler, safer language struggling to get out." -- Bjarne Stroustrup
The C++ Core Guidelines are a collaborative effort led by Bjarne Stroustrup, much like the C++ language itself. They are the result of many person-years of discussion and design across a number of organizations. Their design encourages general applicability and broad adoption but they can be freely copied and modified to meet your organization's needs.

The latest update is September 2022.
Just take a look at how the two authors present it from the main page[140].

---

[137] https://github.com/isocpp/CppCoreGuidelines

[138] https://isocpp.github.io/CppCoreGuidelines/CppCoreGuidelines

[139] https://github.com/Microsoft/GSL

[140] https://isocpp.github.io/CppCoreGuidelines/CppCoreGuidelines

September 23, 2022

Editors:

- Bjarne Stroustrup
- Herb Sutter

This is a living document under continuous improvement. Had it been an open-source (code) project, this would have been release 0.8. Copying, use, modification, and creation of derivative works from this project is licensed under an MIT-style license. Contributing to this project requires agreeing to a Contributor License. See the accompanying LICENSE file for details. We make this project available to "friendly users" to use, copy, modify, and derive from, hoping for constructive input.

Comments and suggestions for improvements are most welcome. We plan to modify and extend this document as our understanding improves and the language and the set of available libraries improve. When commenting, please note the introduction that outlines our aims and general approach. The list of contributors is here.

Problems:

- The sets of rules have not been completely checked for completeness, consistency, or enforceability.
- Triple question marks (???) mark known missing information
- Update reference sections; many pre-C++11 sources are too old.
- For a more-or-less up-to-date to-do list see: To-do: Unclassified proto-rules

You can read an explanation of the scope and structure of this Guide or just jump straight in:

- In: Introduction
- P: Philosophy
- I: Interfaces
- F: Functions
- C: Classes and class hierarchies
- Enum: Enumerations
- R: Resource management
- ES: Expressions and statements
- Per: Performance
- CP: Concurrency and parallelism
- E: Error handling
- Con: Constants and immutability
- T: Templates and generic programming
- CPL: C-style programming
- SF: Source files
- SL: The Standard Library

Professional C++ - Philosophy and Principles

> This work is the best of breed of 40 years of C++. Juts give your motivation to eat it, live with it and dream, breath and love this manual from Herb Sutter and Bjarne Stroustrup.

Look at the Abstract part[141].

Abstract

This document is a set of guidelines for using C++ well. The aim of this document is to help people to use modern C++ effectively. By "modern C++" we mean effective use of the ISO C++ standard (currently C++20, but almost all of our recommendations also apply to C++17, C++14 and C++11). In other words, what would you like your code to look like in 5 years' time, given that you can start now? In 10 years' time?

The guidelines are focused on relatively high-level issues, such as interfaces, resource management, memory management, and concurrency. Such rules affect application architecture and library design. Following the rules will lead to code that is statically type safe, has no resource leaks, and catches many more programming logic errors than is common in code today. And it will run fast – you can afford to do things right.

We are less concerned with low-level issues, such as naming conventions and indentation style. However, no topic that can help a programmer is out of bounds.

Our initial set of rules emphasizes safety (of various forms) and simplicity. They might very well be too strict. We expect to have to introduce more exceptions to better accommodate real-world needs. We also need more rules.

You will find some of the rules contrary to your expectations or even contrary to your experience. If we haven't suggested you change your coding style in any way, we have failed! Please try to verify or disprove rules! In particular, we'd really like to have some of our rules backed up with measurements or better examples.

You will find some of the rules obvious or even trivial. Please remember that one purpose of a guideline is to help someone who is less experienced or coming from a different background or language to get up to speed.

Many of the rules are designed to be supported by an analysis tool. Violations of rules will be flagged with references (or links) to the relevant rule. We do not expect you to memorize all the rules before trying to write code. One way of thinking about these guidelines is as a specification for tools that happens to be readable by humans.

The rules are meant for gradual introduction into a code base. We plan to build tools for that and hope others will too.

---

[141] https://isocpp.github.io/CppCoreGuidelines/CppCoreGuidelines#S-abstract

Comments and suggestions for improvements are most welcome. We plan to modify and extend this document as our understanding improves and the language and the set of available libraries improve.

Professional C++ - Philosophy and Principles

22. Herb Sutter's CPPCon 2022 Talk "Can C++ be x10 Simpler and Safer"

The title of this chapter is from herb Sutter on its CppCOn 2022 presentation PDF file[142].
The video of the live presentation CPPCon 2022 is available on YouTube[143].

> ## Can C++ be 10× simpler & safer ... ?
>
> Herb Sutter
>
> "Inside C++, there is a **much smaller and cleaner language** struggling to get out."
> — B. Stroustrup (D&E, 1994)
>
> "Say **10% of the size of C++** in definition and similar in front-end compiler size. ... **Most of the simplification would come from generalization**."
> — B. Stroustrup (ACM HOPL-III, 2007)

---

[142] https://github.com/CppCon/CppCon2022/blob/main/Presentations/CppCon-2022-Sutter.pdf

[143] https://www.youtube.com/watch?v=ELeZAKCN4tY

C++ Core Guidelines

 `as` = implemented using as

Pro.safety: Type-safety profile

- Type.1: Avoid casts:
   1. Don't use `reinterpret_cast` ; A strict version of Avoid casts and prefer named casts.
   2. Don't use `static_cast` for arithmetic types; A strict version of Avoid casts and prefer named casts.
   3. Don't cast between pointer types where the source type and the target type are the same; A strict version of Avoid casts.
   4. Don't cast between pointer types when the conversion could be implicit; A strict version of Avoid casts.
- Type.2: Don't use `static_cast` to downcast: Use `dynamic_cast` instead.
- Type.3: Don't use `const_cast` to cast away const (i.e., at all): Don't cast away const.
- Type.4: Don't use C-style `(T)expression` or functional `T(expression)` casts: Prefer construction or named casts or `T{expression}`.
- Type.5: Don't use a variable before it has been initialized: always initialize.
- Type.6: Always initialize a member variable: always initialize, possibly using default constructors or default member initializers. TODO classes
- Type.7: Avoid naked union: Use `variant` instead.
- Type.8: Avoid varargs: Don't use `va_arg` arguments.

C++ Core Guidelines

Pro.bounds: Bounds safety profile

 - Bounds.1: Don't use pointer arithmetic. Use `span` instead: Pass pointers to single objects (only) and Keep pointer arithmetic simple.

 - Bounds.2: Only index into arrays using constant expressions: Pass pointers to single objects (only) and Keep pointer arithmetic simple.

 - Bounds.3: No array-to-pointer decay: Pass pointers to single objects (only) and Keep pointer arithmetic simple.

TODO `std::` - Bounds.4: Don't use standard-library functions and types that are not bounds-checked: Use the standard library in a type-safe manner.

C++ Core Guidelines

Pro.lifetime: Lifetime safety profile

Accessing through a pointer that doesn't point to anything is a major source of errors, and very hard to avoid in many traditional C or C++ styles of programming. For example, a pointer might be uninitialized, the `nullptr`, point beyond the range of an array, or to a deleted object.

See the current design specification here.

Lifetime safety profile summary:

Lifetime — partial, mostly to-do
- Lifetime.1: Don't dereference a possibly invalid pointer: detect or avoid.

P1179
CppCon 2015/18

Roadmap

Motivation & approach
History (since 2015)
Safety
    Type safety — CppCon 2021
    Bounds safety
    Lifetime safety — CppCon 2015
    Initialization safety — CppCon 2020
Simplicity examples
    Parameter passing — CppCon 2020

Metrics to aim for

"50× safer" means
98% fewer CVEs & bugs
in these categories

"10× simpler" means
90% less total guidance
to teach in C++ books
and courses

what if we could do "C++11 *feels like* a new language" again, but broadly for the whole language?

support all C++20/23... evolution

embrace C++20/23... (e.g., default to C++20 modules, C++23 import std;)

"directed evolution" of C++ itself —
compiling to C++20/23... keeps us honest

bring any results to ISO C++ evolution

Cpp2	Cpp1
	preprocessor, #define, #include, which std header to include, auto, [[nodiscard]], forward declarations, ordering dependencies, unsafe casts, uninitialized variables
one l-to-r decl syntax	most vexing parse, east const vs west const, inside-out declaration syntax, two variable declaration syntaxes, two free function declaration syntaxes, two irregular member function declaration syntaxes, lambda function declaration syntax
in, copy, inout, out	X vs X const params, deciding X vs X const& params, T vs T const& in templates references (&, X&&, T&&) throughout the language, and explaining X&& vs T&&
move	std::move, why std::move doesn't move, general overuse of std::move, why not "return std::move," why && isn't rvalue reference for template types, how to write move parameters for template types
forward	std::forward, spelling perfect forwarding idiom right, why forwarding && is only for templated types, how to write forwarding && params for non-template types
named return values	how to enable NRVO, how to return multiple values via anonymous pair/tuple, how to return multiple named values using separately defined struct
new<T>, span	new, delete, owning raw *, memory leaks, 0 as int/pointer, NULL, null dereference pointer arithmetic, out of bounds subscripting, raw arrays, implicit array→ptr decay
postfix operators	(*x)++, ++x vs x++, and (int)-for-postfix dummy parameter convention
is	is_same_v, is_base_of_v, dynamic_cast, std::holds_alternative<T>, my_any.type() == typeid(T), my_optional.has_value
	union, va_arg arguments, C-style casts, reinterpret_cast, const_cast, function-style casts, static_cast, dynamic_cast, std::get<T>/<T&>, std::any_cast<T>/<T*>, opt.value()
as, gsl::narrow	don't use reinterpret_cast, don't use static_cast for arithmetic types, don't cast between pointer types that are the same, don't cast between pointer types where the conversion could be implicit, don't use const_cast, don't use static_cast to downcast, don't use a variable before it has been initialized
$	lambda capture introducers (+ postcondition 'old' values? + string interpolation?)

23. Herb Sutter's Work on CPP2

Some weeks ago in September 2022, Herb Sutter shipped an idea, a prototype named CPP2[144].

The GitHub README is presented here:

Cppfront is a experimental compiler from a potential C++ 'syntax 2' (Cpp2) to today's 'syntax 1' (Cpp1), to learn some things, prove out some concepts, and share some ideas. This compiler is a work in progress and currently hilariously incomplete... basic functions work, classes will be next, then metaclasses and lightweight exceptions.

```
main: () -> int = {
    std::cout << "hello world!";
}
```

```
$cat hello.cpp2

// left-to-right, order-independent,
// context-free, "import std;" default

main: () -> int = {
    hello("world\n");
}

hello: (msg: _) =
    std::cout << "hello " << msg;

$cppfront hello.cpp2 -p
hello.cpp2... ok (all Cpp2, passes safety checks)

hello.cpp

$hello
hello world
```

---

[144] https://github.com/hsutter/cppfront

Goals and History

My goal is to explore whether there's a way we can evolve C++ itself to become 10x simpler, safer, and more toolable. If we had an alternate C++ syntax, it would give us a "bubble of new code that doesn't exist today" where we could make arbitrary improvements (e.g., change defaults, remove unsafe parts, make the language context-free and order-independent, and generally apply 30 years' worth of learnings), free of backward source compatibility constraints.

In 2015-16 I did most of the 'syntax 2' design work. Since then, my ISO C++ evolution proposals and conference talks have come from this work (see list below) — each presenting one part of the design as a standalone proposal under today's syntax, usually with a standalone prototype implementation, to validate and refine that part. Since 2021, I've been writing this cppfront compiler to prototype all the parts together as a whole as originally intended, now including the alternative 'syntax 2' for C++ that enables their full designs including otherwise-breaking changes.

ANNEXES

Bibliography

Here is a list of books and links to view:

[Boost]	The Boost Libraries: free peer-reviewed portable C-source libraries. www.boost.org.
[C,2011]	ISO/IEC 9899. Standard - The C Language. X3J11/90-013-2011.
[C-,1998]	ISO/IEC JTC1/SC22/WG21 (editor: Andrew Koenig): International Standard - The C-Language. ISO/IEC 14882:1998.
[C-,2004]	ISO/IEC JTC1/SC22/WG21 (editor: Lois Goldtwaite): Technical Report on. Performance. ISO/IEC TR 18015:2004(E).
[C-,2011]	ISO/IEC JTC1/SC22/WG21 (editor: Pete Becker): International Standard - The C-Language. ISO/IEC 14882:2011.
[C-,2014]	ISO/IEC JTC1/SC22/WG21 (editor: Stefanus du Toit): International Standard - The C-Language. ISO/IEC 14882:2014.
[C-,2017]	ISO/IEC JTC1/SC22/WG21 (editor: Richard Smith): International Standard - The C-Language. ISO/IEC 14882:2017.
[ConceptsTS]	ISO/IEC JTC1/SC22/WG21 (editor: Gabriel Dos Reis): Technical Specification: C-Extensions for Concepts. ISO/IEC TS 19217:2015.
[CoroutinesTS]	ISO/IEC JTC1/SC22/WG21 (editor: Gor Nishanov): Technical Specification: C-Extensions for Coroutines. ISO/IEC TS 22277:2017.
[Cppreference]	Onlinesource for C-language and standardlibrary facilities. www.cppreference.com.
[Ellis,1989]	Margaret A. Ellis and Bjarne Stroustrup: *The Annotated Reference Manual*. Addison-Wesley. Reading, Massachusetts. ISBN 0-201-51459-1.
[Garcia,2015]	J. Daniel Garcia and B. Stroustrup: *Improving performance and maintainability through refactoring in C-11*. Isocpp.org. August 2015. http://www.stroustrup.com/improving_garcia_stroustrup_2015.pdf.
[Friedl,1997]:	Jeffrey E. F. Friedl: *Mastering Regular Expressions*. O'Reilly Media. Sebastopol, California. ISBN 978-1565922570.
[GSL]	N. MacIntosh (Editor):*Guidelines Support Library*. https://github.com/microsoft/gsl.
[Hinnant,2018]	Howard Hinnant: *Date*. https://howardhinnant.github.io/date/date.html. Mr. Github. 2018.
[Hinnant,2018b]	Howard Hinnant: *Timezones*. https://howardhinnant.github.io/date/tz.html. Mr. Github. 2018.
[Kernighan, 1978]	Brian W. Kernighan and Dennis M. Ritchie: *The C Programming Language.* Prentice Hall. Englewood Cliffs, New Jersey. 1978.
[Kernighan, 1988]	Brian W. Kernighan and Dennis M. Ritchie: *The C Programming Language, Second Edition.* Prentice Hall. Englewood Cliffs, New Jersey. ISBN 0-13-110362-8.

Professional C++ - Philosophy and Principles

[Knuth, 1968]	Donald E. Knuth: *The Art of Computer Programming*. Addison-Wesley. Reading, Massachusetts. 1968.
[Koenig,1990]	A. R. Koenig and B. Stroustrup: *Exception Handling for C* . Proc USENIX C-Conference. April 1990.
[Maddock,2009]	John Maddock: *Boost.Regex*.www.boost.org. 2,009. 2017.
[Stepanov,1994]	Alexander Stepanov and Meng Lee: *The Standard Template Library*. HP Labs Technical Report HPL-94-34 (R. 1). 1994.
[Stepanov,2009]	Alexander Stepanov and Paul McJones: *Elements of Programming*. Addison-Wesley. ISBN 978-0-321-63537-2.
[Stroustrup,1994]	B. Stroustrup: *The Design and Evolution of C.* Addison-Wesley. Reading, Massachusetts. ISBN 0-201-54330-3.
[Stroustrup,1997]	B. Stroustrup: *The C-Programming Language, Third Edition*. I'm AddisonWesley. Reading, Massachusetts. ISBN 0-201-88954-4. Hardcover ("Special") Edition. ISBN 0-201-70073-5.
[Stroustrup,2002]	B. Stroustrup: *C and C: Siblings*, *C and C: A Case for Compatibility*, and *C and C: Case Studies in Compatibility*. The C/C-Users Journal. July-September 2002. www.stroustrup.com/papers.html.
[Stroustrup,2007]	B. Stroustrup: *Evolving a language in and for the real world: C-1991-2006*. ACM HOPL-III. June 2007.
[Stroustrup,2009]	B. Stroustrup: *Programming - Principles and Practice Using C.*. Addison-Wesley. ISBN 0-321-54372-6.
[Stroustrup,2010]	B. Stroustrup: *The C-11 FAQ*. www.stroustrup.com/C++11FAQ.html.
[Stroustrup,2012a]	B. Stroustrup and A. Sutton: *A Concept Design for the STL*. WG21 Technical Report N3351-12-0041. January 2012.
[Stroustrup,2012b]	B. Stroustrup: *Software Development for Infrastructure*. compute. January 2012. doi:10.1109/MC.2011.353.
[Stroustrup,2013]	B. Stroustrup: *The Fourth Edition*. I'm AddisonWesley. ISBN 0-321-56384-0.
[Stroustrup,2014]	B. Stroustrup: C- Applications. http://www.stroustrup.com/applica.html.
[Stroustrup,2015]	B. Stroustrup and H. Sutter. https://github.com/isocpp/CppCoreGuidelines/blob/master/CppCoreGuidelines.md.
[Stroustrup,2015b]	B. Stroustrup, H. Sutter, and G. Dos Reis: *A brief introduction to C-'s model for type- and resource-safety.* Isocpp.org. October 2015. Revised December 2015. http://www.stroustrup.com/resource-model.pdf.
[Stroustrup,2018]	B. Stroustrup: *A Tour of C (Second Edition)*. I'm AddisonWesley. ISBN 0-13-499783-2.
[Sutton, 2011]	A. Sutton and B. Stroustrup: *Design of Concept Libraries for C*. Proc. SLE 2011 (International Conference on Software Language Engineering). July 2011.

[WG21]   ISO SC22/WG21 The C-Programming Language Standards Committee: *Document Archive*. www.open-std.org/jtc1/sc22/wg21.

Professional C++ - Philosophy and Principles

ANNEXE A - Interview with Bjarne Stroustrup (24th Feb 2020 – 19:00 GMT+)

The interview is a common idea of François Tonic and me following Professional Opportunities. François is the Chief Editor of French magazine Programmez[145].

For several months now, Programmez! wants to create a new series of articles and more specifically interviews with language creators. To inaugurate this section, we offer an exceptional interview with the creator of C++: Bjarne Stroustrup. Christophe Pichaud, a well-known C++ contributor in the magazine, spoke to Bjarne at length on 24 February, a few days after the official availability of C++ 20. The first version dates back to 1983.

---

[145] www.programmez.com

INTERVIEW

Bjarne Stroustrup, créateur de C++

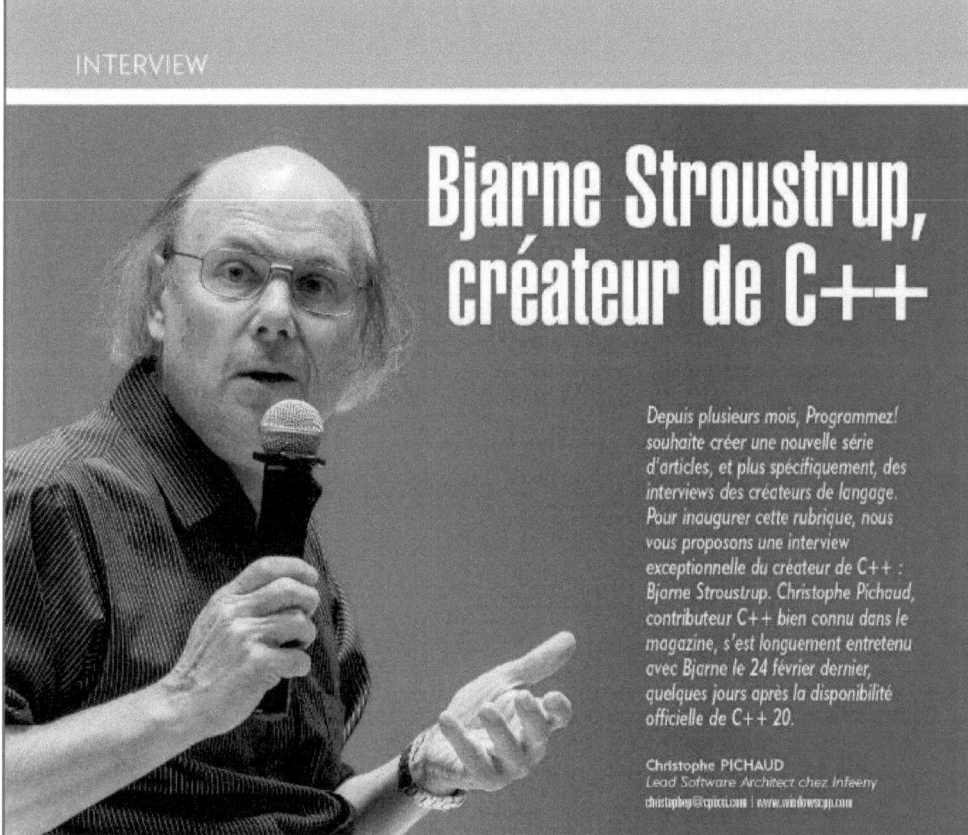

Depuis plusieurs mois, Programmez! souhaite créer une nouvelle série d'articles, et plus spécifiquement, des interviews des créateurs de langage. Pour inaugurer cette rubrique, nous vous proposons une interview exceptionnelle du créateur de C++ : Bjarne Stroustrup. Christophe Pichaud, contributeur C++ bien connu dans le magazine, s'est longuement entretenu avec Bjarne le 24 février dernier, quelques jours après la disponibilité officielle de C++ 20.

Christophe PICHAUD
Lead Software Architect chez Infeeny
christophep@cpixel.com | www.windowscpp.com

Comment naît un langage de programmation ? Comment avez-vous créé C++ ? Expliquez-nous son histoire.
Bjarne Stroustrup : C++, comme la plupart des langages que j'aime le mieux, a commencé avec un besoin, un problème. Je ne voulais pas particulièrement concevoir un langage de programmation. Je voulais construire un système, mais j'ai décidé que je ne pouvais pas construire ce système - une version d'Unix pour fonctionner comme un système distribué - avec les langages existants. J'avais besoin d'un langage capable de faire des choses de bas niveau comme des gestionnaires de mémoire, des pilotes de périphériques et des planificateurs de processus. J'avais aussi besoin d'un langage qui pouvait faire des choses de haut niveau comme spécifier les composants d'un programme et comment ils communiquaient. Aucun langage ne pouvait faire les deux, j'ai donc construit C++. Je n'ai jamais pu construire mon système distribué, mais d'autres ont construit de tels systèmes en C++.

Nous sommes une communauté de plusieurs millions de développeurs C++, en Amérique du Nord, en Australie, en Europe, en Asie. Nous avons traversé les époques et nous ne sommes pas là par hasard. Nous sommes des survivants. Même quand Java est sorti, nous avons survécu et ce sans marketing, sans organe de presse.
C++ doit être bon dans l'abstraction et dans la génération du code, le code bas-niveau, bon dans la gestion du hardware. Il permet de faire aussi bien du C que des templates. C++ n'est pas un full langage OOP au sens strict du terme, cependant il comporte de nombreuses fonctionnalités qui en font un bon candidat.

Les MFC n'utiliscient pas la STL. Dans mon apprentissage, j'ai appris le C++ puis la STL. Dans les MFC, il y avait des macros car le compilateur ne supportait toutes les fonctionnalités des templates. Comment avez-vous réagi quand vous avez vu la première version de la STL écrite par Stepanov pour HP ?
Quand j'ai vu la STL pour la première fois, nous avons discuté et j'ai trouvé cela bizarre. Puis, j'ai fait le compte de tout ce qui était utilisé comme fonctionnalités. Tout y était utilisé. Les templates sont complexes mais

Professional C++ - Philosophy and Principles

Bjarne Stroustrup, creator of C++

Beginning – General questions

1° How does a programming language is born ? How did you create C++ ? Explain us the story !

> C++, like most of the languages I like best, started with a need, a problem. I didn't particularly want to design a programming language. I wanted to build a system, but I decided that I couldn't build that system – a versions of Unix to run as a distributed system – with the existing languages. I needed a language that could do low-level things like memory managers, device drivers, and process schedulers. I also needed a language that could do high-level things like specifying components of a program and how they communicated. No language could do both, so I built C++. No. I never got to build my distributed system, but others built such systems using C++.

2° Are you surprise by the success of C++ ?

> Yes, definitely. I was – and am – quite amazed. There never was a time where C++ didn't have several better financed and heavily marketed competitors. Many aspects of the design were not fashionable, just responses to real-word challenges. Yet the C++ community grew and still grows. C++ serves real needs.

3° C++ is ISO. It is crucial and important ? To maintain an ecosystem and have the guarantee it runs on various platforms.

> For C++, the ISO standards committee (WG21) is essential. We don't have a rich owner and to collaborate, competing organizations need an open forum like WG21 in which to collaborate. Where else can people from competing organizations sit down and solve problems together? Having a standards committee doesn't guarantee anything; only the quality of the standard give success. It is crucial that the standard is based on consensus, so that all compiler and standard-library providers find it worth-while to adhere to it. In Prague, the vote for C++20 was 79-0 in favor! That means that C++20 will become official in the fall. Most parts of C++20 are already shipping in various compilers and much is in production use. C++20 is not Science Fiction.

4° Making enhancement to a programming language is difficult. We saw it with Sun and Oracle with Java, the Kotlin case, making the risk to break compatibility. What is your feeling with C++ ?

> Stability is an important feature, especially for people who build systems than must last for decades. C++ has evolved into a much more expressive and performant language than what I had in the 1980s, but we have been very careful to maintain a great degree of compatibility. Everybody wants a smaller, simpler language. They also want more features. Furthermore, most C++ developers insists that their old code should not be broken. Delivering all three is impossible. I try to maintain compatibility while adding ways to simplify the use of C++.

5° C++ has evolved among years with a rapid growth during the last decade. It is a good thing ?

Yes. New challenges emerge and new ideas are needed to meet them. A living language changes to keep up with a changing world. That is true for both natural and artificial language. Also, I always knew that C++ wasn't yet the best match for my ideals. For example, in 1981 I wrote that generic programming was needed. I conjectured that macros could be used to meet that need, but that didn't scale, so I implemented templates. However, templates met only part of my ideals for generic programming. Only with 'concepts' are we getting close.

Another example is concurrency and parallelism where we had to standardize a strongly typed threads-and-locks level of support. As a systems programming language, C++ had to provide direct support to what the operating systems offered. Then, we have to offer better standard support for lock-free programming, and only later could we address the higher-level models of concurrency and parallel algorithems. C++20 provides parallel algorithms and C++23 is likely to provide a general model of concurrency.

Over the ysear, C++ has also provided many facilities to simplify programming. 'Make simple things simple !' is a common comment. In modern C++, we have to write far less code to manage resources, to express general algorithms, to write simple loops, etc. than in older versions of C++. We canno simplify the language without breaking code, but we can simplify the use of the language.

6° What is your best award ? Tell us more.

The Charles Stark Draper Prize from the US National Academy of Engineering (https://en.wikipedia.org/wiki/Charles_Stark_Draper_Prize). It's one of the world's highest honors for an engineer. It was founded to compensate for the fact that there is no Nobel Prize for engineering. Very few computer scientists have received 'The Draper' ; it is for all fields of engineering. The engineers always appreciated my work and I am proud of having done something that's useful at a large scale.

7° Can you give us your feeling when young developers think about C++ as old legacy stuff compared to Rust, Kotlin and more ?

Everyone like something new and shiny and we'd all like to ignore the messy real-world complexities, many of which relates to past work. I'm somewhat amused when someone accuses me of borrowing something from Rust that I invented decades earlier. Every successful language will become "legacy" and have to deal with older ideas and older code; the alternative is failure.

8° What is the most important features in language that will be popular for you ?

The most important single feature in C++ is the class with constructors and destructors to handle resource management. That's a feature that distinguishes C++ from most other language and it is foundational to C++ programming. After that, I'll point to templates with concepts to support generic programming.

It is typically a mistake to focus on individual language features. I often characterize C++ like this

- A static type system with equal support for built-in types and user-defined types • Value **and** reference semantics
- Systematic and general resource management (RAII)
- Support for efficient object-oriented programming

385

Professional C++ - Philosophy and Principles

- Support for flexible and efficient generic programming
- Support for compile-time programming
- Direct use of machine and operating system resources
- Concurrency support through libraries (where necessary implemented using intrinsics)

This is for C++, of course ; other languages are designed for different application domains and different developer populations, so they have different design criteria.

Core C++ Questions

- assignment:
  - Is move semantic a good thing (what about the fuzzy &&) ?

Move semantics is a very good thing in that it completes C++'s resource management model by allowing resources to be move from scope to scope with little or no overhead and without fiddling with pointers or explicit resource management. This dramatically simplifies code and completes the developments started by the return value optimization (which I implemented in 1984). I almost exclusively use move semantics implicitly through return statements where it is safe and implicit once you have defined move constructors and move assignments. I am very suspicious about explicit use of && and std::move() because such use is error-prone and usually unnecessary.

- class:
  - Still the heart of c++ ; express what you think ! o Do we need enhancements to classes ?

Classes with constructors and destructors (when needed) are the heart of C++. I think they are pretty good and don't need significant improvements.

- concept:
  - Tell us more about C++ 20 concepts

When I designed templates, I wanted three things:

- Generality – to allow people to do more that I could imagine
- Zero overhead
- Precisely-specified interfaces

I didn't know how to do all three simultaneously, so we got just the first two. However, the first two were enough for templates to become a major success, but also caused a lot of problems and confusion.

"Concepts" gives us the that last point: precisely-specified interfaces without run-time overheads or restrictions on what you ca express; it's simply compile-time predicate logic on properties of types and values.

Finally, we can say just

> sort(v);

And get a decent error message if **v** isn't sortable. We might declare **sort()** like this: **void**

> sort(sortable_range auto&);

That **auto** is redundant, but many standards committee members felt that leaving it out would confuse people because then they wouldn't be able to see that **sort()** was a template.

- constructor:
    - A good constructor is easy to use. It's not easy.

???

- Coroutines o Tell us more about C++ 20 coroutines

Coroutines was part of the original conception of C++ and the very first C++ library (when C++ was still called "C with Classes") provided coroutines. I'm very pleased to see them back. Coroutines makes many forms of otherwise complicated code simple by allowing state state of a computation to be automatically saved between computations. The runtime representation of C++20 coroutines is very small and efficient so that they can be used to handle hundreds of thousands of asynchronous computations in a single program. They are already in heavy use in Facebook and Microsoft.

- derived class:
    - then you realize if it's well designed… when you use it or derive it. o Do we need enhancements to this stuff?

No. I don't think we need to add to the derived class mechanisms.

- destructor:
    - When the dirty job is done for you when you have called Close() or not…

Probably my favorite C++ feature. It is key to general resource management. Just managing memory isn't sufficient. We need to handle non-memory resources such as file handles, locks, and database connections.

- exception:
    - I am not an exception guy but I like the catch all… (…)

Well, I am "an exception guy" and I don't mind "catch(…)."

Professional C++ - Philosophy and Principles

Exception used with RAII immensely simplifies code and eliminates whole classes of errors at very minor costs. Sometimes, it provides speedups compared with code littered with tests of error codes. It keeps exceptional control flows from complicating the source code.

Most problems with exceptions come from people who use try-catch as simply a form of ifthen-else or in a codebase that is such a mess of pointers and manual resource management that exceptions become a source of errors and run-time cost. Another class of problems comes in systems that don't try to catch errors and in tiny systems where any form of runtime support can crowd out needed functionality.

- for:
    - for-range is quite cool. Tell us more !

What more is there to tell ? Traversing a range is one of the most common actions in our code so we should have a simple and relatively safe way of expressing it. Most of the common errors with traditional C for loops cannot be made with range-for and it is easier to optimize. Together with **std ::span()** is eliminates most buffer-overflow style errors.

- function:
    - lambda is good. I appreciate a lot for STL stuff.

Yes. They have become key to callbacks of all sorts, including specifying arguments for algorithms parameterized with predicates and other operations. Lambdas are often faster and more convenient than alternatives. Note that in C++, a lambda is simply a convenient notation for defining and instantiating a function object.

- operator:
    - operator overloading is quite good ; it's wonderful.

Indeed. I couldn't do without overloading (for function and operators). They are one of the key to generic programming and to many forms of elegant code.

- public, private, and protected:
    - the separation between things can be marvelous, and sometimes a friend comes at the rescue!

Indeed, though I don't find all that many uses for "protected" these days.

- template:
    - the hard stuff of C++
    - with the experience, it's the pure beauty of abstraction, with the specialization feature.
    - Do we need enhancements to templates ?

We need to polish a few rough corners on the use of contracts, but otherwise I think we are fine for now. For example, I'd like to be able to constrain template arguments in variable definitions:

```
pair<integral,derived_from<Shape>*> p = {27,new Circle{p,30}};
```

With concepts many of our designs will become simpler and easier to use.

If we don't need to constrain, we can simplify

```
pair p = {27,new Circle{p,30}};   // p becomes a pair<int,Circle*>
```

We have had template argument deduction since C++17.

- `virtual`:
    - We could not live without it...

Well, quite often we can. Class hierarchies and virtual functions are great, but somewhat overused.

Various questions

1° When I teach C++ lessons, I tell my students that C++ is everywhere. A friend of mine was in NewYork in June and saw the 66 seconds about "the engine of everything" with you in picture. I was so happy. It's so the truth. From medical to military, from databases to operating systems, from virtual machines (Java, NET) to Office suite, from industry to video games : EVERYWHERE ! Herb Sutter told "the world is built on C++". What about to be a 40-years old personage (C++) and be so simple : no starlight, no ads, no commercial machine, no ownership and a wide adoption by all tech companies. How do you feel when you hear that and because you know the truth ?

> Obviously, I feel happy when I see C++ being so widely used to do well. I also feel a bit scared because it is a great responsibility. C++ really is just about everywhere. Mostly it is invisible as part of some system that we depend on, say our phone, our television set, our movies and games, our car, our bank, our camera, the farm that produces our food.

> Though it was an honor, and not an ad for C++, seeing myself on a three-story-tall video display in Times Square was a bit spooky.

2° When tech people think about C++, they think about C and pointers. I know that, my students tell me. When they realize that smart pointers can do the job, with RAII, they are with no voices. All they have learned with Java and NET is useless.

> Well, those other languages have their place, but yes, it's sad that many have a completely warped view of C++. I wrote "A Tour of C++" to help people get a feel for modern C++. It has the obvious advantage of being thin. If you have already mastered programming, you can read it over a weekend.

3° Some weeks ago, on the MVP Channel, I send a passionate post about Rust popular usage and that some part of the kernel may be written in Rust for Windows Operating systems. Some researcher (who has never written an O.S) was arguing that. Herb replied me and I liked the way he wrote it. He called those guys the believers: like the project singularity, longhorn all those R&D efforts but cost effort. Longhorn was a trauma for Microsoft and was stopped at Vista pre-released. It was planned to incorporate NET stuff into the OS at kernel ad user layers. Windows Division reported that NET was to weak, not robust, not reliable and to slow and asked the Developer Division to address these issues. Because, it was not possible, WinDiv ignore DevDiv and it's still the war 15 years later. How do you feel when all new students learn only Java and NET at school? In my opinion, it's a shame. What is your feeling with those so-called productive languages like Java and NET/C#?

> I don't do language comparisons. They are hard to do well. I think many would benefit from being taught modern C++. Sadly, much C++ teaching is stuck in the 1980s. The C++ standards committee (WG21) now have a study group on education, aiming at providing some easily accessible guidelines for teaching.

4° How did you planned to write the Core C++ Guidelines with Herb Sutter on isocpp github ? Can you give us the under the scene aspect of that ? It could be Addison Wesley C++ Series book but it's free. Was it wanted ? The price to be again the number one is to be free ?

> I was working on a set of guidelines for Morgan Stanley based on the advice sections in my books (e.g., "A Tour of C++") with the aim of making them widely available. It occurred to me that I could not be the only one doing that. After all, C++11 and C++14 were bringing many new people to modern C++ and they needed guidlines. So I asked around and Herb had started similar work at Microsoft. Obviously, to be able to collaborate freely and to share our work on a timely basis, we made it an open-source project. The guidelines and the tiny support library (GSL) are on Github:
>
> - https://github.com/isocpp/CppCoreGuidelines
> - https://github.com/microsoft/gsl
>
> The (essential) static analysis support is mainly in Visual Studio with a bit of support in Clang Tidy.
>
> This is an ambition project. For starters we want to ensure a style of C++ that's type-safe and resource-safe. Beyond that, we'd like to eliminate needless complex use and common performance problems.
>
> The Core Guidelines is another good way of looking at modern C++. Don't read it all at once, though. It's meant to be used with a static analyser, but the introduction can be quite helpful and the individual guidelines can be used much as an FAQ. Obviously, people are encouraged to contribute. It's not just Herb and me. We have many contributors and several regular editors.

5° Some people in marketing, said some years ago that C++ is "unsafe and unsecure" ? I explain them that smart pointers, auto , nullptr, vector ,string do the job and it's a non-sense to emit such a sentence. What is your opinion again a so stupid sentence?

> Safety and security are system properties. Some people seem obsessed with the possibility of language insecurities, but every language that can manipulate hardware directly will have some. Any language that can use the operating systems API directly have some. If I wanted to break into a computer, I wouldn't start messing with C++, there are easier ways in.
>
> That said, most of the things that people complain about can be avoided in modern C++; just look at the C++ Core Guidelines (and enforce them). The feature you mention are among the features that helps.

6° The engine of everything. It's so cool. C++ is a diamond tool. For people who need to allocate dynamic memory it fits, for people who need constant memory it fits, for building all kind of software fits. With the success of native tooling and specially LLVM or GCC backend, a series of languages adopt the native style because it's that that works well and works best. What are you feeling with the eco-system of programming languages that go native?

> Hard to say because there is not just one such ecosystem. It is actually nice to see all those new languages built on a C++ infrastructure.

7° Some companies invest in Java, Kotlin, others Rust, others Go, others Swift. What do you think of diversity ?

> It's good to see developments in programming languages and programming techniques. I just wish more people would realize that there is no language that is best for everything and everybody and try to learn from the best in all and benefit from the variety of languages where they have their strength. C++ is often "the one to beat." There is a reason for that: C++ is pretty good for many things, efficient, and stable. Any language that survives for a couple of decades will have some of C++'s problems.

8° Everything on my pc laptop is made with C/C++ : Windows, Sysinternals Suite, Office (Word, Excel, PowerPoint, Outlook), Chrome, VLC, Winamp, Gimp, Acrobat Reader, SQL Server, my Video games. ALL. Is there best achievements? C++ rulez the world.

> Personally, I am happiest with C++'s role in science and engineering: Think of CERN, the human genome project, the Mars Rovers.

> Also, C++ is spreading into new application domains. For example, through TensorFlow, it is the foundation for most AI/ML.

Professional C++ - Philosophy and Principles

ANNEXE B – BJARNE STROUSTRUP'S ARTICLE in ACCU Overload No 161

The web page is here : https://accu.org/journals/overload/29/161/stroustrup/

The Acknowledgements if presented here because I just put their paper notes.

Acknowledgements

This note is mostly direct or paraphrased quotes from the referenced papers, so many thanks to the contributors to those as listed in their acknowledgement sections. Also thanks to Gabriel Dos Reis, J.C. van Winkel, Herb Sutter, J-Daniel Garcia, Roger Orr and the unnamed *Overload* reviewers who made constructive comments on earlier drafts.

Bjarne Stroustrup is the designer and original implementer of C++. To make C++ a stable and up-to-date base for real-world software development, he has stuck with its ISO standards effort for almost 30 years (so far). You can contact him via his website: www.stroustrup.com.

C++ – AN INVISIBLE FOUNDATION OF EVERYTHING

C++ – an Invisible Foundation of Everything

By Bjarne Stroustrup

Overload, 29(161):8-11, February 2021

What is C++ and why do people still use it? Bjarne Stroustrup provides a short note answering these questions.

I am often asked variations of the questions 'What is C++?' and 'Is C++ still used anywhere?' My answers tend to be detailed, focused on the long term, and slightly philosophical, rather than simple, fashionable, and concrete. This note attempts a brief answer. It presents C++ as 'a stable and evolving tool for building complex systems that require efficient use of hardware'. Brief answers are necessarily lacking in depth, subtlety, and detail – for detailed and reasoned explanations backed by concrete examples, see 'References and resources'. This note is mostly direct or paraphrased quotes from those sources.

Overview

This note consists of:

- *Aims and means* – the high-level aims of C++'s design and its role in systems
- *Use* – a few examples of uses of C++ focusing on its foundational uses
- *Evolution* – the evolutionary strategy for developing C++ based on feedback
- *Guarantees, Language, and Guidelines* – the strategy for simultaneously achieving evolution, stability, expressiveness, and complete type-and-resource safety

- *People* – a reminder of the role of people in software development
- *References and resources* – an annotated list of references that can lead to a deeper understanding of C++
- *Appendix* – a very brief summary of C++'s key properties and features

Aims and means

C++ was designed to solve a problem. That problem required management of significant complexity and direct manipulation of hardware. My initial ideals for C++ included

- **The efficiency of C for low-level tasks**
- **Simula's strict and extensible type system**

What I did not like included

- **C's lack of enforcement of its type system**
- **Simula's non-uniform treatment of built-in types and user-defined types** (classes)
- **Simula's relatively poor performance**
- **Both languages' lack of parameterized types** (what later became templates)

This set off a decades-long quest to simultaneously achieve

- **Expressive code**
- **Complete type-and-resource safety**
- **Optimal performance**

I did not want a specialized tool just for my specific problem (support for building a distributed system), but a generalization to solve a large class of problems:

- **C++ is a tool for building complex systems that require efficient use of hardware**

That's a distillation of my initial – and current – aims for C++. Suitably fleshed out with details and implications, this explains much about modern C++. That statement is not a snappy slogan of the form *C++ is an <<adjective>> language* but I have never found a sufficiently accurate and descriptive adjective for that. Shifting the focus from language use to language technicalities, we can say:

- **C++ is a general-purpose language for the definition and use of light-weight abstractions**

That leaves the definition of 'general-purpose', 'light-weight', and 'abstraction' open to debate. In C++ terms, I am primarily thinking about classes, templates, and concepts; about expressiveness and efficient use of time and space.

To elaborate a bit further:

Professional C++ - Philosophy and Principles

- **C++ supports building resource-constrained applications and software infrastructure**
- **C++ supports large-scale software development**
- **C++ supports completely type-and-resource-safe code**

Technically, C++ rests on two pillars:

- **A direct map to hardware**
- **Zero-overhead abstraction in production code**

By 'zero-overhead', I mean that roughly equivalent functionality of a language feature or library component cannot be expressed with less overhead in C or C++:

- **What you don't use, you don't pay for** (aka 'no distributed fat')
- **What you do use, you couldn't hand-code any better** (e.g., dynamic dispatch)

It does not mean that for a more-specific need you can't write more efficient code (say in assembler).

Use

Many well-known applications/systems are written in C++ (e.g., Google search, most browsers, Word, the Mars Rovers, Maya). All systems need to use hardware and large systems must manage complexity. Supporting those fundamental needs has allowed C++ to prosper over decades :

- **C++ is an invisible foundation of everything**

'Everything' is obviously a bit of an exaggeration, but even systems without a line of C++ tend to depend on systems written in C++. 'Everything' is a good first approximation.

Foundational uses of C++ are typically invisible, often even to programmers of systems relying on C++: to be usable by many, a complex system must protect its users from most complexities. For example, when I send a message, I don't want to know about message protocols, transmission systems, signal processing, task scheduling, processor design, or provisioning. Thus, we find C++ in virtual machines (HotSpot, V8), numerics (Eigen, ROOT), AI/ML (TensorFlow, PyTorch), graphics and animation (Adobe, SideFx), communications (Ericsson, Huawei, Nokia), database systems (Mongo, MySQL), finance (Morgan Stanley, Bloomberg), game engines (Unity, Unreal), vehicles (Tesla, BMW, Aurora), CAD/CAM (Dassault, Autodesk), aerospace (Space-X, Lockheed Martin), microelectronics (ARM, Intel, Nvidia), transport (CSX, Maersk), biology and medicine (protein folding, DNA sequencing, tomography, medical monitoring), embedded systems (too many to mention), and much more that we never see and typically don't think of – often in the form of libraries and toolkits usable from many languages. C++ is also key in components and implementations of many different programming languages (GCC, LLVM).

We also find C++ in 'everyday' applications, such as coffee machines and pig-farm management. However, the role as a foundation for systems, tools, and libraries has critical implications for C++'s design, use, and further evolution.

Evolution

Since its inception, C++ has been evolving. That reflects both necessity and an early deliberate choice:

- **No language is perfect for everything and for everybody** (that includes C++)
- **The world changes** (e.g., there were no mobile apps until about 2005)
- **We change** (e.g., few industrial programmers appreciated generic programming in 1985)

Thus

- **C++ must evolve to meet changing requirements and uses**
- **Design decisions must be guided by real-world use** – all good engineering relies on feedback

To evolve, C++ must

- **Offer stability** – organizations that deliver and maintain systems lasting for decades can't constantly rewrite their systems to keep up with incompatible changes to their foundations.
- **Be viable at all times** – must be effective for problems in its domain at all times; you can't take a 'gap year' from improving the language and its implementation.
- **Be directed by a set of ideals** – to remain coherent, the development of language features must be guided by a framework of principles and long-term aims.

Why continue to evolve after years of success? There never was a shortage of people who would prefer to stay with C or move to one of the latest fashionable languages. People can to do exactly that if it makes sense to them, but

- **C++ is a good solution to a wide range of problems**
- **There are hundreds of billions of lines of working C++ code 'out there'**
- **There are millions of C++ programmers**

It takes significant time for a language to mature to be adequate for a range of uses far beyond the understanding of its original designers. Some design tensions are inherent

- **Every successful language will eventually face the problem of evolution vs. stability**
- **Every general-purpose language must serve both (relative) novices and seasoned experts**

Successful language design – like all successful engineering – requires good fundamental ideas and a careful balancing of constraints. Optimizing for just a single desirable property can offer advantages for one application area for one moment of time, but eventually the result dies for lack of adaptability. By now, C++ has survived for 40 years by carefully balancing concerns, learning from experience, and avoiding chasing fashions.

- **A general-purpose language must maintain a careful balance of user needs**

Professional C++ - Philosophy and Principles

Essential concerns that must be balanced include:

- simplicity, expressiveness, safety, run-time performance, support for tool building, ease of teaching, maintainability, composability of software from different sources, compilation speed, predictability of response, portability, portability of performance, and stability

'Simplicity' refers to how ideas are expressed in source code, 'expressiveness' determines the range of uses, 'safety' to type safety and absence of resource leaks, and 'predictability' is essential for many embedded systems.

Guarantees, language, and guidelines

C++ is complicated, but people don't just want a simpler language, they also want improvements and stability:

- Simplify C++
- Add these new features
- Don't break my code

These are reasonable requests so we need a way out of this 'trilemma'. We cannot simplify the language without breaking billions of lines of code and seriously disrupt millions of users. However, we can dramatically simplify the use of C++:

- Keep simple tasks simple
- Ensure that nothing essential is impossible or unreasonably expensive

To do that

- Provide simpler alternatives for simple uses
- Provide simplifying generalizations
- Provide alternatives to error-prone or slow features

Often, a significant improvement involves a combination of those three.

- Design C++ code to be tunable

A high-level abstraction presents a simple, safe, and general interface to users. When needed, a user – not just a language implementer – can provide an alternative implementation or an improved solution. This can sometimes lead to orders-of-magnitude performance improvements and/or enhanced functionality. By using lower-level or alternative abstractions, we can eventually get to use the hardware directly, sometimes even to directly access special-purpose hardware (e.g., GPUs or FPGAs).

From the earliest days, a major aim for the evolution of C++ was to deliver

- Complete type-and-resource safety

Much of the evolution of C++ can be seen as gradually approaching that ideal, starting with adding function declarations (function prototypes) to C. By 'type safety', I mean complete static (compile-time) checks that an object is used only according to its defined type augmented by guaranteed run-time checks where static checking is infeasible (e.g., range checking). Simula offered that but at significant cost implying lack of applicability in key areas.

- **Making the type system both strict and flexible is key to correctness, safety, and performance**

Type-safety is not everything, though:

- **Correctness, safety, and performance are system properties, not just language features**
- **A type-safe program can still contain serious logic errors**
- **Test early, often, and systematically**

To simplify use, we need tools and guidelines. The *C++ Core Guidelines* (see 'References and resources' on page 10) offer rules for simple, safe, and performant use:

- **No resource leaks** (incl. no leaks of non-memory resources, such as locks and thread handles)
- **No memory corruption** (an essential pre-condition for any guarantee)
- **No garbage collector** (to avoid indirections in access, memory overheads, and collection delays)
- **No limitation of expressiveness** (compared to well-written modern C++)
- **No performance degradation** (compared to well-written modern C++)

These guarantees cannot be provided for arbitrarily complex C++ code. Therefore, the Core Guidelines include rules to ensure that static analysis can offer the needed guarantees. The guidelines are a key part of my strategy for a gradual evolution of C++:

- **Improve C++ by adding language features and libraries**
- **Maintain stability/compatibility**
- **Provide a variety of strong guarantees through selectively enforced guidelines**

The Core Guidelines are in production use, often supported by static analysis. The guidelines can be enforced by a compiler, but the aim is not to impose a single style of use on the whole C++ community. That would fail because of the widely varying needs and styles of use. By default, enforcement must be selective and optional. A separate static analyzer – usable with any ISO C++ compatible implementation – would be ideal. If a specific 'dialect' (that is, a specific set of rules and enforcement profiles) is to be enforced, it can be done through control of the build process (possibly supported by compiler options).

People

Code is written by people. A programming language is a tool, just one part of a tool chain for a technical community. This was recognized from the start. Here is the opening statement of the first edition of *The C++ Programming Language*:

Professional C++ - Philosophy and Principles

C++ is a general-purpose programming language designed to make programming more enjoyable for the serious programmer.

By 'serious programmer' I meant 'people who build systems for the use of others'. This concern for the human side of system development has also been expressed as:

- **Design and programming are human activities; forget that and all is lost**

C++ serves a huge community. To improve software, we need not just to improve the language. We must also bring the community along – supported by education, libraries, and tools. This must be done carefully because no individual can know every use of C++ or every user need.

References and resources

B. Stroustrup: 'Thriving in a crowded and changing world: C++ 2006-2020' *ACM/SIGPLAN History of Programming Languages conference, HOPL-IV.* June 2020. This is the best current description of C++'s aims, evolution, and status. At 160 pages, it is not a quick read. Available at https://dl.acm.org/doi/abs/10.1145/3386320

H. Hinnant, R. Orr, B. Stroustrup, D. Vandevoorde, M. Wong: *DIRECTION FOR ISO C++*. WG21 P2000. 2020-07-15. Outlines the direction of C++'s evolution, co-authored and continuously updated by the ISO C++ Standard committee's Direction Group as a guide to members. Available at http://www.open-std.org/jtc1/sc22/wg21/docs/papers/2020/p2000r2.pdf

B. Stroustrup: The Design and Evolution of C++ Addison Wesley, ISBN 0-201-54330-3. 1994. This book contains lists of design rules for C++, some early history, and many code examples.

B. Stroustrup: A Tour of C++ (2nd Edition) ISBN 978-0134997834. Addison-Wesley. 2018. A brief – 210 page – tour of the C++ Programming language and its standard library for experienced programmers.

B. Stroustrup: Programming – Principles and Practice Using C++ (2nd Edition). Addison-Wesley. ISBN 978-0321992789. May 2014. A programming text book aimed at beginners who want eventually to become professionals.

The C++ Core Guidelines. A set of guidelines for safe and effective use of modern C++. Many of the guidelines are enforceable through static analysis. 2014-onwards. Available at https://github.com/isocpp/CppCoreGuidelines/blob/master/CppCoreGuidelines.md

Infographic: C/C++ Facts We Learned Before Going Ahead with CLion. A 2015 report on a survey of C++ use, estimating the C++ user community to be 4.5 million strong and listing major industrial use. Today, there are more users. Available at https://blog.jetbrains.com/clion/2015/07/infographics-cpp-facts-before-clion/

B. Stroustrup, H. Sutter, and G. Dos Reis: 'A brief introduction to C++'s model for type- and resource-safety'. Isocpp.org. October 2015. An early summary of the aims of the core guidelines as they relate to type safety and resource safety. Available at https://www.stroustrup.com/resource-model.pdf

B. Stroustrup: How can you be so certain? P1962R0. 2019-11-18. A caution against shallow arguments for fashionable causes. Language design requires a certain amount of humility. Available at http://www.open-std.org/jtc1/sc22/wg21/docs/papers/2019/p1962r0.pdf

B. Stroustrup: Remember the Vasa! P0977r0. 2018-03-06. A note of warning about overenthusiastic 'improvement' of the language. Available at https://www.stroustrup.com/P0977-remember-the-vasa.pdf

The C++ Foundation's Website describes the organization and progress of the standards effort. https://isocpp.org/std

www.stroustrup.com offers many of my videos, papers, interviews, and quotes, including:

- My CppCon'14 keynote: 'Make Simple Tasks Simple!' at https://www.youtube.com/watch?v=nesCaocNjtQ
- My Cppcon'17 keynote: 'Learning and Teaching Modern C++' at https://www.youtube.com/watch?v=fX2W3nNjJlo
- My Cppcon'19 Keynote: 'C++20: C++ at 40' at https://www.youtube.com/watch?v=u_ij0YNkFUs&t=235s
- Lex Fridman's 2019 'Interview with Bjarne Stroustrup' at https://www.youtube.com/watch?v=uTxRF5ag27A&t=1s

Appendix: The C++ language

The description of C++ above does not mention any language features or give any code examples. This leaves it open to serious misinterpretation. I cannot give serious examples of good code here – see 'References and resources' – but I can summarize.

There is a reasonably stable core of ideals that guides the evolution of C++ (the references are to my 2020 'History of Programming Languages' paper):

- A static type system with equal support for built-in types and user-defined types (§2.1)
- Value and reference semantics (§4.2.3)
- Systematic and general resource management (RAII) (§2.2)
- Support for efficient object-oriented programming (§2.1)
- Support for flexible and efficient generic programming (§10.5.1)
- Support for compile-time programming (§4.2.7)
- Direct use of machine and operating system resources (§1)
- Concurrency support through libraries (often implemented using intrinsics) (§4.1) (§9.4)

Key language features with their primary intended roles:

- **Functions** – the basic way of defining a named action. Functions with different types can have the same name. The function invoked is then chosen based on the type of its arguments.
- **Overloading** – allowing semantically similar operations on different types is a key to generic programming.
- **Operator overloading** – a function can be defined to give meaning to an operator for a given set of operand types. Overloadable operators includes the usual arithmetic and logical operators plus () (application), [] (subscripting), and -> (member selection).
- **Classes** – user-defined types that can approach built-in types for ease of use, style of use, and efficiency, while opening up a whole new world of general and application-specific types. Classes offer (optional) encapsulation without run-time cost. Class objects can be allocated on the stack, in static memory, in dynamic (heap) memory, or as members of other classes.
- **Constructors and destructors** – the key to C++'s resource management and much of its simplicity of code. A constructor can establish an invariant for a class and a destructor can release any resources an object has acquired during its lifetime. Systematic resource management using constructors and destructors is often called RAII ('Resource Acquisition Is Initialization').

Professional C++ - Philosophy and Principles

- **Class hierarchies** – the ability to define one class in terms of another so that the base class can be used as an interface to derived classes or as part of the implementation of derived classes. The key to traditional object-oriented programming.
- **Virtual functions** – provide run-time type resolution within class hierarchies.
- **Templates** – allow types, functions, and aliases to be parameterized by types and values. The workhorse of C++ generic programming.
- **Concepts** – compile-time predicates on sets of types and values. Mostly used as precise specifications of a template's requirements on its parameters, thereby allowing overloading. A concept taking a single type argument is roughly equivalent to a type, except that it does not specify object layout.
- **Function objects** – objects of classes (often class templates) supporting an application operator ( ). Acts like functions but are objects that can carry state.
- **Lambdas** – a notation for defining function objects.
- **Immutability** – immutable objects can be defined. Access through pointers or references can be declared to be non-mutating.
- **Modules** – a mechanism for encapsulating a set of types, functions, and objects with a well-defined interface offering good information hiding. To use a module, you import it. A program can be composed out of modules.
- **Namespaces** – for separating major components of a program and avoiding name clashes.
- **Exceptions** – for signaling errors that cannot be handled locally. The backbone of much error handling. Exceptions are integrated with constructors and destructors to enable systematic resource management.
- **Type deduction** – to simplify notation by not requiring the programmer to repeat what the compiler already knows. Essential for generic programming and simple expression of ideas.
- **Compile-time functions** – part of comprehensive support for compile-time programming.
- **Concurrency** – lock-free programming, threads, and coroutines.
- **Parallelism** – parallel algorithms.

In addition, there is a relatively large and useful standard library and loads of other libraries. Don't try to write everything yourself in the bare language.

Acknowledgements

This note is mostly direct or paraphrased quotes from the referenced papers, so many thanks to the contributors to those as listed in their acknowledgement sections. Also thanks to Gabriel Dos Reis, J.C. van Winkel, Herb Sutter, J-Daniel Garcia, Roger Orr and the unnamed *Overload* reviewers who made constructive comments on earlier drafts.

Bjarne Stroustrup is the designer and original implementer of C++. To make C++ a stable and up-to-date base for real-world software development, he has stuck with its ISO standards effort for almost 30 years (so far). You can contact him via his website: www.stroustrup.com.

ANNEXE C – LINUS TORVALD   : C++ is CRAP LANGUAGE

Source: https://developers.slashdot.org/story/21/04/17/009241/linus-torvalds-says-rust-closer-for-linux-kernel-development-calls-c-a-crap-language

Linus Torvalds Says Rust Closer for Linux Kernel Development, Calls C++ 'A Crap Language' (itwire.com)
Posted by EditorDavid on Saturday April 17, 2021 @01:34PM from the Rust-never-sleeps dept.

Google's Android team supports Rust for developing the Android operating system. Now they're also helping evaluate Rust for Linux kernel development. Their hopes, among other things, are that "New code written in Rust has a reduced risk of memory safety bugs, data races and logic bugs overall," that "abstractions that are easier to reason about," and "More people get involved overall in developing the kernel, thanks to the usage of a modern language."

Linus Torvalds responded in a new interview with IT Wire (shared by Slashdot reader juul_advocate):The first patches for Rust support in the Linux kernel have been posted and the man behind the kernel says the fact that these are being discussed is much more important than a long post by Google about the language. Linus Torvalds told iTWire in response to queries that Rust support was "not there yet", adding that things were "getting to the point where maybe it might be mergeable for 5.14 or something like that..." Torvalds said that it was still early days for Rust support, "but at least it's in a 'this kind of works, there's an example, we can build on it'."

Asked about a suggestion by a commenter on the Linux Weekly News website, who said, during a discussion on the Google post, "The solution here is simple: just use C++ instead of Rust", Torvalds could not restrain himself from chortling. "LOL," was his response. "C++ solves _none_ of the C issues, and only makes things worse. It really is a crap language.

"For people who don't like C, go to a language that actually offers you something worthwhile. Like languages with memory safety and [which] can avoid some of the dangers of C, or languages that have internal GC [garbage collection] support and make memory management easier. C++ solves all the wrong problems, and anybody who says 'rewrite the kernel in C++' is too ignorant to even know that."

He said that when one spoke of the dangers of C, one was also speaking about part of what made C so powerful, "and allows you to implement all those low-level things efficiently".
Torvalds added that, while garbage collection is "a very good thing in most other situations," it's "generally not necessarily something you can do in a low-level system programming."

----- -> Linus: If you come in Paris, France, tell me. I may change your mind as a kernel farmer boy. You will be a different man. But for that, you will have to buy of a pair of balls. I will explain you real life out your fucking California state. But I promise you "memories for life" so don't forget to travel with a pair of balls. In France we use C and C++ for things you can't imagine so we have to show you things to you. And please, don't smile with all the Diversity and Inclusion of Rust minorities with red and blue hair and all the propaganda of the LGBTQIA+. Please, be a man my friend. Let those daemons using Javascript. You think about JS in your kernel Linus ?

Chris | France.

Professional C++ - Philosophy and Principles

ANNEXE D – RUST WILL REPLACE C AND C++ as System Programming Language ?

My answer is definitively: no.
But let the kids play. We will see.
Make your own opinion. Try the samples. Read the docs.

Copyright © Christophe Pichaud, 2022
Édition : BoD – Books on Demand, info@bod.fr
Impression : BoD – Books on Demand, In de Tarpen 42, Norderstedt (Allemagne)
Impression à la demande
ISBN : 978-2-3224-3548-7
Dépôt légal : Novembre 2022